Educational Documents

Educational Documents provides a valuable introduction for students of education, and anyone with an interest in this field, to some important extracts from reports which run to many thousands of pages.

The main theme is the creation of an administrative framework – a genuine *national* education system. This in turn leads to the subsidiary themes – the relations between Church and State in public education, the training of teachers, the progressive development from elementary to primary and secondary education for all and the growth of technical education from a private to a public activity.

This book was first published in 1965 and is a reissue of the fifth edition published in 1986.

Educational Documents

ENGLAND and WALES · 1816 to the present day

Edited by
J. Stuart Maclure

Routledge
Taylor & Francis Group
London and New York

First published 1965 by Routledge

This edition published 2006 by Routledge
2 Park Square, Milton Park, Abingdon, Oxon, OX14 4RN

Simultaneously published in the USA and Canada
by Routledge
250 Madison Ave, New York, NY 10016

Routledge is an imprint of the Taylor & Francis Group

Typeset in 10/12 Imprint by TechBooks New Delhi, India
Printed and bound in Great Britain by MPG Books Ltd, Bodmin, Cornwall

British Library Cataloguing in Publication Data
A catalogue record for this book is available from the British Library

Library of Congress Cataloging in Publication Data
A catalog record for this book has been requested

ISBN 0-415-38287-4 (set)
ISBN 0-415-38289-0 (volume II)

Publisher's Note

The Publisher has gone to great lengths to ensure the quality of this reprint but points out that some imperfections in the original book may be apparent.

Educational Documents

ENGLAND and WALES · 1816 to the present day

Educational Documents

ENGLAND and WALES · 1816 to the present day

J. Stuart Maclure

Methuen
LONDON and NEW YORK

First published 1965 by
Chapman & Hall Ltd
Second edition 1968
First published 1968 as an Education Paperback by
Methuen & Co. Ltd
11 New Fetter Lane, London EC4P 4EE
Third edition 1973
Fourth edition 1979
Fifth edition 1986
Published in the USA by
Methuen & Co.
in association with Methuen, Inc.
29 West 35th Street, New York NY 10001

Printed in Great Britain at
J.W. Arrowsmith Ltd, Bristol

British Library Cataloguing in Publication Data

Educational documents: England and Wales,
1816 to the present day. – 5th ed. –
(Education paperbacks)
1. Education – England – History – Sources
I. Maclure, Stuart
370'.942   LA631.7

ISBN 0-416-39470-1

Contents

Preface

My debts are too numerous to be acknowledged exhaustively, but I must mention the advice and encouragement of Mr H. C. Dent of the University of London Institute of Education, both at the planning stage and later on. He is not, of course, in any way responsible for the contents of this book.

Like all who have occasion to use the Library at the Department of Education and Science, I have every reason to be grateful to Miss Phyllis M. Downie, the librarian, and her staff for their unfailing helpfulness and long suffering.

And without my wife's help in typing manuscripts and copying documents this book would never have been completed.

ACKNOWLEDGEMENT

Extracts from the following Crown Copyright documents are reproduced by permission of the Controller of Her Majesty's Stationery Office: Industrial Training Act 1973; White Paper on a New Training Initiative 1981: a Programme for Action, Cmnd 8455; The Thompson Report 1982, Cmnd 8686; White Paper on Teaching Quality 1983, Cmnd 8836; White Paper on Training for Jobs 1984, Cmnd 9135.

Introduction

This is not a history of education; it does not set out to provide a connected narrative. It has a strictly limited, mundane purpose – to bring together, in a form which may be useful to students of education and others, selected extracts from the leading official documents which plot the development of a public system of education in England and Wales since 1816.

There is no need to stress the richness of the material, nor yet the extent to which any selection must tend to be arbitrary and idiosyncratic. For all its haphazard and uneven course, English education has been copiously documented. At least every ten years or so – often more frequently – there seems to have been some major report, Act of Parliament, administrative measure or what-you-will, which has crystallized some aspect of educational thought and practice. The Department of Education library – that admirable institution to which any student of these matters must pay a heartfelt tribute – groans beneath the weight of reports, often in half a dozen volumes, and the evidence given to Royal Commissions and Departmental Committees.

This continuity of documentation is one of the key facts about English education. Most of the burning issues of the day have histories which can be traced in the reports which span the years. For example, the Newsom Committee (1961–3) on the secondary education of children of average and below average ability had its roots in the *Education of the Adolescent* produced by the Hadow Committee in 1926, which in turn began by reviewing the history of elementary and post-elementary education since the early nineteenth century. Examples could be multiplied many times. Anyone who wants to contribute seriously to a discussion of educational policy must reckon with these historical threads.

This selection has not sought the recondite and the recherché. It has been less concerned to chase ghosts and embryos than to arrange the famous and the obvious passages in a useful form. The documents themselves are splendid examples of the outstanding work which usually goes into the blue books, and, especially the early ones, are often expressed with a refreshing freedom of language. But few students have access to them and to the vivid commentary on the developing educational scene which they provide. It may be that this collection will persuade more to go back to these secondary but fascinating sources and to dig for themselves.

The main theme of this collection of extracts is the slow and often tortuous process by which a public system of education has been built. The first edition ran from before 1833 – when the first State grants for education were provided – to 1963, when the Robbins Report marked, in a sense, the ultimate recognition that even the universities must be brought within the framework of a public system; and on into the 1970s when the tone of voice of the educational discussion changes.

Alongside this main theme there are others to be traced intermittently over the years. There is the record of the changing relationships between Church and State which dictated many of the lines of school development till well into the twentieth century. There is the steady raising of the educational sights – the outgrowing of elementary education and the acceptance of the idea of secondary education for all, leading on to the transformation of technical education and, in due course, the comprehensive secondary school. There is the recurring dialogue between social class and educational provision, from the mid-Victorian self-confidence of the Taunton Report (see p. 89) to the sociological doubts in the Newsom Report a century later. And – an aspect of all of them – there is the ever-present preoccupation with the training of teachers, linked first with the elementary school system and its social assumptions and, since the end of the nineteenth century, moving into the main stream of higher education.

The documents are arranged in chronological order. At first sight there might seem merit in seeking to group them according to subject and not according to date, but there are snags about this because many of the leading documents range widely over a variety of topics and an involved and repetitious system of cross-referencing would be required.

. . . . .

The starting point of any collection of extracts of this kind is bound to be arbitrary, but the early nineteenth century offers a plausible imitation of a new beginning in English education.

The years which followed the Napoleonic wars, and the economic and social distress which they saw, brought with them a new awareness of educational destitution. The ingenuity of Bell and Lancaster and the activities of the National Society and the British and Foreign Schools Society won a response from the well-to-do section of society to the mass of ignorance allied to poverty among the children of the poor. Political radicalism joined with the Evangelical Revival and the stirrings of Benthamite reform to bring education to the fore.

The first extracts in this book are taken from the evidence to the Parliamentary Committees of 1816–18 and to the similar inquiry in 1834. The large and weighty volumes which contain the answers of clergymen, lawyers, public benefactors and educational enthusiasts provide a bewilderingly rich source of background material. The picture of poverty-stricken London emerges with Dickensian vividness as witnesses tell of Fagins with apprentice-pickpockets in tow, of the wonders of the monitorial system, of children who could only come to school when it was their turn to wear the family suit of clothes.

Many of the themes which recur in the course of more recent educational history can be found in these parliamentary pages.

What sort of education should be given as the basic minimum? What duties, if any, should the State perform in this? What is the true status of religion in education? How should Church and State co-operate in the provision and the running of the schools? How far should the State underwrite the religious dogmas of the Established Church? How far must the State act as honest broker between the Dissenters and the Establishment? What about the mass of the urban working class, largely untouched by the claims of Anglicanism or Rome or Dissent whose children still had to be schooled? Where were the teachers to come from? Who was to train them? What social level should they aspire to?

No one knew how many children there were in any kind of school. No one knew what proportion should be classified as belonging to the poorer classes. These gaps were only filled as the machinery of central and local government was painfully and often reluctantly created.

Throughout the nineteenth century, the evidence of official ignorance and impotence is widespread. The Taunton Commission had to check its guess of the size of the middle and upper classes by calculating the number of weddings by special licence – a luxury of the well-to-do – and comparing this with the number of plebeian unions for which banns were published. In the 1870 debates on the Elementary Education Act, rule-of-thumb techniques hardly less rough and ready were used by W. E. Forster to emphasize the shortcomings of the schools, and by his opponent, Lord Robert Montague, to minimize them.

Many more examples could be given, not all from the distant past. But what these illustrate, often enough, is not just the absence of figures, but the absence of government.

The 1850s and 1860s brought to a climax the public response to educational development begun by voluntary agencies during the preceding forty years. The great reports of the Royal Commissions on Oxford and Cambridge, the Clarendon (Public Schools), Newcastle (Elementary Schools) and Taunton (Endowed Schools) commissions, and the legislation which flowed from them (not to mention the changes they stimulated without legislation) leading through to the Act of 1870 represented a mammoth achievement for institutions of government entirely inadequate for the administrative consequences which they inevitably entailed.

These same inadequate institutions were at the same time grappling with the public health and factory legislation, with road and bridge building, with reform of the Civil Service, law reform, penal reform and electoral reform. To isolate the educational developments is to project a false picture. The reality is that England in mid-century was faced with the incipient problems of a modern state and had to improvise the administration to tackle them.

The lack of an administrative machine is the key to much English educational history in the nineteenth century. There were many other reasons, no doubt, why the Church of England and the other voluntary agencies provided elementary education; reasons which derived from the historic privileges of the church in education, and the religious sentiments, Anglican and Dissenting, of the time. But not least among the reasons why the Government channelled public money for education through the National Society, the British and Foreign Schools Society and the Catholic Poor Schools Committee was that there was no cheap alternative to the parochial system, and the subsidization of voluntary bodies was, in that sense, inevitable.

This undoubtedly coincided strongly with the views of the well-to-do whose philanthropy provided the main source of money for education. The education of the children of the poor was a matter of conscience. It was a religious duty for those who had money to subscribe to the parish school or to one of the voluntary school organizations. The costs of elementary education were very low indeed. With a clutch of monitors one master could teach a hundred children. The pennies of the poor were collected to preserve their self-respect and the well-to-do could devote much of their liberality to the setting up of new schools. About £400 was a fair cost for a large school house (300–400 pupils).

Not only was it a religious duty to support the educational charities, but religion was the basis of education. For those who belonged to the Established Church it was, by right as well as by tradition, a function of the Establishment. The Tractarians were particularly strong in this view. The sanctions of religion were the ultimate sanctions of school discipline. When conscience clauses and withdrawal rights for Dissenters were under discussion in 1870, hands were raised in horror at the idea of a school in which religious instruction was banned, for how else could the schoolmaster impose a godly discipline? Religion and philanthropy were joined by utilitarian motives. The violence and poverty of the time, the sharpness of social distinctions, the prevalence of pauperism and the links between poverty, ignorance and crime made it inevitable that the better-off classes should look for practical advantages from their benevolence. They expected much from religious instruction and Bible reading, including social peace, industrial skill and the arts of self-government.

Though the Anglicans had more money and more support, and through the National Society could establish more schools, Dissent was no less acutely concerned with education. Methodists, Congregationalists and Baptists were all prepared to set up denominational schools. But being unable to create as many schools or as comprehensive a network as the Church of England – and lacking the Anglican sense of divine and prescriptive right – Dissenters were more ready to support schemes for the State to set up schools free from Church control. They were content that the rights of conscience should be preserved by the right of withdrawal, or by schemes under which only a non-sectarian form of Christian or Biblical teaching was allowed. Some went further (see p. 135) and wanted all religious education left to the Sunday Schools and the Churches, as in the United States.

Between Brougham's abortive Bill of 1820 and the Education Act of 1944 one report after another addressed itself to the relationship of Church and State in education. From the outset it was clear that the voluntary bodies needed subventions, but even with grants, could they cover the whole field? Some witnesses for the voluntary organizations had high hopes that they could; they feared and resented the intervention of a godless State. Others disputed this, arguing that where the need was greatest, the voluntary bodies were weakest. 'In the eastern districts of London' a clergyman told the 1834 Inquiry 'the population of some of the parishes amount to 60,000. The utter impossibility of any clergyman or any set of gentlemen undertaking to provide funds for a comprehensive system of education under such circumstances must be evident.' He added: 'Another great obstacle is the very low scale of intellectual power and of moral feeling in the lower orders.'

Bit by bit an administrative structure was created. It was not till 1833 that the first parliamentary funds were voted – some £20,000 was paid to the two voluntary societies, without strings attached. Six years later the Committee of Council on Education was created to administer government grants. Dr James Kay became its first secretary. The principle of inspection was there to be borrowed from the factory legislation of the time and the elements of a central authority could thus be brought into being.

Inspection of voluntary schools required the co-operation of the Church of England which, in a period of militant Anglican revival, was only forthcoming after lengthy and bitter controversy. The resulting compromise took the form of the *concordat* between the Archbishop of Canterbury and the Government (see p. 46) which gave the Church the right to approve inspectors chosen to visit Church schools. In effect this meant that clergymen were appointed to this office. This was the formal link in the dual system.

In practice the Committee of Council extended the same principle to the non-conformists and Roman Catholics so that several separate sets of denominational inspectors worked side by side with lay inspectors.

The system of grants and inspection was only capable of limited extension. From the beginning it was clear that there had to be a workable local administration. The Newcastle Commission looked at this, wanting not only a more active central education department, but also county boards formed from the Justices of the Quarter Sessions. These were to have strictly limited functions mainly connected with the examination of pupils in voluntary and private schools (by a class of inferior local inspectors, to be known as examiners) and the raising of a county rate in relation to this (see p. 71). These education authorities, had they come into being, would not have been popularly elected bodies. But the Newcastle Committee hoped that, nevertheless, they would succeed in enlisting popular interest and support.

For secondary education, the issue was complicated by the existence of endowments. The Taunton Commission (1868) attempted to sort out the endowed schools as the Clarendon Commission (1864) had tried to clear up the nine 'public' schools. As the 1818 report of the Parliamentary Commission had noted after struggling to discover the secrets of the trust deeds of Eton and Winchester, the endowments had been (in many cases) 'misapplied through ignorance or mismanaged through carelessness'. 'Unauthorized deviation' had been made 'more by a regard to the interests of the fellows than of the scholars who were the main object of the foundation and of the founder's bounty.' (Nothing better demonstrated the static economic assumptions of the trustees than the fact that in the main the trusts are better described as unmanaged than mismanaged.)

The Taunton Commission (see p. 89) as well as outlining a system of graded secondary schools to correspond with the social demands of the middle classes, suggested that the Boards of Guardians, joined together, county by county, might form a scheme of provincial government, working closely with district commissioners appointed by the Charity Commissioners, and they wanted a new central authority presided over by a Minister of Education taking over some of the functions of the Charity Commission.

They funked the idea of *ad hoc* school boards adopted two years later in the Forster Act – direct suffrage came from amendments to the original Bill – but their eloquent expression of the case for popular participation in school administration (see p. 97) remains a classic statement of educational democracy.

By 1870, when Forster introduced his Bill in Mr Gladstone's first administration, the weight of evidence at last was great enough to overcome the denominational difficulty and push through the compromise which preserved the Dual System but enabled public authorities to fill the gaps in elementary education.

The 1870 Act (see p. 98) was a milestone from which there was no going back. By setting up elected local bodies the Act created a new source of initiative, independent of either the voluntary bodies or the remote austerity of the Education Department. The Taunton Commission's insight into the importance of popular participation was vindicated.

Elementary education surged ahead. Competition between the School Boards and the Churches (which was bitterly resented by the out-and-out voluntarists and wickedly enjoyed by the militant secularists) was hot. In the ten years which followed the passing of the Act, the number of voluntary schools rose from 8,000 to 14,000; between 3,000 and 4,000 schools were started or taken over by the school boards; in the years 1870–83, the Anglicans spent £12¼m on school building compared with a total of £15m spent by the National Society between 1811 and 1870. Yet by 1900 there were nearly as many children in Board schools as in Church schools.

The effect of progress in elementary education was to emphasize what still needed to be done. Much of it happened in an atmosphere of crude competitive conflict between the Churches and the School Boards which intensified religious conflict and made more difficult the next step which had inevitably to be the provision of rate aid for the voluntary schools.

The controversies of this period undoubtedly had something to do with the lasting hostility of the English middle classes towards educational expenditure. At this period they reckoned they were being taxed twice – once by the rates and once through their charitable obligations to the voluntary schools – and all for the education of other people's children. The behaviour of the representatives of the denominational interest set a pattern for the cruder forms of 'rate-payers representation' on education authorities. It is one of the ironies of English educational history that the supporters of denominational schools who included many of those who had done most and cared most for the education of the people, helped during this fateful thirty-year period to denigrate that public initiative and finance on which they had increasingly to depend.

Much of this background was described by Mr Balfour, when introducing the 1902 Act (see p. 149). And it was the subject of lengthy investigation by the Cross Commission which reported its own divisions in 1888 (see p. 131).

The thirty years before 1902 were formative in many ways: they established attitudes which have proved hard to shake; and the creation of a system of elementary education, complete in itself, had consequential effects on secondary education. The distinctive, highly selective grammar school type of secondary education with its conscious minority function, and its university orientation, was able to take the form it did because the elementary schools were deemed to provide all that was needed for the great majority.

The success with which the School Boards filled up the gaps in elementary education only exposed the need for a similar expansion of secondary education. In 1884 the Samuelson Commission on Technical Education had adverted to this (see p. 125): 'The best preparation for technical study', they wrote, 'is a good modern secondary school of the type of the Manchester Grammar School. . . . We must look to some public measure to supply this . . . [the want of a sufficient number of such schools] . . . the greatest defect of our educational system. . . .'

The School Boards were, for the most part, far too small to carry out responsibilities in secondary education. As the Samuelson Report suggested, this was a job for the new County and County Borough Councils formed after the 1888 Local Government Act. Once again, till the administrative structure had been created there was no way forward. Once it had been formed progress was relatively rapid.

Parallel with the need to create new education authorities capable of administering secondary education was the need to clear up the mess caused by improvisation. This came under two heads. First, School Boards, unable to restrict themselves strictly to elementary education where secondary education was manifestly inadequate, had formed higher-grade schools and pupil-teacher centres, stretching the 1870 Act to do so. The Cockerton judgement arising from the action brought by a District Auditor of that name against the London School Board (a case prompted indirectly by Mr Robert Morant, a member of the Education Department) held that in providing post-elementary education, the London authorities were acting *ultra vires*. A new Act was needed to enable this work to go on within the framework of secondary education, albeit in modified form.

The second was the chaotic developments in scientific and technical education with which the Devonshire and Samuelson Reports were concerned (see pp. 107 and 121).

The Science and Art Department was formed at the Board of Trade in 1853 after the Great Exhibition. It moved to the Education Department in 1856 and from 1859 began to make grants for science classes on a payment-by-results basis. The build-up was rapid and vested interests formed about the Department and its largesse. At first, most of the grants went to evening work carried out by elementary school teachers. Standards steadily rose and by the time of the Bryce Report in 1894–5, S and A grants amounted to £143,000 a year. The pattern had changed: a large part of the money now went to 'ex-standard' – that is, senior classes in day elementary schools. In fact the Science and Art Department was sponsoring a kind of one-eyed secondary education without an Act, and this made for artificial distortion which was plain to all.

Two other complicating factors were the Technical Instruction Act of 1889 empowering Counties and County Boroughs to spend a penny rate on technical or manual instruction, and the Whisky Money (under the Local Taxation (Customs and Excise) Act of 1890) which made additional funds available to counties and boroughs for a similar purpose. Thus the counties and county boroughs, and the Science and Art Department were all nibbling at secondary education. Only a major Act of Parliament could straighten matters out.

The 1902 Act (see p. 149) did this by making the counties and county boroughs education authorities; the counties had, in some areas, small authorities for primary education acting within their boundaries. (These latter small authorities were known as the Part III authorities because of the part of the Act from which their powers derived.)

The new education authorities were not, like the School Boards, *ad hoc* bodies, directly elected for the sole object of administering education. They were the councils elected for all the purposes of local government; but by the Act they were obliged to appoint an education committee to which non-elected people with educational knowledge could be co-opted.

The separate grants from the Science and Art Department stopped. The new county authorities did not need to get round the law by running higher-grade schools: they could (and did in large numbers) found grammar schools, and training colleges and technical colleges. The Act conferred great powers on the local authorities, who for all their preoccupation with the rates, initiated a period of strong and substantial advance. The financial crises of the inter-war years to some extent veiled the magnitude of what was in fact achieved, but no one can reflect on the changes which took place during the forty-odd years after the 1902 Act without being impressed by what it made possible, when allied to strong local demands for education.

The Bryce Commission (see p. 140) had proposed other administrative changes in addition to the county authorities for secondary education, including a much stronger central authority under a Minister of Education, to unify the various activities of the Science and Art Department, the Education Department and the Charity Commissioners. In the event the Government would not make the function of the central authority so unambiguous. They compromised in the matter of a departmental title by making the minister president of an imaginary board composed of the senior members of the Cabinet. But the new minister's authority was greatly strengthened even though his relationship with the local education authorities was supervisory only, and even though the Act depended in part on the extent to which the L.E.A.s availed themselves of the powers they received. The power of the central government continued to be largely indirect, using the Inspectorate and the Codes to make the most effective use of local and voluntary agencies.

A need no less important than the clearing up of the administrative jungle of secondary, scientific and technical education was the overhaul of the content of secondary education. The Bryce Commission (see p. 140) made out the case for the unity of secondary education comprising technical education and scientific studies as well as the more traditional subjects. In so doing it followed up the recommendations of both Devonshire and Samuelson. Huxley's evidence to the Devonshire Commission (see p. 110), advocating science in the primary school and illustrated by mischievous comparison with the teaching of dogmatic theology to infants, was an attempt to argue that scientific study was basic to all education. As an *avant garde* contribution to primary education it was an interesting piece of prophecy: but as an observation about education in general and secondary education in particular it was of more immediate importance.

The Aberdare Report on Education in Wales (see p. 112) and the Welsh Intermediate Act of 1889 had gone some way along these lines, giving Wales a start in the provision of maintained secondary schools, and an early taste for a liberal interpretation of secondary education (and making amends, in part anyway, for the 'treachery of the Blue books' – the report on Welsh elementary education of 1848, see p. 56).

As for elementary education and the perennial religious problems, the 1902 Act brought Rome on to the rates, making the L.E.A.s responsible for secular instruction. The denominational schools received rate aid for their current expenditure while remaining entirely responsible for capital spending. One-third of the managers of a 'non-provided' school, as the Act termed them, were appointed by the L.E.A. Religious instruction continued to be governed by the trust deed, subject to conscience clauses and the right of withdrawal. The denominational interests were pleased to be relieved of an ever-increasing financial burden. The School Boards and the supporters of *ad hoc* authorities attacked the change to many-purpose local authorities. The non-conformists opposed the subsidization of the Church schools, and the Liberals in Parliament found an issue to unite their divided supporters and voiced their opposition with splenetic fury. The Welsh non-conformists threatened passive resistance and withheld their rates. But the storm was weathered. After the Liberals came to power in 1906, there were efforts to overturn the Bill, and tussles between the Lords and Commons on the issue. Gradually the argument died down as the 1902 Act proved itself in practice to be effective and tolerably equitable. In the late 1960s the dying embers of religious controversy in Welsh education were raked by the Gittins

Report (see p. 324) with the suggestion that compulsory worship and instruction should cease to be a legal requirement.

1902 onwards

As the record unfolds and the story is carried forward to the present, it is inevitable that any selection tends to become more diffuse. Many of the same themes have still to be followed out: the growth of secondary education; the abandonment of elementary education as a separate system; the steady improvement of teacher training; sensitiveness to the sociological background; science and technology and their relation to national economic needs, the place of higher education in a national system. And alongside these there is the progressive building up of a national machine and, the consequence of this, the emergence of the Education Department, as a powerful and purposeful force filling out the key central role.

Both the majority and minority reports of the Cross Commission in 1885 had made important recommendations about teacher training (see p. 131). The Departmental Committee of 1925 (see p. 176) carried a stage further the process by which the training of teachers was to be emancipated from its origins in elementary education and brought into a working relationship with the universities and higher education in general – a theme taken up again and further developed in the McNair Report of 1944 (see p. 216), in the relevant chapter of the Robbins Report of 1963 (see p. 288), and in the James Report of 1972 (see p. 354).

The years following 1902 saw a surge forward in secondary education comparable with that in elementary education after 1870. I have included various extracts from Board of Education documents during the first few years which effectively ensured that the new secondary schools should be modelled on the old grammar schools and not on the other forms of post-elementary education which had begun to develop. I have also included the classic description of the aims of elementary education which marked a more liberal trend (see p. 160).

The seal was set upon the grammar school curriculum by the development of external examinations. An extract from the Report of the Consultative Committee of the Board of Education in 1911 records the proposals for the School Certificate Examination (see p. 163) which in turn the Norwood Report (see p. 200) replaced with the General Certificate of Education.

The progressive extension of grammar school facilities marched with the increase in free places and scholarships. From 1907 it became a condition that any school receiving grant from the Board must offer 25 per cent of its places free (see p. 162).

A growing number of free places meant a growing interest in the criteria on which selection for grammar school education could be based.

This is one of the recurring themes in the reports of the inter-war period, notably the Hadow Report (see p. 179) and the Spens Report (see p. 193), as the extracts reproduced in this collection show. Preoccupation with mental testing influenced the development of ideas about other forms of secondary education and buttressed the bipartite and tripartite arrangements which, by the time the 1944 Act was drafted, had become the orthodox forms of secondary organization. The White Paper on *Educational Reconstruction* in 1943 (see p. 206) showed how the ideals of wider opportunity and of selective secondary education were held in uneasy balance, while the 1944 Education Act itself was non-committal on matters of organization, except in that its insistence on secondary education according to 'age, ability and aptitude' was consistent with the interpretation placed on it by most educational administrators who presumed a form of selective education in separate schools.

Nothing was more important in 1944 than the determination to replace elementary education and secondary education – two separate systems – by a single educational process in successive stages. This implied big changes in secondary education which the Hadow Report on *The Education of the Adolescent* had explored. It also implied a reorientation of primary education. The changes in the theory of infants' education, which were beginning to affect the schools, strengthened the trend towards new ideals elsewhere in primary education, and had been reflected in the Hadow Report on the Primary School in 1931 (see p. 188).

The movement towards comprehensive education represented an attempt to carry the concept of secondary education a step beyond the Hadow notions which dominated the thinking of educational administrators in the years immediately following the 1944 Act. Projected to the political level, it became a major item of Labour Party policy. Circular 10/65 (see p. 301) was the result, followed by the threat of legislation and countered after the Conservative victory in 1970 with Circular 10/70 (see p. 352). In due course the wheel turned again, and the 1976 Act was passed (see p. 381).

Since the 1944 Act, the air has been thick with reports and surveys and, as the volume of research and inquiry has grown, the emphasis on the sociological approach has grown also. From the concept of secondary education for all – the acceptance of equality of opportunity as a supreme educational aim – there can be traced in the documents the dethronement of educational psychology and mental-testing and the elevation of educational sociology. This has taken the form of a preoccupation with the effects of the class structure on education, which produces a looking-glass image of the mid-Victorian assumptions of the Taunton Report. The sociological approach can be seen clearly in extracts from the Early Leaving Report of 1954 (see p. 233), the Crowther Report of 1959 (see p. 245), the Albemarle Report of 1960 (see p. 259), the Newsom and Robbins Reports of 1963, and the Plowden Report of 1967, and the Newsom Report of 1968. It can also be noted by its absence in the Fleming Report of 1944 (see p. 210).

By the time the Newsom commission returned to the subject of the public schools (see p. 332) the sociological and political aspects had merged and the dominant questions concerned ways in which the boarding schools could be opened up to children whose parents could not afford large fees, while at the same time forcing them to become more comprehensive in their intakes and restricting financial support to those pupils with an overwhelming social or academic need to board.

The lengthy debates about the pool of ability and the relationship of opportunity to family background also reflected a growing concern about the practical importance which the waste of natural talent might have in national economic terms. And this approach to education as a factor in national prosperity coincided with the need to expand facilities for technical and technological education. Politically, the easily recognized connexion between technology and production made it inevitable that scientific and technical education should be used as a stalking horse for the advancement of education as a whole – as, for instance, in the Barlow Report of 1946 (see p. 230) where the need for an increased output of science graduates enabled a committee on scientific manpower, by an *obiter dictum*, to recommend a big increase in the number of university places in non-scientific subjects as well.

With the concern for science and technology which finds expression in reports (see pp. 226 to 239) such as the Percy Report (1945) and the White Paper on Technical Education (1956), and for the related field of industrial education, which was the subject of the report on Technical Education in Wales (1961) and the Industrial Training White Paper in 1962, went the attempt to build up a structure of higher technical education outside the universities. This meant the creation of the Colleges of Advanced Technology and the hierarchy of colleges and polytechnics in which numbers were limited only by demand.

By the time the Robbins Report came to be written this growth of advanced work in non-university institutions – together with the rapid growth of the teacher training colleges – had become large enough to require the redefinition of higher education and a new structure capable of comprehending it.

Most of the twentieth-century documents have to be read against a background of the growth of power in policy-making and administration at the centre. This growing central power and authority has been the consequence of the growth of government in general, as well as of education in particular.

The Act of 1918 did much less than the projected Bill of 1917 to extend the writ of the Board of Education, though, of course, had the large-scale development of part-time day continuation schools come about this would sooner or later have enhanced the power of the central government. Section 1 of the Act laid the duty of establishing 'a national system of public education' squarely on the local authorities. It was not until the 1944 Act that this duty was shouldered by the Minister of Education, acting through local education authorities 'under his control and direction' (see p. 223). The change was intended to be material, and during the twenty years after 1944 it became apparent how significant it was going to be.

The chief administrative consequence which stemmed from the 1918 Act was the institution of specific percentage grants made by the Board of Education in respect of approved expenditure by education authorities. This had the effect of giving automatic financial support to any local development provided it came within the provisions of the Act and the grant regulations. It cannot be said to have brought about uniform standards, but it encouraged initiative. More significant than this, its local effect was to strengthen the hand of the education committees of the local authorities, and to increase the element of independence they enjoyed as statutory bodies under the 1902 Act.

This quasi-independence of education committees was one of the reasons which prompted the Government in 1958 to end the specific percentage grants introduced by Mr H. A. L. Fisher in 1918, and to substitute a general grant, worked out on a complicated weighted-population formula, paid as a grant in aid of all local authority expenditure, though the education element within it was still computed by reference to the aggregated expenditure of all local authorities on education. This was done in the belief that it would strengthen local government as a whole without harming education.

The 1944 Act carried a stage further the incorporation of the denominational schools into the public system (see p. 222), introducing capital grants of 50 per cent (raised in 1959 to 75 per cent) for 'Aided' schools, on certain carefully specified conditions, and creating a new status of 'Controlled' school for denominational schools in which the L.E.A.s appoint a majority of the managers. In 1967 the grants were raised to 80 per cent and the conditions extended.

At the same time, the Act abolished the Part III authorities, making the counties and county boroughs the education authorities for all purposes. A system of divisional administration based on the old Part III organization survived in some counties and this was somewhat strengthened by the local government reorganization of the early 1960s, but the delegated functions of the divisions and excepted districts were different in kind from the powers of the Part III authorities.

The Ministry of Education – the title was at last enacted by an amendment to the 1944 Bill – has been cautious in assuming the strong central role attributed to the department under the Act. Though it made clear the over-riding authority of the Ministry, the Act was drafted on the assumption that power would continue to be shared with the teachers on the one hand and the local authorities on the other.

The idea of partnership between Minister, teachers and L.E.A.s is not easily reconciled with the positive and purposive leadership which some would like to see exercised by the Department of Education. In practice, however, the execution of policies which a Minister might wish to pursue depends extensively on the co-operation of the teachers and the local authorities, and more than this, the formulation of the policies themselves must largely be a co-operative effort. The importance of the various advisory councils – the Central Advisory Council (successor to the Consultative Committee), the National Advisory Council for the Training and Supply of Teachers, the National Advisory Council on Education for Industry and Commerce – has been that these (like the day-to-day contacts of the Ministry with the teachers' organizations and the local authority associations) have been part of a process by which central direction has been strengthened without being concentrated in the hands of the Minister.

Quite clearly this was not the end of the administrative story. The cost of education continued to rise. Governments had become committed to educational developments in the years since 1944 in a sense that they had never been committed before. Local government failed to arouse any public enthusiasm; people regarded local variations in the character and quality of education with impatience, expecting elected representatives in Parliament to iron out differences, not strengthen the local autonomy which had produced them.

By the middle 1950s the Ministry of Education had begun to flex muscles which had not been brought into play before. The bickering between successive Ministers and the Burnham Committee was a symptom of this. In higher technical education, the Ministry of Education published a White Paper (1956 – see p. 239) which led eventually to the removal of the largest technical colleges from local control to become direct grant institutions financed directly by the Ministry of Education. The two periods of office as Minister of Sir David Eccles (later Lord Eccles) marked the steady extension of the powers and initiative of the Ministry.

His second spell as Minister (from 1959–62) coincided with the conversion of the Conservative Government to economic planning, and the upsurge of interest, on both sides of the Atlantic, in education as a factor in economic growth. To this might be added the growth of activity in the United States in the reform of school science teaching under the stimulus of Russian advances in space technology.

The Treasury had recognized the need for planning. The economists had pointed out education's part in this. The Americans had shown how by research and development, liberally financed by charitable foundations, new syllabuses and new teaching techniques could revolutionize the effectiveness of class teaching and speed up change.

It was in these circumstances that the Ministry of Education began to strengthen its statistical department and to take a modest interest in research. The formation of the Curriculum Study Group in 1962 was the most important move towards creating some central control over curriculum and examinations. This was followed a year later by the proposals for a Schools Council to plan the strategy of development work, and to act as the instrument by which its results were mediated to the schools. Between 1963 and its winding up in 1984, the Schools Council became an important agency for curriculum development. It also became caught in the crossfire of argument about the control of the curriculum and the respective powers and responsibilities of the teachers, the local authorities and the Department of Education and Science. This argument culminated in the Great Debate and Green Paper of 1977 (see p. 394), and the beginning of a new era of intervention by the central Government in the curriculum, signalled by the curriculum review and the reform of the 16 plus examination system in the first half of the 1980s, and by the resurgence of the Inspectorate.

This period of reassessment or – as some would say – reaction, ushered in by the Great Debate, coincided with the increase in youth unemployment and the arrival of the Manpower Services Commission (see p. 381–3) which became a potent and well-funded instrument of policy which often impinged on education. The increased emphasis on technical education, a feature of the rhetoric, was given a boost in 1982 by the announcement of the MSC's Technical and Vocational Education Initiative, a five-year funded pilot scheme aimed at encouraging developments at the secondary stage oriented towards the world of work.

At the same time, the launching of the Youth Training Scheme was an attempt by the MSC to provide a comprehensive programme of vocational preparation and work experience for 16–17-year-old school-leavers, along with some formal education and training.

By the middle 1960s the British Government had been forced to prepare themselves for the last stage in the creation of an administrative structure for British education – the integration of the Universities into the framework of the public education system.

The Robbins Report (see p. 288) is a document of the first importance for many reasons: for the magnitude of the expansion which it proposed and the strength of the statistical evidence on which the recommendations were based; for the underlying principle that it propounded: that higher education should be provided for all qualified and wishing to receive it; for the specific recommendations about teacher training and higher technological education and the methods of financial control. But by no means the least important achievement of the Robbins Committee was to bring higher education formally and unavoidably inside the arena of public responsibility. Till the 1960s the mysteries of the links between the University Grants Committee and the Treasury, which enabled public money to be used to finance the universities with the minimum of Government policy on higher education, had been accepted on almost every side as the guarantee of academic freedom.

The appointment of the Robbins Committee was an essential part of stiffening the public sinews and summoning up the blood. By spelling out the size of the sums of public money involved in the expansion programme – from £200 millions a year in the early 1960s to £700 millions by 1980 – they showed the impossibility of continuing to pretend that the universities were private institutions whose affairs could be settled by the Treasury with the minimum of fuss or parliamentary discussion. The retention of a grants committee went without saying; so, by the time the report appeared, did the need to have a Minister of the Crown responsible for higher education. In the event Parliament and public opinion proved more ready than the Robbins Committee to recognize the logic of the situation and the case for a single Secretary of State for Education who, at last, might be in some sort of a position to carry out his charge under the 1944 Education Act of promoting 'the education of the people'.

* * * * *

This, then, is the barest skeleton. The extracts themselves provide the flesh and blood.

Without speculating at length on the 'usefulness' of educational history, or its place in the education of the men and women who enter the teaching profession, it seems fair to observe that while dominating issues change, the underlying problems remain the same.

The administrative structure has been erected. But most of the interesting questions remain open.

How will the central government fill out the role apportioned to it in the 1944 Act and the Robbins Report? How will power be shared between the Department of Education and Science, the teachers, the local authorities and the autonomous institutions of higher education? How will the expansion of higher education affect academic freedom? What will be the upshot of attempts to define and delimit it? What new forms will the argument take about education as a potential instrument of social control? What new compromise will be found between opportunity and equality? Between professional and academic interests in the education of teachers? Between social, economic and academic pressures in the curriculum?

These documents will not begin to answer the open questions but they will provide a guide to the point of departure. They may explain, too, why the educational folk memory is long and powerful, and why in English education there can be few revolutions, only changes in tempo and direction.

1 · Reports of the Parliamentary Committees on the Education of the Lower Orders in the Metropolis and Beyond. 1816–18

The 1816 inquiry was promoted by Henry Brougham, later Lord Brougham and Vaux. It was confined to London at first, but in the next two years was extended to the rest of the country. It set out to establish the facts about elementary schools, how great the deficiencies were and what was the state of secondary education and of endowed schools originally founded for the education of the children of the poor. The inquiry revealed the existence of tractless wastes of educational destitution and pointed the way to the 1820 Bill. By this Brougham attempted to get parish schools set up at the expense of industry and maintained by the rates. By giving a special place in the scheme to the clergy and requiring schoolmasters to be members of the Church of England it roused strong opposition from Dissenters and Roman Catholics and never became law.

The reports of the committee were short – two of them are reprinted here. The evidence was published at the same time. Extracts are included on some of the major topics about which witnesses were questioned: the extent of the unmet demand for elementary schools, the poverty and degradation of the slum school population, the cost of elementary schooling and the level at which it should aim.

REPORT OF THE PARLIAMENTARY COMMITTEE, 1816

The Select Committee appointed to inquire into the Education of the Lower Orders in the Metropolis, and to report their Observations thereupon . . .

. . . have found reason to conclude, that a very large number of poor Children are wholly without the means of Instruction, although their parents appear to be generally very desirous of obtaining that advantage for them.

Your Committee have also observed with much satisfaction, the highly beneficial effects produced upon all those parts of the Population which, assisted in whole or in part by various Charitable Institutions, have enjoyed the benefits of Education.

Your Committee have not had time this Session fully to report their

Opinion upon the different branches of their Inquiry, but they feel persuaded that the greatest advantages would result to this Country from Parliament taking proper measures, in concurrence with the prevailing disposition in the Community, for supplying the deficiency of the means of Instruction which exists at present, and for extending this blessing to the Poor of all descriptions.

Although Your Committee have not been instructed to examine the state of Education beyond the Metropolis, they have, in addition to what has appeared in Evidence, received communications, which show the necessity of Parliament as speedily as possible instituting an inquiry into the management of Charitable Donations and other Funds for the Instruction of the Poor of this Country, and into the state of their Education generally, especially in the larger Towns . . .

[20th June, 1816

REPORT OF THE PARLIAMENTARY COMMITTEE · 1818

The Select Committee appointed to inquire into the Education of the Lower Orders . . .

. . . Since the inquiries of Your Committee have been extended to the whole Island, they have had reason to conclude, that the means of educating the Poor are steadily increasing in all considerable towns as well as in the Metropolis. A circular Letter has been addressed to all the clergy in England, Scotland and Wales, requiring Answers to Queries . . .

. . . It appears clearly from the Returns, as well as from other sources, that a very great deficiency exists in the means of educating the Poor, wherever the population is thin and scattered over country districts. The efforts of individuals combined in societies are almost wholly confined to populous places.

Another point to which it is material to direct the attention of Parliament, regards the two opposite principles, of founding schools for children of all sorts, and for those only who belong to the established church. Where the means exist of erecting two schools, one upon each principle, education is not checked by the exclusive plan being adopted in one of them, because the other may comprehend the children of sectaries. In places where only one school can be supported, it is manifest that any regulations which exclude dissenters, deprive the Poor of that body of all means of education.

Your Committee, however, have the greatest satisfaction in observing, that in many schools where the national system is adopted, an increasing degree of liberality prevails, and that the church catechism is only taught, and attendance at the established place of public worship only required, of those whose parents belong to the establishment; due assurance being obtained that the children of sectaries shall learn the principles and attend the ordinances of religion, according to doctrines and forms to which their families are attached.

It is with equal pleasure that Your Committee have found reason to conclude, that the Roman Catholic poor are anxious to avail themselves of those Protestant Schools established in their neighbourhood, in which no catechism is taught; and they indulge a hope, that the clergy of that persuasion may offer no discouragement to their attendance, more especially as they appear, in one instance, to have contributed to the support of schools, provided that no catechism was taught, and no religious observances exacted. It is contrary to the doctrine as well as discipline of the Romish Church, to allow any protestant to interfere with those matters, and consequently it is impossible for Romanists to send their children to any school where they form part of the plan.

Your Committee are happy in being able to state, that in all the returns, and in all the other information laid before them, there is the most unquestionable evidence that the anxiety of the poor for education continues not only unabated, but daily increasing; that it extends to every part of the country, and is to be found equally prevalent in those smaller towns and country districts, where no means of gratifying it are provided by the charitable efforts of the richer classes.

In humbly suggesting what is fit to be done for promoting universal education, Your Committee do not hesitate to state, that two different plans are advisable, adapted to the opposite circumstances of the town and country districts. Wherever the efforts of individuals can support the requisite number of schools, it would be unnecessary and injurious to interpose any parliamentary assistance. But Your Committee have clearly ascertained, that in many places private subscriptions could be raised to meet the yearly expenses of a School, while the original cost of the undertaking, occasioned chiefly by the erection and purchase of the schoolhouse, prevents it from being attempted.

Your Committee conceive, that a sum of money might be well employed in supplying this first want, leaving the charity of individuals to furnish the annual provision requisite for continuing the school, and possibly for repaying the advance. . . .

In the numerous districts where no aid from private exertions can be expected, and where the poor are manifestly without adequate means of instruction, Your Committee are persuaded, that nothing can supply the deficiency but the adoption, under certain material modifications of the Parish School system, so usefully established in the Northern part of the Island, ever since the latter part of the seventeenth century. . . .

. . . It appears further to Your Committee, that it may be fair and expedient to assist the parishes where no schoolhouses are erected, with the means of providing them, so as only to throw upon the inhabitants the burthen of paying the schoolmaster's salary, which ought certainly not to exceed twenty-four pounds a year. It appears to Your Committee, that a sufficient supply of schoolmasters may be procured for this sum, allowing them the benefits of taking scholars, who can afford to pay, and permitting them, of course, to occupy their leisure hours in other pursuits. The expense attending this invaluable system in Scotland, is found to be so very trifling, that it is never made the subject of complaint by any of the Landholders.

Your Committee forbear to inquire minutely in what manner this system ought to be connected with the Church Establishment. That such a connection ought to be formed appears manifest; it is dictated by a regard to the prosperity and stability of both systems, and in Scotland the two are mutually connected together. But a difficulty arises in England, which is not to be found there. The great body of the Dissenters from the Scottish Church differ little, if at all, in doctrine from the Establishment; they are separated only by certain opinions of a political rather than a religious nature, respecting the right of patronage, and by some shades of distinction as to church discipline; so that they may conscientiously send their children to parish schools connected with the Establishment, and teaching its catechism. In England the case is widely different; and it appears to Your Committee essentially necessary that this circumstance be carefully considered in the devising arrangements of the system. To place the choice of the schoolmaster in the parish vestry, subject to the approbation of the parson, and the visitation of the diocesan; but to provide that the children of sectarians shall not be compelled to learn any catechism or attend any Church, other than those of their parents, seems to Your Committee the safest path by which the Legislature can hope to obtain the desirable objects of security to the Establishment on the one hand, and justice to the Dissenters on the other.

The more extended inquiries of Your Committee this session have amply confirmed the opinion which a more limited investigation had led them to form two years ago, upon the neglect and abuse of Charitable Funds connected with education. . . .

. . . they must add, that although in many cases those large funds appear to have been misapplied through ignorance, or mismanaged through carelessness, yet that some instances of abuse have presented themselves, of such a nature, as would have led them to recommend at an earlier period of the session, the institution of proceedings for more promptly checking misappropriations. . . .

. . . It unquestionably shows, that considerable unauthorized deviations have been made, in both Eton and Winchester, from the original plans of the founders; that those deviations have been dictated more by a regard to the interests of the Fellows than of the Scholars, who were the main object of the foundations and of the founder's bounty . . .

[3rd June, 1818

SCHOOL BUILDING COSTS

Evidence of Mr William Allen, Treasurer to the British and Foreign School Society – 1816

What should you calculate would be the expense, upon the British and Foreign school plan, of giving education to [those who lack it]? Expense will vary according to local circumstances; where the number of children are sufficient to form a school of 500 or 600 in one place, the total expense per annum, in my opinion, need not exceed £200 or so much. We generally calculate that the expense per head in the largest schools, should not exceed five or six shillings; but it is obvious that local circumstances, such as the price of provisions, the rent of premises, etc. will cause a difference in different places.

Should you think twelve shillings a head a fair average, taking schools of all sizes into account, one with another? Yes.

Do you mean thereby to cover the expenses of school-rooms? All expenses, except those requisite for the first erection of the building . . .

Then do you mean to calculate that from three to four hundred thousand pounds a year would suffice for the education of all the poor now uneducated? Certainly, if the sum of £400,000 could be devoted to that purpose, every child requiring this sort of education might be provided with it throughout England and Wales, so as to leave not an uneducated person in the country; and in my opinion a much smaller sum would suffice. . . .

Can you give the Committee any estimate, generally, of the expenses of a school-room? The school-room at Kingsland, in the neighbourhood of London, was erected for a less sum than £400 and will contain 300 children; but in many parts of the country, an old barn or an old warehouse might be found, which would prevent the necessity of erecting a new building.

Suppose a grant were made merely of the money required to build the school, and the annual expenses were to be defrayed by subscriptions, would such meet with assistance, in your apprehension, in the progress of the system? In my apprehension it would do every thing, because it would encourage benevolent persons in the neighbourhood to promote school associations throughout their districts, on the plan recommended by the British and Foreign School Society, in which the poor themselves would become interested in the education of their children, and receive it, not merely as an act of charity, but as a thing which they themselves had subscribed for.

[1816: pp. 161–2

EDUCATIONAL DESTITUTION IN LONDON
Evidence of the Rev. William Gurney, Rector of Saint Clement Danes

Are you acquainted with the state of education among the lower orders in those parts of the town? I know a great deal about it in Saint Giles's, because there I have the greatest establishment for children. . . . We found there were a great many who did not go to any school; the reason assigned in some measure for it was, their ragged condition, and their being unfit, from their great poverty, to appear decently at any school; and we found also, that a great many children went to Sunday schools belonging to Dissenters of various denominations, who had begun long before us to open schools; we found there was a very large Sunday school in Drury-lane, in which there were from 5 to 600 children; a very large number of our children I believe, went there. But there are a great many mendicants in our parish, owing to the extreme lowness of some parts of the neighbourhood, and the more children they have, the more success they meet with in begging, and they keep them in that way; so that in the weekday we could not get them to a day-school without some different measures were adopted; neither are they fit to appear in them as they are; and on a Sunday they get more by begging than they do on any other day in the week, because more people are out and about; we tried the experiment in several instances, by giving clothes to some of the most ragged, in order to bring them decent to school; they appeared for one Sunday or two, and then disappeared, and the clothes disappeared also. . . .

What is the annual expense of your Sunday school? Very trifling; I have one collection a-year at the church, at which we generally get about £40; we do not go round to collect, it is a private thing done by the Teachers themselves; we have no master, or mistress, or any expense of that kind; the Teachers are all gratuitous and voluntary; the whole expense consists in the books and rent of the rooms; in fact now I have by great exertion got part of the vestry for a Sunday, which saves us the expense of paying rent.

Then the whole expense of this school does not exceed sixty or seventy pounds? Seventy or eighty pounds; we give a good many rewards, according to our funds; and we have a writing school in the week, for the children who behave the best.

What hours do the children attend on a Sunday? From about half-past eight or nine till twenty minutes before the church service commences in the morning, and again at two till five in the afternoon; we have not proper accommodation at the church for them, that is one great grievance to me; and if we had, we could have four times the number attend the school; we cannot accommodate them at the church, and I am forced to send a detachment of them to another chapel; I wanted to have a gallery erected; and I would have done it without any expense to the parish; two or three charity sermons would have done it.

How long does a child take, at the Sunday school, in learning to read, having no other instruction? Several have learnt to read in the course of about eighteen months; we would rather they would stay about two years, so as to be able to read a chapter in the Testament; but others, of course, will take much longer, in consequence of the difference of abilities and attention. . . .

At what age do the children come to your school, generally? We take them as soon as ever the boys have got breeches; we do not consult their age, but their size; we keep them till they are fit to go out; they generally leave us before they are twelve years of age; they are generally five years of age before we take them. I think altogether we have had four thousand children pass through the school during the last eight years; there are about three hundred out of the four hundred attend regularly; that is a very good proportion; and we are open to all parishes, without distinction.

[1816: pp. 14–17

THE CURRICULUM AND REGIME AT NEW LANARK. £1 A CHILD FOR SEVEN YEARS AS AN INVESTMENT IN EDUCATION
Evidence of Robert Owen, Esq. – 1816

What is the plan adopted by you? The children are received into a preparatory or training school at the age of three, in which they are perpetually superintended, to prevent them acquiring bad habits, to give them good ones, and to form their dispositions to mutual kindness and a sincere desire to contribute all in their power to benefit each other; these effects are chiefly accomplished by example and practice, precept being found of little use, and not comprehended by them at this early age; the children are taught also whatever may be supposed useful, that they can understand, and this instruction is combined with as much amusement as is found to be requisite for their health, and to render them active, cheerful and happy, fond of the school and of their instructors.

The school, in bad weather is held in apartments properly arranged for the purpose; but in fine weather the children are much out of doors, that they may have the benefit of sufficient exercise in the open air. In this training-school the children remain two or three years, according to their bodily strength and mental capacity; when they have attained as much strength and instruction as to enable them to unite, without creating confusion, with the youngest classes in the superior school, they are admitted into it; and in this school they are taught to read, write, account and the girls, in addition, to sew; but the leading object in this more advanced stage of their instruction, is to form their habits and dispositions.

The children generally attend this superior day school until they are ten years old; and they are instructed in healthy and useful amusements for an hour or two every day, during the whole of this latter period. Among these exercises and amusements, they are taught to dance; those who have good voices, to sing; and those among the boys who have a natural taste for music, are instructed to play on some instrument.

At this age, both boys and girls are generally withdrawn from the day school, and are put into the mills or to some regular employment. Some of the children, however, whose parents can afford to spare the wages which the children could now earn, continue them one, two or three years longer in the day school, by which they acquire an education which well prepares them for any of the ordinary active employments of life.

These children who are withdrawn from the day school at ten years of age . . . are permitted to attend, whenever they like, the evening schools, exercises and amusements, which commence as from one to two hours, according to the season of the year, after the regular business of the day is finished, and continue about two hours; and it is found that out of choice about 400, on an average, attend every evening. During these two hours there is a regular change of instruction, and healthy exercise, all of which proceed with such order and regularity as to gratify every spectator, and leave no doubt on any mind, of the superior advantages to be derived from this combined system of instruction, exercise, and amusement. The 400 now mentioned are exclusive of 300 who are taught during the day.

On the Sunday, the day scholars attend the school an hour and half in the morning and about the same time in the afternoon; and the evening scholars, as well as their parents and other adults belonging to the establishment, attend in the evening, when either some religious exercises commence, or a lecture is read, and afterwards the regular business of the evening Sunday school begins. These proceedings seem to gratify the population in a manner not easily to be described, and, if stated much below the truth, would not be credited by many; inspection alone can give a distinct and comprehensive view of the advantages which such a system affords to all parties interested or connected with it.

How many masters have you in the day schools? Generally ten or eleven; in the evening schools usually two or three more.

Is the expense of this institution considerable? It is, apparently; but I do not know how any capital can be employed to make such abundant returns, as that which is judiciously expended in forming the character and directing the labour of the lower classes.

I have made out a short statement of the expense of the instruction of the Institution at Lanark, and the expense of the instruction for 700 scholars, part taught in the day and part in the evening, supposing schools to be erected and furnished: One rector or superior master, at £250 per annum; ten assistants, males and females, at £30 each on the average; light, heat and materials of all kinds, £150; making together £700 or 20*s*. per year for each child, which if taken under tuition at three years old, and retained to the age of ten would be £7 each, for forming the habits, dispositions, and general character, and instruction in the elements of every branch of useful knowledge; which acquirements would be of more real value to the individual, and through him to the community, than any sum of money that at present it would be prudent to state. . . .

Do you consider a greater number of masters to be absolutely necessary, than is given upon the new plan? Yes.

Does not this sacrifice the great advantage of the new plan, which consists in enabling one master to teach a great number of children? I consider that circumstance to be a defect in the present system; it is impossible, in my opinion, for the master to do justice to children, when they attempt to educate a great number without proper assistance.

[1816: pp. 240–1

POVERTY

Evidence of Mr W. F. Lloyd, Secretary, Sunday School Union Society – 1818

There is one point which I may allude to, the amazing number of children in the metropolis who are prevented from attending any school whatever, from the absolute want of anything like decent clothing; there are a vast number of children employed in selling matches, sweeping the streets, and various other low employments, whose parents are very careless of their instruction; they will not put themselves to any trouble to procure decent clothing for their attendance at school; many of the parents are likewise so extremely poor, where there are large families, as to be unable to procure clothing. In Southwark, in one district, 2,000 children were found who could not attend any school for want of clothing; in one family, consisting of six children, there was only one suit of clothes, which each child was obliged alternately to use when he went into the street; I should suppose there are 15,000 in the bills of mortality, who are prevented from attending from this cause. . . .

[1818: pp. 8–9

2 · Report of the Parliamentary Committee on the State of Education. 1834

Parliamentary interest in education was stimulated by the Reform Bill of 1832 and the changes in the franchise. In 1833 the first moneys for school building were voted – £20,000 to be paid out as grants in aid of private subscription – and this was channelled through the National Society and the British and Foreign Schools Society.

Roebuck's Bill in 1833 outlined an ambitious State education system which was unacceptable to Parliament, but it was evidence of growing public interest. The parliamentary inquiry of 1834 gives another indication of this, and shows how events have moved since 1818. Support for compulsory, State-provided education remained scant among those who gave evidence.

These extracts include evidence from some of the chief witnesses. They were closely questioned on the denominational issue and the attitude of Church and Dissent in areas where there could only be one school. The drift of their thinking is brought out by the questions about inspection, teacher training and the social status of the teaching profession. An extract is included from the evidence of the Lord Chancellor, Lord Brougham, who opposed compulsory free schooling as contrary to the English tradition, and supported the principles of the Dual System.

1834 REPORT ON THE STATE OF EDUCATION

DENOMINATIONAL REQUIREMENTS IN CHURCH SCHOOLS

Evidence of the Rev. William Johnson, Clerical Superintendent of the National Society

Will you state to the Committee what are the general rules of the society with respect to religious instruction in the schools of the National Society? They are taught according to the doctrine and discipline of the Church of England.

The children are always taught the catechisms of the Church of England? Yes, there is no exception; none that go there refuse to be taught.

None are allowed to come to the schools without? The question has never been started; the impression is such that those who come there are instructed in the liturgy and catechism of the Church of England. . . .

Is there any obligation on the part of the parents of such children to allow their children to go to attend the worship of the Established Church on the

Sunday? I think I may refer the Committee to the 'plan of Union' which will define that very clearly. It is left to local committees to decide that as they see proper, and as may be satisfactory to the committees having charge of the local schools. As regards our own school, we are certainly always most anxious to have the children with us on the Sunday, but there are continually some absent on that day; reasons are assigned for their absence, and those reasons admitted; but I should not think myself justified according to the understood principle and practice on which the directing committee of the society act, to allow children to go to a dissenting place of worship. I wish to state that distinctly, because it is a point to which I apprehend the Committee mean to refer. . . .

In speaking of the central school, over which you have a sort of personal control, supposing, for example, that a child had attended during the whole week regularly, and that on the next Monday morning, having absented himself from the place of worship of the Established Church, should be asked why he was absent, and had stated that he had gone to the place of worship that his parents usually attended, would that child in your school be excluded? Certainly not. I should send for the parents and say such are my instructions, your child is expected to be here on the Sunday; and I can assure you that in no place where the child can possibly go, will greater kindness be shown to the child than by me, and occasionally have the parents been overcome in that way. . . .

TEACHER TRAINING AND SOCIAL COMPOSITION OF TEACHING FORCE

Are you in the habit of supplying the schools connected with you with masters and mistresses from the central school? That is one principal object of the society; . . . Since its institution in 1811, one of the principal objects of the National Society has been to promote the training of masters and mistresses in its own central schools and in the central schools of district societies throughout the country. . . .

Are there comparatively few instances of masters who take up the profession of masters who began in their youth devoting themselves to that particular walk of life; what proportion do those to whom you allude form of the whole of those who began with the profession of teaching? They must all have had some employment before the age of twenty one, and therefore I should say that they have all tried some profession or calling. The exception is so small that it is not worth mentioning; the greater number have been in some other business than that of keeping school; I think the majority have, certainly.

Do you think if you were to select one of your school boys distinguished by their proficiency, and were to give them a superior education as schoolmasters you would have a superior class of schoolmasters? I think we should be worse supplied than at present, considering that those children are connected with the very lowest of the people, and that their principles are not thoroughly matured, I should not recommend it as a general principle, fearing that it would not succeed.

Would you see any advantage in having a school entirely separate for boys rather higher than the lower class of society, of the middle class of society, who should be brought up from their youth with the intention of their being schoolmasters? I should also apprehend that this might not succeed. I would rather take the masters as we do, though they may not have succeeded in life. The greatest care is taken to investigate thoroughly their histories and previous mode of life. No master is received when there is any thing like a flaw in his moral or religious character; we have, therefore, now a kind of security that the parties admitted are equal to what we require of them, as well in regard to character and religious knowledge as in reading, writing and cyphering, and a knowledge of the English language. . . .

If a man were sufficiently well skilled in writing, reading and arithmetic, he could learn in five months the difficult art of teaching? Yes, decidedly; and it may be learnt in three months, if he has tact. . . .

What are the emoluments of the masters in those various district schools, can you state between what sums they vary? From £45 to £100 a year.

One hundred pounds a year is the highest salary that is now received? Yes, I think it is; latterly they have been falling off in amount. . . .

POVERTY AND SCHOOL FEES

You stated that the children of the national schools, make excuses for not attending on the Sunday at service, from want of clothes; has there been any alteration within your experience in the clothing of the children, either for the better or the worse? Those who come to us are better clothed than they were, certainly.

Are they the same class of society? I think they are; but we are establishing a penny clothing society, not only as regards their upper habiliments, but also their shoes; they subscribe a penny or two-pence a week, and are allowed to have shoes at one-half or a third less than their cost, as the case may be. . . .

Do you think that the habits of the children who apply for admission, are more cleanly than they were thirty years ago? There is not a question of that.

Should you from that infer an improvement in the lower orders of society? Yes. And the system is such as must produce a beneficial result on the population generally. Among other practices, with us, after prayers every morning, a regular inspection of the hands and faces of the children takes place; so that cleanliness growing into a habit, attaches itself to the child as he grows into life; and numerous proofs of the good effects of attention to it have shown themselves. . . .

Where instruction is given is it not more valued by parents where payment is received than where it is not? I am inclined to believe that it is more valued; and I think if the National Society were to be formed again, it is probable that all children might be required to pay. It is keeping up the honourable independence of the English labourer. The money could be well spared, as the very poorest of the children have been in the habit of spending upon trash and sweetmeats at least a penny a week.

Therefore you are not of opinion that a small payment of that kind being required prevents the poorest classes from attending the school? No, the poorest children that I have seen have their spending money; and about 18 years ago, in Baldwin's Gardens, I made a careful inquiry and search into the habit of spending this money. Our numbers were at that time much larger than since district schools have been established, which have of course reduced them. We had then a thousand children, and each of those children spent a penny a week, which forms a considerable sum at the end of the year. I have reason to believe that those scholars altogether, on an average, did not spend less than at the rate of £250 a year.

[1834 Report: pp. 4–15

TRAINING AND PAYMENT OF TEACHERS

Evidence of Mr W. F. Lloyd, Secretary to the Sunday School Union

From your extensive knowledge, what is your opinion of the general state of education among the industrious classes of society; is it very imperfect, and are some improvements, in your estimation, exceedingly desirable? There are some improvements which I think very desirable.

Will you state your opinions upon that subject? The first improvement which I think of very great importance is that of training up suitable persons for teachers, and that those teachers should have adequate encouragement; for the fact is, if a man is very clever as a teacher, he is generally picked up for some other employment, and it is not worth his while to continue in that pursuit; and for a man to be a clever teacher, he must have qualifications that would entitle him to double the remuneration he would get in average day schools.

What would be the lowest remuneration which you consider would be adequate to induce him to remain in that situation? It would depend upon the neighbourhood, whether it was a town population or an agricultural neighbourhood. I should be glad to see every efficient teacher of a day school have £100 a year in a town.

You mean that his place should be worth £100 a year, taking all things together, including any fees derived from the children, and any home that might be allotted to him? Yes.

PERIPATETICS?

With regard to the country districts, what would you propose? A plan has struck me with regard to country districts, that if there were a teacher who could have under his charge a school, say in each of three parishes, and could be furnished with a horse, so that he could be able to devote two hours to each of those parishes daily, it might be the means of carrying education into many neighbourhoods which are at present entirely destitute of daily instruction. If they could have two hours a day in agricultural neighbourhoods, it would be a wonderful advantage to them. The population in many of them is too small to support a school in one place, but if there were three villages under one master, and he had a horse furnished, he could visit those three schools in one day; and the schools might be taught in a cottage, so that there would be very little expense of that kind. And in that way, I think, the dense ignorance of many of our agricultural villages might thus be penetrated.

DEEP POVERTY

You think it very dense then? I do, in many places. . . .

Will you state any further suggestions that have occurred to you? A very important part of the population we cannot touch at all; I refer to the most degraded of the poor; I mean the children of trampers, and beggars and gipsies, and people of that kind. Sometimes by extraordinary efforts, we get some of those children into the school, but they are off again almost immediately; and those are the children from whom a very large proportion of our prisons are peopled. Now the difficulty is, how to get those children under instruction, and how to keep them under instruction.

What would you suggest? I hardly know any plan, unless someone connected with the administration of the poor could in some way or other be made binding on the parents to have their children educated. It is a very difficult question.

Does the difficulty arise in a great degree from the bad habits of the parents?

The great impediment we have in Sunday schools, and in all schools, is the bad example and bad habits of the parents. The teacher is pulling one way, and the parents are pulling directly the opposite, and that is the greatest impediment to the usefulness of schools. . . .

INSPECTION

Do you think it is desirable, that in any system of education inspectors should be appointed, whose duty it should be to superintend establishments and to ascertain the defects of education, and the progress it has made in any particular parts? I think next in importance to the system of training, would be a system of inspection. . . . There should be with respect to education a vigilant eye everywhere; and many schools have for want of that, sunk very materially indeed. Schools cannot be too much inspected and examined; and in proportion as the respectable people in the neighbourhood look after them or neglect them, in that proportion, generally speaking, they either flourish or decay. Such an inspection of all the schools throughout the kingdom, I think, would be an unspeakable blessing to society, and would be the means of conveying improvement, and suggesting information to teachers, and stirring them up and leading them to increase their efforts.

You stated it to be a desirable object that better teachers than those now existing should be trained; have you considered the details of any plan by which that could be accomplished? So far as relates to general matters, I think with respect to the two leading societies, if their training department were materially extended it would have a very good effect; the National School Society and the British and Foreign School Society, do good as far as they go in this respect. The training system I think should be extended very largely. . . .

Supposing the system of inspectors were considered desirable, would you see any objection to the Government supplying means for the maintenance of the inspectors? I think it would be a most desirable appropriation of money to inspectors, and I think it is a thing which cannot be done for the whole country unless it be done by the Government.

What schools would you submit to the inspection, would you submit to it all the schools in the country? I think all the schools throughout the kingdom for gratuitous education, or that are supported by the public in any way, should be examined by those inspectors. . . .

TRAINING COLLEGES AND THE SOCIAL STATUS OF TEACHING

Besides establishing a system of inspection, do you think the Government should also allot a sum of money for the establishment of schools for the training of teachers? I think it would be a very useful appropriation of money to the training of suitable teachers; I think it would be a very desirable thing to raise up a body of suitable teachers.

And that a grant from Government would be very well bestowed for that purpose? Very well bestowed.

Do you apprehend there would be the least want of adequate teachers, if the different schools could afford a salary which you think adequate? If you wanted 200 new teachers for schools now, you would hardly know where to find them; there is no system of supplying teachers who are trained and competent to convey instruction to others.

Do you happen to know ten good teachers unemployed? I do not think there are any thoroughly good teachers unemployed, but there are a great many indifferent ones now employed, because the conductors of schools cannot get better. I think 500 thoroughly good teachers, if they were adequately encouraged, could obtain instant employment; but if teachers are to have the wages of porters or ploughmen, you will never get fit persons for teachers. . . .

Supposing you had trained 500 masters, there would still be the difficulty arising from the smallness of the salary, which any particular school needing a master would be able to give him; how would you provide for that case? The only alternative would be to raise some extraneous means to increase his salary.

And you think it would be better to have extraneous means, than that the district itself in which he taught should pay him? I think it would lead to continued caballing in the district, and squabbling as to the election of the master.

Would not it lead in many cases to the district being contented with a person of very insufficient attainments, who would do the thing cheap? Yes; like some parishes where they have a pauper that can just read, and they make him schoolmaster, just to effect a little saving in the funds. I think local abuses of that kind would occur under such circumstances.

[1834 Report: pp. 101–5

COMBINATION OF PUBLIC AND PRIVATE EFFORT

Evidence of Mr H. Althans, Secretary to the East London Auxiliary Sunday School Union

You consider that nearly one half of our infant population are not adequately taught; have any means occurred to you by which this evil might be most effectually remedied? I am not aware of any means that have not been already mentioned for such purpose, that is, the supply of school-rooms to aid the voluntary principle and encourage it; if anything can be done in addition to train more competent teachers and to give them a better remuneration, I think education would thus be very greatly extended.

Supposing that the Government were to build schools upon the present principle, are there not a vast number of districts in the country where there are no persons who are willing to come forward to pay any portion towards the erection of those buildings? I am aw ıre there are such districts.

Then in those districts would it be possible to raise (unless the Government undertook the whole support of those institutions) this adequate remuneration to the master that you state to be indispensable for general improvement? I think in those districts, which we may call the most destitute, a considerable portion of the funds must be supplied; but in other districts I think that a smaller proportion of the funds being supplied would be quite sufficient.

Are there districts in which you think we cannot rely upon the voluntary principle? I do not say that you cannot rely upon it entirely in any district; I say, aid the voluntary principle, and then you will advance education.

You would like the voluntary principle to be acting in conjunction with the amount you receive from the parliamentary fund? My plan is to aid those that will help themselves.

Are there many that cannot help themselves? They ought to be obliged to raise something, if ever so little, to show a disposition. 'Let us know what you can raise, and then we will do what we can to aid you.'

Does it not appear to you that the poorest districts have the greatest need for assistance? I have known instances of poor districts doing wonderfully; the poor, when you can get them to give, will do much, and, therefore, the principle should be encouraged. I should fear, if the poor could have day school education for nothing, they would not sufficiently value it.

[1834 Report: p. 123

THE NATIONAL SOCIETY'S RELUCTANCE TO COMPROMISE

Evidence of the Rev. J. C. Wigram, Secretary to the National School Society

Although you have a million scholars in the Church of England schools, do not you think it is desirable that some additional system should be introduced, which should be more comprehensive of the youthful population at large? I think that wherever there is a population requiring it, there are the means of establishing additional schools of the same kind which now exist, and that if there are a sufficient number of dissenters in any place there may be a dissenters' school, and a Church of England school.

Supposing there are not a sufficient number of dissenters, then inasmuch as you have stated that of course they will be less likely to entertain the doctrines and the habits of their parents, after they have profited by the instruction of your school, is it not somewhat of a hardship that dissenters must either submit to that inconvenience, or leave their children uninstructed? That suggests a question to my mind, which is, supposing there are ten dissenters' families in a place, is it worth while risking the evil effects of having two institutions for the sake of a very limited number of scholars?

Might you not so regulate your institution as to include them? I have said that I do not know how it could be done, if the present schools are to be maintained with their religious character, to satisfy those that have established them. I do not know how they could give up so much as would, in the view of dissenters, make them more acceptable than they now are.

That is to say, the persons that have established these schools think it of greater importance to adhere to their peculiar plan, than to teach the whole population? They find their plan working admirably well; they do not find the difficulties alluded to in these questions, and they say let well alone. . . .

There can be no doubt of the right of each denomination to educate its own children from its own resources; but if aid is to come from the public purse, the question is, whether that aid shall be afforded to schools that comprehend all classes, or to schools affording education for different denominations, and how far you shall carry the system of separation; do you think that if a system of separation is adopted, it should be sufficient to say that there shall be one class for the Church and one class for all other denominations? I do not like to give an opinion upon a subject which I feel an aversion to go into; I am only concerned for one sort of school both officially and upon principle.

Do you think that the religious feelings of a great majority in a parish should be sacrificed with respect to education to the religious feelings of a small minority? I do not hesitate to say that as a clergyman of the Church of England I could only promote education upon those principles which I approve.

[1834 Report: pp. 69–70

THE CASE FOR GOVERNMENT NORMAL SCHOOLS

Evidence of the Rev. Samuel Wood, Secretary of the school on the British system in Harp-alley

Supposing that the Government were willing to take any active steps for the promotion of education, have you ever considered in what way this interference would be most beneficial? I would first establish normal schools in all our principal towns, and connected with each there should be houses for lodging young men and women, who were learning the system. I would make those schools strictly Government schools, that is to say, I would place the management of them entirely in the hands of the Government; for this reason, that if any attempt were made to associate together Government officers and a committee chosen from mere subscribers, I am morally certain that the mere subscribers would spoil the scheme. You would have people associated with you, who knew nothing at all about the subject, whereas if you make them entirely Government schools, you have a chance of their being formed on a good model, and of one uniform system being established. At the same time I think it would be possible to interest the middle and higher class of the people in such institutions, by having annual or half-yearly examinations, to which the public might be invited. If I may judge from what I have seen at the Borough Road and at Harp-alley, I am certain that one of the best means of interesting the public in national education, is to call them together to see the results of some system in actual operation. At our annual examination, which is on the second Monday in October at seven in the evening, we have generally about two hundred boys present, and from 250 to 300 strangers; and the general impression made on all the company present is a most favourable one as to the progress which the boys make on such a system as we adopt. I think that is the best way to interest the public in education, to establish normal schools, and to have public examinations. . . .

In the schools of actual education all over the country would you not feel disposed to leave as much as possible the superintendence to the local residents? Certainly, it must be left as much as possible to the local committees.

You would leave a great part to be played by the local committees in any system of education to be established over the country? I think that if Government were to establish good model schools, and invite the public to come and see what the children actually learn under the system, each of those establishments would be a focus of light and improvement, and would excite people to form similar schools in all that neighbourhood; and the schools thus founded should be under the management of committees of private individuals.

[p. 166

BETTER TEACHER TRAINING AND ITS EFFECT ON TEACHERS' STATUS

Evidence of Mr W. Cotton, member of the Committee of the National Society

Suppose that the National Society, by expending a larger sum of money on its central or training school, and offering other pecuniary inducements to persons while in training, were to draw a superior class of persons into its service, and, by retaining them for a longer time in training, were to furnish them with qualifications altogether of a higher and more intellectual kind than those which the schoolmasters throughout the country generally enjoy, is it your opinion that the superiority of such schoolmasters would cause a general rise and increase in the remuneration made for teaching schools? I am of opinion that it would not, and for this reason, that I do not think there is a general demand through the country for that education which those masters, under the superior training, would be calculated to afford; and until that demand exists, it is needless to pay for the supply.

Do you think that schoolmasters possessed of such superior abilities would continue contented and settled in their occupation as schoolmasters, under such circumstances and in the manner it is understood they now do? Under present circumstances, I think not; I am supposing that the schoolmasters are raised above the ordinary information of persons in their rank of life. I am not one of those that think any body can know too much, whatever rank of life he may be in; but I think that if you were to raise the intellectual qualifications of the schoolmaster, without very materially raising his salary, he would find more profitable occupation by competition with others in another situation, and therefore you would not retain him. . . .

THE MAGNITUDE OF THE PROBLEM

Have you anything to offer in illustration or further confirmation of the evidence which you have now given? I am not aware of any other observation that I can offer, excepting this, which has long pressed upon my attention, and which I have endeavoured to urge upon the attention of others, that the great obstacle to the education of the great mass of the poor of this country is from the enormous extent of the parishes. In the eastern district of London, the populations of some of the parishes amount to 60,000. The utter impossibility of any clergyman or any set of gentlemen undertaking to provide funds for a comprehensive system of education, under such discouraging circumstances, must be evident. Another great obstacle is, the very low scale of intellectual power and of moral feeling in the lower orders.

[1834 Report: pp. 144–5

EDUCATION AS A PRIVATE VENTURE WITH PUBLIC HELP: THE CASE AGAINST FREE COMPULSORY SCHOOLING
Evidence of the Lord Chancellor, Lord Brougham and Vaux

Do you consider that the aid or interference of the Legislature is required for promoting general education in this country? I am of opinion that much good may be done by judicious assistance; but legislative interference is in many respects to be either altogether avoided or very cautiously employed because it may produce mischievous effects.

Do you think that a system of primary education, established by law would be beneficial? I think that it is wholly inapplicable to the present condition of the country, and the actual state of education. Those who recommend it on account of its successful adoption on the Continent, do not reflect upon the funds which it would require, and upon the exertions already made in this country by individual beneficence. In 1818, there were half a million of children taught at day schools supported by voluntary contributions; and if I may trust the accuracy of returns which I received in 1828 from nearly 500 parishes taken at random all over the country, that number had more than doubled. It is probable that day schools for 1,200,000 at the least are now supported without endowment, and endowed schools are established for above 170,000, making, in all, schools capable of educating nearly 1,400,000 children. But if the State were to interfere, and obliged every parish to support a school or schools sufficient for educating all children, two consequences would inevitably follow; the greater part of the funds now raised voluntarily for this purpose would be withdrawn, and the State or the rate-payers in each parish would have to provide schools for 2,000,000 of children, because the interference would be quite useless, unless it supplied the whole defect, which is the difference between schools for one-tenth, the present amount, and schools for one-seventh, the amount required to educate the whole people. Now, to establish and maintain such a number of schools, would be a most heavy expense. Suppose the average capacity of each to be 50 children, and the average number of those taught at the present unendowed day schools is under 35, there would be no less than 40,000 schools required, which, allowing only £50 a year for all expenses of salary and rent, would cost £2,000,000 a year. But supposing the expense provided for, I am clearly of opinion that one great means of promoting education would be lost, namely, the interest taken by the patrons of schools supported by voluntary contributions . . . By degrees, as the parents themselves become better educated, the indifference to the advantage of schooling for their children will disappear. That the funds now raised by subscription, and which amount to near a million a year, will entirely fail, I take to be the inevitable consequence of establishing a school rate. All will think they do enough by paying that . . . To which I must add, that my belief is, that a surer way to make education unpopular, and thus arrest its progress, could not be devised, than making it the cause either of a general tax, or of an increase in the parish rate.

Do you consider that a compulsory education would be justified, either on principles of public utility or expediency? I am decidedly of opinion that it is justifiable upon neither; but, above all, I should regard anything of the kind as utterly destructive of the end it has in view. Suppose the people of England were taught to bear it, and to be forced to educate their children by penalties, education would be made absolutely hateful in their eyes, and would speedily cease to be endured. They who have argued in favour of such a scheme from the example of a military government like that of Prussia, have betrayed, in my opinion, great ignorance of the nature of Englishmen. . . .

Are there any other objections to a national system of education, beside those you have stated? There is one which would make me pause before I consented to it; suppose the funds were easily to be had, and no diminution to be apprehended from the interference of the Government, I do not well perceive how such a system can be established, without placing in the hands of the Government, that is of the Ministers of the day, the means of dictating opinions and principles to the people. . . .

In the first of these questions reference is made to legislative assistance being given to the efforts made by individuals for educating the people; in what way does your Lordship think that such assistance ought to be given? I consider that it should by no means be afforded in the shape of yearly supplies to meet the current expenses of schools, that is, of ordinary schools; but it may safely and beneficially be given in the form of moderate sums, to defray the first cost of establishing a school, the outfit as it were.

It may also be made a condition of the grant, that an equal sum, or at least some portion of the outfit, should be provided by the patrons of the scheme. . . .

But I regard the mere planting of schools as wholly inadequate to meet the exigencies of the case. Mere reading, writing, ciphering, is not enough; the elements of historical and geographical knowledge, a little natural history and drawing, with grammar and singing, I regard as essentially necessary in even the most elementary education. What is done in Mr Wood's sessional school at Edinburgh, and in the Borough Road school of the British and Foreign Society, proves how easily this improvement of education may be effected, and what is now of so little avail as hardly to merit the name of instruction, be made most profitable and useful. For this purpose, I am of opinion that it is expedient to establish schools for the instruction of teachers, or what Mr Fellenberg did in 1809, under the name of a Normal school, or what the Prussian and the French systems have adopted. The expense thus bestowed is perfectly free from the objections which I have stated against a general national school system; and the Government having nothing to apprehend, in any manner of way, from such an interposition, has, in my clear opinion, no more imperative duty cast upon it than to make this provision for teaching masters. The beginning might be made in London, and a hundred teachers be qualified in a year, by fit instruction, in an establishment connected with some such good school as that in the Borough Road, at an expense not exceeding £4,000 for all charges, including rent and maintenance, as well as tuition. There should be another at York, for half the number; a third at Lancaster; and a fourth at Exeter. Two hundred and fifty accomplished masters could thus be sent out in a year, at an expense of not more than £10,000; but if it cost twice as much, I am clearly of opinion that it is the best manner of bestowing the money. . . .

The establishment of useful libraries is another object in promoting which the Government may safely and most advantageously interfere. The exertions of the Society for the Diffusion of Useful Knowledge have so greatly reduced the price of books, maps and prints, and are so constantly multiplying good elementary treatises of every kind, that nothing can be less difficult than the arranging a plan for parish libraries. I look forward to a measure of this sort being without much delay laid before the Government, and, if need be, recommended to Parliament. It has for some time past occupied our attention in the Society, where one of my colleagues has devoted a considerable portion of his time to the subject.

[From pp. 220-5

3 · Creation of the Committee of Council for Education. 1839

In 1839, six years after the first State grants for education had been voted and paid through the National Society and the British and Foreign School Society) the Committee of Council for Education was set up as an embryo education department. Dr James Kay (who later changed his name to Kay-Shuttleworth) was appointed secretary.

As Lord John Russell's letter to Lord Lansdowne (Lord President of the Council) on the occasion of the setting up of the Committee indicated, one of its prime tasks was to be the foundation of a national college for the training of teachers. The sum of £10,000 had been voted by Parliament in 1835 for this purpose.

But the same religious difficulties which had defeated Whitbread's Bill in 1806, Brougham's Bill in 1820, Roebuck's Bill in 1833 and other attempts, both inside and outside Parliament to promote legislation during the 1830's, made it impossible to obtain the agreement of the denominational interests affected by the proposal, and the money in the end was distributed to the two great voluntary societies in capital grants of £50 a student place. A number of new training colleges were founded at this time, including St Mark's, Chelsea, and the Borough Road Training College.

LETTER FROM LORD JOHN RUSSELL TO LORD LANSDOWNE · February 4, 1839

My Lord,

I have received Her Majesty's Commands to make a communication to your Lordship on a subject of the greatest importance. Her Majesty has observed with deep concern the want of instruction which is still observable among the poorer classes of Her subjects. All the inquiries which have been made show a deficiency in the general Education of the People which is not in accordance with the character of a Civilized and Christian Nation.

The reports of the chaplains of gaols show that to a large number of unfortunate prisoners a knowledge of the fundamental truths of natural and revealed religion has never been imparted.

It is some consolation to Her Majesty to perceive that of late years the zeal for popular education has increased, that the Established Church has made great efforts to promote the building of schools, and that the

National and British and Foreign School Societies have actively endeavoured to stimulate the liberality of the benevolent and enlightened friends of general Education.

Still much remains to be done; and among the chief defects yet subsisting may be reckoned the insufficient number of qualified schoolmasters, the imperfect mode of teaching which prevails in perhaps the greater number of the schools, and examination of the nature of the instruction given, the want of a Model School which might serve for the example of those societies and committees which anxiously seek to improve their own methods of teaching, and, finally, the neglect of this great subject among the enactments of our voluminous Legislation.

Some of these defects appear to admit of an immediate remedy, and I am directed by Her Majesty to desire in the first place, that your Lordship, with four other of the Queen's Servants should form a board or Committee, for the consideration of all matters affecting the Education of the People.

For the present it is thought advisable that this Board should consist of:

the Lord President of the Council
the Lord Privy Seal
the Chancellor of the Exchequer
the Secretary of State for the Home Department
the Master of the Mint.

It is proposed that the Board should be entrusted with the application of any sums which may be voted by Parliament for the purposes of Education in England and Wales.

Among the first objects to which any grant may be applied will be the establishment of a Normal School.

In such a school a body of schoolmasters may be formed, competent to assume the management of similar institutions in all parts of the country. In such a school likewise the best modes of teaching may be introduced, and those who wish to improve the schools of their neighbourhood may have an opportunity of observing their results.

The Board will consider whether it may not be advisable for some years to apply a sum of money annually in aid of the Normal Schools of the National and of the British and Foreign School Societies.

They will likewise determine whether their measures will allow them to afford gratuities to deserving schoolmasters; there is no class of men whose rewards are so disproportionate to their usefulness to the community.

In any Normal or Model School to be established by the Board, four principal objects should be kept in view, viz.

1. Religious Instruction

2. General Instruction
3. Moral Training
4. Habits of Industry

Of these four I need only allude to the first; with respect to Religious Instruction there is, as your Lordship is aware, a wide or apparently wide difference of opinion among those who have been most forward in promoting education.

The National Society, supported by the Established Church, contend that the schoolmaster should be invariably a Churchman; that the Church Catechism should be taught in the school to all the scholars; that all should be required to attend Church on Sundays, and that the schools should be in every case under the superintendence of the clergyman of the parish.

The British and Foreign School Society, on the other hand, admit Churchmen and Dissenters equally as schoolmasters, require that the Bible should be taught in their schools, but insist that no Catechism should be admitted.

Others again contend that secular instruction should be the business of the school, and that the ministers of different persuasions should each instruct separately the children of their own followers.

In the midst of these conflicting opinions there is not practically that exclusiveness among the Church Societies, nor that indifference to Religion among those who exclude dogmatic instruction from the school, which their mutual accusation would lead bystanders to suppose.

Much therefore may be effected by a temperate attention to the fair claims of the Established Church, and the religious freedom sanctioned by the law.

On this subject I need only say that it is Her Majesty's wish that the youth of this Kingdom should be religiously brought up, and that the right of conscience should be respected.

Moreover, there is a large class of children who may be fitted to be good members of society without injury or offence to any party – I mean pauper orphans, children deserted by their parents, and the offspring of criminals and their associates.

It is from this class that the thieves and housebreakers of society are continually recruited. It is this class, likewise which has filled the workhouses with ignorant and idle inmates.

The Poor Law Commissioners have very properly undertaken to amend the vicious system which has hitherto prevailed, and in the neighbourhood of the metropolis much has already been done under their auspices.

It is in this direction likewise that certain good can be accomplished. It sometimes happens that the training which the child of poor but virtuous parents receives at home, is but ill exchanged for the imperfect or faulty instruction which he receives at school debased by vicious association; but for those whose parents are dead, or who have no home but one of habitual vice, there can be no such danger.

In all such instances, by combining moral training with general instruction, the young may be saved from the temptations to crime, and the whole community receive indisputable benefit.

These and other considerations will, I am persuaded, receive from your Lordship the most careful attention. I need not enter, at present, into any further plans in contemplation for the extension of the blessings of sound and religious education.

4 · Inspection of Church Schools. Order in Council. 1840

The denominational struggles affected the relationship between the Government and the Church of England, now under the influence of the Oxford Movement on the threshold of an Anglican revival. The Inspection of Schools was one of the issues on which there were long and bitter battles. The Concordat was an attempt to spell out the nature of the dual control implied by State grants for church schools, by defining the peculiar status and responsibilities of the clerical inspector. The Government later (after 1847) extended the same procedures to the appointment and control of the inspectors for schools run by other denominations, including the Roman Catholics.

ORDER IN COUNCIL DATED AUGUST 10, 1840, RECORDING THE CONCORDAT WITH THE ARCHBISHOP OF CANTERBURY CONCERNING THE INSPECTION OF SCHOOLS

At the Court at Buckingham Palace, the 10th of August, 1840

Present,

THE QUEEN'S MOST EXCELLENT MAJESTY IN COUNCIL.

WHEREAS there was this day read at the Board a Report from the Lords of the Committee of Council on Education, dated the 15th July ultimo, in the words following, viz.:

'We, the Lords of the Committee of Council on Education, beg leave humbly to recommend to your Majesty that the following arrangements be made for the inspection of such Schools as are in connexion with the National School Society, or with the Church of England.

'1. – That before we recommend to your Majesty any person to be appointed to inspect Schools receiving aid from the public, the promoters of which state themselves to be in connexion with the National Society or the Church of England, we should be authorized to consult the Archbishops of Canterbury and York, each with regard to his own province, and that the Archbishops should be at liberty to suggest to us any person or persons for the office of Inspector, and that without their concurrence we should recommend no person to your Majesty for such appointment.

'We further beg leave to recommend to your Majesty that if either of the Archbishops should at any time, with regard to his own province, withdraw his concurrence in our recommendation of such appointment, your Majesty would be graciously pleased to permit us to advise your Majesty to issue your Order in Council, revoking the appointment of the said Inspector, and making an appointment in lieu thereof.

'We further beg leave humbly to recommend to your Majesty to direct that such portions of the Instructions to these Inspectors as relate to religious teaching shall be framed by the Archbishops, and form part of the general instructions issued by us to the Inspectors of such Schools, and that the general instructions shall be communicated to the Archbishops before they are finally sanctioned by us.

'We are further of opinion that each of the said Inspectors, at the same time that he presents any Report relating to such Schools to the Committee of the Privy Council, should be directed to transmit a duplicate thereof to the Archbishop of the province, and should also send a copy to the Bishop of the Diocese in which the School is situate, for his information.

'We are further of opinion that the grants of money which we may recommend to your Majesty should be in proportion to the number of children educated and the amount of money raised by private contribution, with the power of making exceptions in certain cases, the grounds of which will be stated in the annual Returns to Parliament.'

Her Majesty, having taken the said Report into consideration, was pleased, by and with the advice of Her Privy Council, to approve thereof; and the Lord President of the Council is to take the necessary steps herein accordingly.

5 · Instructions to Inspectors. 1840

Instructions to H.M. Inspectors were set out in the Minutes of the Committee of Council on Education, dated August 1840. These are notable for the modesty of the aims set forth and for the limits to the functions of the H.M.I. set out in paragraph 5.

The instructions about the inspection of church schools at the end were to carry out the requirements of the Concordat of the same date.

MINUTES OF THE COMMITTEE OF COUNCIL ON EDUCATION · 1840–1

I. – Instructions to Inspectors of Schools.

Committee of Council on Education.
Council Office, Whitehall, August, 1840,

Sir,

1. Her Majesty having been graciously pleased, on the recommendation of the Committee of Council, to appoint you one of the Inspectors of Schools, the Committee request your attention to the enclosed paper of instructions, with the documents thereto annexed, for your guidance in the discharge of the duties which will devolve on you.

2. While an important part of these duties will consist in visiting, from time to time, schools aided by grants of public money made by the authority of the Committee, in order to ascertain that the grant has in each case been duly applied, and to enable you to furnish accurate information as to the discipline, management, and methods of instruction pursued in such schools, your appointment is intended to embrace a more comprehensive sphere of duty.

3. In superintending the application of the Parliamentary grant for public education in Great Britain, my Lords have in view the encouragement of local efforts for the improvement and extension of elementary education, whether made by voluntary associations or by private individuals. The employment of Inspectors is therefore intended to advance this object, by affording to the promoters of schools an opportunity of ascertaining, at the periodical visits of inspection, what improvements in the apparatus and internal arrangement of schools, in school management and discipline, and in the methods of teaching, have been sanctioned by the most extensive experience. . . .

5. A clear and comprehensive view of these main duties of your office is at all times important; but when a system of inspection of schools

aided by public grants is for the first time brought into operation, it is of the utmost consequence you should bear in mind that this inspection is not intended as a means of exercising control, but of affording assistance; that it is not to be regarded as operating for the restraint of local efforts, but for their encouragement; and that its chief objects will not be attained without the co-operation of the school committees; – the Inspector having no power to interfere, and not being instructed to offer any advice or information excepting where it is invited.

6. The Committee will furnish you from time to time with a list of schools not aided by public grants, the school committees or chief promoters of which may have expressed a desire that they should be visited in the route of the Inspectors, when they are able conveniently to do so, in order that the school committees may have the advantage of the Inspectors' advice and assistance in the further improvement of their schools. In submitting the route of your visits of inspection for the approval of this Committee, my Lords request you to include these schools in your arrangements. When engaged in the inspection of a school aided by a public grant, a requisition may be presented to you from the promoters of some school, in the same town or village, not aided by a public grant, requesting you to visit their school. Whenever the special requirements of the public service permit your compliance with this request, my Lords are of opinion it is desirable that you should visit the school, and should convey to the parochial clergyman, the school committee, or chief promoters (whenever solicited to do so), the results of your experience in school management and education. You will specially report any such application to this Committee.

7. Acting on the principle of assisting local exertions, the Committee of Council have prepared a series of plans of school-houses for small parishes, villages, and towns, in which are exhibited those improvements which are suggested by an extensive comparison of the results of experience, and which they intend to render available to the promoters of schools, by furnishing them with an explanation of each plan in detail, together with specifications, working drawings, and estimates, and with forms for making contracts with builders, &c.

8. Their Lordships are strongly of opinion that no plan of education ought to be encouraged in which intellectual instruction is not subordinate to the regulation of the thoughts and habits of the children by the doctrines and precepts of revealed religion.

9. The reports of the Inspectors are intended to convey such further information, respecting the state of elementary education in Great Britain, as to enable Parliament to determine in what mode the sums voted for the education of the poorer classes can be most usefully applied. With this view, reports on the state of particular districts may

be required to ascertain the state of education in such districts, and how far the interference of Government or of Parliament can be beneficially exerted, by providing additional means of education. Your reports will be made to the Committee, but it is intended that they shall be laid before both Houses of Parliament.

10. The Committee doubt not you are duly impressed with the weight of the responsibility resting upon you, and they repose full confidence in the judgment and discretion with which your duties will be performed.

My Lords are persuaded that you will meet with much cordial co-operation in the prosecution of the important object involved in your appointment; and they are equally satisfied that your general bearing and conduct, and the careful avoidance of whatever could impair the just influence or authority of the promoters of schools, or of the teachers over their scholars, will concilate the confidence and good-will of those with whom you will have to communicate; you will thus best fulfil the purposes of your appointment, and prove yourself a fit agent to assist in the execution of Her Majesty's desire, that the youth of this kingdom should be religiously brought up, and that the rights of conscience should be respected.

By order of the
Committee of Council on Education,
JAMES PHILLIPS KAY.

INSTRUCTIONS FOR THE INSPECTORS OF SCHOOLS.

THE Lords of the Committee of Council on Education consider that the duties of the Inspectors of Schools may be divided into *three distinct branches*.

1st. Those duties relate, in the first place, to inquiry in neighbourhoods from whence applications have been made for aid to erect new schools, in order to enable the Committee of Council to determine the propriety of granting funds in aid of the expenses proposed to be incurred, or to the examination of certain special cases in which claims of peculiar urgency are advanced for temporary aid in the support and improvement of existing schools.

2ndly. To the inspection of the several schools aided by public grants issued under the authority of the Committee, and an examination of the method and matter of instruction, and the character of the discipline established in them, so as to enable the Inspector to report thereon to this Committee, for the information of both Houses of Parliament. In obedience to Her Majesty's Order in Council, dated August 10, 1840, a duplicate of such reports respecting schools connected with the

Established Church is to be forwarded by the Inspector to the Archbishop, and a copy to the Bishop of the diocese in which the school is situate, for his information.

3rdly. As incidental to and in furtherance of these duties, Inspectors may also be required by the Committee to make inquiries respecting the state of elementary education in particular districts.

In the case of Schools connected with the National Church the Inspectors will inquire, with special care, how far the doctrines and principles of the church are instilled into the minds of the children. The Inspectors will ascertain whether church accommodation of sufficient extent, and in a proper situation, is provided for them; whether their attendance is regular, and proper means taken to ensure their suitable behaviour during the service; whether inquiry is made afterwards by their teachers how far they have profited by the public ordinances of religion which they have been attending. The Inspectors will report also upon the daily practice of the school with reference to Divine worship: whether the duties of the day are begun and ended with prayer and psalmody; whether daily instruction is given in the Bible; whether the Catechism and the Liturgy are explained, with the terms most commonly in use throughout the authorized version of the Scriptures.

They will inquire likewise whether the children are taught private prayers to repeat at home; and whether the teachers keep up any intercourse with the parents, so that the authority of the latter may be combined with that of the former, in the moral training of the pupils. As an important part of moral discipline, the Inspectors will inform themselves as to the regularity of the children in attending school – in what way registered – and how enforced; as to manners and behaviour, whether orderly and decorous; as to obedience, whether prompt and cheerful, or reluctant, and limited to the time while they are under the master's eye; and as to rewards and punishments, on what principles administered, and with what results. The Inspectors will satisfy themselves whether the progress of the children in religious knowledge is in proportion to the time they have been at school; whether their attainments are showy or substantial; and whether their replies are made intelligently or mechanically and by rote. The Inspectors will be careful to estimate the advancement of the junior as well as of the senior class, and the progress in each class of the lower as well as of the higher pupils. And in every particular case the Inspector will draw up a report, and transmit a duplicate of it through the Committee of Council on Education to the Archbishop of the Province.

[From Minutes of the Committee of Council, 1840–41: pp. 1–11

6 · Pupil Teachers. 1846

The Committee of Council adopted in 1846 a scheme of apprenticeship for pupil teachers. This was a logical extension and development from the old, discredited monitorial system. Kay-Shuttleworth had observed attempts to train monitors in Poor Law Schools and had seen a pupil teacher scheme working in Holland. The introduction of the new regulations followed public controversy, arising from a published letter from Dr W. F. Hook (acting in collaboration with Kay-Shuttleworth) *On the means of Rendering more efficient the education of the People.*

There were various inter-related features of the scheme: a syllabus of training for pupil teachers with annual examinations, grants towards their stipends, bounties for masters taking apprentices, grants to schools, scholarships and bursaries for selected student teachers to attend the training colleges, grants to training colleges based on their student population, and a system of grants in aid of the salaries of schoolmasters appointed to schools under inspection.

MINUTES OF THE COMMITTEE OF COUNCIL ON EDUCATION · AUGUST 25TH, 1846

. . Their lordships had further under their consideration the report of the Inspectors of Schools, memorials from certain Boards of Education, and letters from the clergy and others, representing the very early age at which the children acting as assistants are withdrawn from school to manual labour, and the advantages which would arise if such scholars as might be distinguished by proficiency and good conduct were apprenticed to skilful masters, to be instructed and trained, so as to be prepared to complete their education as schoolmasters, in a normal school.

Resolved, – That the Lord President cause Regulations to be framed, defining the qualifications of the schoolmaster, the condition of instruction in the school, and the local contributions to be required as conditions on which annual grants of money may be made towards the stipends of apprentices in elementary schools; and further cause indentures of apprenticeship to be prepared, declaring the duties of the apprentice and the nature of the instruction he is to receive; the periods of examination by the Inspectors of Schools, and the circumstances under which the indenture may be dissolved, in order that stipends, increasing in each year of the apprenticeship, may be granted in aid of local contribution.

It was further resolved, – that as the masters having charge of the instruction and training of school apprentices will be selected for their character and skill and as the education of the apprentices will increase the labour and responsibilities of such masters, it is expedient that the successful performance of these duties be rewarded by annual grants in aid of their stipends. . . .

[1846. From Volume 1, pp. 1–2

MINUTES OF THE COMMITTEE OF COUNCIL ON EDUCATION DATED 21 DECEMBER, 1846

REGULATIONS RESPECTING THE EDUCATION OF PUPIL TEACHERS AND STIPENDIARY MONITORS

General Preliminary Conditions . . . That the master or mistress . . . is competent to conduct the apprentice through the course of instruction . . .

That the school is well furnished and well supplied . . .

That it is divided into classes; and that the instruction is skilful and is graduated according to the age of the children and the time they have been at school, so as to show that equal care has been bestowed on each class:

That the discipline is mild and firm, and conducive to good order:

That there is a fair prospect that the salary of the master and mistress, and the ordinary expenses of the school, will be provided during the period of the apprenticeship. . . .

Pupil Teachers – Qualifications of Candidates . . . They must be at least 13 years of age, and must not be subject to any bodily infirmity likely to impair their usefulness . . .

In schools connected with the Church of England, the clergyman and managers, and, in other schools, the managers must certify that the moral character of the candidates and of their families justify an expectation that the instruction and training of the school will be seconded by their own efforts and by the example of their parents. If this cannot be certified of the family the apprentice will be required to board in some approved household.

Candidates will also be required:

1. To read with fluency, ease and expression.
2. To write in a neat hand with correct spelling and punctuation, a simple prose narrative slowly read to them.

3. To write from dictation sums in the first four rules of arithmetic, simple and compound; to work them correctly, and to know the table of weights and measures.
4. To point out the parts of speech in a simple sentence.
5. To have an elementary knowledge of geography.
6. *In schools connected with the Church of England* they will be required to repeat the Catechism, and to show that they understand its meaning and are acquainted with the outline of Scripture history. The parochial clergyman will assist in this part of the examination.

In other schools the state of the religious knowledge will be certified by the managers.

7. To teach a junior class to the satisfaction of the Inspector.
8. Girls should also be able to sew neatly and to knit.

[*Then follow details of the requirements for examination at the end of each of the five years of apprenticeship. The Minute also provides for a less complete, four-year course of apprenticeship and training for Stipendiary Monitors because 'the Inspectors may, for some time, find in the rural districts schools in which all the general conditions required for the apprenticeship of a pupil teacher may be satisfied, but the master or mistress of which may be unable to conduct an apprentice . . . through the foregoing course'.*

The Minute provides for stipends paid by the Committee of Council 'irrespective of any other sum that may be received from the school or from any other source' – for a pupil teacher £10 at the end of the first year, rising to £20 at the end of the fifth, and for the Stipendiary Monitor £5 at the end of the first year rising to £12. 10. 0 at the end of the fourth.]

Renumeration and Duties of Schoolmasters and Mistresses:

At the close of each of these years, if the pupil teachers have received a certificate of good character and of satisfactory progress, the master or mistress by whom they have been instructed and trained shall be paid the sum of £5 for one, of £9 for two, of £12 for three pupil teachers, and £3 per annum for every additional apprentice; and on the like conditions, £2. 10s. for one stipendiary monitor, £4 for two, £6 for for three, and £1. 10s. in addition in each year for every additional stipendiary monitor. . . .

In consideration of the foregoing gratuity, and of the assistance obtained from the pupil teachers and stipendiary monitors in the instruction and management of the school, the master will give them instruction in the prescribed subjects, during one hour and a half at least during five days in the week, either before or after the usual hours of school-keeping. . . .

[1846. From Volume 1, pp. 2–9

SUPPORT OF NORMAL SCHOOLS
EDUCATION OF SCHOOLMASTERS AND MISTRESSES, AND GRANTS IN AID OF THEIR SALARIES

. . . The Lord President should authorize one or more of Her Majesty's Inspectors, together with the Principal of a normal school . . . to submit . . . from among the pupil teachers who had successfully terminated their apprenticeship, a certain number . . . who, upon competition in a public examination, to be held annually . . . might be found most proficient . . .

That the Committee of Council . . . should award, for as many as they might think fit, an exhibition of £20 or £25 to one of the normal schools . . .

that the pupil teachers to whom such exhibitions should be awarded should be thenceforward denominated 'Queen's Scholars' . . .

. . . In order still further to reduce the burden of such establishments, [i.e. normal schools], their Lordships will award to every normal school subject to inspection a grant for every student . . . Such grants shall be £20 at the close of the first year, £25 at the close of the second, and £30 at the close of the third . . .

Their Lordships will further grant, in aid of the salary of every schoolmaster appointed to a school under their inspection, and who has had one year's training in a normal school . . . £15 or £20 per annum; and in aid of the salary of every such schoolmaster who has had two years of such training, £20 or £25 per annum; and of every such schoolmaster who has had three years of such training £25 or £30 per annum . . . on the following conditions:

1. that . . . the school provide the master with a house rent-free and a further salary, equal at least to twice the amount of this grant.
2. that . . . his character, conduct and attention to his duties are satisfactory.
3. that the Inspector report that his school is efficient . . .

[1846. From Volume 1, pp. 10–11

7 · Report of the Commissioners of Inquiry into the State of Education in Wales. 1847

Commissioners: *R. R. W. L. Lingen; J. C. Symons; H. V. Johnson*

The Parliamentary Commission was set up after a motion was introduced in 1846 praying the Queen 'To direct an inquiry to be made into the State of Education in the Principality of Wales'. Kay-Shuttleworth's letter of instructions included a reference to the need to form an estimate 'of the influence which an improved education might be expected to produce on the general condition of society, and its moral and religious progress'.

This opened the way to the strictures on Welsh morality which are a feature of the reports.

Concern about the state of Welsh education had been aroused by Hugh Owen, whose *Letter to the Welsh People* appeared in 1843, advocating non-denominational schools, supported by Government grants. He formed the Cambrian Educational Society in 1846, working closely with the British and Foreign Schools Society.

The 1847 Departmental Committee investigated and described the state of elementary education in the principality in scathing terms. Examination proved the prevalence of learning by rote and the ignorance of the scholars, even of the set-piece Biblical lessons in which they were ready to be tested. The Commissioners also took evidence from the clergy and other leading citizens on the moral state of the populace which turned out to be shameless in certain respects. The report was bitterly attacked in Wales and by nonconformity as part of a campaign against the Welsh. In particular it was alleged that the Established Church used the occasion to traduce the nonconformists. (Evening prayer meetings were held partly responsible for illegitimacy because young people were encouraged to attend and walk home alone afterwards.) In fact, though prejudiced and unsympathetic, the Commissioners were more ignorant than malicious. Sweeping comments on moral degradation were not reserved for the Welsh. Compare the report of Rev. Henry Moseley, M.A., F.R.S., Inspector of Schools, on the elementary schools of the Midland District which appeared a year earlier (in the Minutes of the Committee of Council, 1846, vol. 1).

Mr Moseley, like the Welsh Commissioners, relied much on local clergy for information. In south Staffordshire there was good money to be earned. 'The earnings of these men', wrote Mr Moseley, 'were at the time of my visit, probably greater than those of any equally large body of workmen in the Kingdom. Of the numerous class employed in the manufacture of wrought iron from cast, called puddlers, the average wages were £2. 10s. a week. The weekly wages of others were £3 and of some as much as £6 or £7. . . . These men and their families, nevertheless, live in more squalid and miserably dirty and worse furnished abodes, their children appear worse clad and more neglected, their wives more slatternly and poverty stricken, and about each of them fewer appliances of comfort, and fewer sources of happiness, have been collected, than I have observed in respect to any other labouring population. The country, not less in its moral than in its physical aspect, seems to be scorched up. . . .

'The miners of Bilston are 5000 in number, and it is computed that £50,000 are spent by them annually in the purchase of ale. In . . . Moxley there are said to be 440 houses and from 30 to 40 beer-shops, being one beershop to every 12 houses. . . .

'If the wages of the entire labouring community could be doubled tomorrow, their happiness would not be thereby necessarily increased, or their position elevated but rather, I fear, degraded.

'It is stated on good authority that of the 5000 miners of Bilston there are 4000 who attend no place of worship, and that the whole number of persons arrived at years of discretion in that place and in the district immediately surrounding it, who thus entirely neglect the public ordinances of religion, is 11,000 out of a population of 24,000.

. . . 'In no schools that I have visited has it been found necessary to fix the fees of admission lower . . .

. . . 'An opulent proprietor, had, at the period of my last visit to the schools in his district, withdrawn his annual subscription of £1 because writing had, against his judgement, been added to the subjects of instruction.'

But there was a ray of hope. The Savings Bank had begun to attract depositors – 800 of them. A gentleman had told Mr Moseley of his success in encouraging a workman to start to save. 'At the end of five years he drew out the fund he had accumulated, amounting, I think, to £13, bought a piece of land, and has built a house on it. I think if I had not spoken to him, the whole amount would have been spent in feasting, or clubs, or contributions to the trade union.' Mr Moseley treats himself to italics to sum up the moral of salvation through property. '*That man's eyes are now open* – his social position is raised – *he sees and feels as we do*, and will influence others to follow his example.'

The interest in education aroused by the Welsh Report, notwithstanding its offensive tone, was maintained. It extended to higher education, and built up into the popular movement which enabled the University College of Wales to be founded at Aberystwyth in 1872 with money collected from rich and poor alike throughout Wales.

REPORT OF THE COMMISSIONERS OF INQUIRY INTO THE STATE OF EDUCATION IN WALES · 1847

From Part Two: Report of Mr J. C. Symons on Brecknock, Cardigan, Radnor and Monmouth

A PENNY FOR AN ANSWER

After the master or teacher had heard one or two classes read, and I had seen him give in his own way all the instruction I could prevail on him to exhibit, I have invariably requested permission to have the children to myself and to examine them *ad libitum*, which without a single exception has been willingly granted; and in a majority of cases I have been earnestly begged to examine the scholars myself before it comported with my object to release the teacher from the exercise of his functions. The lesson selected was almost invariably a chapter in the Bible in the first instance, and, with the exception of one or two superior schools, it was the only lesson capable of exhibition. When, upon asking a few simple initiatory questions on the subject of the lesson, I perceived any bashfulness or any very striking ignorance, or any reluctance to answer, I have made it a constant practice to promise pence to the children who in a short time should have answered the most promptly and the most correctly. I did this not only in cases of bashfulness, in order to counteract it, but in cases of gross ignorance, in order to test its reality. When assured by a child that it had never heard for instance of the Apostles or of our Lord, or that it did not know the number of months or weeks in a year, or whether Ireland was a town, a man, or a country, I invariably offered a penny to that child if it would tell me rightly; nor did I allow myself to be satisfied of its ignorance until its genuine anxiety to get the penny had prompted the wild guesses. . . .

[p. 206

IGNORANCE

I found children who read fluently constantly ignorant of words such as 'observe', 'conclude', 'reflect', 'perceive', 'refresh', 'cultivate', 'contention', 'consideration', 'meditation', &c. . . .

No working-class child is in the habit of saying 'I *observed* my brother pass by', &c.; the expression used is, 'I *see'd* him go by'. Another reason why there is so little comprehension by the child of what he reads is that the poorer classes are either British, or Saxon retaining only Anglo-Saxon terms, whilst the books they read are chiefly written in language a large portion of which is of Norman or Roman derivation.

The proficiency of the children in spelling is wonderful. . . . I attribute this proficiency in spelling to its being that which gives the master the least trouble to teach and test, and to the very great power of memory which the children possess.

There is next to no religious instruction in the day-schools. In the adventure* schools the masters and mistresses, when they spoke out, admitted that they did not teach it, and that the parents would be dissatisfied if they did. One master said to me, 'Why, they all go to Sunday-schools: is not that enough?' The Holy Scriptures are, as I have said, read in every school I have been in with one exception, but almost universally as a text-book to learn reading by, selected chiefly on account of its cheapness, and in some measure because it is considered a test of education 'to read in the Bible'. Of scriptural knowledge the children have no idea, except in the few superior schools. . . .

[p. 256

SUNDAY SCHOOLS

The Sunday-schools, where grown-up persons constitute a large portion of the scholars, afforded me some slight insight into the information possessed by the adult classes. I desired to improve the means of ascertaining their mental state, and I therefore lost no available opportunity of engaging them in conversation wherever I met with them, and probing their amount of information and opinions. This was a work of some difficulty and delicacy; to the satisfactory execution of which my note-book was a complete barrier. The natural suspicion attaching to an Englishman questioning a peasant at all, and especially where it was known that he was likewise an emissary of the Government, generally closed their mouths the moment any attempt was made to reduce their answers to writing, unless my questions were confined to the means of education for their children, which always propitiated them.

[p. 207

TEACHERS

No person, really qualified for the office of schoolmaster by moral character, mental energy, amiability of temper, and proficiency in all the elementary branches of education, together with aptitude in imparting knowledge, will doom himself to the worst paid labour and almost the least appreciated office to be met with in the country.

Were even the means of training schoolmasters as ample as they are defective, and were the number of men adequately trained to the work

* That is, private schools run for profit.

at hand, the generality of schools would be not one jot the better supplied, for such training would fit men for employment in other spheres, where they would realize four or five times the emolument and enjoy a much higher social position than they can hope for as schoolmasters in Wales under existing circumstances.

[p. 252

MORAL AND PHYSICAL CONDITION

I have hitherto, my Lords, treated of the actual state of education in my district. It remains alone for me to advert to the moral character and condition of the population, the general state of intelligence and information of the poorer classes, and to the influence which an improved education might be expected to produce on the general condition of society and its moral and religious progress. . . .

The people in my district are almost universally poor. In some parts of it wages are probably lower than in any part of Great Britain. . . .

. . . The farmers themselves are very much impoverished, and live no better than English cottagers in prosperous agricultural counties . . .

The evidence given me of the immoral character of the people, with a few exceptions, tells the same tale. The Welsh are peculiarly exempt from the guilt of great crimes. There are few districts in Europe where murders, burglaries, personal violence, rapes, forgeries, or any felonies on a large scale are so rare. On the other hand, there are, perhaps, few countries where the standard of minor morals is lower. Petty thefts, lying, cozening, every species of chicanery, drunkenness (where the means exist), and idleness, prevail to a great extent among the least educated part of the community, who scarcely regard them in the light of sins. There is another very painful feature in the laxity of morals voluntarily attested by some of those who have given evidence. I refer to the alleged want of chastity in the women. If this be so, it is sufficient to account for all other immoralities, for each generation will derive its moral tone in a great degree from the influences imparted by the mothers who reared them. Where these influences are corrupted at their very source, it is vain to expect virtue in the offspring. The want of chastity results frequently from the practice of 'bundling', or courtship on beds, during the night—a practice still widely prevailing. It is also said to be much increased by night prayer-meetings, and the intercourse which ensues in returning home. These are not the only causes of this vice. It results also from the revolting habit of herding married and unmarried people of both sexes, often unconnected by relationship, in the same sleeping rooms, and often in adjoining beds without partition or curtain. Natural modesty is utterly suppressed by this vile practice, and the instinctive delicacy alike in men and women is destroyed in its very germ. These practices obtain in the classes immediately above as well as among the labouring people. . . .

The Reverend R. Harrison, the Incumbent of Builth, says–

'The Welsh are more deceitful than the English; though they are full of expression, I cannot rely on them as I should on the English. There is more disposition to pilfer than among the English, but we are less apprehensive of robbery than in England. There is less open avowal of a want of chastity, but it exists; and there is far less feeling of delicacy between the sexes here in every-day life than in England. The boys bathe here, for instance, in the river at the bridge in public, and I have been insulted for endeavouring to stop it. There is less open wickedness as regards prostitution than in England. Drunkenness is the prevailing sin of this place and the country around, and is not confined to the labouring classes, but the drunkenness of the lower classes is greatly caused by the example of those above them, who pass their evenings in the public-houses. But clergymen and magistrates, who used to frequent them, have ceased to do so within the last few years. I have preached against the sin, and used other efforts to check it, though I have been insulted for doing so in the street. I think things are better than they were in this respect. . . . I do not think they are addicted to gambling, but their chief vice is that of sotting in the public houses.

'They are very dirty. I found a house in Builth where, in the bedroom down stairs, I found two pigs in one corner, and two children ill with the scarlet fever in the other. The dunghills are placed in the front of the houses in some parts of the town.'

I can speak in very strong terms of the natural ability and capacity for instruction of the Welsh people. Though they are ignorant, no people more richly deserve to be educated. In the first place, they desire it to the full extent of their power to appreciate it; in the next, their natural capacity is of a high order, especially in the Welsh districts. They learn what they are even badly taught with surprising facility. Their memories are very retentive, and they are remarkably shrewd in catching an idea. In the words of a clergyman who has lived among them, they 'see what you mean before you have said it'.

[pp. 292–309

WELSH LANGUAGE

The evil of the Welsh language . . . is obviously and fearfully great in courts of justice. . . . It distorts the truth, favours fraud, and abets perjury, which is frequently practised in courts, and escapes detection through the loop-holes of interpretation. This public exhibition of successful falsehood has a disastrous effect on public morals and regard for truth. The mockery of an English trial of a Welsh criminal by a Welsh jury, addressed by counsel and judge in English, is too gross and shocking to need comment. It is nevertheless a mockery which must continue until the people are taught the English language; and that will not be done until there are efficient schools for the purpose.

[pp. 309-10

8 · Reports of the Royal Commissions on the Universities of Oxford and Cambridge

Published: *1852–3*

OXFORD

Chairman: *Rt Rev. Dr Samuel Hinds, Bishop of Norwich*

Members: *Dr A. C. Tait; Dr Francis Jeune; H. G. Liddell; J. L. Dampier; Professor Baden Powell; G. H. S. Johnson*

Secretary: *Rev. A. P. Stanley*

CAMBRIDGE

Chairman: *Rt Rev. Dr John Graham, Bishop of Chester*

Members: *Dr G. Peacock; Sir John Herschel, Bart.; Sir John Romilly, Attorney General; Professor Adam Sedgwick*

Secretary: *Rev. W. H. Bateson*

Terms of Reference: *To inquire into the State, Discipline, Studies and Revenues of our University (Oxford and Cambridge) and of all and singular the Colleges in our said University(ies).*

The Royal Commissions on Oxford and Cambridge were the first in the remarkable series of mid-century full-dress inquiries into education at all levels. The origin of this upsurge of interest was both simple and complex – simple, in that no-one who examined the schools or the universities could doubt that a great deal needed to be done; complex in that the sixth decade of the nineteenth century saw the combination of circumstances, political and economic, in which new departures became possible.

Internal reform had already begun at both Oxford and Cambridge, Oxford being the more slow and resolutely hidebound. In 1849, there was a petition for a Royal Commission signed by Fellows of the Royal Society from both Universities. When Lord John Russell accepted a parliamentary request for a Royal Commission, Oxford resisted the Commissioners and refused to co-operate. (The Hebdomadal Board told Lord John Russell via the Duke of Wellington, Chancellor of the University: 'Two centuries ago – in 1636 – the University revised the whole body of its statutes, and the academic system of study was admirably arranged at a time when not only the nature and faculties of the human mind were exactly what they are still, and must, of course, remain, but the principles also of sound and enlarged intellectual culture were far from being imperfectly understood.')

Cambridge, where Prince Albert was Chancellor, welcomed them. The tone of the two reports was quite different. The Oxford Commission was radically critical; the Cambridge Commission commented favourably on the changes already taking place to liquidate unwanted traditional restrictions and open up new courses of study.

The extracts which follow are from the Oxford Report. While some influential Oxford figures such as Jowett and Stanley, who later became Secretary of the Commission, wrote to offer as much help as they could, the Commissioners clashed with certain basic Oxford ideas about the nature of the University.

Dr Hinds, Chairman of the Oxford Commission, had been an undergraduate of Queen's, and later vice-principal of St Alban Hall. He was a close associate of Archbishop Whately. Dr Jeune was the only College head (Pembroke). Dr A. C. Tait was a Glasgow graduate who had been a don at Balliol, and was later to become Archbishop of Canterbury (1869–82). As a group, the Commissioners were regarded as undoubted liberals.

The Commissioners tended to see the University point of view as conflicting with that of the Colleges. They stood for the professoriate and the lecture system as against the tutors and the College teaching. They saw the University as a place of universal research and learning, where the dons were wedded to a particular form of liberal education. Their notion of what was needed had a strangely modern ring: 'to place the best education within reach of all qualified to receive it' (see p. 67).

Both Committees proposed reform of University government, the Hebdomadal Board and the Council of the Senate, to make it more democratic, less dominated by *ex-officio* representatives. They proposed that English should be allowed as the language for discussion in Congregation and Senate, instead of Latin. Both reports approved of wider courses of study, and rejected closed fellowships. The Oxford Report favoured more students in non-collegiate halls and lodgings to make it possible for poorer students to attend. The Cambridge Report, which was less antagonistic to the Colleges, opposed non-collegiate students.

The Oxford University Act of 1854 and the Cambridge University Act of 1856 reformed the methods of University government and placed the Colleges and the Universities under notice to reform themselves or receive statutory commissioners. Powers were given to alter trusts more than fifty years old, and amend College statutes. Nonconformists were enabled to become members of Colleges, and take first degrees, but were still unable to become fellows.

The Acts were successful in stimulating and directing the impetus towards reform already present at both Universities.

REPORT OF ROYAL COMMISSION ON OXFORD . 1852

Preamble

To the Queen's Most Excellent Majesty.

On three of the points to which our attention was directed . . . the State, Discipline and Studies of the University and of the Colleges – we have received evidence from the great majority of the professors and from many persons of note . . . in Oxford . . .

The Governing Body has withheld from us the information which we sought through the Vice-Chancellor as its chief resident officer; and this, as has been since intimated to us, with the purpose of disputing the legality of your Majesty's Commission. We have had, however, the means of learning the opinions of the Heads of Houses, as a body, on several of the subjects which we have considered, and to some extent the reasons which determined their conclusions . . .

DISCIPLINE

It is satisfactory to find that when we compare the discipline, the order and the morals of the University with what they are reported to have been even within the memory of living men, that a decided reform has taken place . . . The grosser exhibitions of vice, such as drunkenness and riot have in Oxford, as in the higher classes generally, become rare. The intercourse of the undergraduates with their tutors has, in many cases, become more confidential and more frequent . . .

There still remains, however, much to be done . . . Of existing evils the most obvious are sensual vice, gambling in its various forms and extravagant expenditure . . . In the villages round Oxford . . . the opportunities to vice are too abundant . . .

Gambling is carried on in the University, as elsewhere, in such a manner as to make it extremely difficult of detection . . . A system of espionage would be wholly uncongenial to the spirit of the place . . .

Between the small class which is guilty of disgraceful extravagance and the larger body which is prudent, there is still a considerable number of young men who spend far more than they have any right to spend . . .

Driving, riding and hunting are . . . causes of great expense. Of these amusements the most expensive is hunting. It seldom costs less than four guineas a day. Some of those who indulge in it are accustomed to it at home and can afford it; on this ground as well as on the supposition that it often takes the place of worse pursuits, it is in several colleges overlooked or permitted. It is, however, a matter which ought to be under strict control . . .

It is important to observe that no permanent good results can be expected from these or any other means, unless a change is effected in the habits and the temper of the students themselves. Those who are studious at present are, for the most part, moral and frugal. But a large proportion of students are now unemployed and require additional incentives to study. Without this there is no effectual security against vice.

[From pp. 22–7

UNDERGRADUATE EXPENSES

On the whole, we believe that a parent, who, after supplying his son with clothes and supporting him at home during the vacations, has paid for him during his university course not more than £600, and is not called upon to discharge debts at its close, has reason to congratulate himself. . . .

[From p. 33

POVERTY NO BAR TO SCHOLARSHIP

[*After quoting from a Royal Commission Report on the Scottish Universities describing how students lived on a pittance in term-time and returned 'to hold the plough and cut the harvest' in the vacation, the report continues*]

Such brave struggles might perhaps be witnessed in Oxford, too, if the poor were admitted to the University without being forced to join any college or hall, as of old.

It may not be likely that any considerable number of students so poor as those to whom we have just alluded will resort to Oxford, as it is not proposed that the literary qualifications of any candidates for admission should be lowered. Yet, as there have been, so there might still be men of genius who could adequately prepare themselves for the University even while pursuing mechanical or menial occupations, and who would confer honour on it as well as derive honour from it. The training institutions for masters of schools for the poor are likely to produce pupils of great powers, who would probably desire a University education if they considered it within their reach, and would submit to great privations in order to obtain it. The loss of one such person would be a serious loss . . . We believe that, without the necessity of any great self-denial, young men might be supplied with all that is necessary, on very moderate terms, in private lodging houses . . .

[From p. 49

AIMS DEFINED

What is needed is to make the University a great seat of learning; to bring together the ablest instructors and the ablest students; to enable many who could not otherwise become members of the University to avail themselves of the advantages attached to its training and society; to cause the rewards and stimulants of its endowments to bear on the largest possible number of minds . . . What is needed is to place the best education within the reach of all qualified to receive it; not to offer some solace to those who are excluded. . . .

[From p. 54

RELIGIOUS TESTS

There is one large class of the community which is excluded though not by poverty . . ., namely those who are unwilling to subscribe to the Thirty Nine Articles of the Church of England.

The question respecting the admission of Dissenters to the University is one which we are instructed not to entertain. We merely call attention to the fact that several members of the University have recorded in their evidence a strong opinion that the present policy in this matter should be abandoned . . . It may be observed that the Subscription is found practically neither to exclude all who are not members of the Church of England, nor to include all who are. On the one hand it is no obstacle to the admission of some persons who are known to be members of other Communions such as the Evangelical Church of Prussia, the Evangelical Society of Geneva, the Wesleyan body, and the Established Church of Scotland. On the other hand there are persons who, though members of the Church of England are unwilling to declare that they adopt all that is contained in the Articles, and therefore feel themselves excluded from taking the higher degrees. It, certainly, is singular that a lay Corporation should require laymen, simply as a condition of membership, that which the Church of England does not require for participation in its most sacred Ordinance . . . We do not offer any suggestions as to the manner in which this evil should be remedied; but we must express our conviction that the imposition of Subscription, in the manner in which it is now imposed in the University of Oxford, habituates the mind to give a careless assent to truths which it has never considered, and naturally leads to sophistry in the interpretation of solemn obligations.

[From pp. 54–6

NEED FOR WIDER COURSES OF STUDY

Following the Examination Statute of 1850. All students will henceforward be permitted to choose . . . the special studies of Law and History, or Mathematical Science or Natural Science; but previously to his examination in any of these branches, each candidate for a degree must still present himself in the School of Literae Humaniores, to be there examined in Classics for the third time, as well as Philosophy and History.

No doubt this restriction was maintained in consequence of an opinion which has long prevailed at Oxford with regard to the nature of a liberal education. It has been held to be the sole business of the University to train the powers of the mind, not to give much positive or any professional knowledge; and the study of the classical books is regarded as the best means of refining and invigorating the mind. The education given has hitherto been the same for all, whether clergymen or barristers, medical men or private gentlemen . . .

A different theory of education prevailed . . . when the ancient statutes were drawn up . . . Youths usually came to the University at a very early age, and stayed many years. At first they found it a mere grammar school, but afterwards a place where all the knowledge of the age might be deeply studied. At the present day, young men come into residence at a much more advanced age, and yet the University is for the majority of them a mere grammar school from first to last . . .

It is important to note the extent to which all separate branches of learning both professional and preparatory to professions have been suffered to decay. . .

Oxford still educates a large proportion of the clergy; but learned theologians are very rare in the University, and in consequence, they are still rarer elsewhere . . .

Oxford has ceased altogether to be a school of medicine . . . The connexion of Oxford with the profession of the law is also unsatisfactory. The number of barristers not educated at either University is increasing; and of those who have graduated, the majority are of Cambridge . . .

[From pp. 70–1

CLOSED FELLOWSHIPS

Of the changes required, perhaps the most important is that of removing restrictions on the Elections to Fellowships. The most injurious are those which confine the Fellowships to natives of particular localities, to members of particular families and to those who are or have been Scholars in the College . . . Such a measure is absolutely necessary in order to render the revenues of the Colleges available for the services of learning and education. The wealth of Oxford is commonly laid to the account of the University. But this is a serious misapprehension. It is to the Colleges that large landed estates are confined. They receive, it is said, not much less than £150,000 per annum between them from endowments, exclusively of what is paid by the students. This might be rendered a noble provision for learning and science, but if these endowments were multiplied tenfold, and distributed to a tenfold number of Fellows elected without reference to their talents and acquirements, little would result but increased odium to the University. The architectural magnificence of Oxford would be diminished and many excellent men would suffer, and great opportunities of future good will* be lost, if several of its richest Colleges were swept away; but little present loss would be sustained by the University, the church or the country.

[From pp. 149–51

* *Sic.*

9 · Report of the Commissioners appointed to inquire into the State of Popular Education in England. [*The Newcastle Report*]

Published: *1861*

Chairman: *Henry Pelham, Duke of Newcastle**

Members: *Sir John Taylor Coleridge; William Charles Lake, M.A.; William Rogers, M.A.; Goldwin Smith, M.A.; Nassau William Senior, M.A.; Edward Miall*

Terms of Reference: *To inquire into the present state of Popular Education in England, and to consider and report what Measures, if any, are required for the extension of sound and cheap elementary instruction to all classes of the people.*

The Newcastle Commission was set up in 1858, two years after the creation of the Education Department as the administrative instrument of the Committee of Council. The Royal Commission was a recognition that the new department was bound to pursue a policy of 'the extension of sound and cheap elementary instruction to all classes of the people'.

Everything pointed to the need for legislation. But every attempt to persuade Parliament to intervene had run into trouble on denominational grounds. Bills seeking to extend public elementary education through Church schools had continued to make their appearance, but with no more success than before.

Sir John Graham's Factory Bill (1843) was defeated by the Dissenters who, like the Anglicans, had begun to think in terms of building and maintaining their own schools free of State interference.

On the other hand, all the religious groups joined in opposing the secularists – W. J. Fox's Bill in 1850 providing for free and secular schools was easily defeated. It was not till later that some of the nonconformists came round to the view that denominational religion ought to be kept out of all schools (see extract from Cross Report, p. 135). A conscience clause was the answer in most minds.

A succession of Education Bills between 1847 and 1857, including Sir

* Henry Pelham Fiennes Pelham Clinton, fifth Duke of Newcastle (1811–64), was educated at Eton and Christ Church, sitting in Parliament (as Lord Clinton) as M.P. for South Notts (1832–46) and Falkirk Burghs from 1846 till he succeeded to the Dukedom in 1851. At the Colonial Office and War Office he was responsible for the state of the army at the outbreak of the Crimean War, and the attempts to make up for the decades of neglect. (*D.N.B.*)

John Russell's Borough Bill, and three others in 1855, were defeated mainly on the denominational issue.

The Newcastle Report was the first comprehensive survey of English elementary education. The Commission interpreted the terms of reference to mean the education of the independent poor, but it also made inquiries into the education of pauper, vagrant and criminal children, schools supported by the State (the Army and Navy) and certain other charitable foundations. The Commission in turn appointed 10 assistant commissioners each to 'examine minutely' a specimen district, agricultural, manufacturing, mining, maritime and metropolitan, two to each district. In addition, Matthew Arnold visited and reported on France, French Switzerland and Holland, and Mark Pattison on Germany. It also studied the reports of inspectors of schools from 1839 onwards.

Much of the report takes the form of statistics based on inquiries made by the Commission, and on estimates of doubtful value. The Commissioners recognized this, but concluded that, of the 2,655,767 children of the poorer classes with whom they were concerned, no fewer than 2,535,462 were in schools of some kind. They estimated that the majority of pupils left school at 11, only about 5·4 per cent remaining after 13. Average school life was 4–6 years.

The main recommendations of the Commission were that the Committee of Council should extend its operations, but that the chief features of the old system should remain – no interference with the denominational bodies, and no central control over school management.

The Commission proposed changes in the methods of paying grants. They wanted capitation grants from the State, with additional grants for pupil teachers, to be supplemented by new payments from local rates.

With the proposal for local rates went a plan for county and borough education boards, charged with the responsibility of examining secular instruction, and paying certain grants. They were not to be concerned with starting new schools, nor would they have been in any sense school boards of the kind set up after 1870. The principle of inspection, and the continued special status of clerical inspectors, was endorsed.

The role of the State was considered in principle in Part I, Chapter VI. The majority advocated the continuation of State grants towards the cost of education, while rejecting the suggestion that education should be free or compulsory. The minority reckoned that aid should be limited to the children of the poorest classes.

The only recommendation of the Newcastle Commission adopted by the Government of the day was payment by results.

But in this respect Mr Robert Lowe, the vice-president of the Council, went much further than the Commission. The Government were unwilling to broach the question of putting some of the cost of education on the rates. Had they done so, this would have raised every kind of denominational issue, and this was not a proposition which appealed to the Administration. Therefore, instead of using payment by results as a method of distributing supplementary grants by local authorities, Lowe in his Revised Code of 1862 (see

p. 79) made it the main way of dispensing central Government grants for elementary school running expenses. The county boards envisaged by the Newcastle Commission were, of course, never set up.

The report was important also for the light it shed on the status of teachers and the efficiency of the schools. The poor light in which the schools appeared was used by Lowe to justify his down-to-earth approach to educational finance.

Extracts selected here show the lines along which the committee approached the fundamental administrative and financial questions of elementary education, the size of the problem, and the sketchy nature of the statistics, the state of the argument for and against public intervention in elementary education, and the low level of esteem in which the Commission held the teaching profession (a point on which Mr Robert Lowe fastened in commending his Revised Code of 1862).

THE NEWCASTLE REPORT · VOLUME I · 1861

PAYMENT BY RESULTS

General Plan for Modifying and Extending the Present System. . . .

1. *General Principles.* All assistance given to the annual maintenance of schools shall be simplified and reduced to grants of two kinds.

The first of these grants shall be paid out of the general taxation of the country, in consideration of the fulfilment of certain conditions. . . .

The second shall be paid out of the county rates, in consideration of the attainment of a certain degree of knowledge by the children in the school. . . .

The existence of this degree of knowledge shall be ascertained by examiners appointed by the County Board of Education. . . .

2. *Distribution of the Grant from the State Fund*

[The Report goes on to prescribe how this is to be allocated – from 4s. 6d. to 6s. a head according to the size of school, provided a certificated teacher is employed, with additional sums according to the number of pupil-teachers and assistant teachers.]

3. *Grant from the County Rate* . . . The examiner shall examine every child presented to him . . . individually in reading, writing, and arithmetic. . . .

The managers of all schools fulfilling the conditions specified . . . shall be entitled to be paid out of the county rate a sum varying from 22s. 6d. to 21s. for every child who has attended the school during 140 days in the year preceeding . . . and who passes an examination. . . .

[From Chapter 6, pp. 328–30

CONSIDERATIONS IN FAVOUR OF THE PROPOSED PLAN

. . . The direct effects which we anticipate from this recommendation are, first, that such a measure will enable many schools to obtain public aid, which at present have no prospect of doing so; secondly that it will excite local interest, and secure as much local management as is at present desirable; and, thirdly, that the examination will exercise a powerful influence over the efficiency of the schools, and will tend to make a minimum of attainment universal. . . .

. . . Till something like a real examination is introduced into our day schools, good elementary teaching will never be given to half the children who attend them. At present, the temptation of the teachers is to cram the elder classes, and the inspector is too cursory to check the practice, while there are no inducements to make them attend closely to the younger children. . . . Everyone who has been at a public school knows how searching and improving is the character of a careful examination, even down to the very youngest children. . . .

We have carefully considered all that may be urged against such a plan, both upon the grounds of its employing the agency of school-masters, a class inferior to the present inspectors, and of the probable variations in . . . standard . . . We consider it to be one of the most valuable parts of inspection that the Inspector, moving in the same class of society, understands the objects and the feelings of the managers of schools. It would be a great mistake to introduce a person of inferior manners and education as an advisor or an authority into the schools. But nothing of this sort is contemplated. . . . The work of the examiner will be of a limited and technical character, and will give no room for the expression of opinion as to the school, and still less for interference with its arrangements.

[From Chapter 6, pp. 338–42

TOO FEW SCHOOL PLACES

. . . The whole population of England and Wales, as estimated by the Registrar-General in the summer of 1858, amounted to 19,523,103. The number of children whose names ought, at the same date, to have been on the school books, in order that all might receive some education, was 2,655,767. The number we found to be actually on the books was 2,535,462, thus leaving 120,305 children without any school instruction whatever. The proportion, therefore, of scholars in week-day schools of all kinds to the entire population was 1 in 7·7 or 12·99%. Of these 321,768 are estimated to have been above the condition of such as are commonly comprehended in the expression 'poorer classes', and hence are beyond the range of our present inquiry. Deducting these from the whole number of children on the books of some school, we find that 2,213,694 children belonging to the poorer classes were, when our statistics were collected and compiled, receiving elementary instruction in day schools. Looking, therefore, at mere numbers as indicating the state of popular education in England and Wales, the proportion of children receiving instruction to the whole population is, in our opinion, nearly as high as can be reasonably expected. In Prussia, where it is compulsory, 1 in 6·27; in England and Wales it is, as we have seen, 1 in 7·7; in Holland it is 1 in 8·11; in France it is 1 in 9·0. . . .

. . . One other point deserves attention; it relates rather to the kind than to the amount of the instruction given in our public elementary schools to the children attending them. The children do not, in fact, receive the kind of education they require. We have just noticed the extravagant disproportion between those who receive some education and those who receive a sufficient education. We know that the uninspected schools are in this respect far below the inspected; but even with regard to the inspected, we have seen overwhelming evidence from Her Majesty's Inspectors, to the effect that not more than one-fourth of the children receive a good education. So great a failure in the teaching demanded the closest investigation; and as the result of it we have been obliged to come to the conclusion that the instruction given is commonly both too ambitious and too superficial in its character, that (except in the very best schools) it has been too exclusively adapted to the elder scholars to the neglect of the younger ones, and that it often omits to secure a thorough *grounding* in the simplest but most essential parts of instruction. . . .

[From Chapter 6, pp. 293–6

AGAINST COMPULSION

. . . Any universal compulsory system appears to us neither attainable nor desirable. In Prussia, indeed, and in many parts of Germany, the attendance can scarcely be termed compulsory. Though the attendance is required by law, it is a law which entirely expresses the convictions and wishes of the people. Such a state of feeling renders the working of a system of compulsion, among a people living under a strict government, comparatively easy. Our own condition, it need scarcely be stated, is in many respects essentially different. But we also found that the results of this system, as seen in Prussia, do not appear to be so much superior to those which have been already attained amongst ourselves by voluntary efforts, as to make us desire an alteration which would be opposed to the feelings, and, in some respects, to the principles of this country.

An attempt to replace an independent system of education by a compulsory system, managed by the Government, would be met by objections, both religious and political, of a far graver character in this country than any with which it has had to contend in Prussia; and we have seen that, even in Prussia, it gives rise to difficulties which are not insignificant. And therefore, on the grounds of a long-established difference between our own position and that of the countries where a compulsory system is worked successfully; on the grounds of the feelings, both political, social and religious, to which it would be opposed; and also on the ground that our education is advancing successfully without it, we have not thought that a scheme for compulsory education to be universally applied in this country can be entertained as a practical possibility.

[From Chapter 6, p. 300

LIMITED HORIZONS OF ELEMENTARY EDUCATION

Evidence of Rev. James Fraser, an assistant commissioner who later became Bishop of Manchester.

It is quoted in the Report ('We agree with the following observations . . .')

. . . Even if it were possible, I doubt whether it would be desirable, with a view to the real interests of the peasant boy, to keep him at school till he was 14 or 15 years of age. But it is not possible. We must make up our minds to see the last of him, as far as the day school is concerned, at 10 or 11. We must frame our system of education upon this hypothesis; and I venture to maintain that it is quite possible to teach a child soundly and thoroughly, in a way that he shall not forget it, all that is necessary for him to possess in the shape of intellectual attainment, by the time that he is 10 years old. If he has been properly looked after in the lower classes, he shall be able to spell correctly the words that he will ordinarily have to use; he shall read a common narrative – the paragraph in the newspaper that he cares to read – with sufficient ease to be a pleasure to himself and to convey information to listeners; if gone to live at a distance from home, he shall write his mother a letter that shall be both legible and intelligible; he knows enough of ciphering to make out, or test the correctness of, a common shop bill; if he hears talk of foreign countries he has some notions as to the part of the habitable globe in which they lie; and underlying all, and not without its influence, I trust, upon his life and conversation, he has acquaintance enough with the Holy Scriptures to follow the allusions and the arguments of a plain Saxon sermon, and a sufficient recollection of the truths taught him in his catechism, to know what are the duties required of him towards his Maker and his fellow man. I have no brighter view of the future or the possibilities of an English elementary education, floating before my eyes than this. If I had ever dreamt more sanguine dreams before, what I have seen in the last six months would have effectually and for ever dissipated them.

In such inspection of schools as time and opportunity allowed me to make, I strictly limited myself to testing their efficiency in such vital points as these; never allowing myself to stray into the regions of English grammar, or English history, or physical science, unless I had previously found the ground under the children thoroughly firm, and fit to carry, without risk of settlements, a somewhat loftier and more decorated superstructure. Then it was but common justice to a conscientious teacher to take note of and show that one appreciated the higher mark at which he had aimed. Teachers look for such recognition, and cherish it as one of their best rewards.

[From Chapter 4, p. 243

ABUSE OF RELIGIOUS CONTROLS: SINGLE SCHOOL AREAS

While . . . we have deemed it to be a matter of the highest importance to leave the religious teaching in schools assisted from public funds to the exclusive decision and control of the managers, we feel ourselves compelled to notice a serious evil incident to this arrangement. It sometimes happens that in places too small to allow of the establishment of two schools, the only one to which the children of the poor in those places can resort, is . . . under regulations which render imperative the teaching of the Church catechism . . . and . . . attendance . . . at Church. In such cases it may result that persons of other denominations are precluded, unless at the sacrifice of their conscientious convictions from availing themselves of educational advantages for their children, furnished in the part by public funds to which as taxpayers, they contribute . . . We believe that the evil may safely be left to the curative influence of public opinion and will not necessitate a compulsory enactment. Should events prove that we are mistaken, it may be the duty of the Committee of Council to consider whether the public fund placed at their disposal in aid of popular education may not be administered in such a manner as will insure to the children of the poor in all places the opportunity of partaking of its benefits without exposing their parents to a violation of their religious convictions.

[From Chapter 6, pp. 343-4

ARGUMENTS FOR AND AGAINST STATE AID FOR ELEMENTARY EDUCATION

Majority view

The greater portion of the members of the Commission are of opinion that the course pursued by the Government in 1839, in recommending a grant of public money for the assistance of education, was wise; that the methods adopted to carry out that object have proved successful; and that while it is expedient to make considerable alterations in the form in which this public assistance is given, it would not be desirable either to withdraw it or largely to diminish its amount. Without entering into general considerations of the duty of a State with regard to the education of the poorer classes of a community, they think it sufficient to refer to the fact that all the principal nations of Europe, and the United States of America, as well as British North America, have felt it necessary to provide for the education of the people by public taxation; and to express their own belief that, when the grant to education was first begun, the education of the greater portion of the labouring classes had long been in a neglected state, that the parents were insensible to its advantages, and were (and still continue to be) in most cases incapable from poverty of providing it for their children, and that religious and charitable persons, interested in the condition of the poor, had not the power to supply the main cost of an education which, to be good, must always be expensive.

Minority view

The minority admit that the responsibilities and functions of Government may be enlarged by special circumstances, and in cases where political disasters have retarded the natural progress of society. But they hold that in a country situated politically and socially as England is, Government has, ordinarily, speaking, no educational duties, except towards those whom destitution, vagrancy, or crime casts upon its hands. They make no attempt at this distance of time to estimate the urgency of the circumstances which originally led the Government of this country to interfere in popular education. They fully admit that much good has been done by means of the grant; though they think it not unlikely that more solid and lasting good would have been done, that waste would have been avoided, that the different wants of various classes and districts would have been more suitably supplied, that some sharpening of religious divisions in the matter of education would have been spared, and that the indirect effects upon the character of the nation, and the relations between class and class would have been better, had the Government abstained from interference and given free course to the sense of duty and the benevolence which, since the mind of the nation has been turned from foreign war to domestic improvement, have spontaneously achieved great results in other directions.

[From Chapter 6, pp. 297–8

TEACHERS AND THEIR SHORTCOMINGS

Whilst it appears to be proved that the character of the teachers is greatly raised by their training, and that they are altogether a superior class to those who preceded them, it is equally clear that they fail, to a considerable extent, in some of the most important of the duties of elementary teachers, and that a large proportion of the children are not satisfactorily taught that which they come to school to learn. . . .

Though children leave school at a very early age, and attend with little regularity, they do attend long enough to afford an opportunity of teaching them to read, write, and cypher. A large proportion of them, however, in some districts do not learn even to read; at least, their power of reading is so slight, so little connected with any intelligent perception of its importance, and so much a matter of mere mechanical routine, as to be of little value to them in after-life, and to be frequently forgotten as soon as the school is left. The children do not generally obtain the mastery over elementary subjects which the school ought to give. They neither read well nor write well. They work sums, but they learn their arithmetic in such a way as to be of little practical use in common life. Their religious instruction is unintelligent, and to a great extent confined to exercises of merely verbal memory. . . .

Other complaints are that the trained teachers are conceited and dissatisfied. The first we do not believe to be true of the class, the second we admit to a certain degree, and account for it by remarking, amongst other causes, that their emoluments, though not too low, rise too soon to their highest level.

[From Chapter 2, pp. 168–9

10 · The Revised Code. 1862

The Code of Regulations made by the Committee of the Privy Council on Education for the administration of grants to schools was revised in the light of the Report of the Newcastle Commission. The revision incorporated the principle of payment by results into the distribution of maintenance grants for elementary schools but (see p. 72) not in the form put forward by the Newcastle recommendations.

The architect of the Revised Code was Mr Robert Lowe, vice-president of the Council and head of the education department. The code was greeted with strenuous protests on all sides and its introduction was twice postponed before coming into operation on August 1, 1863. Lowe told the House of Commons: 'I cannot promise the House that this system will be an economical one and I cannot promise that it will be an efficient one, but I can promise that it shall be one or the other. If it is not cheap it shall be efficient; if it is not efficient it shall be cheap.'

The New Code abolished payments direct to certificated teachers and made them to managers instead, in a single grant, thereby opening the system of grants to schools taught by teachers with poorer attainments. At the same time, it instituted a lower class of certificates than those previously existing and raised the regulation number of pupils allowed for each teacher. No more grants were available for building and improving training colleges.

The rigours of the Revised Code were modified in 1867 and successive Codes over the next thirty years removed the worst features of payment by results till the principle itself was dropped.

FROM THE REVISED CODE · 1862

. . . 40. The Managers of Schools may claim at the end of each year . . . (*a*) the sum of 4s. per scholar . . . at morning and afternoon meetings of their school and 2s. 6d. per scholar . . . at the evening meetings of their school:

(*b*) For every scholar who has attended more than 200 morning and afternoon meetings of their school.
1. If more than six years of age 8s. subject to examination.
2. If under six years of age 6s. 6d. subject to a report by the inspector that such children are instructed suitably to their age, and in a manner not to interfere with the instruction of the older children.

(*c*) For every scholar who has attended more than 24 evening meetings of their school 5s., subject to examination.

. . . 46. Every scholar for whom grants are claimed must be examined according to one of the following standards . . .

48	Standard I	Standard II	Standard III
Reading . .	Narrative in monosyllables.	One of the Narratives next in order after monosyllables in an elementary reading book used in the school.	A short paragraph from an elementary reading book used in the school.
Writing . .	Form on black-board or slate, from dictation, letters, capital and small manuscript.	Copy in manuscript character a line of print.	A sentence from the same paragraph, slowly read once, and then dictated in single words.
Arithmetic .	Form on black-board or slate, from dictation, figures up to 20; name at sight figures up to 20; add and subtract figures up to 10, orally, from examples on black-board.	A sum in simple addition or subtraction, and the multiplication table.	A sum in any simple rule as far as short division (inclusive).

	IV	V	VI
Reading . .	A short paragraph from a more advanced reading book used in the school.	A few lines of poetry from a reading book used in the first class of the school.	A short ordinary paragraph in a newspaper, or other modern narrative.
Writing . .	A sentence slowly dictated once by a few words at a time, from the same book, but not from the paragraph read.	A sentence slowly dictated once, by a few words at a time, from a reading book used in the first class of the school.	Another short ordinary paragraph in a newspaper, or other modern narrative, slowly dictated once by a few words at a time.
Arithmetic .	A sum in compound rules (money).	A sum in compound rules (common weights and measures).	A sum in practice or bills of parcels.

11 · Effects of the Revised Code

FROM MATTHEW ARNOLD'S GENERAL REPORT FOR THE YEAR 1867

In my report to the Royal Commission of 1859 (the Newcastle Commission) I said, after seeing the foreign schools, that our pupil teachers were, in my opinion, 'the sinews of English public instruction'; and such in my opinion they, with the ardent and animated body of schoolmasters who taught and trained them, undoubtedly were. These pupil-teachers and that body of schoolmasters were called into existence by the school legislation of 1846 (see p. 52); the school legislation of 1862 struck its heaviest possible blow at them; and the present slack and languid condition of our elementary schools is the inevitable consequence.

The rate of pupil-teachers to scholars in our elementary schools was, in 1861, one pupil-teacher for every 36 scholars; in 1866 it was only one pupil-teacher for every 54 scholars. . . .

The performance of the reduced number of candidates is weaker and more inaccurate. . . .

The mode of teaching in the primary schools has certainly fallen off in intelligence, spirit, and inventiveness during the four or five years which have elapsed since my last report. It could not well be otherwise. In a country where everyone is prone to rely too much on mechanical processes and too little on intelligence, a change in the Education Department's regulations, which, by making two-thirds of the Government grant depend upon a mechanical examination, inevitably gives a mechanical turn to the school teaching, a mechanical turn to the inspection, is and must be trying to the intellectual life of a school. . . .

More free play for the inspector, and more free play, in consequence, for the teacher is what is wanted. . . . In the game of mechanical contrivances the teacher will in the end beat us; and as it is now found possible, by ingenious preparation, to get children through the Revised Code examination in reading, writing and ciphering, so it will with practice no doubt be found possible to get the three-fourths of the one-fifth of the children over six through the examination* in grammar, geography and history, without their really knowing any one of these three matters.

I observe that one or two of my colleagues say in their reports that

* A reference to new regulations introduced in 1867 which made language, geography and history the subject of grant-bringing examinations.

school managers get pleased with the new mode of examination, and with the idea of payment by results, as they become familiarized with it. I think this is very true; the idea of payment by results was just the idea to be caught up by the ordinary public opinion of this country and to find favour with it; no doubt the idea has found favour with it, and is likely perhaps to be pressed by it to further application. But the question is, not whether this idea, or this or that application of it suits ordinary public opinion and school managers; the question is whether it really suits the interests of schools and their instruction. In this country we are somewhat unduly liable to regard the latter suitableness too little, and the former too much. I feel sure, from my experience of foreign schools as well as of our own, that our present system of grants does harm to schools and their instruction by resting its grants too exclusively, at any rate, upon individual examination, prescribed in all its details beforehand by the Central Office, and necessarily mechanical; and that we have to relax this exclusive stress rather than to go on adding to it.

The growing interest and concern in education will of itself tend to raise and swell the instruction in the primary schools; if we wish fruitfully to co-operate with this happy natural movement we shall, in my opinion, best do so by some such relaxation as that which I have indicated.

Throughout my district I find the idea of compulsory education becoming a familiar idea with those who are interested in schools. I imagine that with the newly awakened sense of our shortcomings in popular education – a sense which is just, the statistics brought forward to dispel it being, as every one acquainted with the subject knows, entirely fallacious – the difficult thing would not be to pass a law making education compulsory; the difficult thing would be to work such a law after we had got it. In Prussia, which is so often quoted, education is not flourishing because it is compulsory, it is compulsory because it is flourishing. Because people there really prize instruction and culture, and prefer them to other things, therefore they have no difficulty in imposing on themselves the rule to get instruction and culture. In this country people prefer to them politics, station, business, money-making, pleasure and many other things; and till we cease to prefer these things, a law which gives instruction the power to interfere with them though a sudden impulse may make us establish it, cannot be relied upon to hold its ground and to work effectively.

[From pp. 121–36

12 · Report of Her Majesty's Commissioners appointed to inquire into the Revenues and Management of certain Colleges and Schools, and the studies pursued and instruction given therein. [*The Clarendon Report*]

Published: *1864*

Chairman: *George William Frederick, Earl of Clarendon**

Members: *William Reginald, Earl of Devon; George William, Lord Lyttelton; Hon. Edward Turner Boyd Twisleton; Sir Stafford Henry Northcote, Bt.; William Hepworth Thompson, M.A.; Henry Holford Vaughan, M.A.*

Terms of Reference: *To inquire into the nature and application of the Endowments, funds and Revenues belonging to or received by the hereinafter mentioned Colleges, Schools and Foundations; and also to inquire into the administration and management of the said Colleges, Schools and Foundations, and into the system and course of studies respectively pursued therein, as well as into the methods, subjects and extent of the instruction given to the students of the said Colleges, Schools and Foundations.* (*Eton, Winchester, Westminster, Charterhouse, St. Paul's, Merchant Taylor's, Harrow, Rugby, Shrewsbury.*)

This Royal Commission was set up to investigate the state of the Public Schools following widespread and well-informed criticism led, amongst others, by Sir John Taylor Coleridge, who was at that time a member of the Newcastle Commission investigating elementary schools. The Commissioners prepared a detailed report on each of the nine schools including recommendations for the revision of their statutes, and the powers of Governing Bodies and headmasters.

They also made general recommendations on the subject of curriculum. They held that 'the classical languages and literature should continue to hold the principal place in the course of study', but advocated also that every boy should be taught mathematics, one modern language, some natural science

* George William Frederick Villiers, fourth Earl of Clarendon (1800–70), was a leading politician and member of governments formed by Lord John Russell, Lord Aberdeen and Lord Palmerston. His early training was in the diplomatic service, and although he held various other high offices between 1839 and 1870, his reputation was based on two important periods as foreign minister—1853–8 and 1868–70. He was Lord Lieutenant of Ireland from 1847–52, which included the period of the Great Famine. (*D.N.B.*)

and either drawing or music. They also thought that all boys should obtain a good general knowledge of geography and ancient history, and 'some acquaintance with modern history'.

Other recommendations included the suggestion that in the later stages of school life boys should be allowed to drop some portion of their classics and specialize in mathematics, languages or natural science (or alternatively, drop these and specialize in classics). 'Care should be taken to prevent this privilege from being abused as a cover for idleness.'

THE CLARENDON REPORT · 1864

CLASSICS VINDICATED, BUT MORE WANTED BESIDES

We shall now state generally the opinions we have formed respecting the course and subjects of instruction proper for these schools.

We believe that for the instruction of boys, especially when collected in a large school, it is material that there should be some one principal branch of study, invested with a recognized and, if possible, a traditional importance, to which the principal weight should be assigned, and the largest share of time and attention given.

We believe that this is necessary in order to concentrate attention, to stimulate industry, to supply to the whole school a common ground of literary interest and a common path of promotion.

The study of the classical languages and literature at present occupies this position in all the great English schools. It has, as we have already observed, the advantage of long possession, an advantage so great that we should certainly hesitate to advise the dethronement of it, even if we were prepared to recommend a successor. . . .

It is not, however, without reason that the foremost place has in fact been assigned to this study. Grammar is the logic of common speech, and there are few educated men who are not sensible of the advantages they gained as boys from the steady practice of composition and translation, and from their introduction to etymology. The study of literature is the study, not indeed of the physical, but of the intellectual and moral world we live in, and of the thoughts, lives, and characters of those men whose writings or whose memories succeeding generations have thought it worth while to preserve.

We are equally convinced that the best materials available to Englishmen for these studies are furnished by the languages and literature of Greece and Rome. From the regular structure of these languages, from their logical accuracy of expression, from the comparative ease with which their etymology is traced and reduced to general laws, from their severe canons of taste and style, from the very fact that they are 'dead', and have been handed down to us directly from the periods of their highest perfection, comparatively untouched by the inevitable process of degeneration and decay, they are, beyond all doubt, the finest and most serviceable models we have for the study of language. As literature they supply the most graceful and some of the noblest poetry, the finest eloquence, the deepest philosophy, the wisest historical writing; and these excellences are such as to be appreciated keenly though inadequately, by young minds, and to leave, as in fact they do, a lasting impression. Beside this, it is at least a reasonable opinion that this literature has had a powerful effect in moulding and animating the statesmanship and political life of England. Nor is it to be forgotten that the whole civilization of modern Europe is really built upon the foundations laid two thousand years ago by two highly civilized nations on the shores of the Mediterranean; that their languages supply the key to our modern tongues; their poetry, history, philosophy, and law, to the poetry and history, the philosophy and jurisprudence, of modern times; that this key can seldom be acquired except in youth, and that the possession of it, as daily experience proves, and as those who have it not will most readily acknowledge, is very far from being merely a literary advantage. . . .

. . . [But] . . . If a youth, after four or five years spent at school, quits it at 19, unable to construe an easy bit of Latin or Greek without the help of a dictionary or to write Latin grammatically, almost ignorant of geography and of the history of his own country, unacquainted with any modern language but his own, and hardly competent to write English correctly, to do a simple sum, or stumble through an easy proposition of Euclid, a total stranger to the laws which govern the physical world, and to its structure, with an eye and hand unpractised in drawing and without knowing a note of music, with an uncultivated mind and no taste for reading or observation, his intellectual education must certainly be accounted a failure, though there may be no fault to find with his principles, character, or manners. We by no means intend to represent this as a type of the ordinary product of English public-school education; but speaking both from the evidence we have received and from opportunities of observation open to all, we must say that it is a type much more common than it ought to be, making ample allowance for the difficulties before referred to, and that the proportion of failures is therefore unduly large. . . .

Natural science . . . is practically excluded from the education of the higher classes in England. Education with us is, in this respect, narrower than it was three centuries ago, whilst science has prodigiously extended her empire, has explored immense tracts, divided them into provinces, introduced into them order and method, and made them accessible to all. This exclusion is, in our view, a plain defect and a great practical evil. It narrows unduly and injuriously the mental training of the young, and the knowledge, interests, and pursuits of men in maturer life. Of the large number of men who have little aptitude or taste for literature, there are many who have an aptitude for science, especially for science which deals, not with abstractions, but with external and sensible objects; how many such there are can never be known, as long as the only education given at schools is purely literary; but that such cases are not rare or exceptional can hardly be doubted by any one who has observed either boys or men. . . .

It quickens and cultivates directly the faculty of observation, which in very many persons lies almost dormant through life, the power of accurate and rapid generalization, and the mental habit of method and arrangement; it accustoms young persons to trace the sequence of cause and effect; it familiarizes them with a kind of reasoning which interests them, and which they can promptly comprehend; and it is perhaps the best corrective for that indolence which is the vice of half-awakened minds, and which shrinks from any exertion that is not, like an effort of memory, merely mechanical. With sincere respect for the opinions of the eminent Schoolmasters who differ from us in this matter, we are convinced that the introduction of the elements of natural science into the regular course of study is desirable, and we see no sufficient reason to doubt that it is practicable.

It may, perhaps, be objected that there is not time for such a course of study as we have described, and that it could not be attempted without injury to classics; that the working hours are already long enough; that not more than a certain quantity of work can be put into a certain number of hours, and that a boy's head will not hold more than a certain quantity of knowledge. . . . Until a few years ago, there was no time for mathematics; at Eton, even now, it is deemed impossible to find time for French. Yet scholarship is none the worse, and general education is much the better, for the introduction of mathematics. . . . There would be reason therefore to distrust the objection, had we no other means of judging of it. But we are persuaded that by effective teaching time can be found for these things without encroaching on the hours of play; and that room may be made for them, by taking trouble, in the head of any ordinary boy. We are satisfied that of the time spent at school by nine boys out of ten much is wasted, which it is quite possible to economize. . . . The great difficulty of a public school as every master knows, is simple idleness, which is defended by numbers and entrenched behind the system and traditions of the place, and against which, if he be active, he wages a more or less unequal war. We are not without hope that, by the changes which we are about to recommend with respect to the schools collectively and separately, this evil may be considerably abated. . .

[From First Part, General Report: pp. 28–33

RECENT IMPROVEMENTS

It remains for us to discharge the pleasantest part of our task, by recapitulating in a few words the advances which these schools have made during the last quarter of a century, and in the second place by noticing briefly the obligations which England owes to them, – obligations which, were their defects far greater than they are, would entitle them to be treated with the utmost tenderness and respect.

That important progress has been made even in those particulars in which the schools are still deficient, is plain. . . . The course of study has been enlarged; the methods of teaching have been improved; the proportion of masters to boys has been increased; the quantity of work exacted is greater than it was, though still in too many cases less than it ought to be. At the same time the advance in moral and religious training has more than kept pace with that which has been made in intellectual discipline. The old roughness of manners has in a great measure disappeared, and with it the petty tyranny and thoughtless cruelty which were formerly too common, and which used indeed to be thought inseparable from the life of a public school. The boys are better lodged and cared for, and more attention is paid to their health and comfort.

Among the services which they have rendered is undoubtedly to be reckoned the maintenance of classical literature as the staple of English education, a service which far outweighs the error of having clung to these studies too exclusively. A second, and a greater still, is the creation of a system of government and discipline for boys, the excellence of which has been universally recognized, and which is admitted to have been most important in its effects on national character and social life. It is not easy to estimate the degree in which the English people are indebted to these schools for the qualities on which they pique themselves most – for their capacity to govern others and control themselves, their aptitude for combining freedom with order, their public spirit, their vigour and manliness of character, their strong but not slavish respect for public opinion, their love of healthy sports and exercise. These schools have been the chief nurseries of our statesmen; in them, and in schools modelled after them, men of all the various classes that make up English society, destined for every profession and career, have been brought up on a footing of social equality, and have contracted the most enduring friendships, and some of the ruling habits, of their lives; and they have had perhaps the largest share in moulding the character of an English gentleman. The system, like other systems, has had its blots and imperfections; there have been times when it was at once too lax and too severe – severe in its punishments, but lax in superintendence and prevention; it has permitted, if not encouraged, some roughness, tyranny, and licence; but these defects have not seriously marred its wholesome operation, and it appears to have gradually purged itself from them in a remarkable degree.

[From First Part, General Report: p. 56

13 · Report of the Royal Commission known as the Schools Inquiry Commission. [*The Taunton Report*]

Published: *1868*

Chairman: *Henry, Baron Taunton**

Members: *Lord Edward Henry Smith Stanley; George William, Baron Lyttelton; Sir Stafford Northcote; The Very Rev. Dr. W. F. Hook, Dean of Chichester; Dr Frederick Temple, Headmaster of Rugby; A. W. Thorold; T. D. Acland; Edward Baines; W. E. Forster; Peter Erle, Q.C.; Dr John Storrar*

Secretary: *H. J. Roby*

Assistant Commissioners: *D. R. Fearon, H.M.I., H. A. Gifford, C. H. Stanton, T. H. Green, J. L. Hammond, J. G. Fitch, James Bryce, H. M. Bompas*

Matthew Arnold, H.M.I., carried out inquiries for the Commission in France, Germany, Switzerland and Italy. Rev. James Fraser visited Scotland and the United States.

Terms of Reference: (*December 1864*) *To inquire into the education given in schools not comprised within the scope of . . . [the Newcastle and Clarendon reports] and also to consider and report what measures, if any, are required for the improvement of such education, having especial regard to all endowments applicable or which can rightly be made applicable thereto.*

The Commission was set up as a direct result of the two previous Royal Commissions into the nine public schools and into elementary education, as part of the fact-finding needed if any concerted attempt were to be made to improve English education. The Clarendon Commission had revealed the unsatisfactory state of the endowments and charters of the public schools, and there was every reason to expect that those of the endowed schools were no better. The spread of elementary education described by the Newcastle Report made an inquiry into secondary education all the more necessary.

The Commission's wide terms of reference covered every kind of school between the elementary schools about which the Newcastle Commission had reported in 1861, and the nine 'great' public schools, considered by the Clarendon report (in 1864). They divided the schools in question into

* Henry Labouchere, first Baron Taunton (1798–1869), was M.P. for Taunton from 1830 till 1859, when he went to the House of Lords. He served in various capacities in Liberal Governments, including Chief Secretary for Ireland 1846–7, President of the Board of Trade 1847–52, and Secretary of State for the Colonies 1855–8.

'endowed', 'private', and 'proprietary' and set about the inquiry by calling for written and oral evidence, by questionnaires, and by appointing assistant commissioners to make on-the-spot investigations.

Evidence was taken from the religious denominations, examining bodies, such as the College of Preceptors, and the Universities of Oxford, Cambridge and London, representatives of the professional bodies, schoolmasters and schoolmistresses in every kind of school. Special investigations were made of Christ's Hospital and King Edward the Sixth's School, Birmingham. Evidence was taken about the state of the law on charitable trusts.

As endowed schools, all the grammar schools received questionnaires and they were then re-classified. Those where Latin or Greek were not required (nearly 2,200 in number) were called 'non-classical schools', the remaining 705 being 'grammar schools'. Most of the non-classical schools were said to be devoted 'both by their foundations and by actual use' to the education of the labouring classes only. Only about 40 of them had endowments worth more than £500 a year.

Very few proprietary schools were investigated (schools, that is, promoted by companies). It was estimated that there were more than 10,000 'private' schools – schools run by individuals for private profit – and the assistant commissioners chose a large sample of these – all in London and Lancashire, and others selected from all over the country.

The General Register Officer estimated that there were some 3,000,000 persons in 'the middle and higher classes' in 1861 – a figure confirmed by estimates based on the number of marriages by licence (middle and upper) compared with those by banns (the rest of the population). On this basis, the number of children in the middle and upper classes, aged 5–20, was estimated at 974,258. It was this section of the community for whom secondary schools existed.

The Commission considered how secondary schools might be arranged according to the social background and wishes of the parents, and the age to which they were prepared to keep their sons (daughters were different) at school. 'First grade' schools were to 18 or 19, 'second grade' to about 16, and 'third grade' to 14 (see extract).

The most important conclusions of the report lay in matters of administration. They tidied up the muddled state of the endowments, which, they said, should be used mainly to maintain the physical structure of the schools, and laid down detailed suggestions for the benefit of boards of governors.

They outlined a scheme of provincial government based on the existing Boards of Guardians, which boards, they thought, might be joined together, county by county, into boards of education, working in conjunction with 'official District Commissioners' appointed by the Charity Commissioners. These would work under a new Central authority presided over by a Minister of Education – perhaps through the enlargement of the Charity Commissioners' powers.

They speculated on the merits of *ad hoc* school boards of the kind adopted a few years later for elementary schools, while rejecting them because the electorate was insufficiently informed, but they were aware of the need to create a direct local interest in education if the schools were to be improved. They recommended that parishes should in certain circumstances be allowed to raise a rate for building a school and providing scholarships for needy children from the elementary school. They laid down the principle that in schools with religious foundations but not 'distinctly and exclusively' denominational, parents of day scholars should be allowed the right of withdrawal for religious instruction. They considered and rejected proposals for a Normal School on French lines for the training of secondary school teachers, preferring a system of registration and certification based on public examinations. They wanted more inspection of schools and more examination of the pupils, including more University examining boards. They deplored the poor state of girls' education without proposing any clear suggestions for improvement.

The report was followed a year later (1869) by the Endowed Schools Act which ignored most of the Taunton Commission's recommendations, concentrating solely on the endowed schools, appointing three Endowed Schools Commissioners, among them Lord Lyttelton, a member of the Taunton Commission. They were charged with supervising and, if necessary, reorganizing the numerous charitable trusts belonging to the Endowed Schools. Special reference was made in the Act to the need to extend the educational opportunity for girls. The Act also carried out the Commission's recommendations that the parent should have the right to withdraw his child from Endowed schools from any period or periods of denominational religious instruction.

THE TAUNTON REPORT · 1868

RIGHT OF WITHDRAWAL

. . . All endowed schools not distinctly and exclusively denominational appear to us to fall under the rules recommended in our first chapter. Parents of day-scholars ought to be allowed to withdraw their children from the religious instruction, if they think fit. . . .

Without this the public character of the school is sacrificed, and in many cases the main intention of the founder, to give education to all who were fit for it in his town or parish, is curtailed by the exclusion of those who are unable to accept the religious teaching of the master. Nor do we think that any serious difficulty will be found to attend such simple rules as these. The master would be free to teach in his own way. He would give religious instruction to those who were not withdrawn, without anything to hamper him. And in the secular lessons he would not fear, that such allusions to religious truths, as grew naturally out of the subject which he was teaching, would be made a handle for condemning him on a charge of attempting to make proselytes. . . .

These rules would protect day-scholars; boarders must stand on a different footing. A master who has boarders in his house, is not merely a teacher; he has for the time the full responsibility of a parent. He ought to be able to regulate their prayers, their conduct, their religious learning, just as a father would. It is not right to require a man in that position to take a boy into his house, and yet not to have the guidance of his religious education. Some men would undertake such work; but many of the best men (such men, for instance, as Dr Arnold) would not, and it is highly inexpedient to put impediments in the professional path of such men as these. . . .

[From Chapter 7, p. 587

SOCIOLOGY OF SECONDARY SCHOOLS

The wishes of the parents can best be defined in the first instance by the length of time during which they are willing to keep their children under instruction. It is found that, viewed in this way, education, as distinct from direct preparation for employment, can at present be classified as that which is to stop at about 14, that which is to stop at about 16, and that which is to continue till 18 or 19; and for convenience we shall call these the Third, the Second, and the First Grade of education respectively. The difference in the time assigned makes some difference in the very nature of the education itself; if a boy cannot remain at school beyond the age of 14 it is useless to begin teaching him such subjects as require a longer time for their proper study; if he can continue till 18 or 19, it may be expedient to postpone some studies that would otherwise be commenced early. Both the substance and the arrangement of the instruction will thus greatly depend on the length of time that can be devoted to it.

It is obvious that these distinctions correspond roughly, but by no means exactly, to the gradations of society. Those who can afford to pay more for their children's education will also, as a general rule, continue that education for a longer time.

First-grade

We shall discuss these grades of education in order, beginning with the *first*, that is, with the one which keeps boys at school for the longest time.

The bulk of those who wish for this grade of education, that is, who wish their children's schooling to continue till 18 or past, consists of two very distinct classes, which must be considered separately.

One class is identical, or nearly so with those whose sons are in the nine schools that have been already reported on by a previous Commission; men with considerable incomes independent of their own exertions, or professional men, and men in business, whose profits put them on the same level. This class appears to have no wish to displace the classics from their present position in the forefront of English education; but there is among them a very strong desire to add other subjects of instruction. Their wish appears to be not to change, but to widen; to keep classics, but to cultivate mathematics more carefully than at present, to add modern languages and natural science. . . .

The other class of parents, who wish to keep their children at school the same length of time, have a somewhat different desire. These are the great majority of professional men, especially the clergy, medical men, and lawyers; the poorer gentry; all in fact, who, having received a cultivated education themselves, are very anxious that their sons should not fall below them. Of this class it should rather be said that they wish to cheapen education than that they wish to widen it. They would, no doubt, in most instances be glad to secure something more than classics and mathematics. But they value these highly for their own sake, and perhaps even more for the value at present assigned to them in English society. They have nothing to look to but education to keep their sons on a high social level. And they would not wish to have what might be more readily converted into money, if in any degree it tended to let their children sink in the social scale. The main evil of the present system, in their eyes, is its expense. The classical education of the highest order is every day to a greater degree quitting the small grammar schools for the great public schools, and others of the same kind. Those who want such education can no longer find it, as they could in the last century, close to their doors, all over the country. They are compelled to seek it in boarding schools, and generally in boarding schools of a very expensive kind.

Second-grade

When we come down to the *second* grade of education, that which is to stop at about 16, the desire to substitute a different system for the classical becomes stronger, and though most of these parents would probably consent to give a high place to Latin, they would only do so on condition that it did not exclude a very thorough knowledge of important modern subjects, and they would hardly give Greek any place at all. These parents consist of two classes. On the one hand, many of them could well afford to keep their children at school two years longer, but intend them for employments, the special preparation for which ought to begin at 16; as, for instance, the army, all but the highest branches of the medical and legal professions, civil engineering, and some others. On the other hand, there are very many parents whose position in life makes them require their boys to begin at 16 wholly or partially to find their own living.

The first of these would no doubt accept Latin as an important element in education, partly because it is in some cases of real practical use in these professions, partly because of its social value, partly because it is acknowledged to facilitate a thorough knowledge of modern languages, partly because almost all teachers agree in praising its excellence as a mental discipline.

But the great mass of the other class seem disposed barely to tolerate Latin, if they will even do that. Mr Fearon has expressed what is no doubt a very general feeling in describing the wishes of the mercantile classes in London.

'Among the mercantile classes in London, that is to say, the tradesmen, shopkeepers, and all who live by trade (who now to a large extent patronize private schools, but many of whom have sons whom they want to educate cheaply and would, under altered circumstances, gladly avail themselves of the grammar schools), I find a great desire for less instruction in classics, and more thorough teaching in modern subjects. This feeling is growing and spreading so much among the mercantile and trading classes, that I have been assured by several men of business that few things would please them better than a successful attack upon classical studies. When I have asked what is the reason of this feeling against the classics, and have endeavoured to explain the value of the cultivation which results from them, the answer has been, "Our sons' school life is not long enough for the production of the fruits of which you speak. They do not come to any maturity in the time; moreover, though classics may be excellent, yet mathematics, modern languages, chemistry, and the rudiments of physical science are essential, and we do not find time enough for all. We must, therefore, either abandon classical teaching altogether, or have it provided in a manner which shall not occupy much time." . . .'

It may be said, that in education of this grade a certain amount of thorough knowledge of those subjects which can be turned to practical use in business, English, arithmetic, the rudiments of mathematics beyond arithmetic, in some cases natural science, in some cases a modern language, is considered by the parents absolutely indispensable, and that they will not allow any culture, however valuable otherwise, to take the place of these. But some of them are not insensible to the value of culture in itself, nor to the advantage of sharing the education of the cultivated classes.

The education of the first grade which continues till 18 or past, and that of the second grade which stops at about 16, seem to meet the demands of all the wealthier part of the community, including not only the gentry and professional men, but all the larger shopkeepers, rising men of business, and the larger tenant farmers.

Third-grade

The *third* grade of education, which stops at about 14, belongs to a class distinctly lower in the scale, but so numerous as to be quite as important as any: the smaller tenant farmers, the small tradesmen, the superior artisans. The need of this class is described briefly by Canon Moseley to be 'very good reading, very good writing, very good arithmetic'. More than that he does not think they care for; or if they do they merely 'wish to learn whatever their betters learn'. To the same effect Mr Green defines their wish to be what is called a clerk's education, namely, a thorough knowledge of arithmetic, and ability to write a good letter. It cannot be said that this is aiming at much, and it is to be wished that parents even of this rank should learn the value of a somewhat higher cultivation. But the more their demand is considered the more thoroughly sensible it seems, and they certainly have a right to insist that what they wish for shall be secured before anything else be added.

The smaller tenant farmers, it is to be feared, do not often aim at so much as this, and if it were not for fear of being outdone by the class below them, would probably not care much for any education at all. But so little of what really deserves the name of secondary education is at present put within the reach of this class, whether in town or country, that they cannot be said to have had fair means of forming an opinion.

[From Chapter 1, pp. 15-21

NEED FOR RATE SUPPORT

We cannot look on the registration of private schools, as sufficient alone to supply the need which we have described. That need will not have been met unless a suitable school shall be within the reach of every parent in England; and for this purpose it seems desirable, that facilities should everywhere be given to the people, to establish public schools of their own.

We believe that recourse must be had to rates, if this object is to be effectually attained. We are not, indeed, prepared to recommend that rates for secondary education should be made compulsory; but we are of opinion, that, if any town or parish should desire to rate itself for the establishment of a school or schools above the elementary, it should be allowed to do so.

In recommending a recourse to rates we are touching on a matter of much controversy. Whilst there are many who would strongly deprecate rates for education altogether, there are others who would advocate a system similar to the American, and propose, as the goal to be ultimately attained, the provision of free public schools of every grade, at which the best education, that the country could give, would be put within the reach of every child without charge. There are many and weighty arguments on both sides. In favour of the American plan it is urged, that no other so effectually stamps the education of the people with its true value, as a great national duty, to be put on a level with the defence of the country or the administration of justice; that the experience of New England proves that gratuitous education does not of necessity in any degree pauperize those who receive it; that it is a matter of national interest that intellectual ability, in whatever rank it may be found, should have the fullest opportunities of cultivation, and that none of it should be lost to the country because poverty has prevented its attaining due development; that a system of free schools secures better than any other that general diffusion of education, which all now concur in considering almost a necessity to the happiness and prosperity of the country. On the other hand it is maintained, that the parental obligation to educate is prior to the national, and that it would be in the highest degree inexpedient to weaken the sense of that obligation by removing from parents the burden of discharging it; that the experience of America, with its comparatively homogeneous society, cannot be taken as a guide in dealing with the complex society of England; that English experience as far as it yet goes, is distinctly against gratuitous education, and that even in elementary schools it is found better to charge low fees than to admit the scholars free of all cost; that under present circumstances it seems more likely that people will learn the value of education by being perpetually urged to make the sacrifices necessary to procure it for their children, than by being set free from all care or labour for the purpose; that the burden cast on the ratepayers as far as they were distinct from the parents would be so heavy, as to run great risk of causing serious discontent, and that such burdens can only be borne, when they have been assumed by slow degrees and all other expenditure has been gradually adjusted to meet them; that the money given grudgingly would be administered grudgingly, and that rate-supported schools would be bad themselves and would keep others out of the field.

We are convinced that it is vain to expect thoroughly to educate the people of this country except by gradually inducing them to educate themselves. Those who have studied the subject may supply the best guidance, and Parliament may be persuaded to make laws in accordance with their advice. But the real force, whereby the work is to be done, must come from the people. And every arrangement which fosters the interest of the people in the schools, which teaches the people to look on the schools as their own, which encourages them to take a share in the management, will do at least as much service as the wisest advice and the most skilful administration. Public schools have a great advantage in the security that can be taken for the efficiency of their teachers, in the thoroughness of the test that can be applied to their work. But they have a far greater advantage, when they have besides these, the support of popular sympathy, and the energy which only that sympathy can inspire. The task before us is great. It is discreditable that so many of our towns should have no means of education on which parents can rely with assured confidence, and that, according to a great weight of evidence, so large a proportion of the children, even of people well able and willing to afford the necessary cost, should be so ill-taught. The machinery to set this right will need skilful contrivance. But, even more than skilful contrivance, it will need energy; and energy can only be obtained by trusting the schools to the hearty goodwill of the people.

[From Chapter VIII, pp. 656–9

14 · Elementary Education Act, 1870

SPEECH BY MR. W. E. FORSTER INTRODUCING ELEMENTARY EDUCATION BILL. HOUSE OF COMMONS· February 17th, 1870

W. E. Forster, son-in-law of Dr Thomas Arnold and brother-in-law ot Matthew, became Vice-President in charge of the Education Department when Gladstone formed his first administration in 1868. He was a Quaker and a Radical, but his Bill had to steer a course between the two policies advocated by the major organizations campaigning for educational reform – the National Education League (a Radical body emanating from Birmingham), and from among the Conservatives and Anglicans the National Education Union of Manchester. Its recipe for avoiding both secularism and Church control was the dual system.

The Act provided for school boards to be set up in areas which were short of schools with the duty of 'filling up the gaps'. The Education Department had the task of causing boards to be formed where necessary, the country being divided up into school districts which were boroughs or, in country areas, civil parishes. London was dealt with separately as a single school district.

Essential to the Bill was a compromise on the religious issue. The right of withdrawal from religious instruction on grounds of conscience in all public elementary schools, including those run by the churches, was guaranteed. The most important amendment accepted by the Government was the famous Cowper–Temple clause which laid down that in schools—'hereafter established by means of local rates, no catechism or religious formulary which is distinctive to any particular denomination shall be taught'.

Voluntary schools received a 50 per cent grant from the Education Department, but building grants came to an end. There was a six months' period of grace for the voluntary schools to put their house in order before the needs of each school district was surveyed.

The school boards, which, as a result of an amendment, were directly elected, and not appointed by borough councils and parish vestries as originally proposed, were empowered to raise a rate in order to finance their activities. School fees were not abolished. Compulsory attendance from 5 to 13 (with exceptions) was a matter for local option and enforcement by bye-laws.

For a discussion of the Act, see Mr Balfour's speech introducing the 1902 Bill (p. 149).

SPEECH BY MR W. E. FORSTER, VICE-PRESIDENT OF THE COUNCIL, INTRODUCING THE ELEMENTARY EDUCATION BILL, IN THE HOUSE OF COMMONS · February 17th, 1870

More or less imperfectly about 1,500,000 children are educated in the schools that we help – that is, they are simply on the registers. But, as I had the honour of stating last year, only two-fifths of the children of the working classes between the ages of six and ten years are on the registers of the Government schools, and only one-third of those between the ages of ten and twelve. Consequently, of those between six and ten, we have helped about 700,000 more or less, but we have left unhelped 1,000,000; while of those between ten and twelve, we have helped 250,000, and left unhelped at least 500,000. Some hon. members will think, I daresay, that I leave out of consideration the unaided schools. I do not, however, leave them out of consideration; but it so happens – and we cannot blame them for it – that the schools which do not receive Government assistance are, generally speaking, the worst schools, and those least fitted to give a good education to the children of the working classes. . . .

Now, what are the results? They are what we might have expected; much imperfect education and much absolute ignorance; good schools become bad schools for children who attend them for only two or three days in the week, or for only a few weeks in the year; and though we have done well in assisting the benevolent gentlemen who have established schools, yet the result of the State leaving the initiative to volunteers, is, that where State help has been most wanted, State help has been least given, and that where it was desirable that State power should be most felt it was not felt at all. In helping those only who help themselves, or who can get others to help them, we have left unhelped those who most need help. Therefore, notwithstanding the large sums of money we have voted, we find a vast number of children badly taught, or utterly untaught, because there are too few schools and too many bad schools, and because there are large numbers of parents in this country who cannot, or will not, send their children to school. Hence comes a demand from all parts of the country for a complete system of national education, and I think it would be as well for us at once to consider the extent of that demand. . . .

The first problem, then, is, 'How can we cover the country with good schools?' Now, in trying to solve that problem there are certain conditions which I think hon. members on both sides of the House will acknowledge we must abide by. First of all, we must not forget the duty of the parents. Then we must not forget our duty to our constituencies, our duty to the taxpayers. Though our constituencies almost, I believe, to a man would spend money, and large sums of money, rather than not do the work, still we must remember that it is upon them that the burden will fall. And, thirdly, we must take care not to destroy in building up – not to destroy the existing system in introducing a new one. In solving this problem there must be, consistently with the attainment of our object, the least possible expenditure of public money, the utmost endeavour not to injure existing and efficient schools, and the most careful absence of all encouragement to parents to neglect their children. . . . Our object is to complete the present voluntary system, to fill up gaps, sparing the public money where it can be done without, procuring as much as we can the assistance of the parents, and welcoming as much as we rightly can the co-operation and aid of those benevolent men who desire to assist their neighbours.

Now I will at once proceed to the main principles that run through all our clauses for securing efficient school provision. They are two in number. Legal enactment, that there shall be efficient schools everywhere throughout the kingdom. Compulsory provision of such schools if and where needed, but not unless proved to be needed. These being the principles, I now come to the actual provisions.

The first provision that would probably suggest itself to the minds of all hon. members would be a system of organization throughout the country. We take care that the country shall be properly mapped and divided, so that its wants may be duly ascertained. For this, we take present known divisions, and declare them to be school districts, so that upon the passing of this Bill there will be no portion of England or Wales not included in one school district or another. . . . We have taken the boundaries of boroughs as regards towns, and parishes as regards the country, and when I say parish, I mean the civil parish and not the ecclesiastical district.

. . . If, then, we get all England and Wales divided into districts, our next duty is to ascertain their educational condition, and for that purpose we take powers to collect returns which will show us what in each district is the number of schools, of scholars, and of children requiring education. We also take power to send down inspectors and officers to test the quality of the schools, and find out what education is given. Then, I may at once state that if in any one of these districts we find the elementary education to be sufficient, efficient, and suitable, we leave that district alone. By sufficient, I mean if we find that there are enough schools; by efficient, I mean schools which give a reasonable amount of secular instruction; and by suitable, I mean schools to which, from the the absence of religious or other restriction, parents cannot reasonably object; and I may add that for the purpose of ascertaining the condition of these districts, we count all schools that will receive our inspectors, whether private or public, whether aided or unaided by Government assistance, whether secular or denominational. If we find the district adequately supplied, we let it alone so long as it continues in that state, retaining for ourselves the power to renew the examination from time to time. It would, however, be vain for us not to suppose that we shall find a vast number of districts – I am afraid the enormous majority throughout the area of the country – where the educational provision is insufficient, and where that is so, as it is by public inquiry that that insufficiency must be ascertained, so it is by public provision that that need must be supplied. . . . We consider that these public elementary schools should in future be subject to three regulations – one of them an old regulation, and the other two new. The old regulation, which is manifestly a necessary one, is that the school should be kept up to the standard of secular efficiency which Parliament from time to time may think it necessary to exact. The next regulation is a new one, and is one which I fear I may have to encounter some difference of opinion upon, though much less than I believe would have been the case last year. Inspection is absolutely necessary. Hitherto the inspection has been denominational; we propose that it should no longer be so. . . . We propose that, after a limited period, one of the conditions of public elementary schools shall be that they shall admit any inspector without any denominational provision. . . .

I come now to another condition upon which also up to this year there would have been much difference of opinion, but as to which I expect there will be very little at present, and that is that after a limited period we attach what is called a Conscience Clause as a condition to the receipt by any elementary school of public money. . . .

. . . Well, then, if these three regulations are accepted – an effectual Conscience Clause; undenominational inspection; and compliance with conditions securing secular efficiency – then no other regulations will be enforced, and, especially, the present restrictions against secular schools will be removed. . . .

Now, then, we come at last to what will undoubtedly be looked upon as the most important part of the Bill – namely, the compulsory provision where it is wanted. I have said that there will be compulsory provision where it is wanted – if and where proved to be wanted, but not otherwise. We come now to the machinery for its application where it is proved to be wanted. How do we propose to apply it? By school boards elected by the district. We have already got the district; we have found out the educational want existing in it – we see that the district must be supplied – we have waited in the hope that some persons would supply it; they have not done so. We, therefore, say that it must be supplied; but by whom? It would be possible for the Government to attempt to supply it by defraying the expenses from the taxes; and I believe that one or two hon. gentlemen think that would be the best way. No doubt it would be possible for the Government to try to do this; but I believe it would be impossible for them to effect it. I believe it is not in the power of any central department to undertake such a duty throughout the kingdom. Consider also the enormous power it would give the central administration. Well, then, if Government cannot do it itself by central action, we must still rely upon local agency. Voluntary local agency has failed, therefore our hope is to invoke the help of municipal organization. Therefore, where we have proved the educational need we supply it by local administration – that is, by means of rates aided by money voted by Parliament, expended under local management, with central inspection and control. I wish to be frank with the House, and I therefore say that undoubtedly this proposal will affect a large portion of the kingdom. I believe it will affect almost all the towns, and a great part of the country. . . .

I cannot leave this point without just alluding to the reason why we have this difficulty at all, which is almost a disgrace to this country. We are behind almost every other civilized country, whether in America or on the Continent of Europe, in respect to rural municipal organization; and this drawback meets us not only in connection with education, but when many other social questions affecting the people come before us. The same difficulty applies to London. . . .

The school boards are to provide the education. Who are to pay for it? In the first place, shall we give up the school fees? I know that some earnest friends of education would do that. I at once say that the Government are not prepared to do it. If we did so the sacrifice would be enormous. The parents paid in school fees last year about £420,000. If this scheme works, as I have said we hope it will work, it will very soon cover the country, and that £420,000 per annum would have to be doubled, or even trebled. Nor would it stop there. This would apply to the elementary education chiefly of the working classes. The middle classes would step in – the best portion of the working classes would step in – and say, 'There must be free education also for us, and that free education must not be confined to elementary schools.' The illustration and example, so often quoted, of America would be quoted again, and we should be told that in the New England States education is free not only in the elementary schools, but free also up to the very highest education of the State. The cost would be such as really might well alarm my right hon. friend the Chancellor of the Exchequer. I hope the country would be ready to incur that cost if necessary; but I think it would be not only unnecessary, but mischievous. Why should we relieve the parent from all payments for the education of his child? We come in and help the parents in all possible ways; but, generally speaking, the enormous majority of them are able, and will continue to be able, to pay these fees. Nevertheless, we do take two powers. We give the school board power to establish special free schools under special circumstances which chiefly apply to large towns, where, from the exceeding poverty of the district, or for other very special reasons, they prove to the satisfaction of the Government that such a school is needed, and ought to be established. . . .

We also empower the school board to give free tickets to parents who they think really cannot afford to pay for the education of their children; and we take care that those free tickets shall have no stigma of pauperism attached to them. We do not give up the school fees, and indeed we keep to the present proportions – namely, of about one-third raised from the parents, one-third out of the public taxes, and one-third out of local funds. Where the local funds are not raised by voluntary subscription the rates will come into action. I know when I talk of rates that I am touching very delicate ground, and I do not for a moment dispute that the whole system and principle of rating is one of the questions which urgently demand the consideration of this House. I trust, however, that no reasonable member present would wish to keep the children throughout England untaught until that question is solved. . . .

I now come to another part of the subject, to that part to which I referred at the beginning of my remarks when I said that the country would expect that we should secure, if possible, the attendance of the children. . . .

. . . It is that, after much thought upon the matter, the Government has permitted me to put before the House the principle of direct compulsion. This may seem to be a startling principle; but, although I feel that I have already occupied the House much longer than I should have wished to do, it is a principle of the Bill which I feel I cannot quickly pass over. . . .

We give power to the school boards to frame bye-laws for compulsory attendance of all children within their district from five to twelve. They must see that no parent is under a penalty – which is restricted to 5s. – for not sending his child to school if he can show reasonable excuse; reasonable excuse being either education elsewhere, or sickness, or some unavoidable cause, or there not being a public elementary school within a mile. These bye-laws are not to come into operation unless they are approved by the Government, and unless they have been laid on the table of this and the other House of Parliament forty days, and have not been dissented from. Thus, with these checks, supplied by the necessary sanction of the Government, of this House, and of the public opinion of the district, every precaution is taken in the application of the principle. . . .

I have now described the principal provisions of this Bill. Before I sit down I hope the House will allow me to say one word upon the spirit in which this measure is submitted by the Government to them. In measures of constructive legislation, it seems to me that the purpose, the end aimed at, matters much; and the precise method matters comparatively little. What is our purpose in this Bill? Briefly this, to bring elementary education within the reach of every English home, aye, and within the reach of those children who have no homes. This is what we aim at in this Bill; and this is what I believe this Bill will do. I believe it will do it eventually, and not only eventually, but speedily. To do it will require enormous labour on the part of the Government; but if the House passes this Bill with the approbation of the country, no Government will be able to refuse that labour. Now this purpose we cannot allow, with our assent, to be frustrated; unless this Bill provides a complete national system of education, our efforts in framing it, your time in considering it, will have been wasted. Again, there are many points which have to be taken into consideration. There are rights of parents; rights of minorities; rights of conscience, which must be respected; but, within these limits, the attainment of our purpose, the due regard to individuals, I hardly need say that in a measure of this kind the Government will receive with the greatest possible attention every suggestion from either side of the House. The Bill will be in the hands of members, I hope, to-morrow; certainly on Saturday. They will find that the clauses have been prepared with care, and I think that they are consistent one with another; but we shall be ready to consider every amendment with the most careful attention.

But I confess I am sanguine, hon. members may think me too sanguine that in its main provisions the Bill will become law. . . .

I am not going to repeat my arguments, I have already detained you too long, and have only one further remark to make before I sit down. I have said that this is a very serious question; I would further say that whatever we do in the matter should be done quickly. We must not delay. Upon the speedy provision of elementary education depends our industrial prosperity. It is of no use trying to give technical teaching to our artizans without elementary education; uneducated labourers – and many of our labourers are utterly uneducated – are, for the most part, unskilled labourers, and if we leave our work-folk any longer unskilled, notwithstanding their strong sinews and determined energy, they will become over-matched in the competition of the world. Upon this speedy provision depends also, I fully believe, the good, the safe working of our constitutional system. To its honour, Parliament has lately decided that England shall in future be governed by popular government. I am one of those who would not wait until the people were educated before I would trust them with political power. If we had thus waited we might have waited long for education; but now that we have given them political power we must not wait any longer to give them education. There are questions demanding answers, problems which must be solved, which ignorant constituencies are ill-fitted to solve. Upon this speedy provision of education depends also our national power. Civilized communities throughout the world are massing themselves together, each mass being measured by its force; and if we are to hold our position among men of our own race or among the nations of the world we must make up the smallness of our numbers by increasing the intellectual force of the individual.

15 · Report of the Royal Commission on Scientific Instruction and the Advancement of Science. [*The Devonshire Report*]

Published: *1872–5*

Chairman: *The Duke of Devonshire**

Members: *Marquess of Lansdowne; Sir John Lubbock, Bart.; Sir James Kay-Shuttleworth, Bart.; Bernhard Samuelson; Dr William Sharpey; Professor T. H. Huxley; Professor G. G. Stokes; Professor H. J. Smith*

Terms of Reference: ***An inquiry with regard to Scientific Instruction and the Advancement of Science, and to inquire what aid thereto is derived from grants voted by Parliament or from Endowments belonging to the several universities in Great Britain and Ireland and the Colleges thereof and whether such aid could be rendered in a manner more effective for the purpose.***

The report takes the form of a detailed survey of scientific education at the universities and other institutions relevant to higher education, including, for instance, the British Museum, the Geological Survey and the Mining Record Office. It also includes a section on science in the public and endowed secondary schools and the elementary schools and training colleges.

It urged that older children in elementary schools should have more science teaching than the New Code (1871) encouraged, and that Training College programmes should be modified to provide teachers with the necessary preparation for this. It wanted the work of the Science and Art Department and the Education Department to be coordinated as harmoniously as possible. It made various suggestions for the training, recognition and payment of qualified science masters, and for building grants for certain kinds of institutions.

* William Cavendish, seventh Duke of Devonshire (1808–91), was a brilliant scholar at Eton and Trinity, Cambridge, passing his tripos as second wrangler and eighth classic. He entered Parliament in 1829 as Member for Cambridge University, supported the Reform Bill and was not re-elected by the University in 1831. He returned to Westminster the same year as member for Malton in Yorkshire, and from 1832–4 he sat for Derbyshire seats. In 1834 he succeeded as second Earl of Burlington, gave up politics, devoted himself to science and industry, setting about restoring the family estates by investing in iron and steel at Barrow-in-Furness and elsewhere and in railways.

Perhaps his most notable benefaction was the gift of the Cavendish Laboratory to the University of Cambridge (of which he was Chancellor from 1861 till his death thirty years later). (*D.N.B.*)

THE DEVONSHIRE REPORT · 1875

NEED FOR MORE SCIENCE TEACHING

. . . In spite of . . . [the] . . . concurrence of authority in favour of the Introduction of Science into Schools, it appears that, not one half of the 128 Endowed Schools from which returns have been received, have even made an attempt to introduce it; and of these, as we have already stated, only 13 have a Laboratory, and only 10 give as much as four hours a week to these subjects.

The neglect of Recommendations [in the Taunton Report] of so weighty and authoritative a character should imply the existence of strong grounds of excuse. The chief of those given for the omission of the Teaching of Science in Schools are – (1) the Absence of Funds; (2) the Uncertainty as to the Educational Value of Science, particularly in the case of young pupils; (3) the Difficulty of finding Time for a New Study in an already overcrowded curriculum. . . .

. . . With reference to the wealthier Foundations, and the great Proprietary Schools, the want of funds cannot be properly alleged as a reason for not providing appliances proper for the Teaching of Natural Science. Indeed, there is already considerable evidence of improvement in this respect. Laboratories have been built, or are in the course of construction, at Eton, Harrow and Rugby; and there is reason to hope that the example will be generally followed, as the Special Commissioners appointed for the Purposes of the Public Schools Act of 1868 have included in their Regulations a Clause requiring the Governing Bodies of the nine Public Schools to which their powers extended to provide and maintain Laboratories and Collections of Apparatus and of Specimens. We desire to record our opinion that School Laboratories should be constructed so as to supply accommodation for Practical Work in Physics, as well as in Chemistry. It will be seen from the Secretary's Report that many persons of experience in education have arrived at the conclusion that Chemistry is not so well fitted for the practical instruction of young pupils as Physics. Without attempting to decide this disputed question, we would express our conviction that neither of these forms of practical work ought to be neglected in School Teaching. . . .

SHORTAGE OF SCIENCE TEACHERS

. . . We regret to observe that in many of the Larger Schools the number of Science Masters is totally inadequate. The Special Commissioners have found it necessary to insist that there should be at least one Science Master for every 200 boys; a provision which appears to point to a still greater deficiency at present. Until this state of things is remedied, no considerable improvement can be expected in the Standard of Scientific Education at present prevailing in English Schools. We fear that the fewness of the Science Masters in the great Public Schools, and the slowness with which their number is allowed to increase must, to a certain extent, be attributed to an inadequate appreciation, on the part of the Authorities of those Institutions, of the importance of the place which Science ought to occupy, and which the country desires it should occupy, in School Education. But we are also disposed to believe that the difficulty of disturbing existing arrangements, and the increased expense entailed by additions to the staff of Masters, are among the principal causes of the delay in remedying an evil of such magnitude. It might seem, at first sight, that the provision of an adequate number of Science Masters ought not to involve any heavy charge upon the income of a large school; because, in proportion as the time of the pupils is occupied with Natural Science, fewer teachers of other subjects would be required. It has, however, been found in practice that whenever the subjects of instruction in a school become more varied, the whole number of persons employed in teaching has to be increased. But, as there is a well-founded impression that the large English Schools have suffered from being insufficiently supplied with Assistant Masters, we cannot regard it as any disadvantage that a more general introduction of Natural Science Teaching would call for an increase in the number of such Assistants. . . .

AIMS OF SCIENCE TEACHING

. . With regard to the second objection, it is obvious that all branches of Science do not possess an educational value of the same kind; and we are not prepared to assert that the mere communication to the mind of the pupil of the facts of Science would contribute very materially to the training of his intellectual powers, although it may supply him with much valuable information, and may render him the still more important service of awakening his desire for further knowledge. But the true teaching of Science consists, not merely in imparting the facts of Science, but in habituating the pupil to observe for himself, to reason for himself on what he observes, and to check the conclusions at which he arrives by further observation or experiment. And it may well be doubted whether, in this point of view, any other educational study offers the same advantages for developing and training the mental faculties by means of a great variety of appropriate exercises. In the Lower Forms of our Public Schools, the youth of the scholars must of course be taken into consideration in the nature of the instruction given, but we nevertheless think it of great importance that the introduction of Science into Education should take place at a very early stage. Elementary Science is certainly not more difficult, and to most young persons is more interesting, than Arithmetic or Grammar, and the most eminent men of Science, as well as some most successful Teachers, are of opinion that there is no reason to apprehend any difficulty in this respect. The Evidence which we have received on this point is very strong; and its force is not diminished by the fact that much of it related to Primary Schools.

PRESSURE OF TIME

. . . The third of the difficulties most frequently urged is want of Time. While we cannot deny the reality of this difficulty, it seems to us to offer no justification whatever for the total or almost total exclusion from Education of any great branch of Human Knowledge. The difficulty is one which can only be met by carefully economizing time, by employing the best methods of teaching, and by discarding superfluous subjects of study. To meet it by making education one-sided and incomplete, cannot be for the interest of the pupil. Nor does it appear to us impossible to make a fair adjustment between the claims of the different branches of Instruction. The number of hours of study in our Public Schools may be taken at not less than 35 per week, including in the estimate the number of hours on an average employed in preparation. Now, if six hours per week be devoted to Science, and if we suppose six hours also to be given to Mathematics, there would still remain at least 23 hours a week for the study of Languages and other subjects.

We are not prepared to admit that the classical Scholarship of the Pupil would, by the close of his school career, have suffered in consequence of the subtraction of the 12 hours which we have assigned to Mathematics and Science: since we believe that the influence of Instruction in Natural Science on the Development of his intellectual powers might be such as to promote his success in Classical Learning. Be this as it may, it is quite certain that his Education, if confined to one class of subjects, would be an unbalanced one, that his intellectual tastes and powers would have been developed in one direction only, and that so far he would be the worse prepared, whether for the continuance of study, or for the active business of life. We have already expressed the opinion that the Student who has given evidence that he possesses a fair amount of both Literary and Scientific Culture, may with advantage be allowed to choose for himself among the main lines of study pursued at an University. But, while he is still at school, and before he can have given such evidence, we do not think that the same liberty of choice ought to be conceded. . . .

. . . On a review of the present state of the Public and Endowed Schools, it appears to us that though some progress has no doubt been achieved, and though there are some exceptional cases of great improvement, still no adequate effort has been made to supply the deficiency of Scientific Instruction pointed out by the Commissioners of 1861 and 1864. We are compelled, therefore, to record our opinion that the Present State of Scientific Instruction in our Schools is extremely unsatisfactory. The omission from a Liberal Education of a great branch of Intellectual Culture is of itself a matter for serious regret; and, considering the increasing importance of Science to the Material Interests of the Country, we cannot but regard its almost total exclusion from the training of the upper and middle classes as little less than a national misfortune.

[From the Sixth Report (1875): pp. 4–10

EVIDENCE GIVEN BY A MEMBER OF THE COMMISSION

Professor T. H. Huxley: 'A plea for science in the elementary school'

Are you not also of opinion that the teachers, in giving this elementary instruction in science, ought not to be engaged in day-school instruction? My own feeling is that I should rather put it in another way; that is to say, that scientific teaching ought to be made a fundamental part of all primary teaching in the kingdom, and be made a part of the day's work. Unless I am greatly misinformed, the scientific instruction which is now current in the kingdom was the result, so to speak, of a battle between two official departments. I do not know whether I am rightly or wrongly informed, that it was in the teeth of the Educational Department that this scientific instruction was introduced; but, if such be the case, the fact accounts, I think, for the nocturnal, and somewhat surreptitious, position which science at present occupies. . . . I think that is the way that we have dealt with science, not only in primary education, but in the larger educational bodies in the country; and my hope is to see science made an integral part of the elementary teaching everywhere in the country, and not to have it merely forced upon one department by another, as it seems to have been the case formerly.

You are aware that so far as positive legislation yet has extended, the school age has been defined by the revised code as 11 years of age, and by the Factories' Act as 13 years of age, for half time. Have you much hope that any elementary scientific instruction which deserves the name could be given to a child before the age of eleven? Considering the difficult matters with which elementary education is now made to deal, such as the exceedingly difficult problems connected with dogmatic theology and the like, I think science might be taught quite as well. I think that the time which is devoted to the one might with equal success be devoted to the other. . . .

Have you also observed in what standards the scholars ordinarily pass in the very best elementary schools, and under the largest and most efficient staff of educational machinery yet employed, up to the highest school age, in respect of ordinary elementary instruction, such as reading, writing, arithmetic, and geography? I am not aware, I have not paid attention to that; but I may say in relation to this matter, that I have no doubt whatever that a certain amount of scientific teaching of a very valuable kind might be given to children of the ages now specified. I think that the nature of your scientific teaching must be very carefully determined, but I think that a great deal of what may be fairly called elementary science, with respect to the ordinary phenomena of nature, is information which might be made very complete in its way, although, of course, it would be very elementary; indeed, I am quite sure, from my own knowledge of children, that that may be given to children under 12 years of age, with extreme benefit.

That, of course, would be of a very different character from that which at present comes under the review of the examiners of the Science Department? I do not think necessarily so. I think, for example, that children of that age may be taught elementary physical geography. I think it might be made a most important and most valuable subject of instruction, and not only of instruction, but of training, under that age. The elementary facts of physics (I am now using physics, of course, in its most elementary sense), I imagine may be taught with perfect ease. . . .

If science teaching were introduced into elementary schools, would it not be desirable that there should be a more intimate connexion between the Education Department, and the Science and Art Department, than that arising simply out of both being under one chief? I must confess that I think the present state of affairs is an anomaly which could only exist in our own country. Separating the teaching of science from education, is like cutting education in half. It is a wonderful state of affairs, and the result is that practical antagonism, which I believe does not exist now, but which for a number of years, I am told, did exist, when one half of the department of the state which had charge of education was opposed to that which the other half was doing.

[From Volume I (1872), Minutes of Evidence, pp. 23–6

16 · Report of the Departmental Committee on Intermediate and Higher Education in Wales. [*The Aberdare Report*]

Published: *1881*

Chairman: *Lord Aberdare**

Members: *Lord Emlyn, M.P.; Prebendary H. G. Robinson; H. Richard, Esq., M.P.; Professor John Rhys; Lewis Morris*

Terms of Reference: *To inquire into the present condition of Intermediate and Higher Education in Wales and to recommend the measures which they may think advisable for improving and supplementing the provision that is now or might be made available for such education in the principality.*

The Aberdare Committee – twelve years after the corresponding Taunton Report for England – was set up as a result of the growing interest in higher education in Wales, and the manifest need to reform secondary education.

The Commission examined existing facilities for Intermediate (secondary) and higher education and found them wanting in amount and also in kind because they were mainly in Anglican schools unsuited to a nonconformist population. It recommended the setting up of two more university colleges (at Cardiff and Bangor) and a series of steps calculated to increase the number of places in non-denominational grammar schools, administered by popularly elected governors.

The Welsh Intermediate Education Act of 1889 set up quasi-representative authorities for 'intermediate' and 'technical' education, charged with the duty of working out schemes of intermediate and technical education for each county. The definition of intermediate education in Section 17 of the Act

* Henry Austin Bruce, first Baron Aberdare (1815–95), became closely involved with Welsh education in the last fifteen years of his life. In addition to being chairman of the Departmental Committee, he was president of the University College at Cardiff from its foundation in 1883, and having worked hard for a University of Wales he became first Chancellor in 1894.

He was educated at Swansea Grammar School and called to the Bar at Lincoln's Inn. Before he had time to become established as a barrister his father became very rich when coal was discovered in large quantities under the Duffryn Estate.

He entered Parliament as a Liberal for Merthyr Tydfil in 1852 – he switched to Renfrewshire in 1869 – and served in Liberal governments in various capacities, among them Under-Secretary of State at the Home Office (1862); Vice-President of the Council (1864), Charity Commissioner (1864) and Home Secretary (1869). He retired from active politics in 1874, having been made a baron and briefly served as Lord President in the closing months of Mr Gladstone's government. Thereafter he devoted himself to educational and social matters. (*D.N.B.*)

described a course of education which did not consist chiefly of elementary education in reading, writing and arithmetic, but which included instruction 'in Latin, Greek, the Welsh and English language and literature, Modern languages, Mathematics, Natural and Applied Science, or in some of such studies, and generally in the higher branches of knowledge'.

Technical education was defined as including instruction in

'(i) Any of the branches of science and art with respect to which grants are for the time being made by the Department of Science and Art;
(ii) The use of tools, and modelling in clay, wood, or other material;
(iii) Commercial arithmetic, commercial geography, book-keeping, and shorthand;
(iv) Any other subject applicable to the purposes of agriculture, industries, trade or commercial life and practice, which may be specified in a scheme, or proposals for a scheme, of a joint education committee as a form of instruction suited to the needs of the district;

but it shall not include teaching the practice of any trade, or industry, or employment.'

By opening the way to developments in secondary education which did not follow strictly the traditional lines of the English grammar school, the Aberdare Report can be said to be responsible for the present shape of Welsh secondary education, and the large number of secondary school places which were to be found in many parts of Wales before the 1944 Act required secondary education for all. It also helped to promote further expansion of higher education in Wales by the opening of the University College of South Wales and Monmouthshire at Cardiff (1883) and the University College of North Wales at Bangor (1884) each with a Parliamentary grant of £4,000 a year.

THE ABERDARE REPORT · 1881

SPECIAL CHARACTERISTICS

The first thing to be noted is that Wales has a distinct nationality of its own. . . .

The spirit which elsewhere manifests itself in struggles against the central authority, and in protests against the supremacy of a dominant race, is in Wales content with maintaining the continuity of the national life, preserving the traditional sentiments of the race, and fostering those ideas and usages which are distinctive and characteristic of the nation.

The sentiment of nationality cannot be ignored, and ought not in our opinion to be discouraged. Some of the witnesses who gave evidence before us expressed themselves strongly as to what they designated Welsh narrowness and provincialism, and seemed to be of opinion that whatever is specially characteristic of the people should be got rid of. . . .

That narrowness or provincialism, whether Welsh or English, should be corrected, and, as far as may be, replaced by breadth of view and comprehensiveness of thought, will probably be admitted without controversy, but this may be done without destroying the Welsh type of character or converting the people of Wales into Englishmen. . . .

The existence, therefore, of a distinct Welsh nationality is in our opinion a reason for securing within the limits of Wales itself a system of intermediate and higher education in harmony with the distinctive peculiarities of the country.

In close connexion with the subject of Welsh nationality are the existence and prevalence of the Welsh language.

The question of language is, and must be for a long time to come, a very important factor in estimating the condition, both social and educational, of the people of Wales. To those who are resident in Wales, the prevalence of the Welsh language is a matter of daily experience. According to calculations made after the census of 1871 by Mr Ravenstein in his work on the Celtic-speaking population of the British Isles, out of a population of 1,426,514 in Wales and Monmouthshire no less than 1,006,100 habitually spoke Welsh. It has also been stated that of the Nonconformist bodies of Wales, 686,220, or including children under 10 years of age 870,220, used the Welsh language in worship, as against 36,000 who worship in English.

Twelve newspapers with a weekly circulation of 74,500; 18 magazines with a circulation of 90,300; and two quarterly publications with a circulation of 3,000, are published in Welsh. A large number of useful books, translations for the most part, are yearly published in Welsh. We were told by one witness, that in the year 1875 no less a sum than 100,000*l.* was spent in Welsh literature of all kinds.

The fact being thus established, the question will arise what effect does this prevalence of the Welsh language produce upon the education of the Welsh child? On this important subject we have received much evidence, far the greater part of which tended to show that such prevalence was very disadvantageous to proficiency in those branches of knowledge, such as the classics, philosophy, &c., where a copious command of English was necessary to success in competing for the prizes and honours of the University. . . .

It may be asked how far this state of things is likely to be permanent; and, in answer to this question, we feel bound to say that, in spite of the progress which, under the influence of the elementary schools, of railways, and other causes, the knowledge of English has made and is making, such is the attachment of the Welsh to their language and literature, so deeply interwoven are they with their daily life, their religious worship, and even their amusements, that in dealing with the subject of education, speculations as to the probable duration or disappearance of their native tongue are hardly of practical bearing. There is every appearance that the Welsh language will long be cherished by the large majority of the Welsh people, and that its influence upon the progress of their education and upon their prospects in competing with English-born students will be for an indefinite time but little less in the future than it has been in the past.

Hardly less marked in its bearing on the educational position of the Welsh people is the question of their RELIGION. In the absence of an authoritative census of religious opinions, it is impossible to frame any estimate of the comparative numbers of the various denominations which may not be open to dispute, but there can be no doubt, as already stated, that the Nonconformists constitute a very large majority of the population of Wales and Monmouthshire.

Moreover it is indisputable that nonconformity in Wales is the outward expression of deep-seated religious convictions among the people. The Welsh, turning aside from the ecclesiastical system recognized by the State, have created their own and maintain it at a large annual cost voluntarily incurred. . . .

This condition of things must be recognized in any steps that are taken for the improvement of intermediate or higher education in Wales. . . . The progress of education has been injuriously affected by the distrust entertained of the endowed schools generally on account of the Church influences prevalent in them, and in the recommendations we shall have to make it will be our duty to suggest some mode of reconciling the national convictions with the institutions that exist for the educational interests of the nation.

Great prominence has been given in the evidence to the desire among the Welsh people for a better education. That such a desire exists cannot be questioned. But with this desire there undoubtedly prevails . . . an imperfect estimate on the part of parents of what constitutes a good education . . . Hence, in large part, the very inadequate state of preparation in which boys present themselves, whether at the intermediate schools or the colleges, and the necessity for masters devoting much time, which ought to be applied to the proper studies of the place, to the merest elementary instruction. A year or two's schooling is supposed to be a sufficient preparation for Lampeter or Aberystwith. . . .

The result is that the ardent desire for an advanced education, which undoubtedly exists in Wales, is more strongly exhibited in the youths themselves than in their parents. Numerous instances, which might have been almost indefinitely multiplied, of the struggles of youths, conscious at once of their ignorance and abilities, to obtain a better education, were adduced before us; and have deeply impressed us with the extreme importance of supplying means of education which should be at once sound and economical.

[From Chapter IV, pp. xlvi–xlviii

Conclusion and Recommendations

1. *Intermediate Education*

The provision for intermediate education in Wales and Monmouthshire first claim our attention. On the adequacy and suitableness of this provision the advancement of higher education in the Principality depends.

The conclusion forced upon us by the evidence received and the facts brought under our notice is that at present it is far from adequate in amount, and not wholly suitable in character.

Testimony is practically unanimous as to the defective state of preparation of the great majority of Welsh students who enter the provincial colleges or the universities and the deficiency is due, in part at least, to the want of facilities for early methodical training in those subjects which supply the material for more advanced intellectual culture.

It is a significant fact that, so far as we can ascertain, few Welsh candidates present themselves for the public appointments which are made on the results of competitive examinations, and that in 1879, none of the Endowed Schools in Wales furnished a candidate for the Indian Civil Service. . . .

It has been shown that in the Endowed Grammar Schools there is accommodation for not more than 2,846 scholars, a number which must . . . fall very far short of the number for which accommodation ought to exist in a population of more than 1,500,000. . . .

But . . . the accommodation . . . is not at present made use of to anything approaching its full extent, since the number in attendance in all the grammar schools together is only 1,540: not very much in excess of half the number for whom accommodation exists. . . . The general conclusion . . . is that the existing grammar schools are not accessible to a large part of the population of Wales, or do not offer the kind of education required, or fail to command general confidence from the character of their governing bodies and the conditions under which they are generally managed.

The first thing therefore to be insisted on in the interests of Welsh education is that these schools should not only be made as efficient as possible, but should be so dealt with as to ensure their adaptation to local requirements and their hold on public confidence. . . .

While we adopt the view that the reconstitution of the endowed schools of Wales and Monmouthshire, so as to ensure their usefulness and popularity, can be effected under existing legislative provisions, and that to this extent no fresh appeal to the Legislature is called for, we think it necessary to point out that there are certain matters connected with the reorganization of the endowments, with regard to which the framers of schemes have a wide discretion under the Endowed Schools Acts, but which can only, in the case of Welsh endowments, be treated in one way, and on one very definite principle, if a satisfactory system of intermediate education is to be attained.

In the first place, if the schools are to have the confidence of the people, and to be freely resorted to by the classes for whose use they are intended, it is essential that they should have no sectarian or denominational character. . . .

It may be safely assumed that the Welsh grammar schools are generally, so far as regards their legal status, undenominational. But while legally and nominally, undenominational, they are, with few exceptions, practically in the hands of one religious body, which constitutes what is comparatively a small minority of the population. We found during the time of our inquiry that, in several instances, the whole of the governing body were members of the Church of England. That was the case at Ruthin, Cowbridge, Monmouth, and the two endowed schools for girls at Llandaff and Denbigh . . . to which must be added that the head master and most of the other masters are almost always members of the Church of England.

It was the unanimous contention of Nonconformist witnesses that the fact of the governing body and the teaching body belonging to one religious denomination gives a denominational character to the school. If, therefore, the schemes under the Endowed Schools Acts are to satisfy popular feeling and to give real effect to what is now the legal status of the foundations, they must ensure that any religious teaching given shall be undenominational, and that the governing bodies shall be of a properly representative character. But it is contended that the schemes as at present framed fail to do this, inasmuch as the provisions they contain for religious instruction leave it in the power of the governing body to decide what the particular character of the religious instruction shall be, and thus a majority of governors of one way of thinking might at any time insist that the instruction given shall be in accordance with the doctrines and formularies of their own or any other denomination.

We recommend, therefore, that in schemes for Welsh schools, other than schools of a denominational character, any provision made for religious instruction shall be confined to the reading and explanation of Holy Scripture and shall not include instruction in the doctrines or formularies of any church, sect, or denomination.

We further recommend that no such instruction shall be given to any scholar unless the written consent of the parent or guardian has been previously obtained.

We make this recommendation because we believe that if the endowed schools of the Principality are hereafter to be used by the people without distinction of class or creed and are no longer to be regarded with distrust and suspicion by large sections of the community, there is no alternative than the adoption of what we propose or the absolute exclusion from the schools of every kind of religious instruction.

Although we are not prepared to include in our recommendations the exclusion of ministers of any religious denomination from the masterships of intermediate schools, it would, in the present state of public opinion, be undoubtedly considered by many as an additional security for religious equality that these offices should be filled by laymen.

THE NEXT THING which seems to us to be of vital importance is the management of the schools, and more particularly the nature and constitution of the governing bodies to whom that management is to be entrusted. . . .

The people of Wales have shown themselves sufficiently alive to this fact, and therefore it is that they insist with such unanimity on popular and representative management.

The grammar schools have generally in times past been in the hands of trustees for the most part self-elective, belonging to the upper classes, and differing from the main body of the people in religious and political opinions. It is desired that an end should be put to this state of things, and that, practically, the control of the schools should be transferred to the classes who may be expected to make use of them.

[From Chapter V, pp. l–liii

II. *Higher Education*

We now proceed to state what recommendations we desire to make with reference to the provision for higher education in Wales. . . .

We have no hesitation in avowing our conviction that colleges of this kind [University colleges] which have recently been founded in many of the larger towns of England are desirable in the circumstances of Wales, and would be found conducive to the advancement of higher education in the country. Amongst a people like the Welsh who, though defective in regular scholastic training, have a natural turn for some forms of literary culture and self-improvement, such institutions would tend to stimulate the desire for more advanced education by providing opportunities for obtaining it under conditions most suited to the position and requirements of the nation.

The experience of the University College at Aberystwith, where various adverse causes have operated, must not be taken to be conclusive against the success of such colleges in Wales. . . .

It is important that the colleges should be adapted, as regards their management and the course of instruction given, to the particular circumstances of the country.

The more practical the education, the more it takes account of the requirements of commercial or professional life, the more will it be in demand amongst a people who, in all the efforts they make and the sacrifices they undergo, have very definitely before them the importance of fitting themselves for a career.

Science, therefore, especially in its application to arts and manufactures, should occupy a prominent place in the curriculum of the colleges, and, while classical studies are not overlooked, a leading position must be given to English literature and to those modern languages, the knowledge of which, in places like Cardiff and Swansea, is found most conducive to commercial success. . . .

We would urge that the colleges should be altogether unsectarian, and should not undertake to provide any kind of theological instruction. The principal should, in every case, be a layman.

We think that the advantages of the teaching staff should as far as possible be thrown open to girls or young women requiring a higher education than can be given to them in schools.

We contemplate the admission of students at a much earlier age than is now the practice at the English universities. We are persuaded that if a college in Wales is to succeed it must provide a course, which in ordinary cases shall not last beyond the twentieth year, or earlier, so as to take in the large class of persons, who, after leaving the second grade schools, may be able to devote to the higher education the not over long interval which may elapse before they enter into active business life.

It now only remains to state the conclusions at which we have arrived with regard to the necessity or expediency of creating in Wales a university, with the power of conferring degrees. The arguments advanced either in favour of or against such an institution by those interested have been summed up in a previous chapter, and they may be taken to embrace nearly all that can be said on the subject. That a Welsh university if established, would at once take rank, we do not say with the older universities of the kingdom, but with the London or Victoria University, or the Queen's University in Ireland, is not to be expected. Its influence would necessarily be restricted to a much narrower field of operations. It would only in very exceptional cases attract *alumni* from places outside the Principality, and would therefore almost necessarily be a university for Welshmen only. Nor can it be anticipated that all Welshmen would give it the preference over other universities. As a rule, those only would use it to whom for any reason the universities of established repute were inaccessible. It has been questioned whether this class would present itself in sufficient numbers to give the university a solid status, and to justify the maintenance of its somewhat elaborate machinery for their benefit.

Apart from these drawbacks and difficulties the existence of a Welsh university would almost certainly exercise a beneficial influence on higher education in Wales.

It would bring such education more closely home to the daily life and thoughts of the people. It would gratify the national sentiment and furnish new motives for the pursuit of learning. It might, under favourable circumstances, tend to develop new forms of culture in affinity with some of the distinctive characteristics of the Welsh people. A lesser luminary in close proximity will shed more light than a far greater orb shining from a distant sphere, and so a Welsh university crowning the educational edifice might help to diffuse the light of knowledge more generally through the Principality than has been or can be done by Oxford or Cambridge with all their prestige.

[From Chapter V, pp. lxv–lxvii

17 · Report of the Royal Commission on Technical Instruction. [*The Samuelson Report*]

Published: *1882–4*
Chairman: *Bernhard Samuelson, F.R.S.**
Members: *Henry Enfield Roscoe, F.R.S.; Philip Magnus, B.A., B.Sc.; John Slagg; Swire Smith; William Woodall.*
Terms of Reference: *To inquire into the instruction of the industrial classes of certain foreign countries in technical and other subjects for the purpose of comparison with that of the corresponding classes in this country; and into the influence of such instruction on manufacturing and other industries at home and abroad.*

The Samuelson Commission was set up in 1881 as a result on the one hand of widespread concern about the capacity of English industry to stand up to European competition, and on the other, of the unregulated growth of various forms of technical education in England.

The report recommended that 'rudimentary drawing should be incorporated with writing as a single elementary subject', and fully inspected. The Commission advocated more object lessons, more craft work, more agriculture, less part-time employment for children. They wanted more teaching of science and art in training colleges; more endowed schools with 'modern' curricula; powers for local authorities to set up technical and secondary schools. Other recommendations urged industry to provide more systematic training for young workers in works schools, and more support for the City and Guilds of London Institute.

Three specific recommendations dealt with secondary and technical schools:

'(*a*) that steps be taken to accelerate the application of ancient endowments, under amended schemes, to secondary and technical instruction.

(*b*) that provision be made by the Charity Commissioners for the establishment, in suitable localities, of schools or departments of schools, in which the

* Bernhard Samuelson (1820–1905) was apprenticed as a merchant, but by the nature of his business, exporting machinery to Europe, became an engineer and ironmaster. He sat as M.P. for Banbury briefly in 1859, and from 1865–95, being a Liberal and a devoted supporter of Mr Gladstone. His interests ranged over mathematics, music, modern languages and technical education. In 1867, fourteen years before his appointment as Chairman of the Royal Commission, he had made his own comparative study of European technical education. As a member of the Devonshire Commission he had been responsible for the Science and Art Section of the Report. He later served on the Cross Commission, signing the minority report. He was made a baronet in 1884. (*D.N.B.*)

study of natural science, drawing, mathematics and modern languages shall take the place of Latin and Greek.

(*c*) that local authorities be empowered, if they think fit, to establish, maintain, and contribute to the establishment and maintenance of secondary and technical (including agricultural) schools and colleges'.

The Local Government Act of 1888 which set up the County and County Borough Councils was followed in 1889 by the Technical Instruction Act which authorized the new local authorities to spend up to the product of a penny rate on technical and manual instruction. This in turn was followed by the Whisky Money grants from 1890, which diverted more funds to the counties and county boroughs, to be spent on technical and scientific education.

THE SAMUELSON REPORT · VOLUME I · SECOND REPORT · 1884

DEFICIENCIES

Great as has been the progress of foreign countries, and keen as is their rivalry with us in many important branches, we have no hesitation in stating our conviction, which we believe to be shared by Continental manufacturers themselves, that, taking the state of the arts of construction and the staple manufactures as a whole, our people still maintain their position at the head of the industrial world. . . .

In two very important respects, however, the education of a certain proportion of persons employed in industry abroad, is superior to that of English workmen; first, as regards the systematic instruction in drawing given to adult artizans, more especially in France, Belgium and Italy; and secondly, as to the general diffusion of elementary education in Switzerland and Germany. . . .

[From Part IV, pp. 506–11

SPREAD OF TECHNICAL EDUCATION

. . . Not many years have passed since the time when it would still have been a matter for argument whether, in order to maintain the high position which this country has attained in the industrial arts, it is incumbent upon us to take care that our managers, our foremen, and our workmen, should, in the degrees compatible with their circumstances, combine theoretical instruction with their acknowledged practical skill.

No argument of this kind is needed at the present day. In nearly all the great industrial centres – in the Metropolis, in Glasgow, in Manchester, Liverpool, Oldham, Leeds, Bradford, Huddersfield, Keighley,

Sheffield, Nottingham, Birmingham, the Potteries, and elsewhere – more or less flourishing schools of science and art of various grades, together with numerous art and science classes exist, and their influence may be traced in the productions of the localities in which they are placed.

The schools established by Sir W. Armstrong at Elswick; by the London and North-Western Railway Company at Crewe; and those of Messrs Mather and Platt of Salford, in connection with their engineering works, testify to the importance attached by employers to the theoretical training of young mechanics. The efforts of Messrs Denny, the eminent shipbuilders of Dumbarton, for encouraging the instruction of their apprentices and for rewarding their workmen for meritorious improvements in details applicable to their work, are proofs of this appreciation. The evidence of Mr Richardson, of Oldham, and of Mr Mather, of Salford, is emphatic as to their experience of its economical value.

Without more particularly referring to the valuable work in the past, accomplished by the numerous Mechanics' Institutes spread over the country, many of them of long standing, we may point out that they are now largely remodelling their constitutions in order to bring up their teaching to the level of modern requirements, as regards technical instruction. The example of the Manchester Mechanics' Institute may be studied in this connection.

Moreover, as evidencing the desire of the artisans themselves to obtain facilities for instruction both in science and art, we must not omit to mention the classes established and maintained by some of the leading co-operative societies. The Equitable Pioneers' Society of Rochdale has led the way in this, as in so many other social movements. It is much to be wished that the various trades' unions would also consider whether it is not incumbent on them to promote the technical education of their members.

The manufacturers of Nottingham speak with no uncertain voice of the important influence of the local school of art on the lace manufacture of that town. Without the Lambeth School, the art productions of Messrs Doulton could scarcely have come into existence. The linen manufacturers of Belfast are becoming alive to the necessity of technical instruction if competition on equal terms with foreign nations in the more artistic productions, is to be rendered possible. The new generation of engineers and manufacturers of Glasgow has been trained in the technical schools of that city. The City and Guilds of London Institute owes its existence to the conviction of the liverymen that technical instruction is a necessary condition of the welfare of our great industries.

Natural science is finding its way surely, though slowly, into the curriculum of our older English universities, and of our secondary schools. It is becoming a prominent feature in the upper divisions of the elementary board schools in our large towns. There are scarcely any important metallurgical works in the kingdom without a chemical laboratory in which the raw materials and products are daily subjected to careful analysis by trained chemists. The attainments of the young men who have been trained in the Royal Naval College at Greenwich recommend them for remunerative employment by our great ship-building firms.

[From Part IV, pp. 513–14

NEED FOR LOCAL SOURCES OF REVENUE

. . . In dealing with the question of technical instruction in this country we would, at the outset, state our opinion that it is not desirable that we should introduce the practice of foreign countries into England, without considerable modification. As to the higher education, namely, that for those intended to become proprietors or managers of industrial works, we should not wish that every one of them should continue his theoretical studies till the age of 22 or 23 years in a Polytechnic School, and so lose the advantage of practical instruction in our workshops, (which are really the best technical schools in the world) during the years from 18 or 19 to 21 or 22, when he is best able to profit by it.

We have, also, in the science classes under the Science and Art Department, to the intelligent and able administration of which it is our duty to bear testimony, a system of instruction for the great body of our foremen and workmen, susceptible certainly of improvement, but which, in its main outlines it is not desirable to disturb.

Moreover, in considering by whom the cost of the further development of technical instruction should be borne, we must not forget that, if it be true that in foreign countries almost the entire cost of the highest general and technical instruction is borne by the State, on the other hand, the higher elementary and secondary instruction in science falls on the localities to a much greater extent than with us; whilst, as to the ordinary elementary schools, the cost in Germany and Switzerland is almost exclusively borne by the localities; and this was also the case in France and Belgium until the people of those countries became impatient of the lamentable absence of primary instruction on the part of vast numbers of the rural, and in some instances, of the town population; an evil which large State subventions alone could cure within any reasonable period of time. With the exception of France, there is no European country of the first rank that has an Imperial budget for education comparable in amount with our own. In the United Kingdom at least one-half of the cost of elementary education is defrayed out of Imperial funds, and the instruction of artisans in science and art is almost entirely borne by the State. Hence, it will be necessary to look, in the main, to local resources for any large addition to the funds required for the further development of technical instruction in this country. . . .

[From Part IV, pp. 514–15

GAPS IN SECONDARY EDUCATION

. . The best preparation for technical study is a good modern secondary school of the types of the Manchester Grammar School, the Bedford Modern School, and the Allan Glen's Institution at Glasgow. Unfortunately our middle classes are at a great disadvantage compared with those of the Continent for want of a sufficient number of such schools. . . .

We must look to some public measure to supply this, the greatest defect of our educational system. . . . Power should be given to important local bodies, like the proposed County Boards and the municipal corporations, to originate and support secondary and technical schools . . .

Intelligent youths of the artizan classes should have easy access to secondary and technical schools by numerous scholarships . . .

For the great mass of our working population, who must necessarily begin to earn their livelihood at an early age, and from whom our foremen will be mostly selected, it is essential that instruction in the rudiments of the sciences bearing upon industry should form a part of the curriculum of the elementary schools, and that instruction in drawing, and more especially in drawing with rule and compass . . . should receive far greater attention than it does at present. . . . In all infant schools, simple lessons on objects and the more commonly occurring phenomena of nature have been made obligatory. . . .

When, however, the child enters the elementary school the teaching of science practically ceases . . . It appears to us that geography, if properly taught, is a branch of elementary science which need not be separated from science generally, and can well be taught along with other branches of science, by means of object lessons. . . .

[From Part IV, pp. 516–17

SPECIALIST INSTITUTIONS OF HIGH RANK

. . . We may remark concerning the colleges that it is not necessary that all of them should be of the highest type. To enable the relatively small number of persons capable of occupying the highest industrial positions to acquire the most complete education of which modern science admits, only a few well equipped institutions of high rank are needed. It is, however, of national importance that these few should be placed in such a position of efficiency as to enable them to carry out successfully the highest educational work in the special direction for which circumstances, particularly of locality, have fitted them; your Commissioners believe that no portion of the national expenditure on education is of greater importance than that employed in the scientific culture of the leaders of industry.

[From Part IV, p. 525

[*The report included an account of some of the institutions visited.*]

Messrs Mather and Platt's Workshop School. This is a private technical evening school, established and supported by the firm for the benefit of their apprentices.

Under the guidance of Mr Mather, we inspected the school room and examined specimens of the students' drawings.

Mr Mather stated that there are 68 scholars in the school, which is designed to provide science teaching for the apprentices employed in the works. No strangers are admitted for instruction. The drawings are of work actually in progress in the works. The teacher lectures upon them, and explains and makes calculations, and the boys the next day at the works see the very thing they have heard about here. They are allowed to go through the shop in all directions with the teacher from time to time. Everything required (patterns and models) is brought here full size. The great feature is that in the workshop they have the actual things being made under their own observation, and which have to be sold. The parts upon which they are working here in detail, they afterwards see made up as a whole.

In Mr Mather's opinion, you must bring the school to the workshop; you cannot bring the workshop to the school. Bringing the school to the workshop is simple and inexpensive. The teachers here are draughtsmen in the works, and by this teaching they add to their ordinary income. The teacher explained that the boys are not allowed to copy drawings; everything is drawn to a different scale from the flat copy, or the pupils have to draw from actual patterns or pieces of machinery used in the shops. . . .

Mr Mather pointed out that the advantage of the teachers being persons employed in the works, and being trained in this school, rather than in science classes, is that he knows what each person is working at every day, and has the opportunity of pointing out something connected with the work he is doing. The teaching has an actual bearing on his every day work. The students are rewarded not only for proficiency in drawing, but for regular attendance, and actual proficiency in their manual work. It is also a condition of employment that they should be regular in their attendance here.

In reply to the question as to the advantage which the works have derived from the establishment of these schools, Mr Mather replied: 'An incalculable advantage. We desire to send out abroad yearly one, two, or more, thoroughly competent men, who shall not be simply mechanics in the ordinary sense of the word, but who shall be able to turn their attention to anything coming under their notice, whether they have done the thing before, or not (they are sent out simply as mechanics). We had the greatest difficulty in finding such men, until we began to take them from this school, and since the school has been established we have been able to send boys at 20 to 21 to long distances from England, and to place in their hands work which they have not had much to do with before, and by their own intelligence they have made competent teachers of others, and given the greatest satisfaction. Thus one was sent out only a few years ago not quite out of his apprenticeship, and is now getting £4 a week.'

Again, he stated that most of his mechanics are members of the Amalgamated Society of Engineers, and this society not only shows no jealousy in any way of the systems adopted, either of tuition or of giving early employment to boys when they are fit for putting on good jobs; but, on the contrary, they seem to like it, and are pleased at the lads' progress; and he can say the same with respect to the trades generally that are employed in the works.

In reply to the question whether the foremen had any jealousy of the teacher, Mr Jones, the teacher, replied, 'There is no jealousy whatever. They are always ready to give me assistance as a teacher.' . . .

The manager of Messrs Mather and Platt's works remarked, as regards the influence of the school upon the workshop: 'Instead of requiring draughtsmen to look after every separate job, the young fellows who are growing up now can make their own drawings, work to them, and fit the work together and erect it, where it used to require a separate man for each department. The men are most intelligent, and understand, and can execute, their work much better and at a much earlier age. We form thus our own foremen from the boys who have been in the school. We do not find any dissatisfaction or awkwardness with the trade union.'

[From Part III, pp. 429-30

18 · Report of the Royal Commission on the Elementary Education Acts. [*The Cross Report*]

Published: *1888*

Chairman: *Lord Cross**

Members: *Cardinal Manning; Lord Harrowby† ; Lord Beauchamp; The Bishop of London (Dr Temple); Lord Norton; E. L. Stanley; Sir Francis Sandford; Sir John Lubbock; Sir Bernhard Samuelson; Rev. J. R. Rigg; Rev. R. W. Dale; Canon Robert Gregory; Canon B. F. Smith; Rev. T. D. Cox Morse; C. H. Alderson; J. G. Talbot, M.P.; S. C. Buxton; T. E. Heller; B. C. Molloy, M.P.; S. Rathbone; H. Richard, M.P.; G. Shipton.*

Secretary: *F. Cavendish Bentinck*

Terms of Reference: *To inquire into the working of the Elementary Education Acts, England and Wales.*

This Royal Commission was appointed after complaints by the Roman Catholics led by Cardinal Manning and backed by the Church of England about the position of the voluntary schools under the 1870 Act.

The large and divergent membership of the Commission prevented it from producing a united report and on almost every issue the commissioners were divided into a majority and a minority, eight of the twenty-three members eventually writing a minority report.

The *majority* report found that, after making due allowance for 'sickness, weather, distance from school, and other reasonable excuses for irregular attendance' – the demand for school accommodation 'has been fairly met'.

The report supported the right of voluntary effort to work '*pari passu* with a school board' in providing accommodation to meet an increase in population.

It advocated higher standards for school buildings – more 'air, light and space'.

The Inspectorate. It said that inspectors should continue to be men of wide and liberal training, but considered it should be possible for elementary teachers to rise to the rank of inspector. More of them should know some natural science.

* Richard Assheton, first Viscount Cross (1823–1914) was Home Secretary from 1874–80 and 1885–6. Before he was raised to the peerage in 1886, he was a prominent Lancashire member of the House of Commons.

† Another leading member of the Committee was Lord Harrowby (1831–1900), who had sat in the House of Commons as Lord Sandon. He was a member of the London School Board for its first year 1871–2, Vice-President of the Council 1874–8, President of the Board of Trade 1878–80, and Lord Privy Seal 1885–6.

Teachers. The majority wanted no high entry qualification for teachers lest this should exclude those 'with a natural aptitude and a love of learning'. It wanted more 'women of superior social position and general culture' (an earlier draft which referred to them as ladies was amended by a majority vote). There ought to be a superannuation scheme. Pupil-teachers should continue to be apprenticed and their training improved.

Training Colleges. The majority supported State grants to denominational training colleges, and proposed that new voluntary colleges should get similar grants. It supported the idea of a third training college year but doubted if this were feasible 'as yet'. It supported some day training colleges as an experiment but reckoned the residential system the best.

Attendance and Compulsion. The report approved the way in which compulsion had gradually been introduced through the Factory Acts by minimum age for half-time exemption 11, full-time exemption 13+.

Religion and Moral Training. The report found that witnesses were practically unanimous in believing that religious training was desired by parents. It supported biblical instruction, rejected the separation of religion and secular instruction, and coupled this with the need to observe the conscience clause scrupulously. H.M.I.s first duty should be to inquire into and report on the moral training and condition of the schools.

Finance. The Commission concluded that 'the present large annual outlay as now distributed does not secure for the nation commensurate results'. They held that the code should be redrawn and the rates of grant increased. The majority proposed the payment of grants to voluntary schools from the rates without the imposition of the Cowper–Temple clause, and that all public elementary schools for which no rent was paid or received should be free of rates. 'The balance of advantage' was greatly in favour of retaining fees for those who could afford to pay.

Cardinal Manning was among five Commissioners who wrote notes of reservation. He thought the report failed to go far enough in support of the voluntary system and providing for its future expansion, for which purpose he sought 'some new and larger statute for national education'.

Among the subjects on which the *minority* report (signed by eight members including Mr E. L. Stanley and Sir Bernhard Samuelson) disagreed was the training of teachers (see extract). They deplored the pupil-teacher system – 'the weakest part of our educational machinery' – and only assented to the continued payment of grants to existing denominational training colleges in the hope that the system of training in force in Scotland might be imitated both in the association of training with higher education and in a big increase of day students.

On the religious issue, the minority accepted the importance of the formation of character but doubted whether 'moral training can be satisfactorily tested by inspection'. They rejected 'any systematic inspection of morals by Her Majesty's Inspectors'.

They objected to the proposal to support Voluntary Schools from the rates.

They recommended that throughout the country 'where there is a reasonable number of persons desiring them' there should be schools of an undenominational character and under popular representative government.

Curriculum. The report urged that standards should be retained. Reading showed 'room for improvement'. 'The establishment of school libraries is strongly to be recommended.' There was too much importance attached to spelling. The report wanted more attention to handwriting, more practical arithmetic, more learning of poetry by heart, more and more varied schoolbooks, more direction of the syllabus by H.M.I.s, only an outline of history, more 'good and economical cottage cookery', more simple physiology, more Welsh in Wales. It was against enforcing singing by note and elaborate apparatus for gymnastics, looking to the training college for a 'safe and scientific system of physical training'.

It advocated, but did not attempt, a definition of 'elementary' education.

Among other recommendations, the report proposed the transfer of technical institutions from the Science and Art Department to the Education Department.

Both the majority and minority reports agreed on the modification and eventual abolition of payment by results and the consequential changes this would bring to inspection.

The denominational tension which was the cause of the Commission being set up, and which led to a divided report, did not grow any less in the years which followed its publication.

As in the Cross Commission, the conflict between the Church party in education and those who supported non-denominational schools was a feature of School Board politics, and at the national level came to divide the Unionists and the Liberals. The supporters of the voluntary schools accused the School Boards of extravagance, but were themselves obliged to spend more and more on their own schools to keep up with their rivals.

The Cross Commission's proposals for rate aid for the denominational schools was recognized by the Unionists to be the only solution, and in 1895 an abortive Bill was introduced to enable the new county and county boroughs to assist the voluntary schools, and to control secondary education. Voluntary schools were to be relieved of paying rates and a clause was included which would have permitted denominational teaching in Board Schools contrary to the Cowper–Temple Clause. The Bill was not carried beyond a second reading, but in 1897 an Act was passed to aid voluntary schools by removing the limit to the grants they could receive from the Government (set at 17s. 6d. a child by Lord Sandon's Act of 1876), excusing them from rates, and creating a special grant for necessitous schools. The 1902 Act eventually grasped the combined nettles – the need to help the voluntary schools, and the need to create education authorities for secondary education – and in so doing drew upon the Cross Report as well as the Bryce Report (see p. 140).

THE CROSS REPORT · 1888 · FINAL REPORT

Majority Report

PUPIL-TEACHERS

There are those who represent the employment of pupil-teachers as the weakest part of our educational system, and as a positive injury to the work of teaching. . . .

'It is at once', says Dr Crosskey,* 'the cheapest and the very worst possible system of supply', and 'it should be abolished root and branch'. Several teachers express a similar opinion in their evidence.

On the other hand, many teachers not only cordially approve of the pupil-teacher system, but they also look upon it as having justified its institution by its results, and as being the best way of securing a supply of trained teachers. 'This country', says Mr Hance, clerk to the Liverpool School Board, 'must always look to the pupil-teachers as being on the whole the best as well as the main source of the supply of certificated teachers'; and this opinion is endorsed by the principals of several training colleges. Thus Canon Daniel, Principal of Battersea Training College, who has had much practical experience, says that he attaches very great importance to the previous training received by teachers as pupil-teachers, for the 'power which is acquired between the ages of 14 and 18 can scarcely ever be acquired to perfection afterwards. We notice the greatest difference between students who have been pupil-teachers, and those who have not, in their ability to handle a class, in their power of discipline, and in their capacity to deal with all the little difficulties of school work.' Canon Cromwell, Principal of St Mark's, says, 'I have a very strong opinion of the great advantage of the pupil-teacher course in preparing young people to be teachers.' Mr Mansford, Vice-Principal of the Wesleyan Training College, thinks that the candidates for admission who have been pupil-teachers are better trained than those who have not been, though he fears that their training is deteriorating rather than improving. The inspectors, too, bear strong testimony to the value of the system. 'It furnishes a very valuable portion of the supply', says Mr Fitch†; 'it needs improvement', says Mr Oakley,‡ but 'the system affords the best means of keeping up the supply'; 'it is the only possible arrangement at present', says Mr

* Dr H. W. Crosskey, a Unitarian, was one of the Secretaries of the Central Nonconformist Committee in Birmingham, and a prominent supporter of the Education League.

† Mr J. G. (later Sir Joshua) Fitch, Chief H.M.I. for Training Colleges for schoolmistresses.

‡ Mr H. E. Oakley, Chief H.M.I. for Training Colleges for schoolmasters.

Sharpe* and Canon Warburton† looks upon the relations between the pupil-teachers and the head teachers as most valuable, and he considers that those who become teachers, without passing through the apprenticeship of pupil-teachers, lose great practical advantages. . . .

On the whole, we concur in the opinion of the inspectors, whose words we have just quoted, that, having regard to moral qualifications, there is no other available, or as we prefer to say, equally trustworthy source from which an adequate supply of teachers is likely to be forthcoming; and with modifications, tending to the improvement of their education, the apprenticeship of pupil-teachers, we think, ought to be upheld.

[From Part III, Chapter 5, pp. 87–8

TRAINING COLLEGES

It has been urged upon us that training should be extended to a third year, or even longer. This was originally provided for by the rules of the Education Department, but so few students were found able or willing to prolong their college life, for whom, nevertheless, an extra teaching staff had to be provided, that training was limited to two years. . . . We think that there is much to be said for a more extended course of training. As is the master, such is the school, and our elementary teachers would be very different if their training were more thorough, and extended over a longer period, for it is not more knowledge that they need, but more penetration of their minds by that knowledge. In all good education, time is an essential element, and the same knowledge if learnt slowly is generally worth far more than if learnt quickly. Moreover, it would kindle a new spirit in the teacher if the history of education were more studied than it is; the teachers of the present day do not know enough of what has been done by the great teachers of past times, and they would learn much of the science of their profession by a study of its history.

It has been suggested that if students were allowed a third year of training, to be spent at Oxford or Cambridge, the benefit would be considerable in completing their equipment for the best class of service in their profession. To any such suggestion the objections seem to us, under existing circumstances, to be very great. . . . Such students would be unsettled and unfitted, rather than prepared for their work as public elementary teachers, and this proposal therefore seems to us to be inapplicable to those who are to become teachers in elementary schools.

* Rev. T. W. Sharpe, one of H.M. Chief Inspectors of Schools.

† Canon W. P. Warburton, Canon of Winchester. Member of the Inspectorate for 1850–85. H.M.I. for female training colleges, 1881–5.

We are, on the whole, of opinion that an additional year of training would be a great advantage for some students, and only hesitate to recommend it from the doubt whether it is as yet feasible. But, at any rate, we think that picked students from training colleges might even now with advantage be grouped at convenient centres, for a third year's course of instruction.

[From Part III, Chapter 6, p. 97

INCOME AND EXPENDITURE

The financial side of the question of education, has, in the course of our inquiry, engaged a large share of our attention. The gross increase in the expenditure on public elementary schools between the year 1860 and 1886 is largely due to the additional number of scholars brought under efficient education, for whereas in the former period the proportion of the population under instruction in aided schools was only 5%, it had increased in 1886 to between 16 and 17%. But there has meanwhile also been a steady growth in the costliness of elementary education. In the year 1876, the average annual cost per scholar in average attendance, taking all descriptions of elementary schools together, was £1. 14s. 8d. In 1886 the sum was £1. 19s. 5d., a rise of 4s. 9d. a head, or of over 13% in ten years. . . .

Lord Lingen* makes the following statement in regard to the increased costliness of education. After allowing that the educational requirements of the present time cause the cost per scholar to be very considerably increased, he goes on to say: 'My own opinion is, be it worth what it may, that the cost per scholar is larger than it need be at this time.' He accounts for the increase of the cost in several ways. One is that, in his opinion, 'the salaries of the teachers in many of the large towns are larger than they need be;' and another is that, since school boards having unlimited funds to deal with, 'the golden rule of "making things do", is very much overlooked in the board schools'. He thinks, too, that the increase of the parliamentary grant has led to extravagance. Two other causes of the increased cost of education he specifies: the first is 'that there has been a great impulse of public opinion in favour of education, and some impression that the more you spend upon it the more efficient it is; the other is that it is largely due to the rivalry between the board and voluntary schools.' . . .

In the year 1886, out of a total income of £6,827,189 contributed for the maintenance of all elementary schools, the amount set down under the head of Government grant is £2,866,700, or about 42%. . . .

* R. R. W. Lingen succeeded Kay-Shuttleworth as secretary of the Committee of Council, 1849–69. Permanent Secretary to the Treasury, 1869–85. Made first Baron, 1885.

The portion of the cost of education which is borne by the rates differs in amount very widely in different localities, and it must be remembered that the amount so raised for school maintenance very inadequately represents the whole of the charge which education now places upon the ratepayers. From the last Report of the Committee of Council it appears that whilst £1,276,917 was raised from rates in England and Wales in the year 1886 for school maintenance, the other charges upon the education rate brought up the sum total to £2,526,495, the average rate in the £ having grown from 6·3 pence in 1883–4 to 7 pence in 1885–6 in England, exclusive of Wales. . . .

Between 1870 and 1884, Mr Cumin* says the amount annually raised in voluntary subscriptions for voluntary inspected schools rose from £418,839 to £732,524, which is an increase of 74%. . . . Many witnesses advert to the heavy pressure on those who not only support voluntary schools, but are called on to contribute to the rates by which board schools are maintained in the same district. . . .

The time indeed, seems to have come for a new departure. The country is now provided with a national system, in the sense in which Mr Forster spoke of his Bill, as 'the first attempt in providing national education', because it would 'provide for the education of every child of the nation'. The supply of schools is complete; a full staff of teachers has been provided and 4½ millions of children are on the registers of inspected schools. The great majority of these schools, containing 64% of the scholars on the rolls, have been erected, and are supported, by voluntary effort; the promoters of which are nevertheless rated for the maintenance of the school board system in school board districts. We think that if, in the impending reorganization of the local government of the country, education were recognized as one of the most important branches of that local government, and arrangements were made for gradually connecting it, more or less, with the civil administration of each locality, much of the unhealthy competition between the two school systems would disappear, and the expenditure caused by their rivalry would be reduced. Such an arrangement would also tend to decentralize the present system in a way of natural local development, relieving the Education Department of innumerable administrative details, and largely reducing the cost of its staff, while retaining for the Education Department powers of general control which have been of the greatest value to education in the past. . . . We think it reasonable and just that the supporters of voluntary schools should retain the management of these schools on the condition of bearing some substantial share of the burden of the cost in subscriptions. But it does not seem either just or expedient to allow the voluntary system to be

* Secretary of the Committee of Council for Education.

gradually destroyed by the competition of board schools possessinh unlimited resources at their command. We therefore recommend that the local educational authority be empowered to supplement from local rates the voluntary subscriptions given to the support of every public State-aided elementary school in their district to an amount equal to these subscriptions, provided it does not exceed the amount of ten shillings for each child in average attendance.

[From Part V, Chapter 3, pp. 191–4

RELIGIOUS TRAINING

... The views of those who would remove from day elementary schools all Religious Teaching and Observance have received our attentive consideration. The Rev. C. Williams, Chairman of the Baptist Union, is personally in favour of the establishment of secular schools, and thinks that they are perfectly consistent with the religious education of the children of the Country, if the churches would do their duty, but he thinks that the majority in almost every district would be found opposed to a purely secular system. Mr Snape, Governor of the Ministerial Training College of the United Methodist Free Churches, desires that in all State-aided schools the State should be responsible for secular instruction, and the Church should be responsible for the religious teaching. Rev. Dr Bruce, a Congregationalist minister and Chairman of the School Management Committee of the Huddersfield School Board, said, 'Our principle is this: that if you have a State system according to our Nonconformist views, it must in the main be either secular or unsectarian.' The Rev. J. Atkinson, President of the Free Churches of the Primitive Methodist Society, would have no distinctive religious teaching, that is to say, no distinctive sectarian teaching; if religious teaching could be given without this, he would not object; but as he does not think this possible, he does not suppose that he would object perhaps to reading the Scriptures, but he sees difficulties in the way even of admitting that. Dr Crosskey, of the Birmingham School Board, thinks it very undesirable, for the sake of religion, that religion should be taught in public elementary schools.

Those who hold this view in favour of purely secular schools did not shrink from urging before us, through the witnesses who represented them, that the State should take the extreme step of prohibiting religious instruction in public elementary schools. These witnesses, however, while affirming as a matter of principle the purely secular character of national public education, stated that they were willing to acquiesce in the compromise of 1870, by which, in board schools, unsectarian biblical teaching was left to the discretion of local representative authorities. Even those witnesses, however, who strenuously advocated the secularization of public elementary education, most emphatically declared that they regarded religion as the true basis of education, and only contended for its exclusion from the day school in the belief that it could be provided in some other and better way.

In questions of this character, it is impossible to have negative provisions which have not also a positive side. Thus, for children to attend day schools in which no religious teaching was given, would, in the opinion of those who think that the daily lessons should be accompanied with religious teaching, be practically leading them to undervalue the importance of religion. They would hold that the impression left upon the children's minds would be that religion was a matter of inferior moment, at all events to that secular teaching which they were acquiring day by day.

In support of the contention that religious instruction should be excluded from the day school, it was further urged by Dr Crosskey that it makes an undesirable tax on the teachers' energies. But, on the other hand, we have had brought before us trustworthy testimony, some of it from teachers themselves, that as a body, they would consider it a great loss if they were debarred from giving Bible lessons to their scholars. Nor can that be matter of surprise if it be remembered that they would thereby be precluded from exercising their trained powers of oral teaching on a subject which they regard as one of the most interesting and profitable to their scholars. Moreover, the religious instruction given by teachers, we have been told by the Rev. J. Duncan,* greatly increases the moral influence of the teacher. The moral character of teachers themselves, Archdeacon Norris, formerly Her Majesty's Inspector of Schools in various populous counties, thinks would suffer if they were forbidden to impart religious instruction. And, finally, against the attempt, on this or any other ground, to prohibit teachers from giving moral and religious instruction in their schools, Mr Cumin, Secretary of the Committee of Council on Education, emphatically protests. He believes that many excellent teachers would absolutely refuse to be restricted in their teaching to secular subjects.

Dr Crosskey advanced as an additional ground in favour of this restriction that religious instruction ought only to be given by religious people. But without denying that religious teaching is liable sometimes to fall into unfit hands, all such instruction is more or less liable to the same objection, and we see no ground for admitting the inference which seems to underlie this objection that elementary teachers as a class have no special fitness for the task for which, nevertheless, a very large pro-

* Rev. James Duncan, Secretary of the National Society, 1870–90.

portion of them have been specially trained. Objection was also raised by the same witness to the Bible being used as a school book, lest it should thereby suffer in the estimation of the scholars, and it was urged that religion was dishonoured by being included in a programme consisting chiefly of secular subjects. But we have no evidence tending to show that these results actually occur, and it can hardly be supposed that if such were found to be practically the result, religious bodies and school boards would still continue to make such great efforts as we find they now do in order to maintain an efficient system of religious instruction in the schools for which they are responsible. On the other hand, we have positive evidence that children who have received religious teaching in the day school are better prepared to profit by Sunday school teaching, and to become themselves teachers in Sunday schools. . . .

After hearing the arguments for a wholly secular education, we have come to the following conclusions:

1. That it is of the highest importance that all children should receive religious and moral training.
2. That the evidence does not warrant the conclusion that such religious and moral training can be amply provided otherwise than through the medium of elementary schools.
3. That in schools of a denominational character to which parents are compelled to send their children the parents have a right to require an operative conscience clause, so that care be taken that the children shall not suffer in any way in consequence of their taking advantage of the conscience clause.
4. That inasmuch as parents are compelled to send their children to school, it is just and desirable that, as far as possible, they should be enabled to send them to a school suitable to their religious convictions or preferences.
5. We are also of opinion that it is of the highest importance that the teachers who are charged with the moral training of the scholars should continue to take part in the religious instruction. We should regard any separation of the teacher from the religious teaching of the school as injurious to the morals and secular training of the scholars.

[From Part IV, Chapter 1, pp. 122–7

Minority Report

TEACHER TRAINING

[*The majority report considered (and rejected) a suggestion that students at training college should be allowed to contract out of religious attendance under a conscience clause.*]

. . . In reference to the conscience clause in residential training colleges, we dissent from the arguments and conclusions of the report of the majority. The statement that its introduction would destroy all unity of christian family life, whether in a denominational or undenominational college, and would interfere fatally with the framework of ordinary domestic and moral discipline, has, in our opinion, no sufficient foundation. . . .

We think that the other schemes suggested to us of training students in connexion with places of higher education deserve a much heartier support than they receive in the report of the majority, and we also think that if professional training is to be extended for our elementary teachers, it is improper to prohibit any aid being derived from the rates. Such aid would be a trifling charge compared with the total cost of education, and would bring an ample return in the increased efficiency of the teachers. If twice as many students were in training as are now, that is, if 3,200 more students were trained in day training colleges, we believe that a Parliamentary grant materially lower than that now made on behalf of a student in existing training colleges with reasonable fees from students and a small subvention, which might often prove unnecessary, from the school board or other public authority would suffice to defray the cost of training in connexion with local colleges existing or to be founded . . .

We assent to the continuance of grants to the existing denominational training colleges, partly in deference to the strenuous desire of the advocates of denominational education to preserve a strongly denominational system of training with vigilant domestic discipline, but we cannot assent to the statement in the report that the existing system of residential training colleges is the best both for the teachers and the scholars of the public elementary schools of the country, and we only acquiesce in the continuance of these grants in the hope that the system of training now in force in Scotland may be largely imitated here, in the association of training with higher education, in the great extension of facilities for day students and in the liberal recognition of the rights of conscience, and we look to the adoption of these reforms as enabling us hereafter to dispense almost entirely with the employment of untrained teachers.

As to pupil teachers, we strongly dissent from the proposition that having regard to moral qualifications, there is no other equally trustworthy source from which an adequate supply of teachers is likely to be forthcoming. Indeed, bearing in mind the statement of our colleagues, in an earlier part of the chapter, as to the valuable influence of women of superior social position and general culture, we can hardly reconcile the two statements, and we are certainly of opinion that the moral securities we should look for in our future teachers are not likely to be diminished, but on the contrary greatly increased by a wider course and a prolonged period of preliminary education before students are trusted with the management of classes.

In general we consider that the pupil teacher system is now the weakest part of our educational machinery, and that great changes are needed in it if it is to be continued in the future. We should deplore the reduction of the commencing age to 13, recommended by our colleagues, and we think rather that no pupil teacher should be entrusted with a class till he or she is at least 15 years of age; the first year or two of apprenticeship being almost entirely employed in learning. . . .

VOLUNTARY SCHOOLS ON THE RATES

. . . We object to the proposal made by our colleagues in their chapter on income and expenditure of schools . . . that voluntary schools should be enabled to receive help from the rates up to a possible maximum of 10s. a head, on the ground already indicated, that such a proposal seems to us unsound in principle, destructive of the settlement of 1870, and certain, if it became law, to embitter educational politics, and intensify sectarian rivalries. . . .

In recording our dissent from so many of the conclusions of our colleagues' report, we would add that we have further this general objection, that their report appears to us too often to approach proposals for the improvement of education from the point of view of considering how such improvements may affect the interests of certain classes of schools rather than how far they are desirable; and that it does not do justice to the wish that we entertain for an expansion of education, a widening of its aims, and its establishment on a broad base of local support and popular management, which would enable us to dispense with much in the present system of State aids and examination which we think unfavourable to the best modes of imparting knowledge.

[From pp. 242–7

19 · Report of the Royal Commission on Secondary Education. [*The Bryce Report*]

Published: *1895*

Chairman: *James Bryce**

Members: *Sir John Hibbert; the Hon. Edward Lyttelton; Sir Henry Roscoe, F.R.S.; Dr E. C. Maclure; Dr A. M. Fairbairn; Professor R. C. Jebb; Dr Richard Wormell; Henry Hobhouse; Michael Sadler; H. L. Smith; G. J. Cockburn; Charles Fenwick; J. H. Yoxall; Lady Frederick Cavendish; Dr Sophie Bryant, Mrs E. M. Sidgwick*

Term of Reference: *To consider what are the best methods of establishing a well-organized system of secondary education in England, taking into account existing deficiencies and having regard to such local sources of revenue for endowments or otherwise as are available or may be made available for this purpose and to make recommendation accordingly.*

The main recommendations were: (1) A central authority for secondary education under a Minister of Education taking over the educational function of such bodies as the Education Department, the Science and Art Department, the Charity Commission. This central authority would be the central authority for elementary education – a fully fledged government department with a permanent secretary.

(2) An Educational Council to assist the Minister in exercise of certain quasi-judicial functions, made up of representatives appointed by the Crown, universities and teachers, which would also act as a body for teachers' registration.

(3) Local Authorities for Secondary Education of which the majority should be chosen by counties and county boroughs with wide power 'to supply, maintain and aid schools'.

The origin of the Royal Commission was quite simply the confusion which had continued to grow out of the hydra-headed administrative structure. The

* James Bryce (1838–1922), jurist, historian, politician and ambassador, was born in Belfast, the son of a schoolmaster. A brilliant scholar at Glasgow University, he went on to Trinity College, Oxford, where he was President of the Union Society and took a first in Greats. A fellow of Oriel, after serving as an assistant commissioner on the Taunton Commission (see p. 89) from 1865–6, he became a barrister in 1867, and Regius Professor of Civil Law at Oxford in 1870. He entered Parliament as a Liberal in 1885, remaining a member till 1906 when he became Ambassador to the United States. He held various offices in Liberal governments between 1886 and 1906. Queen Victoria liked him – 'I like Mr Bryce. He knows so much, and is so modest.' Only a moderate success as a politician, his scholarly diplomacy came into its own as Ambassador in Washington. He was made a Viscount in 1914. (*D.N.B.*)

Aberdare Report, 1881 (see p. 112), and the Welsh Intermediate Education Act, 1889 (see p. 112), did something to remedy this in the Principality. The chaos in England grew worse. After 1889, the Counties and County Boroughs became education authorities for higher technical education. The proliferation of grants from the Science and Art Department and the Whisky Money threatened to distort the development of secondary education in which the Education Department itself had no formal part to play. To sort out the implications of this for secondary education, Lord Rosebery set up the Royal Commission in 1894.

The recommendation of the Bryce Report for the creation of a unified central authority was carried out by the Act of 1899 which set up the Board of Education which took over the educational work of the Charity Commission, together with that of the existing Education Department and the Science and Art Department. At the same time a consultative committee was established corresponding to the Council recommended by the Bryce Commission.

The comprehensive review of educational organization which was required was outside the terms of reference. But it was impossible any longer to deal with the problems of secondary education separately from those of education as a whole – this was plain from the Bryce Report. Mr Balfour took over from Lord Salisbury in 1902 with the promise of early legislation on education, and the Act of that year was the sequel. It in its turn had been prompted by the Cockerton Judgment. This was the decision of the courts upholding a district auditor named Cockerton who disallowed expenditure by the London School Board on the North London School of Art, on the grounds that this was not elementary education, and therefore was outside their legal scope. An emergency Bill had to be rushed through Parliament to legalize the illegality. This was in 1901. The following year, Mr Balfour pushed through his Education Act.

The main driving force behind the legislation was Mr Robert Morant, who from the Office of Special Enquiries and Reports had drawn attention (in a report on education in Switzerland) to the dubious legality of developments in higher elementary education. He was successively Private Secretary to Sir John Gorst and the Duke of Devonshire, and in 1903 he became Permanent Secretary of the Board of Education. He was knighted in 1907. He left the Board of Education in 1910 after a public controversy which arose over an internal circular issued to H.M.I.s which was derogatory to L.E.A. inspectors with elementary school backgrounds. Sir Robert Morant, who held strong views about the strict limits which properly belonged to elementary education, became the target of strong criticism from the National Union of Teachers and in Parliament, and was transferred to work on Mr Lloyd George's insurance scheme.

THE BRYCE REPORT · 1895

PUBLIC INTEREST IN EDUCATION

One of the things the Schools Enquiry Commission deemed most needful, was the intelligent interest of the people in the cause of education. Without this interest, they held, legislation could accomplish little; with it there might be many failures and mistakes, but the end would certainly be correction and improvement. Events have gone far to justify their forecast; the intervening period has been one of constant movement, and experiment in both Elementary and Secondary Education. Between these it has been found easier to draw a theoretical than to maintain a practical division, but wherever the dividing line may be drawn, instruction has been so enlarged on both sides of it that whole regions of knowledge, at one time scarcely thought of as falling within an educational curriculum, have been added to its province. The classical languages are taught more extensively than ever, but less as if they were dead, and more as if they still lived, rich in all those humanities by virtue of which they have been the supreme instruments of the higher culture. And they do not now stand alone; a place and a function have been found for modern languages and literatures, and it is ceasing to be a reproach that our schools have cultivated dead to the exclusion of living tongues. There has been a remarkable and growing use in education of certain physical sciences, while technical and manual instruction has risen and assumed, especially in certain localities, what may in some aspects appear to be rather large proportions. And though some of these extensions represent new departments of knowledge, yet they involve instruction in old subjects, like mathematics and mechanics, and so build on them, that the progress of the scholar depends on the knowledge he already possesses of them. The idea of technical instruction as a means for the formation of citizens capable of producing or distributing wealth, has taken hold, though in varying degrees of intelligence and intensity, of both our old borough councils and our new county councils, and hence has come a concern for that kind of education that we might otherwise have looked for in vain. In a word, we have two excellent things, an enlarged education and a wider and more intelligent interest in it; and out of these may come a development which it will require all the wisdom of the legislature to guide. . . .

But there is one feature in this growing concern of the State with education which must not be here overlooked. The growth has not been either continuous or coherent; i.e. it does not represent a series of logical or even connected sequences. Each one of the agencies whose origin has been described was called into being, not merely independently of the others, but with little or no regard to their existence. Each has remained in its working isolated and unconnected with the rest. The problems which Secondary Education present have been approached from different sides, at different times, and with different views and aims. The Charity Commissioners have had little to do with the Education Department and still less with the Science and Art Department. Even the borough councils have, to a large extent, acted independently of the school boards, and have, in some instances, made their technical instruction grants with too little regard to the parallel grants which were being made by the Science and Art Department. Endowments which, because applied to elementary education, were exempted from the operation of the Endowed Schools Acts, have been left still exempt; though the public provision of elementary education in 1870 and the grant of universal free elementary education in 1891 have wholly altered their position. The University Colleges, though their growth is one of the most striking and hopeful features of the last 30 years, remain without any regular organic relation either to elementary or to Secondary Education, either to school boards or to county councils. This isolation and this independence, if they may seem to witness to the rich variety of our educational life, and to the active spirit which pervades it, will nevertheless prepare the observer to expect the usual results of dispersed and unconnected forces, needless competition between the different agencies, and a frequent overlapping of effort, with much consequent waste of money, of time, and of labour.

THE LOCAL AUTHORITY: ITS PLACE AND PURPOSE

On no point were our witnesses more entirely unanimous than on this, – the necessity of local authorities to a national system of Secondary Education. There was, indeed, almost every possible variety of opinion as to how they should be constituted; over what area they should reign; what they should be empowered to do; what schools they should have to do with; and what they should have to do with the schools; but as to some form of local authority being a necessity of the situation, there was no difference of opinion whatever. There was, however, a well-marked distinction of intellectual attitude: on the one side, professional scholastic opinion was, on the whole, though by no means unanimously, fearful of local authorities, and inclined to propose that they should be if not muzzled, yet so constituted and conditioned as to be made as innocuous as possible: on the other side, what we may term the administrative and political mind looked hopefully to such authorities as the most potent and promising factors for the solution of the problem. Each attitude is explicable enough. The schoolmaster, the more competent he is and the more assured in position, wants the more to be let alone. What he needs in order to attain the best results is, on the one side, command of means and possession of pupils, and, on the other, freedom of hand and method; and so he desires what he conceives to be the simple conditions of success. But the administrator sees the other side of the question: – the necessity of creating and maintaining the machinery which the schoolmaster has to work, and he knows that this can best be done by evoking popular interest and allowing parental or family care for posterity to inspire the educational work and agencies of the present. It would be a serious evil if education were allowed to become the business of the schoolmaster alone; the more completely it grows into the concern of the whole people, and is made an integral part of their common life and civil policy, the more will it flourish, and the better will it become. . . .

CENTRAL AUTHORITY. THE MINISTER OF EDUCATION

There has been a remarkable consensus of opinion on this point: – That in order to constitute an efficient and satisfactory Central Authority there must be a Minister of Education, the head of a Department, responsible to Parliament, with a seat in the Cabinet, a Minister who, as Sir William Hart-Dyke said, would be a Secretary of State. On this matter witnesses of all orders . . . were agreed . . . that as he was to be responsible he must be supreme, though his supremacy was not always heartily or willingly accepted. This general agreement was made the more significant by an occasional voice of protest, or of dissent more or less qualified.

The Bishop of London, whose position was one with which many secondary teachers would probably agree, thought that the central authority would be better 'dissociated from any particular "Ministry;" its policy ought not to change with the Ministry of the day' . . .

We believe that education has more chance of a vigorous and a beneficent life if treated as a public question than were it allowed to become the concern of a special order; and it is of the very essence of our problem to find the means by which public control and educational policy, instead of counteracting, may supplement and fortify each other. . . .

On the whole then, it is well, in the face of what is now actual fact, to recognize, with Sir Henry Longley, that political control goes necessarily with the bestowment of public money.

It was suggested that the Department should be organized under this Minister, he being assisted by a parliamentary under secretary, and 'a permanent official' or 'common secretary', 'who would be the head of all departments', with 'under secretaries at the head of each (separate) department'. He ought to have the charge of education, both primary and secondary, though there was division of opinion as to whether, while the Minister was one, the Departments ought to remain distinct. In every case it was held that the Minister was to be the centre of unity, and generally, though not universally, that there should be unification of all the bodies concerned with Secondary Education. The ideas of unification and how it was to be acomplished were very various, but the necessity was admitted almost quite universally. The reasons for it were economy, efficiency, harmony of idea and purpose, as well as of legislative and administrative control.

TEACHERS

The fact is that the body of teachers must necessarily occupy a somewhat anomalous position in the economy of national life. The service which they render is one over which the State must in self-defence retain effective oversight; the provision of teaching and the conduct of education cannot be left to private enterprise alone. Nor, on the other hand, do the teachers stand in the same relation to Government as does the Civil Service. Education is a thing too intimately concerned with individual preference and private life, for it to be desirable to throw the whole of it under Government control. It needs organization, but it would be destroyed by uniformity; it is stimulated by inspection, but it could be crushed by a code. In the public service, where the chief object is administrative efficiency, the individual officer is necessarily subordinate; in education, where a chief object is the discovery of more perfect methods of teaching, the individual teacher must be left comparatively free. Every good teacher is a discoverer, and, in order to make discoveries, he must have liberty of experiment.

REGISTRATION

Upon no subject, of all those on which we have taken evidence or received memoranda was there more general agreement than as to the necessity of some measure for the registration of teachers. The demand has come from all the associations of teachers alike; from the Headmasters' Conference; from the four several Associations of Head and Assistant Masters and Mistresses; from the Teachers' Guild, the College of Preceptors and the National Union of Teachers; from the Private Schools Association and from the Association of Headmasters of Preparatory Schools. . . .

As to the basis of the register there was sharp difference of view. Some witnesses wished to include in one register all teachers who could produce the required qualification; others, however, declared that registration was required only for teachers in secondary schools, the objects of registration being already secured for teachers working in elementary schools by arrangements of the Education Department. Hence the latter witnesess protested emphatically against the admission to the new register of any certificated teachers engaged in public elementary schools. Those who took this more exclusive attitude urged that, in any election on a common register, the teachers in elementary would swamp those in secondary schools, the latter being less united and therefore, for electoral purposes, comparatively weak. They also dwelt on the arguments that the spheres of Elementary and Secondary Education should be kept distinct and separate; that, as a secondary school teacher, much as he would often like to do so, cannot at will enter into certificated service in a public elementary school, an elementary school teacher would be unfairly favoured if, preserving his own territory for his own exclusive use, he was free to make excursions at pleasure into the field of Secondary Education, and finally that, when this partial registration became soundly established, the method might be extended downwards, so as to make registration take the place of certification. The rejoinder of those who desire that employment in a public elementary school should form no bar to registration, was that one of the causes of weakness in English education is the social estrangement between different grades of teachers; that the middle wall of partition should be broken down, and facilities given for good teachers to pass, as the case may be, from secondary to elementary, from elementary to secondary, schools; that the present separation between elementary and secondary instruction has its roots, not in the nature of things, but in the diversity of administrative regulations which can be more easily reformed by a united profession than by one divided into sections; that distinctions between teachers in different grades of schools are artificial and unreal, save only as they correspond to differences in intellectual attainment or professional competence; that a register which drew a line between secondary and elementary schools, irrespective of the attainments or aptitude of the teachers engaged in them, would include many who should be shut out, and shut out many who would satisfy any reasonable test of mental qualification or of technical skill; that the simple policy of having one register of all duly qualified teachers is also the sound one; that any other plan would fail to achieve its fundamental object of marking off the skilled teacher from the unskilled. . . .

While we are far from denying the weight of the arguments urged by those who would confine the right of admission to the register to qualified teachers actually engaged in secondary schools, we are nevertheless of opinion that the course of events has materially altered the conditions under which such a limitation was originally proposed. So long as the establishment of a register was regarded as the initial step in the organization of Secondary Education, and as the means by which information as to the state of secondary schools could be most easily obtained, there were obvious reasons for restricting it to those persons who might be actually engaged in the kind of schools about which it was desired to collect statistics with a view to further legislation. But as we conceive that the advantages, which it was thus sought to obtain indirectly through registration, will be otherwise secured by the labours of the Central and Local Authorities, we think that the way is now clear for the establishment of a register on a more comprehensive basis. We therefore propose that there should be one register for teachers who fulfil the conditions of registration hereafter mentioned. . . .

We think that, after the lapse of a reasonable time, – say seven years after the establishment of the register – no unregistered person should be allowed to be appointed as a teacher of a public secondary school, or of a school recognized by the Local Authority as contributing to the supply of efficient Secondary Education.

CONCLUSION

In dwelling on the need for a systematic organization of Secondary Education we have more than once had occasion to explain that we mean by 'system' neither uniformity nor the control of a Central Department of government. Freedom, variety, elasticity are, and have been, the merits which go far to redeem the defects in English education, and they must at all hazards be preserved. The 'system' which we desire to see introduced may rather be described as coherence, an organic relation between different authorities and different kinds of schools which will enable each to work with due regard to the work to be done by the others, and will therewith avoid waste both of effort and of money. Of the loss now incurred through the want of such coherence and correlation, it is impossible to speak too strongly. It is the fault on which all our witnesses and all our Assistant Commissioners unite in dwelling. Unfortunately, so far from tending to cure itself, it is an evil which every day strikes its roots deeper. The existing authorities and agencies whose want of co-operation we lament are each of them getting more accustomed to the exercise of their present powers, and less disposed to surrender them. Vested interests are being created which will stand in the way of the needed reforms. Instances occur in which large sums of money are being expended in buildings, or otherwise upon institutions, which, if not superfluous, are planned upon imperfect lines, and with reference to one area or one purpose only where others should have been equally regarded, while at the same time many plans of admitted excellence cannot be carried out owing to the precarious position in which the money available under the Customs and Excise Act of 1890 now stands. Thus the difficulty of introducing the needful coherence and correlation becomes constantly greater, and will be more serious a year or two hence than it is at this moment. . . .

Upon the magnitude of those questions, and their influence on the future of the country we need not enlarge. Elementary education is among the first needs of a people, and especially of a free people, as appears by the fact that all, or nearly all, modern constitutional States have undertaken to provide it. But it is by those who have received a further and superior kind of instruction that the intellectual progress of a nation is maintained. It is they who provide its literature, who advance its science, who direct its government. In England, those classes which have been wont to resort to the universities have, during the last sixty or seventy years, fared well. Those who could afford to pay the very high charges made at some of the great endowed schools have had an education which, if somewhat one-sided, has been highly stimulative to certain types of mind. But the great body of the commercial and professional classes were long forced to content themselves with a teaching which was usually limited in range and often poor in quality, and whose defects had become so familiar that they had ceased to be felt as defects.

Things have improved within the last thirty years, as may be seen by whoever compares the picture drawn by our Assistant Commissioners with that contained in the reports of the Assistant Commissioners of 1865. But the educational opportunities offered in most of our towns, and in nearly all our country districts, to boys or girls who do not proceed to the universities, but leave school at sixteen, are still far behind the requirements of our time, and far less ample than the incomes of the parents and the public funds available might well provide.

Not a few censors have dilated upon the disadvantages from which young Englishmen suffer in industry and commerce owing to the superior preparation of their competitors in several countries of continental Europe. These disadvantages are real. But we attach no less importance to the faults of dullness and barrenness to which so many lives are condemned by the absence of those capacities for intellectual enjoyment which ought to be awakened in youth. In an age of increasing leisure and luxury, when men have more time and opportunity for pleasure, and pursue it more eagerly, it becomes all the more desirable that they should be induced to draw it from the best sources. Thus, it is not merely in the interest of the material prosperity and intellectual activity of the nation, but no less in that of its happiness and its moral strength, that the extension and reorganization of Secondary Education seem entitled to a place among the first subjects with which social legislation ought to deal.

20 · The Education Act. 1902

The 1902 Act was the first comprehensive education Bill to reach the Statute Book. For the circumstances in which the Bill was brought forward, see the notes on the Cross Report (p. 128) and the Bryce Report (p. 140). The administrative structure which the Bill set up was foreshadowed in the Bryce Report, and by the logic of events since the creation of County and County Borough Councils in 1888. The need for unified control of primary and secondary education had become manifest, and the Counties and the County Boroughs were the obvious authorities for the job. In the event, though authority was unified at the centre through the new Board of Education (set up by the 1899 Act) local pressure forced Balfour to give way during the passage of the Bill. The Counties and County Boroughs became the L.E.A.s. Under Part III of the Act, Borough Councils with 10,000 population and urban districts with 20,000 population became authorities for elementary education only.

By the 1899 Act the Board of Education had been charged with 'the superintendence of matters relating to education in England and Wales'. The 1902 Act made clear the limitations on this superintendence: 'the local education authority shall consider the educational needs of their area and take such steps as seem to them desirable, to supply or aid the supply of education other than elementary, and to promote the general coordination of all forms of education . . .' Expenditure by L.E.A.s on higher education was initially limited to a twopenny rate.

The power of the Board of Education was exercised through the codes of regulations which, having laid on the table in the House of Commons for a month, became law. The codes, and the system of inspection, gave the Board of Education close control over what went on in the schools, while the absence of any positive initiating power to the Board enabled L.E.A.s to proceed as fast or as slowly as they chose.

The results of the Education Act of 1902 were – as Mr Balfour had hoped that they would be – seen most dramatically in the provision of county secondary schools and teacher training colleges. But the aim of unifying the education system was far from achieved.

EDUCATION ACT · 1902

Speech by Mr A. J. Balfour, Prime Minister, introducing the Bill, House of Commons. March 24th, 1902

Nobody can be more impressed than I am with the difficulty of the task the Government have undertaken . . . It is only because we are of the opinion that it cannot with national credit be much longer delayed, that we have resolved to lay before the House our solution of the great problem which, for so many years past, education has embarrassed the legislature and the reformer . . .

So far as primary education is concerned . . . the system under which we now work is practically the system adopted . . . more than a generation ago . . . The Legislature in 1870 . . . aimed at supplying a gap . . . filling up the vacuum which voluntary effort had left empty. It was for that object and that object alone that School Boards were called into existence . . .

The Act of 1870 successfully carried out this great if . . . limited object . . . But two unforeseen consequences arose . . . and three considerable omissions made themselves felt as time went on. The first of the two unforeseen consequences was the embarrassment into which the Voluntary Schools were thrown by the rivalry of the rate-aided Board Schools . . . Mr Forster and the Government of that day greatly underrated the . . . cost. Mr Forster contemplated that a threepenny rate would do all that had to be done . . . There was a wholly unexpected expenditure by School Boards . . . and the voluntary schools were subjected to a competition which, however good for education, was certainly neither anticipated nor desired by the framers of the Act of 1870. The second result was that a strain . . . was put upon local finances . . . through the action of a body responsible indeed to the community so far as regards education, but having no responsibility for general expenditure, which was, of course, in the hands of the local authority . . .

Let me just enumerate hurriedly the three important omissions . . . In the first place, the Act of 1870 provided no organization for voluntary schools. Board schools . . . were organized under the School Boards. But voluntary schools . . . were isolated and unconnected . . . The second omission was . . . that there was no sufficient provision for the education of the great staff of teachers required for our national schools. And . . . third . . . our primary system was put in no kind of rational or organic connection with our system of secondary education, and through the system of secondary education, with the University education which crowns the whole educational edifice. . . .

[*Mr Balfour went on to refer to the Endowed Schools Act and the Act of 1889 giving County and Town councils certain duties in connexion with technical education – 'the first great step taken in the direction of municipalizing education'.*]

There are omissions and defects . . . which it is the bounden duty of Parliament to remedy. One of these is . . . the insufficiency of the supply of secondary education. Another is that by the very fact that you have given to County Councils and Borough Councils the right and the duty to intervene in respect of technical instruction . . . alone, the normal and healthy growth of a true scheme of secondary education has been inevitably warped. Higher technical instruction can . . . only do its work well when that work is based on a sound general secondary education . . .

We find dealing with education . . . two elective authorities . . . in rivalry . . . Around these two rival authorities . . . are scattered independent endowed schools and independent voluntary schools . . .

I cannot believe that is a sound system of local government. It is not a system we should tolerate in any other administrative branch of our business . . . I do not believe that this system of *ad hoc* authority with unlimited rating is one which really has any important experimental endorsement behind it at all . . .

The second of the evils . . . relates to the imperfect coordination of educational effort above the limiting line of elementary education. I am not one of those who throw blame on the School Boards because they have, in many cases, trespassed on the territories of secondary education . . . there was a great vacuum to fill . . . But frankly, I must add that . . . these authorities for primary education have exaggerated their capacity for dealing with . . . secondary education . . . If we are considering the whole field of secondary education . . . no mere addition of higher classes at the top of the elementary schools will carry out the objects we have in view . . .

The third defect . . . has relation to the education of teachers . . . Any child who wishes to become a teacher gets made a pupil teacher, and when he has reached that *status* half his time goes to teaching and the other half . . . to learning . . . What is the result? . . . I find that 36% . . . have never got through the examination for the certificate, and that 55% of the existing teachers have never been to a training college of any sort . . . We spend £18,000,000 a year on elementary education. Can anybody believe that under the system I have described we get the best results . . . for so vast an expenditure?

There is yet a third point on which I wish to say a word or two. It relates to the deplorable starvation of voluntary schools. Some of the opponents of voluntary schools put down their difficulties to the want of liberality on the part of the subscribers. I do not think there is any justification for that charge . . . The fact . . . remains that after all their great efforts on the part of the voluntary subscriber and after all the aid given from the National Exchequer, the voluntary schools are in many cases not adequately equipped and not as well fitted as they should be to carry out the great part which they are inevitably destined to play in our system of national education . . . At this moment the number of voluntary schools is over 14,000 as compared with about 5,700 Board Schools and . . . while the Board Schools educate 2,600,000 odd, the voluntary schools educate over 3,000,000. . . .

We are agreed about secular education. We are not agreed about religious education . . . We have as a community, repudiated responsibility for teaching a particular form of religion . . . As we have . . . left to the parents the responsibility for choosing what religion their children are to learn, surely we ought . . . to make our system as elastic as we can in order to meet their wishes . . .

Our reform if it is to be adequate, must in the first place, establish one authority for education – technical, secondary, primary – possessed of power, which may enable it to provide for the adequate training of teachers, and for the welding of higher technical and higher secondary education on to the University system. In the second place . . . this one authority for education being as it is, responsible for a heavy cost to the rate payers, should be the rating authority of the district. In the third place . . . voluntary schools must be placed in a position in which they can worthily play their necessary and inevitable part . . . Our system should be one which will not encourage for the future the perpetual introduction of denominational squabbles into our local and municipal life; and . . . the education authority should have at its disposal all the educational skill which the district over which it presides can supply. . . .

[*Mr Balfour then outlined the main provisions of the Bill.*]

There is another set of possible objectors . . . whom I hardly dare to hope I shall placate – the ardent believers in School Boards . . . I would say to them that though they may prefer an *ad hoc* authority, they must surely know that no *ad hoc* authority now can cover the whole ground of education. The last hope of such a consummation was swept away when this House passed the Act of 1889 and when the new municipalities . . . took the advantage of it . . . No practical man will tell me across the floor of this House that he expects that Parliament or the country will ever deprive the municipalities of powers they have so admirably used. I would therefore say to the advocate of School Boards that . . . if he wants a universal authority – one which can really coordinate education – it can only be to the municipalities that he can turn his gaze.

To the educationalist I think I need make no apologies and offer no excuses . . . He has long seen a vast expenditure of public money which has yet left this country behind all its Continental and American rivals in the matter of education. He has seen a huge average cost per child in our elementary schools, and yet at the same time many of these schools, half starved, inadequately equipped, imperfectly staffed. He has seen in the last 10 or 15 years a development of University life by private liberality which has no parallel except in America, which has covered, and still is covering our great industrial centres with Universities and University Colleges where the very highest type of University instruction is given by men well qualified for their duty. He has seen technological institutions which I am afraid do not yet rival those which America and Germany have produced, but which yet in their measure and within their limits are admirable . . . Yet these University Colleges and these great technological institutions do not, cannot, and never will effect all they might do so long as our secondary education, which is their necessary preparation, is in the imperfect condition in which we find it . . .

It is not upon the opinions or wishes of any particular section of opinion in this House or in the country that the fate of this Bill depends. It depends upon the common sense of the great body of the people, on their growing perception of the need of a really national system of education . . . I count upon the support of our countrymen to enable us to close for ever these barren controversies which for too long have occupied our time, and in the interests alike of parental liberty and of educational efficiency to terminate the present system of costly confusion.

21 · Elementary Code. 1904

This New Code incorporated changes following the Balfour Act of 1902, concerning the computation and payment of grant, intended to liberalize the elementary school. It was prefaced by an introduction, usually attributed on inadequate evidence to Sir Robert Morant, which is the classic statement of the aims of the public elementary school. Professor Eric Eaglesham has suggested that it may have been written by J. W. Mackail, a classical scholar, civil servant in the Education Department from 1884 to 1919, and sometime Professor of Poetry at Oxford.

Introduction

The purpose of the Public Elementary School is to form and strengthen the character and to develop the intelligence of the children entrusted to it, and to make the best use of the school years available, in assisting both girls and boys, according to their different needs, to fit themselves, practically as well as intellectually, for the work of life.

With this purpose in view it will be the aim of the School to train the children carefully in habits of observation and clear reasoning, so that they may gain an intelligent acquaintance with some of the facts and laws of nature; to arouse in them a living interest in the ideals and achievements of mankind, and to bring them to some familiarity with the literature and history of their own country; to give them some power over language as an instrument of thought and expression, and, while making them conscious of the limitations of their knowledge, to develop in them such a taste for good reading and thoughtful study as will enable them to increase that knowledge in after years by their own efforts.

The School must at the same time encourage to the utmost the children's natural activities of hand and eye by suitable forms of practical work and manual instruction; and afford them every opportunity for the healthy development of their bodies, not only by training them in appropriate physical exercises and encouraging them in organized games, but also by instructing them in the working of some of the simpler laws of health.

It will be an important though subsidiary object of the School to discover individual children who show promise of exceptional capacity, and to develop their special gifts (so far as this can be done without sacrificing the interests of the majority of the children), so that they may be qualified to pass at the proper age into Secondary Schools, and be able to derive the maximum of benefit from the education there offered them.

And, though their opportunities are but brief, the teachers can yet do much to lay the foundations of conduct. They can endeavour, by example and influence, aided by the sense of discipline, which should pervade the School, to implant in the children habits of industry, self-control, and courageous perseverance in the face of difficulties; they can teach them to reverence what is noble, to be ready for self-sacrifice, and to strive their utmost after purity and truth; they can foster a strong respect for duty, and that consideration and respect for others which must be the foundation of unselfishness and the true basis of all good manners; while the corporate life of the School, especially in the playground, should develop that instinct for fair-play and for loyalty to one another which is the germ of a wider sense of honour in later life.

In all these endeavours the School should enlist, as far as possible, the interest and co-operation of the parents and the home in an united effort to enable the children not merely to reach their full development as individuals, but also to become upright and useful members of the community in which they live, and worthy sons and daughters of the country to which they belong.

22 · Regulations for Secondary Schools. 1904

Mr Robert Morant, Permanent Secretary of the Board, signed prefatory memoranda to various Codes and Regulations issued after the passing of the 1902 Act. Among them were the *Regulations for Secondary Schools*, 1904, which effectively ensured that the new county secondary schools to be established under the powers given to the L.E.A.s under the Act should follow closely the conventional pattern of the old public and grammar schools.

Behind the decision, and the regulations which enforced it, was the low estimate formed by Morant and his advisers, of the work in the higher grade schools – the extra-legal tops which had been erected as a superstructure to the elementary schools. Morant, not without ulterior motives, entrusted to a brilliant classicist, J. W. Headlam, a staff inspector, the inspection of some of the ex-elementary work and used his crushing indictment of it as part of the reason for insisting on an orthodox grammar school pattern for the new county secondary schools.*

PREFATORY MEMORANDUM

The term Primary as applied to education, though still occasionally used, has since the legislation of 1870 been almost wholly superseded alike in official and in popular language by the term Elementary. The term Tertiary has at no time come into acceptance in this country at all. The intermediate term of Secondary, as applied to education, has consequently been left in the air; and to this fact in no small measure may be attributed the extreme vagueness with which the word is used and the actual misuse of it which may be often observed. Parliament in recent legislation has refrained from employing the term at all; and the Board do not consider that any precise definition of the term Secondary Education is immediately practicable. But a definition of the term 'Secondary School' – which has come to have a recognized meaning in English Education – has become indispensable in order to give to Secondary Schools a definite place in the wide and vague scheme of 'education other than elementary', with the provision and organization of which the Local Education Authorities under the Act of 1902 have been charged, and in respect of which they obtain financial aid and administrative regulation from the Board of Education.

* See *British Journal of Educational Studies*: May, 1962. Article by Professor Eric Eaglesham: '*Implementing the Education Act of 1902*.'

In order to arrive at a proper differentiation of functions, it is important for purposes of central and of local administration, and in particular for considering and properly planning courses of instruction, to distinguish Secondary Schools, on the one hand, from Technical Institutes and Classes which devote themselves mainly to giving specialized instruction and training in certain subjects to young persons and adults who should previously have completed a sound general education, and on the other, from Evening Schools and Classes which, though they may offer instruction to some students in subjects of a general kind and to others in subjects of Art or of pure and applied Science, do not provide a consecutive and complete course of general education, to be followed by each student who attends the School.

For the purposes of these Regulations, therefore, the term 'Secondary School' will be held to include any Day or Boarding School which offers to each of its scholars, up to and beyond the age of 16, a general education, physical, mental and moral, given through a complete graded course of instruction of wider scope and more advanced degree than that in Elementary Schools. The Board desire to emphasize the three following points as being essential to this course of instruction: –

(*a*) The instruction must be general; *i.e.*, must be such as gives a reasonable degree of exercise and development to the whole of the faculties, and does not confine this development to a particular channel, whether that of pure and applied Science, of literary and linguistic study, or of that kind of acquirement which is directed simply at fitting a boy or girl to enter business in a subordinate capacity with some previous knowledge of what he or she will be set to do. . . .

Specialization in any of these directions should only begin after the general education has been carried to a point at which the habit of exercising all these faculties has been formed and a certain solid basis for life has been laid in acquaintance with the structure and laws of the physical world, in the accurate use of thought and language, and in practical ability to begin dealing with affairs.

(*b*) The course of instruction must be complete; *i.e.* must be so planned as to lead up to a definite standard of acquirement in the various branches of instruction indicated above, and not stop short at a merely superficial introduction to any one of them. Secondary schools are of different types, suited to the different requirements of the scholars, to their place in the social organization, and to the means of the parents and the age at which the regular education of the scholars is obliged to stop short, as well as to the occupations and opportunities of development to which they may or should look forward in later life. But in no case can the course of a Secondary School be considered complete which is not so planned as to carry on the scholars to such a point as they may reasonably be expected to reach at the age of 16. It may begin at the age of 8 or 9, or even earlier. Scholars may pass into it from Elementary Schools at various ages beyond this, up to 12 or 13; and in schools of a high grade, which give an education leading directly on to the Universities, it may be continued up to the age even of 18 or 19. But as a rule the years from 12 or 13 up to 16 or 17 will be those during which it is most important that it should be carried on in accordance with a systematic and complete scheme. . . .

All Secondary Schools receiving grants from the Board will in future have to satisfy these conditions, as set forth more at large in the following Regulations. The rules there laid down have been framed with the view of ensuring that the education given shall be general in its nature, while leaving greater freedom than hitherto for schools to frame curricula of varying kinds, as may be required or rendered possible by local conditions. A certain minimum number of hours in each week must be given, in each year of the Course, to the group of subjects commonly classed as 'English', and including the English Language and Literature, Geography, and History; to Languages, ancient or modern, other than the native language of the scholars; and to Mathematics and to Science. Ample time is left for a well planned curriculum to add considerably to this minimum in one or more of these groups of subjects, as well as to include adequate provision for systematic Physical Exercises; for Drawing, Singing, and Manual Training; for the instruction of girls in the elements of Housewifery; and for such other subjects as may profitably be included in the curriculum of any particular school.

In order to secure the best local knowledge and the best educational experience, the functions of the Governors, and their discretion in exercising them, must therefore both be considerable. Nothing should be done to discourage the best men and women available from serving as Governors of schools, or to weaken their sense of responsibility for the effective discharge of their functions; and control exercised too closely or too minutely by the Local Education Authority would leave insufficient scope in these respects to the Governors, except by their encroaching in turn on the sphere of the Head Master or Head Mistress, a result which would be no less undesirable. In the case of Endowed Schools under Schemes having the force of a statute, for the exact observance of which the Board are specially responsible, the Governors have a direct and express liability to the Board. Other schools which receive aid from the Board may receive no aid from the Local Authority, or may receive it in varying degrees short of absolute dependence on it for their continued existence. But in the case of all schools alike the Board attach importance to direct communication with the Governing Body, and to preserving for the Governing Body as much responsibility, independence and freedom of action as is consistent with effective control of educational policy and educational provision, by the Local Authority in its own area, and by the Central Authority in all areas.

REGULATIONS

. . . The Course should provide for instruction in the English Language and Literature, at least one Language other than English, Geography, History, Mathematics, Science and Drawing, with due provision for Manual Work and Physical Exercises, and, in a girls' school for Housewifery. Not less than 4½ hours per week must be allotted to English, Geography and History; not less than 3½ hours to the Language where only one is taken or less than 6 hours where two are taken; and not less than 7½ hours to Science and Mathematics, of which at least 3 must be for Science. The instruction in Science must be both theoretical and practical. When two Languages other than English are taken, and Latin is not one of them, the Board will require to be satisfied that the omission of Latin is for the advantage of the school.*

* The detailed prescription of time-table hours was renounced in 1907. The requirement of a special dispensation for omitting Latin if two other languages were taught was retained.

23 · Handbook of Suggestions for the Consideration of Teachers and others concerned in the work of Public Elementary Schools

Issued as a Blue Book by the Board of Education in 1905.

Prefatory Memorandum

Neither the present volume, nor any developments or amendments of it are designed to impose any regulations supplementary to those contained in the Code. The only uniformity of practice that the Board of Education desires to see in the teaching of Public Elementary Schools is that each teacher shall think for himself, and work out for himself such methods of teaching as may use his powers to the best advantage and be best suited to the particular needs and conditions of the school. Uniformity in details of practice (except in the mere routine of school management) is not desirable even if it were attainable. But freedom implies a corresponding responsibility in its use. . . . (p. 6.)

Introduction

The Teacher and his Work The essential condition of good education is to be found in the right attitude of the teacher to his work. . . .

The teacher must know the children and must sympathize with them, for it is of the essence of teaching that the mind of the teacher should touch the mind of the pupil. He will seek at each stage to adjust his mind to theirs, to draw upon their experience as a supplement to his own, and so take them as it were into partnership for the acquisition of knowledge. Every fact on which he concentrates the attention of the children should be exhibited not in isolation but in relation to the past experience of the child; each lesson must be a renewal and an increase of that connected store of experience which becomes knowledge. Finally all the efforts of the teacher must be pervaded by a desire to impress upon the scholars, especially when they reach the highest class, the dignity of knowledge, the duty of each pupil to use his powers to the best advantage, and the truth that life is a serious as well as a pleasant thing.

The work of the public elementary school is the preparation of the scholars for life; character and the power of acquiring knowledge are valuable alike for the lower and for the higher purposes of life, and though the teachers can influence only a short period of the lives of the scholars, yet it is the period when human nature is most plastic, when good influence is most fruitful, and when teaching, if well bestowed, is most sure of permanent result (pp. 14–15).

24 · Free Places in Secondary Schools. 1907

New secondary school regulations published in 1907 laid down that all secondary schools receiving grants from the Board of Education should provide free places for 25 per cent of their annual entry.

This, formally, was the beginning of the scholarship ladder leading from the elementary school to the university.

There were, of course, scholarships before 1907. The Board of Education called for a return in 1906 which showed that there were over 23,000 awards covering all or part of the fees, but when published this list showed that many authorities were not providing any scholarships. By 1913 scholarships had increased to 60,000 and by 1927 the number approached the 150,000 mark.

As the number of free places grew so did interest in how they were to be awarded, which in part accounted for the concentration on mental testing procedures by educational psychologists working with the local education authorities.

SUPPLEMENTARY REGULATIONS FOR SECONDARY SCHOOLS IN ENGLAND · 1907

The School may be with or without fees, but any scale of fees must be approved by the Board.

In all Schools where a fee is charged, arrangements must be made to the satisfaction of the Board for securing that a proportion of School places shall be open without payment of fee to scholars from Public Elementary Schools who apply for admission, subject to the applicants passing an entrance test of attainments and proficiency such as can be approved by the Board. . . .

The proportion of School places thus required will ordinarily be 25 per cent of the scholars admitted.

[From Chapter 3, pp. 5 and 6

25 · Report of the Consultative Committee of the Board of Education on Examinations in Secondary Schools

Published: *1911*

Chairman: *A. H. Dyke Acland**

Members: *Mr C. W. Bowerman, M.P.; Mrs Sophie Bryant; Rev. James Chapman; Mr R. S. Clay; Miss Isabel Cleghorn; Mr Christopher Cookson; Miss F. Hermia Durham; Mr James Esterbrook; Rev. T. C. Fitzpatrick; Sir Henry F. Hibbert; Mr Marshall Jackman; Mr Albert Mansbridge; Dr Norman Moore; Mr J. L. Paton; Principal Sir Harry R. Reichel; Professor M. E. Sadler; Mr George Sharples; Miss Margaret J. Tuke; Mr Christopher Turnor*

Secretary: *Mr Arthur H. Wood*

Terms of Reference: *To consider when and in what circumstances examinations are desirable in secondary schools (a) for boys and (b) for girls. The committees are desired to consider this question under the following heads:*

(i) *Examination at entrance to school.*
(ii) *Examination during school life.*
(iii) *Examination at leaving school.*

The expansion of secondary education following the 1902 Act acted as a spur to the proliferation of examinations which had already begun in the previous century. (The 1868 Schools Inquiry Commission had drawn attention to the changes.) In 1904 the Consultative Committee made recommendations on the subject which as they noted in 1911 'though not unfruitful in certain indirect ways were to a great extent nullified by the absence of any subsequent driving power'.

* Sir Arthur Herbert Dyke Acland (1847–1926) was chairman of the President of the Board of Education's Consultative Committee from 1907 to 1916. This followed an active political life as an M.P. from 1885 to 1889, which included service as Vice-President of the Committee of Council for Education (1892–5) with a seat in the Cabinet. He was regarded as one of the Liberals' links with the Labour movement. Before entering Parliament he was a don at Keble and Christ Church and remained an honorary fellow of Balliol.

As a backbencher – M.P. for Rotherham and a member of the W. Riding County Council – he had worked hard to support the entry of county councils into education. And he was one of the promoters of the Welsh Intermediate Education Act of 1889 – which was a Private Member's Bill. He inherited the title as thirteenth baronet in 1919. (*D.N.B.*)

By 1911 the situation had got worse and prominent among the examinations being offered to the schools were several varieties of 'junior certificates' taken at 14 or 15. The Consultative Committee recommended the setting up of a representative Examinations Council in which the Board of Education could join with the local education authorities and the university examining bodies, to exercise supervision over all external examinations, and to lay down conditions. In 1917 the Board of Education acted on the lines recommended, introduced the new scheme to replace the junior certificate and other examinations. This was the origin of the School Certificate Examination. The universities were recognized as responsible bodies for the conduct of these examinations, and a body called the Secondary Schools Examination Council was set up to advise the Board on this subject.

The extract which appears below sets out the pros and cons of external examinations with clarity and brevity. Part of it was reprinted in the Report of the Beloe Committee (a subcommittee of the Secondary Schools Examinations Council) in 1960.

EXAMINATIONS IN SECONDARY SCHOOLS · 1911

. . . It will be convenient if we summarize what we believe to be the more important effects of examinations (1) on the pupil, (2) on the teacher.

(1) The good effects of examinations on the pupil are (a) that they make him work up to time by requiring him to reach a stated degree of knowledge by a fixed date; (b) that they incite him to get his knowledge into reproducible form and to lessen the risk of vagueness; (c) that they make him work at parts of a study which, though important, may be uninteresting or repugnant to him personally; (d) that they train the power of getting up a subject for a definite purpose, even though it may not appear necessary to remember it afterwards – a training which is useful for parts of the professional duty of the lawyer, the administrator, the journalist, and the man of business; (e) that in some cases they encourage a certain steadiness of work over a long period of time; and (f) that they enable the pupil to measure his real attainment (i) by the standard required by outside examiners, (ii) by comparison with the attainments of his fellow pupils, and (iii) by comparison with the attainments of his contemporaries in other schools.

On the other hand, examinations may have a bad effect upon the pupil's mind (a) by setting a premium on the power of merely reproducing other people's ideas and other people's methods of presentment, thus diverting energy from the creative process; (b) by rewarding evanescent forms of knowledge; (c) by favouring a somewhat passive type of mind; (d) by giving an undue advantage to those who, in answering questions on paper, can cleverly make the best use of, perhaps, slender attainments; (e) by inducing the pupil, in his preparation for an examination, to aim rather at absorbing information imparted to him by the teacher than at forming an independent judgment upon the subjects in which he receives instruction; and (f) by stimulating the competitive (and, at its worst, a mercenary) spirit in the acquisition of knowledge.

(2) The good effects of well-conducted examinations upon the teacher are (a) that they induce him to treat his subject thoroughly; (b) that they make him so arrange his lessons as to cover with intellectual thoroughness a prescribed course of study within appointed limits ot time; (c) that they impel him to pay attention not only to his best pupils, but also to the backward and the slower amongst those who are being prepared for the examination; and (d) that they make him acquainted with the standard which other teachers and their pupils are able to reach in the same subject in other places of education. On the other hand, the effects of examinations on the teacher are bad (a) in so far as they constrain him to watch the examiner's foibles and to note his idiosyncrasies (or the tradition of the examination) in order that he may arm his pupils with the kind of knowledge required for dealing successfully with the questions that will probably be put to them; (b) in so far as they limit the freedom of the teacher in choosing the way in which he shall treat his subject; (c) in so far as they encourage him to take upon himself work which had better be left to the largely unaided efforts of his pupils, causing him to impart information to them in too digested a form or to select for them groups of facts or aspects of the subject which each pupil should properly be left to collect or envisage for himself; (d) in so far as they predispose the teacher to overvalue among his pupils that type of mental development which secures success in examinations; (e) in so far as they make it the teacher's interest to excel in the purely examinable side of his professional work and divert his attention from those parts of education which cannot be tested by the process of examination.

It will be seen that the dangers of examinations, and especially of external examinations, are considerable in their possible effect both on pupil and on teacher. We have no hesitation, however, in stating our conviction that external examinations are not only necessary but desirable in Secondary Schools. But we are equally convinced that if the admitted advantages of external examinations are to be secured and the dangers of them minimized, such examinations should be subjected to most stringent regulations as to their number, the age at which they are taken, and their general character. . . .

The fundamental principles which . . . must underlie any improved system are as follows:

(i) Examinations which are conducted by external examining bodies and of which the primary object is an educational one, should be brought into intimate connection with inspection, the existing system of inspection being modified and developed so as to meet the new needs.

(ii) The existing multiplicity of external examinations . . . the claims of which at present so frequently interfere with the best work of the schools, should be reduced by concerted action.

(iii) All external examinations should be so conducted as to assist and emphasize the principle that every secondary school should provide, for pupils up to the average age of 16, a sound basis of liberal education which . . . would serve as a foundation upon which varieties of further education could be based. . . .

We would suggest that the examination should be called the Examination for the Secondary School Certificate so that its name may convey a perfectly clear idea to the public of what it really is.

[From Chapter IV, pp. 102–6

26 · Report of the Departmental Committee on Juvenile Education in Relation to Employment after the War. [*The Lewis Report*]

Published: *Interim: 1916. Final: 1917*

Chairman: *J. Herbert Lewis, M.P.**

Members: *Mr W. A. Appleton; Mr R. A. Bray; Mr A. B. Bruce; Mr E. K. Chambers; Mr F. W. Goldstone, M.P.; Mr Spurley Hey; Mr J. P. Hinchliffe; Mr F. Lavington; Miss C. Martineau; Mr F. Pullinger; Mr J. F. P. Rawlinson, K.C., M.P.; Mr C. E. B. Russell; Lady Edmund Talbot; Mr H. M. Thompson; Mr Christopher H. Turnor*

Secretary: *Mr J. Owen*

Terms of Reference: *To consider what steps should be taken to make provision for the education and instruction of children and young persons after the war, regard being had particularly to the interests of those*

(i) *who have been abnormally employed during the war;*
(ii) *who cannot immediately find advantageous employment;*
(iii) *who require special training for employment.*

The Committee was set up in 1916 by Mr Arthur Henderson, Mr H. A. L. Fisher's predecessor at the Board of Education, as part of the elementary planning for reconstruction after the War. The specific problem which concerned the educational planners was the disruption to juvenile employment and industrial training caused by the War and by the industrial mobilization which it involved (see Mr H. A. L. Fisher's speech introducing the Bill, p. 173).

An Interim Report was published in 1916 urging the strengthening of existing systems of juvenile employment bureaux and the local employment committees.

Concern about juvenile employment and the need to end the half-time system had grown during the decade before 1914. There had been various official reports, notably that of the Poor Law Commission which contained a

* The Chairman of the Committee, Mr J. Herbert Lewis, M.P., was Parliamentary Secretary to the Board of Education from 1915 to 1922. He sat as Liberal M.P. for Flint Boroughs, Flintshire, and the University of Wales between 1892 and 1922. He was knighted in 1922. For some reason the report has been neglected by the authors of short histories of English education.

valuable report on *Boy Labour* by Mr Cyril Jackson, and of the Board of Education's Consultative Committee on *Continuation Schools*.

The main report appeared in 1917. The Committee's first recommendation, therefore, was to raise the leaving age to 14 and abolish all half-time arrangements.

This was applied by the 1918 Education Act, as was the second major recommendation which concerned Day Continuation Classes, although the section of the Act which provided for these classes became a dead letter.

JUVENILE EDUCATION IN RELATION TO EMPLOYMENT AFTER THE WAR: FROM THE FINAL REPORT · 1917

We have endeavoured, on the basis of the census returns of 1911 and of figures collected by the Board of Education . . . to arrive at a statistical picture of juvenile education as it stood before the war. The results . . . are for various reasons not precise, but the following table may be taken as showing . . . the proportion of children and young persons . . . under some kind of public educational training

	Children and Young Persons aged between					
	12–13	13–14	14–15	15–16	16–17	17–18
Percentage in full-time courses	91	66	12	4	2	1
Percentage in part-time courses	4	9	16	14	13	10
Percentage unenrolled	5	25	72	82	85	89

From the proportion given as unenrolled . . . should be deducted something for children educated outside the purview of the Board of Education. For this deduction 5 per cent would be a liberal estimate . . .

The story amounts to this . . . Practically . . . public education after the Elementary School leaving age is a part-time affair. And there is very little of it. In 1911–12 there were about 2,700,000 juveniles between 14 and 18, and of these about 2,200,000 or 81·5 per cent were enrolled neither in day schools nor in evening schools . . .

What, then, are the remedies? In a sense there is only one remedy . . . But it is a pretty thorough-going one; nothing less than a complete change of temper and outlook on the part of the people of this country as to what they mean, through the forces of industry and society, to make of their boys and girls. Can the age of adolescence be brought out of the purview of economic exploitation and into that of the social conscience? Can the conception of the juvenile as primarily a little wage-earner be replaced by the conception of the juvenile as primarily the workman and the citizen in training? Can it be established that the educational purpose is to be the dominating one, without as well as within the school doors, during those formative years between 12 and 18? If not, clearly no remedies at all are possible in the absence of the will by which alone they could be rendered effective. . . .

It is, we think, clear that there are two lines of advance which can be pushed forward concurrently . . . Early legislation is required –

(a) to establish a uniform Elementary School leaving age of 14, which entails the abolition of all exemptions, total or partial, from compulsory attendance below that age;
(b) to require attendance for not less than 8 hours a week, or 320 hours a year, at Day Continuation Classes between the ages of 14 and 18.

We come now to the new device of compulsory Continuation Classes. These are, so far as we can judge, the remedy to which educational and social reformers look with the greatest confidence as a step towards the final solution of the juvenile problem. There are, of course, no substitutes for a sound early education, but such education, when it terminates at 14, or even at 15, leaves the child with intellect and character still unformed at perhaps the most critical stage of his development . . . Some handrail is required over the bridge which crosses the perilous waters of adolescence. . . .

We have asked ourselves and have asked others, whether the few hours a week which is all that appears to us practicable at the present time to secure for education, will be of substantial value for the purpose, in view of the numerous hours that will still remain available for counteracting influences. We believe that the answer is in the affirmative. Many will feel that the system of half-time employment and half-time schooling, which has been put forward in some schemes of reform, approaches more nearly to a counsel of perfection. But we do not believe this to be at present attainable, and we are assured by experienced teachers that, if they are given something like eight hours a week during a continuous period of years from the time of leaving school, they will be able so to utilize those hours as to maintain that effective contact with the forces of civilization, which is at present in too many cases so soon broken. Even though the educational obligation may be a small one, it will still be sufficient to establish the principle that a child is no longer to be regarded as at once attaining, when he enters employment, to the fully independent status of wage-earning manhood. He will still be one under authority and open to the influences of encouragement and reproof, of the corporate life and the offered ideals, which, even more than mere instruction, are of the essence of the educational process.

We are clear that the business of the classes is to do what they can in making a reasonable human being and a citizen, and that, if they do this, they will help to make a competent workman also. Though this is wholly true, it is also true that education must be approached, especially at the adolescent stage, through the actual interests of the pupil, and that the actual interests of pupils who have just turned a corner in life and entered upon wage-earning employment are very largely the new interests which their employment has opened out to them.

Although, then, at any rate in the earlier years, Continuation Classes should give a general and not a technical education, we think that they may with advantage from the very beginning have something of a vocational bias. This will not mean very much more than that the children will be as far as possible classified according to their occupations, and that four or five alternative courses will be planned, in which subjects will be differently grouped and differently treated, so as to give them some kind of living relation to the occupations of the children taking them. . . .

Between 16 and 18 a greater amount of specialization will probably be introduced . . . English teaching should now tend towards a deliberate stimulation of the sense of citizenship. For young persons engaged upon highly skilled work, however, technical subjects bearing upon that work will inevitably come to take a leading place in the curriculum, although even for them the civics and the humanities must by no means be excluded. . . . But it is only a minority . . . who find highly skilled work. . . . There is bound to be a good deal of differentiation. In some cases, a desire for knowledge will have established itself . . . which will reach upwards to the admirable ideals of self-education which lie at the heart of the Workers' Educational Association movement. In other cases, and we will hope in a diminishing minority of cases, the capacity for study on anything like academic lines will be approaching saturation point. For these it will be necessary to plan courses in which the general subjects of the earlier period will be diversified by others directed to one or other of those multifarious personal interests which afford the amenities of life. Music, art, local history, home industries, first aid, natural history, will all afford an opportunity for the skilful teacher. . . .

[From the Final Report: 1917, pp. 5–29

27 · Education Act. 1918

The Education Act of 1918, known as the Fisher Act after Mr H. A. L. Fisher, M.P., the President of the Board of Education in Mr Lloyd George's Wartime Coalition, was a compromise. At first in 1917 it was intended to stiffen the powers of the central government. The abolition of the Part III Authorities was proposed and there were plans for achieving a more uniform standard of educational provision by merging authorities in certain circumstances into provincial associations. These centralizing tendencies aroused strong opposition from the local authorities and the Bill was extensively amended when it was re-introduced in 1918.

In the end, the Act strengthened the local authorities and the power of the Board to stimulate them. It reformed the grant system on a basis which ensured that not less than 50 per cent of the cost of education was met from the central government funds, abolished fees in elementary schools, abolished all exemptions from the leaving age of 14 and extended the range of ancillary services an L.E.A. was permitted to provide.

The most important clauses concerned continued part-time education and followed a pattern similar to that adopted in Germany. With this was linked provision for raising the leaving age to 15 at a later date. Compulsory part-time day continuation schools were scotched by the slump and the cuts imposed on Government expenditure of all kinds, surviving only at Rugby, the famous exception.

Section 1

'With a view to the establishment of a national system of public education available for all persons capable of profiting thereby, it shall be the duty of the council of every county and county borough, so far as their powers extend to contribute thereto by providing for the progressive development and comprehensive organization of education in respect of their area and with that object any such council may and shall when required by the Board of Education, submit to the Board schemes showing the mode in which their duties and powers under the Education Acts are to be performed and exercised, whether separately or in cooperation with other authorities.'*

Section 3

(1) It shall be the duty of the local education authority . . . either separately or in cooperation with other local education authorities, to establish

* This may be contrasted with Part 1 of the 1944 Education Act (see p. 223) as an indication of the move towards centralization between 1918 and 1944.

and maintain, or secure the establishment and maintenance under their control and direction, of a sufficient supply of continuation schools in which suitable courses of study, instruction and physical training are provided without payment of fees for all young persons resident in their area who are, under this Act, under an obligation to attend such schools.

Section 10

(1) Subject as hereinafter provided* all young persons shall attend such continuation schools at such times, on such days, as the local education authority of the area . . . may require, for three hundred and twenty hours in each year . . .

* Exceptions included those who had matriculated before leaving school at 16, or who had continued in full-time education at a school recognized as efficient up to the age of 16, or were receiving efficient part-time education in some other form.

28 · Education Act. 1918.
Statement by Mr H. A. L. Fisher, President of the Board of Education, introducing the Education Bill. *Hansard: August 10th, 1917*

I would like very briefly to describe some aspects of the movements of opinion which, in the minds of the Government, have made a considerable measure of advance in education an absolute necessity. In the first place, attention has been increasingly directed to the close connection between educational and physical efficiency. One of the great dates in our social history is the establishment of the school medical service in 1907. We now know, what we should not otherwise have known, how greatly the value of our educational system is impaired by the low physical conditions of a vast number of the children, and how imperative is the necessity of raising the general standard of physical health among the children of the poor, if a great part of the money spent on our educational system is not to be wasted. . . .

Another element is the growing consciousness that there is a lack of scientific correlation between the different parts of our educational machinery. We find an important and populous centre without a secondary school in any shape or form. We find an older and less important centre with four secondary schools. . . .

There is not even a reasonable probability that the child will get the higher education best adapted to his or her needs. The Act of 1902 no doubt contemplated area schemes for higher education, but the duty of considering the whole need of an area was left hanging in the air.

A third feature in the movement of opinion is the increased feeling of social solidarity which has been created by the War. When you get Conscription, when you get a state of affairs under which the poor are asked to pour out their blood and to be mulcted in the high cost of living for large international policies, then every just mind begins to realize that the boundaries of citizenship are not determined by wealth, and that the same logic which leads us to desire an extension of the franchise points also to an extension of education. There is a growing sense, not only in England but through Europe, and I may say especially in France, that the industrial workers of the country are entitled to be considered primarily as citizens and as fit subjects for any form of education from which they are capable of profiteering [*sic*]. I notice also that a new way of thinking about education has sprung up among many of the more reflecting members of our industrial army. They do not want education only in order that they may become better technical workmen and earn higher wages. They do not want it in order that they may rise out of their own class, always a vulgar ambition, they want it because they know that in the treasures of the mind they can find an aid to good citizenship, a source of pure enjoyment and a refuge from the necessary hardships of a life spent in the midst of clanging machinery in our hideous cities of toil. I ask whether there is a single struggling young student in this country to whom a library of good books has not made an elemental democratic appeal.

> 'Unlike the hard, the selfish and the proud,
> They fly not sullen from the suppliant crowd,
> Nor tell to various people various things,
> But show to subjects what they show to kings.'

I will now descend to our specific proposal which may be conveniently though not exhaustively, considered under six heads. Firstly, we desire to improve the administrative organization of education. Secondly, we are anxious to secure for every boy and girl in this country an elementary school life up to the age of fourteen which shall be unimpeded by the competing claims of industry. Thirdly, we desire to establish part-time day continuation schools which every young person in the country shall be compelled to attend unless he or she is undergoing some suitable form of alternative instruction. Fourthly, we make a series of proposals for the development of the higher forms of elementary education and for the improvement of the physical condition of the children and young persons under instruction. Fifthly, we desire to consolidate the elementary school Grants and, sixthly, we wish to make an effective survey of the whole educational provision in the country and to bring private educational institutions into closer and more convenient relations to the national system.

I now come to the most novel if not the most important provision in the Bill. We propose that, with certain exceptions to be defined in the Bill, every young person no longer under any obligation to attend a public elementary school shall attend such continuation school as the local education authority of the area in which he resides may require for a period of 320 hours in the year, or the equivalent of eight hours a week for forty weeks. . . .

The proposal, then, comes to this, that in general young persons who are not undergoing full-time instruction will be liberated from industrial toil for the equivalent of three half-days a week during forty weeks – two half-days to be spent in school, while one will be a half-holiday. . . .

We have reached a point in our history when we must take long views. We are a comparatively small country, we have incurred the hostility of a nation with a larger population and with a greater extent of concentrated territory and with a more powerful organization of its resources. We cannot flatter ourselves with the comfortable notion, I wish we could, that after this War the fierce rivalry of Germany will disappear and hostile feeling altogether die down. That in itself constitutes a reason for giving the youth of our country the best preparation which ingenuity can suggest. And there is another reason. We are extending the franchise, we are making a greater demand than ever before upon the civic spirit of the ordinary man and woman at a time when the problems of national life and of world policy upon which this House will be called upon to decide have become exceedingly complex and difficult, and how can we expect an intelligent response to the demands which the community propose to make upon the instructed judgment of its men and women unless we are prepared to make some further sacrifices in order to form and fashion the minds of the young. . . . .

I have sketched the general features of the measure. . . .

We assume that education is one of the good things of life which should be more widely shared than has hitherto been the case, amongst the children and young persons of the country. We assume that education should be the education of the whole man, spiritually, intellectually, and physically, and it is not beyond the resources of civilization to devise a scheme of education, possessing certain common qualities, but admitting at the same time large variation from which the whole youth of the country, male and female, may derive benefit. We assume that the principles upon which well-to-do parents proceed in the education of their families are valid; also *mutatis mutandis* for the families of the poor; that the State has need to secure for its juvenile population conditions under which mind, body, and character may be harmoniously developed. We feel ourselves that in the existing circumstances the life of the rising generation can only be protected against the injurious effects of industrial pressure by a further measure of State compulsion. But we argue that the compulsion proposed in this Bill will be no sterilizing restriction of wholesome liberty, but an essential condition of a larger and more enlightened freedom, which will tend to stimulate the civic spirit, to promote general culture and technical knowledge, and to diffuse a steadier judgment and a better-informed opinion through the whole body of the community.

29 · Report of the Departmental Committee on the Training of Teachers for Public Elementary Schools

Published: *1925*

Chairman: *Viscount Burnham**

Members: *Alderman F. Askew; Dr Ernest Barker; Mr E. K. Chambers; Miss E. R. Conway; Miss Grace Fanner; Sir John Gilbert; Miss Freda Hawtrey; Mr Spurley Hey; Mr R. Holland; Mr A. W. Hurst; Alderman P. R. Jackson; Dame Margaret Lloyd George; Mr Frank Roscoe; Mr E. J. Sainsbury; Mr H. Ward; Miss A. W. Wark; Professor Helen Wodehouse; Mr H. E. Mann (Secretary)*

Terms of Reference: *To review the arrangements for the training of teachers for Public Elementary Schools, and to consider what changes, if any, in the organization or finance of the existing system are desirable in order that a supply of well qualified teachers adjustable to the demands of the schools may be secured, regard being had to*

(a) *the economy of public funds*

(b) *the attractions offered to young persons by the teaching profession as compared with other professions and occupations*

(c) *the facilities afforded by Secondary Schools and Universities for acquiring academic qualifications.*

The Committee were tied by terms of reference which were based on the administrative distinction between elementary schools and secondary schools. While pointing out that the distinction between the teacher training needs of elementary and secondary schools was more of an administrative convenience than a desirable educational difference to be perpetuated, the Committee recommended that the university courses which included a degree should continue to be four years while the training colleges, concentrating on professional training more exclusively than hitherto, should only have their students for two years.

On the other hand, they sought to bring the universities and training col-

* Lord Burnham, 1862–1933.

Harry Lawson Webster became first Viscount Burnham in 1919. He was M.P. for W. St. Pancras 1885–92, E. Gloucestershire 1893–5, Tower Hamlets 1905–6, 1910–16. He acted as president of the International Labour Conference, Geneva, 1921–2 and 1926. He was invited by Mr H. A. L. Fisher to be chairman of the salary negotiating committees set up in 1919 following widespread unrest and sporadic strikes over teachers' salaries. In due course his name became attached to the committees and their procedures and long outlived him.

leges together along the lines indicated in the extract below. The most effective way of doing this was through the establishment of joint examination boards by the training colleges and the universities to take over from the Board of Education the qualifying examination at the end of the training college course.

This was accepted by the Board of Education and by 1929 the Joint Boards were set up. It was out of the activity of these boards that the nucleus of subsequent area training organization emerged (see *McNair* Report, 1944).

The importance of the 1925 Report was that it carried a stage further the process by which the training of teachers was emancipated from the rigid limitations of elementary education.

These limitations were as much social as educational, as the earlier documents have shown.

Training Colleges and Universities

Other modes of connexion between Universities and Training Colleges:

Examinations . . . A second mode in which a university may co-operate with a Two-Year Training College is by holding a special examination for the whole body of the Training College students. Special syllabuses of work are arranged between the College and the university with the approval of the Board, and the examination on these syllabuses is accepted by the Board in place of their Final Examination as qualifying for the Certificate. Such examinations have for some years past been held by the University of London for those students of the Goldsmiths' College who do not prepare for the university degree examinations, and by the University of Liverpool for the Colleges of Warrington, Edge Hill and Chester, though this arrangement has recently come to an end for financial reasons, the Colleges concerned no longer feeling justified in contributing to the cost of it. The examination of Bangor North Wales Training College has been undertaken under similar arrangements by the Bangor University College. A scheme of a wider scope has recently been suggested by which the University of London would undertake to hold an examination for the Two Year Training Colleges of London as a body. This, we understand, has so far not gone beyond the stage of informal preliminary discussion.

We think this mode might be further developed, not only with the object of interesting the universities more generally in the training of teachers outside their precincts, but incidentally as a means of giving the Training Colleges a greater measure of autonomy, and of relating the examination, upon which students qualify for certification, more closely to the needs of particular Colleges or groups of Colleges, than is possible where the central authority is required to devise and conduct an examination applicable to all but a small minority of the Colleges. From the evidence which we have heard we feel convinced that the universities, as a whole, are anxious to accept a larger responsibility for the training of teachers in its various aspects, in no sense as a means to power but as part of the normal evolution of their function. We feel satisfied also that such arrangements, if carefully planned and undertaken with good will by all the parties concerned, in the interests of greater educational efficiency, need not lead to friction or interference, or to any objectionable increase of inspection. We suggest, therefore, that, as one means of securing the association of universities with Training Colleges, arrangements might be authorized for the establishment of joint examining boards for particular Colleges or groups of Colleges, which would undertake to that extent the Final Examination of students in Training Colleges now conducted by the Board of Education. In our view these boards should normally consist of representatives nominated by the governing bodies of universities and Training Colleges. They would conduct the examination through panels of examiners consisting of internal examiners from the staffs of the Colleges participating, and external examiners. It would be for them to issue certificates or diplomas which the Board of Education could accept as the necessary evidence in that respect of the students' qualification for recognition. With regard to the costs of administering an examination of this kind, we see no reason why students who take it should not be expected to pay a fee, as is, of course, usual with other important qualifying examinations, and we consider that the money thus obtained should be sufficient for the purpose without necessitating any call upon university or College funds.

[From Chapter 8, p. 107

30 · Report of the Consultative Committee of the Board of Education on The Education of the Adolescent. [*The Hadow Report*]

Published: *1926*

Chairman: *Sir W. H. Hadow**

Members: *Mr P. W. H. Abbott; Mr S. O. Andrew; Dr Ernest Barker; Miss E. R. Conway; Rev. Dr D. H. S. Cranage; The Rt Hon. Lord Gorell; Miss Lynda Grier; Mr Ivor H. Gwynne, J.P.; Miss Freda Hawtrey; Sir Percy R. Jackson; Dr A. Mansbridge; Mr A. J. Mundella; Miss E. M. Tanner; Mr R. H. Tawney; Mr S. Taylor; Mr W. W. Vaughan; Mr W. C. Watkins, J.P.; Mr W. H. Webbe; Mr J. A. White; Mr R. F. Young* (*Secretary*)

Terms of Reference (February 1924): (*i*) *To consider and report upon the organization, objective and curriculum of courses of study suitable for children who will remain in full-time attendance at schools, other than Secondary Schools, up to the age of 15, regard being had on the one hand to the requirements of a good general education and the desirability of providing a reasonable variety of curriculum, so far as is practicable, for children of varying tastes and abilities, and on the other hand the probable occupations of the pupils in commerce, industry and agriculture.* (*ii*) *Incidentally thereto, to advise as to the arrangements which should be made* (*a*) *for testing the attainments of the pupils at the end of their course;* (*b*) *for facilitating in suitable cases the transfer of individual pupils to Secondary Schools at an age above the normal age of admission.*

The principal recommendations concerned the raising of the minimum leaving age to 15 and the institution of secondary education for all children, to follow consecutively on six years of primary education, thus extending the concept of secondary education beyond the type of academic course given in grammar schools to cover 'modern secondary schools' where the education might have a 'practical' and 'realistic' bias.

Notable members of the Hadow Committee at this time included Dr R. H.

* William Henry Hadow (1859–1937) was educated at Malvern and Worcester College, Oxford, where he took a first in Greats. His academic studies were in the history of music and music criticism, and he was himself a composer of chamber music and songs. He became principal of Armstrong College, Newcastle-upon-Tyne, in 1909, being Vice-Chancellor of the University of Durham from 1916–18 (when he was knighted), and after war service directing army education he became Vice-Chancellor of the University of Sheffield, where he remained till 1930. He was chairman of the Consultative Committee of the Board of Education from 1920–34.

Tawney and Dr Ernest Barker. The latter, being chairman of the drafting sub-committee, left a clearly recognizable stamp on certain passages of the report.

This report stemmed from the remit given by the first Labour Government within a few weeks of taking office. The notion of 'secondary education for all' had already been adopted by many influential Labour intellectuals, among them Dr Tawney, who had written a book of that title.

By the time the Committee reported, Mr Baldwin had replaced Mr MacDonald at No. 10 Downing Street. Legislation to raise the leaving age to 15 was not an early priority with the new Government. When Labour returned again in 1929, Sir Charles Trevelyan introduced a Bill to raise the leaving age to 15 while paying maintenance grants to those over 14 still at school. The legislation ran into trouble both for its open-ended financial commitment and because of denominational disagreements. The three Bills incorporating the new legislation were defeated.

This was the most important of the Consultative Committee's reports in the inter-war period. It laid down the lines on which development was to take place and was accepted by the Board of Education (without commitment as to date). It paved the way for the tripartite organization of secondary schools (see also the *Spens* and *Norwood* Reports) being influenced by the evidence of the educational psychologists and, while accepting a broader interpretation of secondary education, did so with reservations.

Reorganization of schools on what became known as Hadow lines began in the 1930s, and the 1944 Act formalized the changes. The leaving age was not raised to 15 in 1932 as recommended by the report. By that time the financial crisis of 1931 was forcing new economies on the education service, but this recommendation, too, was incorporated in the 1944 Act and brought into force in 1947.

THE HADOW REPORT

INTRODUCTION

There is a tide which begins to rise in the veins of youth at the age of eleven or twelve. It is called by the name of adolescence. If that tide can be taken at the flood, and a new voyage begun in the strength and along the flow of its current, we think that it will 'move on to fortune'. We therefore propose that all children should be transferred, at the age of eleven or twelve, from the junior or primary school either to schools of the type now called secondary, or to schools (whether selective or non-selective) of the type which is now called central, or to senior and separate departments of existing elementary schools. . . .

We are disposed to believe that we may safely recommend the institution both of an entrance examination, on the lines of the present examination for scholarships and free places in secondary schools, to determine the conditions of entry into selective modern schools, and of a final or leaving examination, *not* on the lines of the First School Examination in secondary schools, to test and to certify the achievement of pupils both of selective and of non-selective central schools and also of senior departments. We recognize that a final examination may to some extent cramp the free growth of these schools. But we feel that their pupils may be handicapped by the absence of any form of guarantee of their work; and we feel that the schools themselves may become uncertain in their aim and vacillating in their methods, if they have no suggestion of a definite standard to guide their work. . . . .

There is a wisdom in the saying of Plato, that 'the life without examination is a life that can hardly be lived'. . . .

We recommend that, as soon as possible, an additional year should be added to the general school life, and the leaving age should be raised to fifteen. Only in that way can the modern schools and senior departments, which will then be able to plan a four years' course, exercise their full influence on their pupils; only in that way can children be guided safely through the opportunities, the excitements and the perils of adolescence; only in that way can the youth of the nation be adequately trained for a full and worthy citizenship. If modern schools thus become the homes of their pupils for a full and consecutive course of four years, they will require, and we hope that they will receive, the services of an ardent, properly trained and adequately qualified teaching staff. In few schools can there be greater opportunities for a teacher of power and of wisdom than there will be in these schools. We earnestly hope that such teachers will be found, and that not only will the trained and experienced teachers of the present elementary schools offer themselves readily for the work, but also University graduates, who have received a fourth year of professional training, will volunteer, and will be accepted with no less readiness.

The scheme which we advocate can be simply stated. It is that between the age of eleven and (if possible) that of fifteen, all the children of the country who do not go forward to 'secondary education' in the present and narrow sense of the word, should go forward none the less to what is, in our view, a form of secondary education, in the truer and broader sense of the word, and after spending the first years of their school life in a primary school should spend the last three or four in a well-equipped and well-staffed modern school (or senior department), under the stimulus of practical work and realistic studies, and yet, at the same time, in the free and broad air of a general and humane education, which, if it remembers handwork, does not forget music, and, if it cherishes natural science, fosters also linguistic and literary studies. It is less easy to state the ideal which lies behind our scheme. But there are three great ends of human life and activity which we trust that our scheme will help to promote. One is the forming and strengthening of character – individual and national character – through the placing of youth, in the hour of its growth, 'as it were in the fair meadow' of a congenial and inspiring environment. Another is the training of boys and girls to delight in pursuits and rejoice in accomplishments – work in music and art; work in wood and in metals; work in literature and the record of human history – which may become the recreations and the ornaments of hours of leisure in maturer years. And still another is the awakening and guiding of the practical intelligence, for the better and more skilled service of the community in all its multiple business and complex affairs – an end which cannot be dismissed as 'utilitarian' in any country, and least of all in a country like ours, so highly industrialized, and so dependent on the success of its industries, that it needs for its success, and even for its safety, the best and most highly trained skill of its citizens.

[From Introduction, pp. xix–xxii

THE REGRADING OF EDUCATION

The first main conclusion which we have reached is concerned with the successive stages in education and with the relations which should exist between them. It is as follows: *Primary education should be regarded as ending at about the age of* 11+. *At that age a second stage, which for the moment may be given the colourless name 'post-primary', should begin; and this stage which, for many pupils would end at* 16+, *for some at* 18 *or* 19, *but for the majority at* 14+ *or* 15+, *should be envisaged so far as possible as a single whole, within which there will be a variety in the types of education supplied, but which will be marked by the common characteristic that its aim is to provide for the needs of children who are entering and passing through the stage of adolescence.*

Such a conception of the relations between primary and post-primary education obviously presents some points of contrast with the arrangement which has hitherto obtained in England, under which, until recent years, approximately 90 per cent. of children have received elementary education up to the age of 13 or 14, and a small minority have been transferred to secondary education, or to that given in central schools, at about the age of 11. . . .

It appears, however, to correspond to the views held by a large and influential section of educational opinion. . . .

There was, indeed, something like unanimity among our witnesses as to the desirability of treating the age of 11 to 12 as the beginning of a new phase in education, presenting distinctive problems of its own, and requiring a fresh departure in educational methods and organization in order to solve them. . . .

The general agreement of administrators and teachers that primary education should be regarded as ending, and post-primary education as beginning, at the age of 11+ seems to us important, as supplying, at any rate, a starting-point from which the further problems involved in our reference may be attacked. The principal reasons for this consensus of opinion are, we think, two. In the first place there is the argument of the psychologist. Educational organization is likely to be effective in proportion as it is based on the actual facts of the development of children and young persons. By the time that the age of 11 or 12 has been reached children have given some indication of differences in interests and abilities sufficient to make it possible and desirable to cater for them by means of schools of varying types, but which have, nevertheless, a broad common foundation. . . .

The arguments derived from educational theory are reinforced by practical considerations. For, in the second place, the tendency of educational organization during recent years has been to mark the years 11 to 12 as the natural turning point up to which primary education leads, and from which post-primary education starts. . . .

In view, then of the administrative developments which are at present taking place, and of the pronouncements of educationalists of experience and authority, we are justified, we think, in stating that the tendency of educational practice and thought is to favour a regrading, and that such a regrading will have as one of its effects to substitute a classification into successive stages, primary up to 11+ and post-primary after that age, for the traditional and overlapping categories of 'elementary' education for nearly all children up to the age of 14 and 'secondary' for a small minority of children from the age of 11. . . . *It is desirable that education up to 11+ should be known by the general name of Primary Education, and education after 11 by the general name of Secondary Education, and that the schools . . . which are concerned with the secondary stage of education should be called by the following designations:* –

(i) *Schools of the 'Secondary' type most commonly existing to-day, which at present pursue in the main a predominantly literary or scientific curriculum, to be known as Grammar Schools.*

(ii) *Schools of the type of the existing Selective Central Schools, which give at least a four years' course from the age of 11+, with a 'realistic' or practical trend in the last two years, to be known as Modern Schools.*

(iii) *Schools of the type of the present Non-selective Central Schools, with a curriculum on the same general lines as in* (ii) *and with due provision for differentiation between pupils of different capacities, also to be known as Modern Schools.*

(iv) *Departments or Classes within Public Elementary Schools, providing post-primary education for children who do not go to any of the above-mentioned types of Schools, to be known as 'Senior Classes'.*

The suggestion that two types of post-primary school (and, if senior classes be counted as a separate category, three types) will be required in addition to secondary schools of the existing type and to junior technical schools, leads naturally to the question of their special characteristics and of the relations which should exist between them. The 'secondary' school, in the sense in which the word 'secondary' is most commonly used to-day, falls outside our terms of reference, and there is only one point on which it is necessary to touch in connection with it. That point is, however, important. It is the necessity of ensuring, in the development of other forms of post-primary education, that nothing is done to cripple the development of secondary schools of the existing types. Exactly what proportion of the children leaving primary schools should pass to such schools in preference to the others suggested, it is not possible, we think, to say. The percentage so passing at present appears to be approximately 8·3 and varies apparently from under 5, to over 27. By general consent it is desirable that it should be largely increased. The growth of secondary education in the last twenty years has been one of the most remarkable movements of our day, and it is vital that nothing should be done to cramp its future development. . . .

On the whole, it seems to us reasonable to anticipate that the development of new forms of post-primary education will assist and strengthen Schools of the existing 'Secondary' type, both by spreading more widely an interest in post-primary education, and by providing a course of education designed to meet the needs of children who cannot stay much beyond the age of 15; thus making it easier for 'secondary' schools to require, as is generally agreed is desirable, a longer period of school attendance from the pupils entering them. At the same time, it is proper to enter a caution to the effect that anything like competition between 'secondary' schools and other forms of post-primary school, which would lead to one attracting to itself pupils better qualified to profit by the other, is to be avoided. In establishing new schools an authority must obviously have regard to the existing supply of post-primary education, to the public demand for further facilities, and to the question which of the existing types of school suggested above is most likely to meet the needs of children for whom satisfactory provision is not yet made. In practice, with the exercise of ordinary care, the risk of undesirable competition will not, we believe, be very serious.

[From Chapter III, pp. 70–96

RECOMMENDATIONS

The general Scheme of Post-Primary Education

Primary education should be regarded as ending at about the age of 11+. A second stage should then begin, and this stage, which for many pupils would end at 16+, for some at 18 or 19, but for the majority at 14+ or 15+, should, as far as possible, be regarded as a single whole, within which there will be a variety of types of education, but which will generally be controlled by the common aim of providing for the needs of children who are entering and passing through the stage of adolescence.

All normal children should go forward to some form of post-primary education. It is desirable, having regard to the country as a whole, that many more children should pass to 'secondary' schools, in the current sense of the term. But it is necessary that the post-primary stage of education should also include other types of post-primary schools, in which the curricula will vary according to the age up to which the majority of pupils remain at school, and the different interests and abilities of the children.

In selective post-primary schools the course should be designed to cover the period from the age of 11+ to that of 15+. In non-selective post-primary schools, so long as the leaving age is 14+, the course should be framed to cover the period from the age of 11+ to that of 14+, but provision should be made for the needs of pupils who remain at school to the age of 15+. . . .

WIDER AIMS

A humane or liberal education is not one given through books alone, but one which brings children into contact with the larger interests of mankind. It should be the aim of schools belonging to the last three types to provide such an education by means of a curriculum containing large opportunities for practical work, and closely related to living interests. In the earlier years the curriculum in these schools should have much in common with that provided in the schools at present commonly known as 'secondary'; it should include a foreign language, but permission should be given to omit the language in special circumstances; and only in the last two years should a 'practical' bias be given to the courses of instruction provided. . . .

[From Chapter III, para. 93

CURRICULUM

The general characteristics of Modern Schools will be as follows:

1. They will plan their courses for a period of 3 or 4 years, and these

courses will accordingly be simpler and more limited in scope than those in Grammar Schools, which are planned for 5 or more years.

2. Though the subjects included in the curriculum of Modern Schools and Senior Classes will be much the same as those in Grammar Schools, more time and attention will be devoted to handwork and similar pursuits in the former.

3. While the courses of instruction in Modern Schools in the last 2 years should not be vocational, the treatment of the subjects of the curriculum should be practical in the broadest sense and brought directly into relation with the facts of every-day life. The courses of instruction, though not merely vocational or utilitarian, should be used to connect the school work with the interests arising from the social and industrial environment of the pupils.

In framing the curricula of Modern Schools and Senior Classes due regard should be paid both to the capacities of the pupils and to the local environment. The curriculum should in each case be planned as a whole, in order that the teaching of the various subjects may be so adjusted as to secure uniformity in the presentation of any matter which is common, and to prevent overlapping. Similarly, in the arrangement of the time-table, any rigid separation of the different sides of a subject should be avoided. In framing the several syllabuses, each subject should again be regarded as a whole; and all detail irrelevant to the purpose in hand should be eliminated, in order that the pupil may not be over-burdened, and an opportunity may be given for the development of individual tastes. Finally, every effort should be made to ensure a close connexion between the work in school and the pupil's further education after leaving.

Practical Bias

Modern Schools and Senior Classes should, as a rule, give a practical bias to the curriculum in the third or fourth year of the course. This bias should be introduced only after careful consideration of local conditions and upon the advice of persons concerned with the local industries. It should not be of so marked a character as to prejudice the general education of the pupils. Adequate provision should be made for the needs of such pupils as may gain greater advantage by following a more general course of study.

Further Education

It is desirable that teachers in Modern Schools and Senior Classes should endeavour to secure the continued education of their pupils after school age by drawing attention to such facilities for further instruction, whether cultural or vocational, as are available in the area . . .

Staffing

The qualifications of the teachers and the standard of staffing in proportion to the number of pupils in the school should approximate to those required in the corresponding forms of Grammar Schools. More teachers, however, will be required in practical subjects. . . .

Equipment

The education of children over the age of 11 in Modern Schools and Senior Classes is one species of the genus 'secondary education.' It is not an inferior species, and it ought not to be hampered by conditions of accommodation and equipment inferior to those of Grammar Schools. . . .

School Life

It is desirable that legislation should be passed fixing the age of 15 years as that up to which attendance at school will become obligatory after the lapse of five years from the date of this Report—that is to say, at the beginning of the school year 1932. . . .

A Leaving Examination

A new Leaving Examination should be framed to meet the needs of pupils in selective and non-selective Modern Schools and in the Senior Classes which retain some of their pupils to the age of 15; but, in order to allow further time for the free development of such schools, this special examination should not be established for at least three years, and the syllabus for it should be carefully adjusted to the needs of broad and varied curricula. Whatever the leaving age may be, this examination should be designed to be taken by pupils at the age of 15+ with the definite object of encouraging them to remain at school up to that age.

The presentation of pupils for any such leaving examination should be wholly optional, both in respect of the individual pupil and of the school as a whole. Any individual pupil should be free to take another examination, such as the First School Examination, if he or she so desires. We attach special importance to the view that entry to the examination should be voluntary.

[From Chapter II, pp. 173–9

31 · Report of the Consultative Committee of the Board of Education on [*The Primary School*]

Published: *1931*

Chairman: *Sir W. H. Hadow*

Members: *Mr J. W. Bispham; Mr W. A. Brockington; Miss E. R. Conway; Dr H. W. Cousins; Mr Evan T. Davis; Lady Galway; Miss Lynda Grier; Miss Freda Hawtrey; The Rev. Sir Edwyn C. Hoskyns, Bart.; Sir Percy R. Jackson; Mr R. J. McAlpine; Mr F. B. Malim; Dr A. Mansbridge; Mr H. J. R. Murray; Miss E. M. Tanner; Dr R. Tawney; Mr S. Taylor; Mr W. C. Watkins; Mr J. A. White; Mr R. F. Young* (*Secretary*)

Terms of Reference (1928): *To inquire into and report as to the courses of study suitable for children (other than children in Infants' Departments) up to the age of 11 in Elementary Schools, with special reference to the needs of children in rural areas.*

This is one of the most neglected of the Consultative Committee's Reports and, in its way, one of the more important. It did much to shape the development of primary education in the years immediately before and after the Second World War. It indicates clearly the currents of psychological and pedagogic thought which were to change the old elementary school into the modern primary school.

Very little of the report is devoted to the rural primary schools, whose problems were found to be mainly due to small size, wide age-spread and excessive demands on a single teacher. Whenever possible, the report recommended, an extra teacher should be provided to look after the infants.

The report endorsed the earlier view of the Consultative Committee (*Education of the Adolescent*) as to the division between primary and secondary education at 11 plus, with transfer from the infants' department at 7 plus. It advocated close co-operation between teachers in primary and secondary schools (and training arrangements to preserve professional mobility). It saw no objection to co-educational primary schools and found no important educational consequences of the difference between the sexes at this age except with regard to physical education and a certain difference of emotional interests.

It recapitulated psychological research which suggested that the difference in intellectual capacity between the brightest and dullest children made it necessary to classify a single age-group in several sections (streams) by the age of 10.

The key to the section on the curriculum is in recommendation 30: 'We are of the opinion that the curriculum of the primary school is to be thought of in terms of activity and experience, rather than of knowledge to be acquired and facts to be stored' (see also extract below).

There is a chapter on retarded children which relates identification and remedial treatment to the extent to which the child's mental age is below his chronological age. It introduces a distinction between mentally deficient children (those whose mental age is below half their chronological age) and retarded children, whose mental age is between a half and eight-tenths of their chronological age.

Other recommendations referred to the staffing of schools – it demanded primary classes of 40, that is, no larger than those then permitted in secondary schools – the training of teachers for backward groups, school building standards, parental co-operation and the importance of discouraging any tendency to base a comparative estimate of the efficiency of schools on success in the 'free place' examination.

REPORT OF THE CONSULTATIVE COMMITTEE ON PRIMARY EDUCATION · 1931

INTRODUCTION

The curriculum . . . has passed in the last hundred years through three main phases, which of course overlap. In the age before the establishment of a public educational system, when even some of those who agreed that it was desirable that children should learn to read, 'if only for the best of purposes, that they may read the Scriptures', were doubtful if it was desirable to teach them to write, since 'such a degree of knowledge might produce in them a disrelish for the laborious occupations of life', questions of curriculum were naturally not a burning issue. In the period immediately preceding and following 1870, the period of the Revised Code and the early school boards, the dominant – and, indeed it is hardly an exaggeration to say, the exclusive concern of most schools was to secure that children acquired a minimum standard of proficiency in reading, writing, and arithmetic, subjects in which their attainments were annually assessed by quantitative standards, with a view to the allocation to schools of pecuniary rewards and penalties. During the last forty years, and with increasing rapidity in the twelve years since 1918, the outlook of the primary school has been broadened and humanized. To-day it includes care, through the school medical service, for the physical welfare of children, offers larger, if still inadequate, opportunities for practical activity, and handles the curriculum, not only as consisting of lessons to be mastered, but as providing fields of new and interesting experience to be explored; it appeals less to passive obedience and more to the sympathy, social spirit and imagination of the children, relies less on mass instruction and more on the encouragement of individual and group work, and treats the school, in short, not as the antithesis of life, but as its complement and commentary.

What is needed now is not to devise any new system or method, but to broaden the area within which these tendencies are at work. It is not primarily a question of so planning the curriculum as to convey a minimum standard of knowledge, indispensable though knowledge is, and necessary as is the disciplined application by which alone knowledge can be acquired. The essential point is that any curriculum, if it is not to be purely arbitrary and artificial, must make use of certain elements of experience, because they are part of the common life of mankind. The aim of the school is to introduce its pupils to such experiences in an orderly and intelligent manner, so as to develop their innate powers and to awaken them to the basic interests of civilized existence. If the school succeeds in achieving that aim, knowledge will be acquired in the process, not, indeed, without effort, but by an effort whose value will be enhanced by the fact that its purpose and significance can be appreciated, at least in part, by the children themselves. . . .

Professor Burt drew in his evidence a moving picture of the effect of a squalid environment not only on physical, but also, if the two can be distinguished, on mental energy. Its result, he writes, is a 'lack of mental vitality . . . and a chronic condition of mental fatigue. . . . Much so-called laziness is really the outcome of a defence mechanism, arising out of genuine physical weakness.' The school cannot eradicate these conditions, but it can do much, and should do more, to counter-act their effects. . . . Formal instruction . . . is less important than the influence of the environment supported by the school itself, and the provision of ample opportunities for healthful activity as part of its normal work. It is idle to give lessons in hygiene and good manners if the surroundings in which children pass 27 hours each week are unhygienic or mean. It should hardly be necessary to insist not only that class rooms must be sunny and airy, but that every school should contain proper accommodation, lavatories with an abundant supply of hot water wherever possible, cloak-rooms with facilities for drying wet clothes and boots, a provision of drinking water, and provision for school meals where necessary. The more closely the design of the primary school approaches that of the open air school the better. . . .

. . . Hitherto the general tendency has been to take for granted the existence of certain traditional 'subjects' and to present them to the pupils as lessons to be mastered. There is, as we have said, a place for that method, but it is neither the only method, nor the method most likely to be fruitful between the ages of seven and eleven. What is required; at least, so far as much of the curriculum is concerned, is to substitute for it methods which take as the starting-point of the work of the primary school the experience, the curiosity, and the awakening powers and interests of the children themselves. . . .

We should deprecate very strongly . . . any tendency to make the improvement of the schools attended by the older children an excuse for offering inferior accommodation to children under the age of eleven, nor can we accept the view that classes in primary schools may properly be of a larger size than those in schools for children over the age of eleven. . . .

The primary school is on the way to becoming what it should be, the common school of the whole population, so excellent and so generally esteemed that all parents will desire their children to attend it. . . .

The root of the matter is, after all, simple. What a wise and good parent would desire for his own children, that a nation must desire for all children.

[From the Introduction, pp. xvii–xxix

CURRICULUM

Our main care must be to supply children between the ages of seven and eleven with what is essential to their healthy growth – physical, intellectual, and moral – during that particular stage of their development. The principle which is here implied will be challenged by no one who has grasped the idea that life is a process of growth in which there are successive stages, each with its own specific character and needs. It can, however, hardly be denied that there are places in our educational system where the curriculum is distorted and the teaching warped from its proper character by the supposed need of meeting the requirements of a later educational stage. . . . No good can come from teaching children things that have no immediate value for them. . . . To put the point in a more concrete way, we must recognize the uselessness and the danger of seeking to inculcate what Professor A. N. Whitehead calls inert ideas – that is, ideas which at the time when they are imparted have no bearing upon a child's natural activities of body or mind and do nothing to illuminate or guide his experience.

There are doubtless several reasons why a principle so obviously sane should in practice be so often neglected. . . . In the earliest days of popular education children went to school to learn specific things which could not well be taught at home – reading, writing and cyphering. The real business of life was picked up by a child in unregulated play, in casual intercourse with contemporaries and elders, and by a gradual apprenticeship to the discipline of the house, the farm, the workshop. But as industrialization has transformed the basis of social life. . . . the schools . . . have thus been compelled to broaden their aims until it might now be said that they have to teach children how to live. This profound change in purpose has been accepted with a certain unconscious reluctance, and a consequent slowness of adaptation. The schools, feeling that what they can do best is the old familiar business of imparting knowledge, have reached a high level of technique in that part of their functions, but have not clearly grasped its proper relation to the whole. In short, while there is plenty of teaching which is good in the abstract, there is too little which helps children directly to strengthen and enlarge their instinctive hold on the conditions of life by enriching, illuminating and giving point to their growing experience.

Applying these considerations to the problem before us, we see that the curriculum is to be thought of in terms of activity and experience rather than of knowledge to be acquired and facts to be stored. Its aim should be to develop in a child the fundamental human powers and to awaken him to the fundamental interests of civilized life so far as these powers and interests lie within the compass of childhood. . . .

[From Chapter VII, pp. 92–3

32 · Report of the Consultative Committee of the Board of Education on Secondary Education with Special Reference to Grammar Schools and Technical High Schools. [*The Spens Report*]

Published: *1938*
Chairman: *Mr Will Spens.**
Members: *Dr M. Dorothy Brock; Mr W. A. Brockington; Dr H. W. Cousins; Miss Lynda Grier; Sir Percy Jackson; Professor Joseph Jones; Mr Hugh Lyon; Dr A. Mansbridge; Mr H. J. R. Murray; Mr J. Paley-Yorke; Miss A. E. Phillips; Mr T. J. Rees; Mr R. L. Roberts; Alderman E. G. Rowlinson; Dr H. Schofield; Lady Simon; Mr J. H. Simpson; Mr J. A. White;* Secretary: *Dr R. F. Young*
Terms of Reference (1933): *To consider and report upon the organization and inter-relation of schools other than those administered under the Elementary Code which provide education for pupils beyond the age of 11 + ; regard being had in particular to the framework and content of the education of pupils who do not remain at school beyond the age of about 16.*

The report recommended the expansion of the technical schools and the continued development of secondary education in separate grammar, technical and modern schools. It recapitulated the psychological evidence and summarized the consensus of opinion at the time about the validity and usefulness of intelligence tests. It rejected the idea of the multilateral or comprehensive school on a variety of grounds (see extract below), related to the size and intellectual composition of the annual intake, while calling for a 'multilateral idea' in separated schools.

Other recommendations were for parity of staffing and staff treatment between the different types of school. It advocated the introduction of courses based on pupils' vocational interest in the later stages of the school life, urged the adoption of a 'tutorial system' and the appointment of careers masters. It reviewed the curricula of various types of secondary schools and the role of the School Certificate Examination. It recommended the raising of the school leaving age to 16, grammar school places for about 15 per cent of the population. It deprecated ideas for centralizing the sixth-form work of grammar schools into a central school.

* Will Spens was born in 1882. Educated at Rugby and King's College, Cambridge, becoming a fellow and tutor of Corpus Christi College, Cambridge, of which college he was Master from 1927–52. He was Regional Commissioner for Civil Defence for the Eastern Region from 1939–45. He was knighted in 1939.

THE SPENS REPORT · 1938

TRADITIONALISM OF THE GRAMMAR SCHOOL

Perhaps the most striking feature of the new secondary schools provided by local education authorities, which have so greatly increased in numbers since 1902, is their marked disinclination to deviate to any considerable extent from the main lines of the traditional grammar school curriculum. That conservative and imitative tendency which is so salient a characteristic in the evolution of English political and social institutions, is particularly noticeable in this instance. The natural tendency, however, to keep within the ambit of the grammar school tradition was greatly re-enforced, and in a sense fostered, by the Regulations for Secondary Schools issued by the Board of Education in 1904–1905 [see p. 156] and succeeding years, and later by the First School (Certificate) Examination as organized in 1917 [see p. 162]. . . .

The Board took the existing Public Schools and Grammar Schools as their general *cadre* or archetype for secondary schools of all kinds. The further development of post-primary schools with traditions somewhat different from those of the Grammar Schools, such as the Higher Grade Schools, the Organized Science Schools and the Day Technical Schools which had sprung into existence in the last quarter of the nineteenth century, was definitely discouraged and new Secondary Schools were in effect compelled to take as their model the curriculum of the existing Public Schools and Grammar Schools. The tendency of Secondary Schools maintained or aided by local education authorities to imitate the Public Schools and Grammar Schools has since 1902 been considerably accentuated by the fact that economic difficulties have forced many of the old endowed schools to accept financial aid from public funds and thus to become an integral part of the public system of education. . . .

On a dispassionate retrospect of the history of post-primary education since 1900 we cannot but deplore the fact that the Board did little or nothing . . . to foster the development of secondary schools of quasi-vocational type designed to meet the needs of boys and girls who desired to enter industry and commerce at the age of 16.

The need in a highly industrialized society for post-primary schools of non-academic type with an orientation towards commerce or industry was shown by the development of the Central Schools in London and Manchester in 1911–12, and of the Junior Technical Schools from 1913 onwards.

The present difficulties in the field of secondary education have arisen largely out of the confusion which began about 1904 between a type of secondary education appropriate to the needs of boys and girls between the ages of 11 to 12 and of 16 to 17 and the traditional academic course orientated towards the Universities.

[From pp. 71–3

SOCIAL BASIS

A careful study of the development of secondary education in England and Wales, particularly since 1900, and an examination of the present position . . . leave us with the general impression that the existing arrangements for the whole-time higher education of boys and girls above the age of 11+ in England and Wales have ceased to correspond with the actual structure of modern society and with the economic facts of the situation.

[From pp. 352–3

PSYCHOLOGICAL EVIDENCE

Intellectual development during childhood appears to progress as if it were governed by a single central factor, usually known as 'general intelligence', which may be broadly described as innate all-round intellectual ability. It appears to enter into everything which the child attempts to think, or say, or do, and seems on the whole to be the most important factor in determining his work in the classroom. Our psychological witnesses assured us that it can be measured approximately by means of intelligence tests. . . .

We were informed that, with few exceptions, it is possible at a very early age to predict with some degree of accuracy the ultimate level of a child's intellectual powers, but this is true only of general intelligence and does not hold good in respect of specific aptitudes or interests. The average child is said to attain the effective limit of development in general intelligence between the ages of 16 and 18 . . .

Since the ratio of each child's mental age to his chronological age remains approximately the same, while his chronological age increases, the mental differences between one child and another will grow larger and larger and will reach a maximum during adolescence. It is accordingly evident that different children from the age of 11, if justice is to be done to their varying capacities, require types of education varying in certain important respects.

[From pp. 357–8

DEMARCATION LINES

There is in fact no clear line of demarcation, physical, psychological or social, between the pupils who attend Grammar Schools and those who attend Modern Schools, and all the evidence that we have heard on the existing methods of selection for one or other type of school confirms us in our opinion that the line as drawn at present is always artificial and often mistaken.

[From p. 140

TECHNICAL SCHOOLS

We are convinced that it is of great importance to establish a new type of higher school of technical character, wholly distinct from the traditional academic Grammar (Secondary) School, and as a first step to this end we recommend that a number of the existing Junior Technical Schools which at present provide a curriculum based on the engineering industries (and among these we include the building industry) and any others which may develop training of such a character as (*a*) to provide a good intellectual discipline, altogether apart from its technical value, and (*b*) to have a technical value in relation not to one particular occupation but to a group of occupations, should be converted into Technical High Schools in the sense that they should be accorded in every respect equality of status with schools of the grammar school type.

We recommend that the age of recruitment for these schools should be 11+ and that the method of recruitment should be through the general selective examination by which children are recruited for the Grammar Schools. The selection of children for the Technical High Schools should be made (from those children who have attained the necessary standard in the examination) in accordance with:

(*a*) the choice of the parents;
(*b*) the report of the Head of the primary school; and
(*c*) the result of an interview of the child and its parent or parents, with the Head of the Technical High School, and a representative of the local education authority.

We attach considerable importance to an interview of this character, both in the interests of the children and their parents, and as constituting a really valuable step in the process of selection.

[From Chapter 8, pp. 274–5

SEPARATE SECONDARY SCHOOLS

We have . . . found it impossible to discuss the problems with which we are immediately concerned without some reference to post-primary schools which are at present administered under the Elementary Code.

We are of opinion that the schools which are directly covered by our reference [*i.e. the grammar schools*] should retain a special character and must retain a special importance. It does not follow that they should enjoy specially favourable conditions: on the contrary, we consider that the existence of different conditions, except in so far as they are justified by differences of curriculum, is open to grave objection.

Before reaching the conclusion that these schools must remain a separate type of school, we considered carefully the possibility of *multilateral schools*. The special characteristics of this type of school are the provision of a good general education for two or three years for all pupils over 11+ in a given area, and the organization of four or five 'streams', so that the pupils at the age of 13 or 14 years may follow courses that are suited to their individual needs and capacity. There would be a common core in these several courses, but they would differ in the time and emphasis given to a certain group of subjects. . . . But . . . we have reluctantly decided that we could not advocate as a general policy the substitution of such multilateral schools for separate schools of the existing types.

The reasons which weighed with us in favour of the existing system are as follows:

(i) In order to secure a satisfactory number of pupils in each 'stream' in a multilateral school, the size of the school would have to be very considerable, say 800 or possibly larger . . . we believe that the majority of pupils gain more from being in smaller schools.

(ii) There is general agreement that much of what is most valuable in the grammar school tradition depends on the existence of a Sixth Form. But a Sixth Form can only play its traditional part in the life of a school if it contains a reasonably high proportion of the pupils in the school. This could scarcely be the case if only half the pupils, or probably less, were on the grammar 'side' and were with comparatively few exceptions the only recruits for a Sixth Form. It is in general difficult enough to secure adequate Sixth Forms in ordinary Grammar Schools as a result of the large proportion of pupils who leave before or about the age of 16.

(iii) Even where geographical and other conditions admit of relatively large schools there is much to be said for their being wholly of the grammar school type. This is so, in view of the importance of having large Sixth Forms which render economically possible a considerable variety of Sixth Form courses.

(iv) We attach great importance to the steady evolution of the curriculum and methods of teaching in Modern Schools, and equal importance to carrying further certain reforms in the curriculum of Grammar Schools. . . . We believe that it would be very difficult, if multilateral schools became common, even in certain areas, to find Heads who would be as competent to control and inspire *both* developments as to control and inspire *one* or *other*. . . .

(v) The special value of Junior Technical Schools depends in our opinion on their contact with the staff and the equipment of a Technical College. In consequence special 'courses' in multilateral schools would not be a satisfactory substitute for Junior Technical Schools. . . .

Any general policy of establishing multilateral schools would now be very expensive, and it would be justified, more especially in view of the 'Hadow reorganization', only if it were clear that a substantial balance of advantage would result. For the reasons given above we do not think this would be the case, and we cannot therefore recommend the general creation of multilateral schools, even as the goal of a long range policy.

[From the Introduction, pp. xix–xx

ORGANIZATION

The multilateral idea, though it may not be expressed by means of the multilateral school, should in effect permeate the system of secondary education as we conceive it. Each type of secondary school will have its appropriate place in the national system with its educational task clearly in view. . . .

The establishment of parity between all types of secondary school is a fundamental requirement.

In . . . Modern Schools, Grammar Schools, and Technical High Schools, there should be Establishments of Teaching Posts, so that the salary of the teacher will no longer depend directly upon the type of school in which he is serving . . .

The maximum size of classes in the Grammar School and in the Modern School should be the same . . .

We recommend that the building requirements . . . should generally be the same, apart from the fuller provision necessary in Grammar Schools for the teaching of certain subjects of the curriculum, and the provision of smaller classrooms for Sixth Form use. . . .

The conditions which apply in Modern Schools, in which no fees are paid, should be extended to other types of secondary school, as soon as the national finances render it possible. . . .

We believe that the selective examination at the age of 11+ . . . is capable of selecting (*a*) those pupils who quite certainly have so much intelligence, and intelligence of such a character, that without doubt they ought to receive a secondary education of grammar school type; and (*b*) those pupils who quite certainly would not benefit from such an education. We consider that the line defining group (*a*) should be so drawn as to allot in this way something of the order of 50 per cent. of the Special Places. . . .

. . . The choice for grammar school places as between pupils who fall into neither of these groups . . . should be made on the result of a method of selection, including an interview, in which facts other than their relative place as determined by the examination are brought into account. . . .

We recommend that there should be a further review, at about the age of 13, of the distribution of children among all schools in the secondary stage. . . .

LEAVING AGE

Parity among schools . . . implies the raising of the minimum leaving age to the same general level in these schools. The adoption of a minimum leaving age of 16 years, which is now the rule in Grammar Schools, may not be immediately practicable, but in our judgment must even now be envisaged as inevitable.

GRAMMAR SCHOOL PLACES

The amount of provision of education of the grammar school type which is desirable cannot be precisely laid down for the country as a whole. It depends in each area in a high degree on the character and traditions of the population, industrial conditions, and the future careers of the children. . . . On the assumption that alternative forms of secondary education will be provided. . . . We think that provision based on an average annual admission to the Grammar Schools of 15 per cent. of the 'secondary school age-group' in the public elementary schools might for the present be accepted as a working figure.

[From the Summary of Recommendations, pp. 376–81

33 · Report of the Committee of the Secondary Schools Examination Council on Curriculum and Examinations in Secondary Schools. [*The Norwood Report*]

Published: *1943*

Chairman: *Sir Cyril Norwood**

Members: *Miss M. G. Clarke; Miss O. M. Hastings; Mr A. W. S. Hutchings; Dr P. D. Innes; Professor Joseph Jones; Dr J. E. Myers; Mr E. W. Naisbitt; Sir Percival Sharp; Mr S. H. Shurrock; Dr Terry Thomas; Mr W. Nalder Williams; Mr R. H. Barrow (Secretary); Mr G. G. Williams, Mr F. R. G. Duckworth, Mr W. J. Williams (Assessors appointed by the Board of Education)*

Terms of Reference (1941): *To consider suggested changes in the secondary school curriculum and the question of school examinations in relation thereto.*

The report contains one of the most explicit descriptions of the tripartite division of secondary education into grammar, technical and modern schools – see extract below. It also envisaged some kind of diagnostic two-year period in the 'lower school' where the curriculum would be broadly similar in the various types of schools.

In addition to sections on the main subjects in the secondary school curriculum the report contains a lengthy consideration of the examinations required by the schools. The report recommended the end of the School Certificate (a group examination conducted by the University Examining Boards). In its place the Examining Boards, assisted by panels of teachers, were to conduct a subject examination (similar to the General Certificate of Education at Ordinary Level) as an interim step towards internal examinations run by the schools themselves. They also recommended a school-leaving examination at 18 for university entrance and professional qualifications. Other recommendations included continued part-time education to 18 for those who left school earlier and a six months break for public service of some kind, between school and university.

* Cyril Norwood (1875–1956) was educated at Merchant Taylors' School and St John's College, Oxford, where he read Classics and Greats. He entered the Home Civil Service (at the Admiralty) in 1899, but resigned in 1901 to become senior classics master at Leeds Grammar School. He was appointed successively, headmaster of Bristol Grammar School in 1906, Marlborough College in 1916 and Harrow School in 1929, where he remained till in 1934 he became President of St John's College, Oxford, from which office he retired in 1946. He was Chairman of the Secondary Schools Examination Council from 1921–46. He was knighted in 1938.

THE NORWOOD REPORT · 1943

TRIPARTITE ORGANIZATION

Even if it were shown that the differences between individuals are so marked as to call for as many curricula as there are individuals, it would be impossible to carry such a principle into practice; and school organization and class instruction must assume that individuals have enough in common as regards capacities and interests to justify certain rough groupings. Such at any rate has been the point of view which has gradually taken shape from the experience accumulated during the development of secondary education in this country and in France and Germany and indeed in most European countries. The evolution of education has in fact thrown up certain groups, each of which can and must be treated in a way appropriate to itself. Whether such groupings are distinct on strictly psychological grounds, whether they represent types of mind, whether the differences are differences in kind or in degree, these are questions which it is not necessary to pursue. Our point is that rough groupings, whatever may be their ground, have in fact established themselves in general educational experience, and the recognition of such groupings in educational practice has been justified both during the period of education and in the after-careers of the pupils.

For example, English education has in practice recognized the pupil who is interested in learning for its own sake, who can grasp an argument or follow a piece of connected reasoning, who is interested in causes, whether on the level of human volition or in the material world, who cares to know how things came to be as well as how they are, who is sensitive to language as expression of thought, to a proof as a precise demonstration, to a series of experiments justifying a principle: he is interested in the relatedness of related things, in development, in structure, in a coherent body of knowledge. He can take a long view and hold his mind in suspense; this may be revealed in his work or in his attitude to his career. He will have some capacity to enjoy, from an aesthetic point of view, the aptness of a phrase or the neatness of a proof. He may be good with his hands or he may not; he may or may not be a good 'mixer' or a leader or a prominent figure in activities, athletic or other.

Such pupils, educated by the curriculum commonly associated with the Grammar School, have entered the learned professions or have taken up higher administrative or business posts. . . .

Again, the history of technical education has demonstrated the importance of recognizing the needs of the pupil whose interests and abilities lie markedly in the field of applied science or applied art. . . .

The various kinds of technical school were not instituted to satisfy the intellectual needs of an arbitrarily assumed group of children, but to prepare boys and girls for taking up certain crafts – engineering, agriculture and the like. Nevertheless it is usual to think of the engineer or other craftsman as possessing a particular set of interests or aptitudes by virtue of which he becomes a successful engineer or whatever he may become.

Again, there has of late years been recognition, expressed in the framing of curricula and otherwise, of still another grouping of pupils, and another grouping of occupations. The pupil in this group deals more easily with concrete things than with ideas. He may have much ability, but it will be in the realm of facts. He is interested in things as they are; he finds little attraction in the past or in the slow disentanglement of causes or movements. His mind must turn its knowledge or its curiosity to immediate test; and his test is essentially practical. He may see clearly along one line of study or interest and outstrip his generally abler fellows in that line; but he often fails to relate his knowledge or skill to other branches of activity. Because he is interested only in the moment he may be incapable of a long series of connected steps; relevance to present concerns is the only way of awakening interest, abstractions mean little to him. Thus it follows that he must have immediate returns for his effort, and for the same reason his career is often in his mind. His horizon is near and within a limited area his movement is generally slow, though it may be surprisingly rapid in seizing a particular point, or in taking up a special line. Again, he may or may not be good with his hands or sensitive to music or art.

Within this group fall pupils whose mental make-up does not show at an early stage pronounced leanings in a way comparable with the other groups which we indicated. It is by no means improbable that, as the kind of education suitable for them becomes more clearly marked out and the leaving age is raised, the course of education may become more and more supple and flexible with the result that particular interests and aptitudes may be enabled to declare themselves and be given opportunities for growth. That a development of this kind yet lies to great extent in the future does not preclude us from recognizing the existence of a group whose needs require to be met in as definite a manner as those of other groups. . . .

The truth seems to us to stand out quite clearly: the Secondary Schools [*i.e.* the Grammar Schools] which alone have provided full time education up to and beyond the age of 16 years, have often been asked to do too much. . . .

The Secondary Schools, being the sole repositories of recognized secondary education, have had to provide for the needs of the pupils who entered them. They have in our opinion faithfully maintained their inheritance, but at the same time they have had to enlarge their horizon immeasurably to cater for very diverse abilities and interests; none the less they have been confined by limitations arising partly from their own nature and partly imposed from without.

. . . Hence the search for new curricula; hence the pressure to relax examination regulations, for under existing conditions the schools cannot suggest that some of their pupils should not seek the Certificate sought by the rest. Meantime a curriculum on the whole suited to some is condemned because it is unsuited to others. That the schools have done their utmost to do justice to all their pupils is undeniable, but there comes a time when adjustment achieves nothing more and when compromise defeats all ends.

The time has come, we believe, when the real meaning of secondary education, the significance of child-centred education, the value of the Grammar School tradition, the difficulties of the present Secondary Schools should all be recognized and admitted. This means that within a framework of secondary education the needs of the three broad groups of pupils which we discussed earlier should be met within three broad types of secondary education, each type containing the possibility of variation and each school offering alternative courses which would yet keep the school true to type. Accordingly we would advocate that there should be three types of education, which we think of as the secondary Grammar, the secondary Technical, the secondary Modern, that each type should have such parity as amenities and conditions can bestow; parity of esteem in our view cannot be conferred by administrative decree nor by equality of cost per pupil; it can only be won by the school itself.

From one type of education to another there should be ease of transfer, particularly, though not exclusively, in the early stages, for the transition from primary to secondary education is not a break but a process in which special interests and aptitudes have further opportunity of declaring themselves and of meeting with appropriate treatment.

Only on some such reorganization of secondary education can the needs of the nation and the individual be appropriately met. The existing Secondary Schools would continue to perform their proper task without distraction; the secondary Technical Schools would receive an access of pupils well able to profit by the courses which they provide; the Modern Schools still in process of formulating their aims and methods would gain the scope necessary to them to fulfil the promise which they already show, and we do not regard it as impossible that eventually pupils of over 16+ may be found in them. What we are concerned with here and now is that the three main types of secondary education would be free to work out their own spheres of usefulness; all would gain and not least the individual child.

[From Chapter 1, pp. 1–15

A 'Lower School'

However carefully devised and sympathetically carried out, differentiation at 10 or 11+ cannot be regarded as final. Opportunity must be given for the rectifying of mistakes, and for dealing with cases of late development or failure to fulfil promise. For this reason we advocate that for an average two years after entry to the secondary school the pupil should belong to a 'Lower School', placed in the general control of a master or mistress responsible to the Head Master or Head Mistress. This master or mistress would be charged with special oversight of the work of the forms comprising the Lower School, he would have the special duty of observing the progress and development of the individual pupils; he would recommend that after due allowance of time pupils for whom the higher forms of that school could not offer a suitable curriculum should be transferred elsewhere. By the end of two years every pupil should have been sympathetically and skilfully reviewed, and at roughly the age of 13+ promotion of suitable pupils should be made into the higher forms. Such promotion should not be automatic or assumed as consequent upon entry to the Lower School; it should be made only because, in the opinion of those qualified to judge, the curriculum of the higher forms offered a course of education suited to the needs of those promoted.

Thus by the use of the records of the primary school together with subsidiary tests, and by a period of observation and trial in the Lower School, differentiation would become a process, in which time and opportunity would be given for study of the relevant considerations, rather than a snap judgment dependent upon performance in an examination.

In order to ease the transition from primary education to the appropriate secondary course and to enable transfer from one type of school to another to be carried out effectively, we would advocate that the curricula of the Lower School in all types of school should be generally common. Some variation must be allowed. Pupils admitted to the secondary Grammar School, for example, clearly should begin one or two foreign languages if their best interests are to be served; at the same time the Grammar School should make it possible for 13-year-old entrants to begin a foreign language, and for this some generosity as regards staffing would be necessary. Pupils who need the most concrete form of education possible in the Modern School should have an appropriate curriculum, though there is no reason why a modern language should not be taught to the pupils for whom it is suitable. But we believe that the variety of course which each type of school should offer would allow a curriculum largely common to those in each school for whom the question of transfer is likely to arise. . . .

[From Chapter 3, pp. 17-18

34 · White Paper on Educational Reconstruction. 1943

This was the document which foreshadowed the 1944 Education Act.

EDUCATIONAL RECONSTRUCTION

'Upon the education of the people of this
country the fate of this country depends.'

INTRODUCTION

The Government's purpose in putting forward the reforms described in this Paper is to secure for children a happier childhood and a better start in life; to ensure a fuller measure of education and opportunity for young people and to provide means for all of developing the various talents with which they are endowed and so enriching the inheritance of the country whose citizens they are. The new educational opportunities must not, therefore, be of a single pattern. It is just as important to achieve diversity as it is to ensure equality of educational opportunity. But such diversity must not impair the social unity within the educational system which will open the way to a more closely knit society and give us strength to face the tasks ahead. The war has revealed afresh the resources and character of the British people – an enduring possession that will survive all the material losses inevitable in the present struggle. In the youth of the nation we have our greatest national asset. Even on a basis of mere expediency, we cannot afford not to develop this asset to the greatest advantage. It is the object of the present proposals to strengthen and inspire the younger generation. For it is as true to-day, as when it was first said, that 'the bulwarks of a city are its men'.

2. With these ends in view the Government propose to recast the national education service. The new layout is based on a recognition of the principle that education is a continuous process conducted in successive stages. For children below the compulsory school age of 5 there must be a sufficient supply of nursery schools. The period of compulsory school attendance will be extended to 15 without exemptions and with provision for its subsequent extension to 16 as soon as circumstances permit. The period from 5 to the leaving age will be divided into two stages, the first, to be known as primary, covering the years up to about

11. After 11, secondary education, of diversified types but of equal standing, will be provided for all children. At the primary stage the large classes and bad conditions which at present are a reproach to many elementary schools will be systematically eliminated; at the secondary stage the standard of accommodation and amenities will be steadily raised to the level of the best examples. The provision of school meals and milk will be made obligatory.

3. When the period of full-time compulsory schooling ends the young person will continue under educational influences up to 18 years of age either by remaining in full-time attendance at a secondary school, or by part-time day attendance at a young people's college. Throughout all the foregoing stages the benefits of medical inspection and treatment will be available without charge. Opportunities for technical and adult education will be increased.

4. Among other important features of the plan are an effective system of inspection and registration of schools outside the public system; new financial and administrative arrangements for the voluntary schools, and the recognition of the special place of religious instruction in school life.

5. It will be appreciated that these and the other changes set out in subsequent paragraphs cannot be achieved at once. The introduction of each portion of the plan will be related to an Appointed Day. In this way it will be possible to fit the schemes for educational reform into the general picture of social reconstruction and to introduce the various portions of the plan as and when the necessary buildings, the equipment and the teachers become available.

6. The reforms proposed involve a steady increase over a series of years in the expenditure which will fall on the taxpayer and the ratepayer. Estimates are given in an Appendix* to this Paper. The rate at which it will be possible to proceed will depend not only on the factors mentioned in the preceding paragraph, but on the financial resources available, having regard to our existing commitments, to the new claims we may have to meet and to such orders of priority as may have to be laid down. The rate of development of the proposals will therefore have to be determined from time to time in the light of these considerations. The Prime Minister, in a recent pronouncement, foreshadowed in relation to general social advancement a four years plan to be undertaken immediately after the War. In that period and within that conception, it should be possible to complete the initial design of the future structure of a reorganized statutory scheme of full-time education, and to take the first steps in the programme of raising the school-leaving age, and

* The estimated 'ultimate' extra cost was £67·4 million, making a total of £190·4 million. By 1961–2, with major parts of the Act as yet unenforced, current and capital expenditure topped £928 million.

of establishing a system of compulsory part-time education for young persons up to the age of 18. The future rate of progress at the end of this period could again be examined in the light of the conditions then obtaining. . . .

OVER-EMPHASIS ON EXAMINATION SUBJECTS IN JUNIOR SCHOOL

Many of the Infant schools are among the most successful of the publicly provided schools. The Junior Schools for children between 7–11 have, however, tended to be the 'Cinderellas' of the public system . . . Little new and up-to-date accommodation has been provided . . . Classes are in many cases far too large . . . More serious still is the effect . . . of the arrangements for transition . . . to the various types of post-primary education . . .

There is nothing to be said in favour of a system which subjects children at the age of 11 to the strain of a competitive examination on which not only their future schooling but their future careers may depend. Apart from the effect on the children, there is the effect on the curriculum . . . Instead of the Junior Schools performing their proper and highly important function of fostering the potentialities of children at an age when their minds are nimble and receptive, their curiosity strong, their imagination fertile and their spirits high, the curriculum is too often cramped and distorted by over-emphasis on examination subjects and on ways and means of defeating the examiners . . .

[From paragraphs 15–17

ASSESSMENT OF APTITUDES, NOT COMPETITIVE TESTS

In the future, children at the age of about 11 should be classified, not on the results of a competitive test, but on an assessment of their individual aptitudes largely by such means as school records, supplemented, if necessary, by intelligence tests, due regard being had to their parents' wishes, and the careers they have in mind. Even so the choice . . . will not be finally determined at 11 . . . At . . . 13 or even later, there will be facilities for transfer . . . The keynote . . . will be that the the child is the centre of education . . .

If this choice is to be a real one, it is manifest that conditions in different types of school must be broadly equivalent. Under present conditions the secondary grammar school enjoys a prestige . . . which completely over-shadows all other types of school . . . Inheriting as it does a distinguished tradition . . . it offers the advantages of superior premises and staffing and a longer school life . . . But . . . an academic training is ill-suited for many of the pupils who find themselves moving along a narrow educational path bounded by the School Certificate and leading into a limited field of opportunity . . .

The senior schools have a recent history . . . Their future is their own to make . . . They offer a general education for life, closely related to the interests and environment of the pupils and of a wide range embracing the literary as well as the practical, e.g. agricultural, sides.

Junior Technical Schools . . . hold out great opportunities for pupils with a practical bent . . .

Such, then will be the three main types . . . grammar, modern and technical schools. It would be wrong to suppose that they will necessarily remain separate and apart. Different types may be combined in one building or on one site . . . In any case, free interchange of pupils from one type of education to another must be facilitated.

[From paragraphs 27–31

35 · Report of the Committee on Public Schools appointed by the President of the Board of Education. [*The Fleming Report*]

Published: *1944*

Chairman: *Lord Fleming, Senator of the College of Justice in Scotland**

Members: *Alderman Sir James Aitken; Mr J. G. Barrington-Ward; Mr A. L. Binns; Mr Robert Birley; Dr M. Dorothy Brock; Mr G. Chester; Mr Harold Clay; Mr G. D. H. Cole; Sir Edward Crowe; Professor W. J. Gruffydd, M.P.; Mr M. L. Jacks; The Bishop of London, Dr Geoffrey Fisher; Mr A. C. Macdiarmid; Mr A. E. Nichols; Mr H. N. Penlington; Dr A. W. Pickard-Cambridge; Sir Ernest Pooley; Mr C. L. Reynolds; Miss E. M. Tanner; Mr G. G. Williams, Mr F. R. G. Duckworth, Mr W. J. Williams (Assessors appointed by the Board of Education); Mr R. N. Heaton, Mr P. Wilson (Joint Secretaries)*

Terms of Reference: *To consider means whereby the association between the Public Schools (by which are meant schools which are in membership of the Governing Bodies Association or the Headmasters' Conference) and the general educational system of the country could be developed and extended; also to consider how far any measures recommended in the case of boys' public schools could be applied to comparable schools for girls.*

The report belongs to the period of educational inquiry leading up to the 1944 Education Act. It was presented by a Committee set up (in 1942) at the request of the public schools themselves, who were conscious of the social changes which were taking place and anxious not to be isolated. A paragraph in the report emphasizes this:

The Public Schools are now less stereotyped, the curriculum is more flexible, the range of interests wider, and the impact of the present war has done much to break down old traditions and to introduce new activities. In an age of revolutionary change it is only to be expected that the Public School should be less aloof and the boys there more directly interested in the world around them. But the trend of social development is leaving the Public Schools out of alignment with the

* David Pinkerton Fleming (1887–1944) was educated at Glasgow High School and Glasgow and Edinburgh Universities, and the Heriot-Watt College. He built up a large legal practice before becoming Solicitor General for Scotland in 1921, M.P. for Dunbartonshire in 1924 and a Scottish judge in 1925.

world in which they exist. Even the movement, which began over sixty years ago, for founding School Missions in the poorer districts of London and the great cities has brought into sharper relief the unreality of an educational system which segregates so thoroughly the boys of one class from those of another in a world where, much more than in the past, they will meet in later life as equals.

[Chapter 2, *Historical Sketch*, p. 30

Members of the Committee included strong representation from the public schools, notably the then Bishop of London, Dr Fisher, who had been headmaster of Repton, and was shortly to become Archbishop of Canterbury, and five headmasters and headmistresses. These included Mr Robert Birley, then headmaster of Charterhouse and later headmaster of Eton, and Miss E. M. Turner, of Roedean. Other members included Sir James Aitken, chairman of the Lancashire Education Committee, Mr A. L. Binns (later Sir Arthur), chief education officer, West Riding of Yorkshire, Mr M. L. Jacks, director of the Oxford University department of education (and a former head of Mill Hill), Dr A. W. Pickard-Cambridge, lately vice-chancellor of Sheffield University, and two trade unionists – Mr G. Chester of the Boot and Shoe Operatives, and Mr Harold Clay of the Transport and General Workers, who later became president of the Workers Educational Association.

The issue of principle was stated in the following terms:

Our conclusion is that while Day and Boarding Schools do not by any means exclude some of each other's characteristic advantages and while many children would be equally well-suited by either, the choice between a day and boarding education is, for others, important and even critical and ought to be made freely and without financial bar. . . . Our evidence suggests that there are thousands of others who, though tolerably well suited by the day school system, would find in the life of a good boarding school the widening of experience or the extra encouragement or stimulation that would develop and strengthen their characters and release their full potentialities. We are convinced that this most important of all educational choices ought not to depend, as it does now, on financial considerations and that the issue ought not to be confused by the social distinctions, real or imaginary, which divide the two types of schools.

[Chapter 2, p. 50

This led the Committee to put forward two schemes.

Scheme A was intended to replace the Direct Grant System. L.E.A.s would have the right to reserve, at schools under Scheme A, a number of places, day or boarding, for pupils for whom they were responsible – the percentage to vary from school to school, to be fixed by negotiation.

'All the places . . . however filled, should be equally accessible to all pupils in the sense that the only criterion for admission should be the capacity of the pupil to profit by education in the school and that no pupil should be precluded from entering . . . by reason of the inability of the parent to pay fees.' At least a third of the Governing bodies of schools in Scheme A would be nominated by L.E.A.s sending pupils.

Scheme B was designed for the boarding schools only. It was to provide bursaries for pupils from primary schools on an income scale. Schools participating would have to provide at least 25 per cent of their places for the scheme. Selection of candidates would be by regional interviewing board and a central advisory committee, final acceptance resting with the schools. The report expressly discounted any suggestion that selection should be competitive in the sense of finding the ablest or most intelligent (see extract). Fees would be paid by the L.E.A.s who would recover from the parents on an income scale and receive grants from the Ministry of Education.

The Committee said that the same principle of choice between boarding and day education, untrammelled by financial considerations, should be given to girls as well as boys and should be applied in Wales where the boarding tradition was weak.

It also recommended the extension of boarding facilities at maintained schools of all kinds.

The report aroused great interest but was never fully accepted by the Ministry of Education. The Direct Grant list was re-opened and extended. Scheme B, which was the revolutionary part of the report, remained a dead letter. Some L.E.A.s used their powers to pay fees at independent schools, both to supplement their secondary school provision and also to provide boarding school places for pupils whose parents were abroad or who, for some specific compassionate reason, required boarding education. A few such as Hertfordshire operated small-scale bursary schemes which enabled a handful of volunteers to be sent each year to famous schools. But the principle on which the Fleming schemes were based – a free choice, uninfluenced by financial considerations – was never accepted, largely because the local education authorities were unable to reconcile the big difference between the cost of educating a pupil at a maintained secondary school and at a public boarding school. No less formidable were the difficulties of selection.

The Committee seems to have had little insight into these aspects of the matter; it entirely misread public reactions at local level. The result was a report full of special pleading which had little influence on the course of events. In particular the report was fatally weakened by its failure either to suggest a workable selection procedure (see extract) or to face squarely the possibility that there might be no workable selection procedure.

THE FLEMING REPORT · 1944

SELECTION OF BURSARS

We hold . . . that any attempt to make use of the Schemes which we propose in order to segregate the abler children and to send them to

Boarding Schools would be socially and educationally wrong. But this does not mean that when a particular school can offer some particular educational advantage otherwise unobtainable, and a child is specially well fitted to benefit from it, it should be denied to him. Provided that it is well understood that intellectual ability by itself should be no criterion for selection for education at a Boarding School, we think that, if it appears to an Interviewing Board that a child would derive special benefit by going to a particular school, the application should be favourably considered. There should be a clear distinction between any attempt, on the one hand, to differentiate Boarding Schools from Day Schools or independent from grant-aided Schools, and, on the other, the recognition that there may be a particular school which is especially well suited for a particular child. . . .

It must be recognized . . . that if there are more applications than places, the wishes of the parent, though necessarily a first consideration, cannot possibly be a final one, and it would be necessary to supplement them by some other criteria.

We have said that there should be no attempt to take only abler children. At the same time, those chosen for bursaries must be able to assimilate the ordinary curriculum of the school to which they go. It is to be noted, further, that in most Public Schools for boys a knowledge both of Latin and of French is required for entrance. Bursars who are selected at the age of 11 should be able to acquire sufficient knowledge of these two languages by the age of 13, either in the Junior School or Preparatory School or in the lower forms of a Secondary Grammar School. It is, however, not at all to be desired that candidates, whether chosen at 11 or at 13, who have little or no knowledge of Latin should be thereby disqualified. While the Central Advisory Committee and the Regional Boards will be in a position to know the standards and curricula current in the different schools and to direct bursars accordingly, the schools themselves should be prepared to make any special provisions which may be necessary to meet the needs of particular bursars. But, generally speaking, they should be able to take their places naturally in one or other of the forms in a school to which new entrants are usually assigned.

The first task of the Interviewing Boards should be to remove from the lists the names of those candidates for whom an education at the school or schools applied for would not seem really suitable. It can never be satisfactory for a child to be educated at a school in which the standard of the work is above his powers, or the curriculum not suited to his particular aptitudes. The Interviewing Boards should therefore reject applications from those children whose school records and Head Masters' reports show that they cannot be expected to profit from the education provided at the school or schools for which application is made. There are also children who are clearly unsuited, for temperamental reasons, for a type of education in which the pressure of the community is inevitably stronger than at a Day School. Here it is particularly difficult to lay down hard and fast rules, to distinguish, to take one instance, between a retiring child, who would find in the closer communal life of a Boarding School just the experience needed to help him to overcome his difficulties, and another who would stand particularly in need of the opportunities to escape from his fellows which life at a Day School more readily provides. Clearly, very considerable reliance will have to be placed here on the reports of Primary School Head Masters and Head Mistresses, supplemented by a report in every case from the Local Education Authority.

But it is when those children are eliminated for whom a Boarding School education is plainly unsuitable that the problem of finding positive criteria begins. There will be children for whom it will be clear that education at a Boarding School is essential if they are to be given any real chance for education to play its proper part in their lives, and there will be others who seem to have qualities of mind or character which such boarding education could best develop. In both cases it will really be the need of the child which is being considered, though the need is not of the same kind in the two types.

We recommend that both the parent or guardian, on making the application, and the Primary or Secondary School Head Master or Head Mistress, when making the reports, should be required to be quite explicit in stating the particular reason why it is considered that the child should have a Boarding School education. An obvious claim to consideration is possessed by children who, though perfectly sound in mind and character, would not derive the fullest benefit in a Day School because of exceptional home circumstances. . . . There are also children who stand in greater need than others of the continuous discipline of a Boarding School and those who would benefit particularly from education in surroundings free from the distractions inseparable from life at a Day School. There are also those who seem lacking in intiative or self-reliance, and who would almost certainly benefit from living in a Boarding School. But we do not consider that Boarding Schools should be regarded as valuable only for children who are in some way handicapped, either by reason of difficulties in their homes or because of some temperamental weaknesses and, so long as places are insufficient in number, the Boards must necessarily face the difficult task of selecting those children of whom it cannot be said that they stand in positive need of a Boarding School education, but for whom such an education would undoubtedly afford special opportunities for the fuller realization of their particular qualities. We recognize that in no part of our Report is it more difficult to make recommendations than here. Educational psychology is still in its infancy; methods of selection can only be improved by the process of trial and error, and mistakes will no doubt be made. But the accumulation of experience in this matter should be rapid.

[From Chapter 6, pp. 71-3

36 · Report of a Committee appointed by the President of the Board of Education to consider the Supply, Recruitment and Training of Teachers and Youth Leaders. [*The McNair Report*]

Published: *1944*

Chairman: *Sir Arnold McNair**

Members: *Sir Fred Clarke; Dr A. P. M. Fleming; Mrs Lionel Hichens; Sir Frederick Mander; Mr P. R. Morris; Miss A. H. Ross; Mrs J. H. Stocks; Mr B. B. Thomas; Mr S. H. Wood (Secretary)*

Terms of Reference: *To investigate the present sources of supply and the methods of recruitment and training of teachers and youth leaders and to report what principles should guide the Board in these matters in the future. March 1942.*

The Report began by considering recruitment and made a series of recommendations intended to raise the status of the profession of teaching.

'Three things in particular must be done,' said the report, 'if the number and quality of teachers required to match the reforms proposed in the White Paper are to be obtained. The field of recruitment must be widened; conditions of service which deter people from becoming teachers must be abolished; and the standing of education must be improved so that a sufficient number of men and women of quality will be attracted to teaching as a profession. . . .'

Without prescribing scales, it recommended that salaries should be substantially increased and that the Burnham Committee should be reformed with a single committee for teachers in primary and secondary schools. It proposed that the 'pledge' to teach should no longer be required from students seeking grants to prepare for the teaching profession. It condemned the ban on married teachers.

It put forward two alternative schemes for the administration of teacher

* Arnold Duncan McNair was born in 1885. He was educated at Aldenham and Gonville and Caius College, Cambridge, where he was president of the Union in 1909. A lawyer, be became a civil servant during the first world war, remaining to serve as secretary of the Sankey Committee on the Coal Industry in 1919. After various academic posts as an international lawyer he held the chair of Whewell Professor of International Law at Cambridge from 1935 to 1937, from which he moved to Liverpool as vice-chancellor from 1937 to 1945. From 1946 to 1955 he was a Judge of the International Court of Justice at the Hague, becoming president in 1952. He was knighted in 1943 and made a baron in 1955.

training. Five members of the Committee wanted each University to establish a School of Education. This would consist of 'an organic federation of approved training institutions'. To these Schools would be given responsibility for 'the training and the assessment of the work of all students seeking to be recognized . . . as qualified teachers'.

The alternative scheme, put forward by five other members of the Committee including the Chairman, proposed the setting up of a Central Training Council to reorganize the existing Joint Boards which would then become responsible for creating 'an area training service'. In each area there would be 'a University training department and training colleges preserving their identity and being in direct relation with the Board of Education and the Central Training Council'.

The report recommended that the course of training should last three years from 18, with a year's probation after qualification. Further recommendations covered specialists in arts and crafts, music, physical education and domestic subjects.

The latter part of the report laid down principles for recruitment and training for the youth service – three years' full-time study or a year's course for those whose past experience made this unnecessary; salaries comparable with teachers, under the area training organization.

The report was hailed as a teachers' charter and led to expectations not fully realized. The Government accepted most of the report in principle, including higher salaries for teachers which were negotiated in the Burnham Committee in 1947 and subsequently, but little attention was paid to the principles of professional status and comparison put forward in the report. The Area Training Organizations were set up, and the National Advisory Council for the Training and Supply of Teachers was created to act as a standing advisory body.

THE McNAIR REPORT · 1944

SALARIES AND RECOGNITION

It is not our task to frame new scales of salaries for teachers. That is the business of the Burnham Committees. But we do suggest certain criteria by which the emoluments of the profession should be judged. Salary scales would satisfy four main tests:

(*a*) a test of personal need: they should make possible the kind of life which teachers of the quality required ought to be enabled to live;

(*b*) a market test: they should bear a relationship to the earnings of other professions and occupations so that the necessary supply of teachers of the right quality will be forthcoming;

(*c*) a professional test: they should not give rise to anomalies or injustices within the teaching profession; and (*d*) an educational test: they should not have consequences which damage the efficiency of the education provided in any particular type of school or area.

[From Chapter 3, p. 32

A CENTRAL TRAINING COUNCIL AND AN AREA ORGANIZATION OF TRAINING

While we are all in agreement upon the recommendations relating to the supply of teachers and to the creation of a Central Training Council we are not all of one mind about the method of securing the integration, on an area basis, of the institutions which are to be responsible for the education and training of teachers. Some of us wish to place general responsibility for the training of qualified teachers upon the universities (in which term we include some of the university colleges) and recommend a scheme which requires the establishment of 'University Schools of Education'. Other members of the Committee recommend what may be called 'The Joint Board Scheme'. The main difference between them lies in the part which should be played by the universities.

[From Chapter 4, p. 48

[*Then follow the two alternative schemes.*]

1. University Schools of Education (proposed by Sir Fred Clarke, Sir Frederick Mander, Mr P. R. Morris, Mr B. B. Thomas and Mr S. H. Wood)

We . . . are of opinion that a major constitutional change is required in the organization and administration of the education and training of teachers.

We wholly dissent, therefore, from any sharp distinction between education and training, as though the one were the proper concern of the best institutions and teachers and the other were not. Training is that part of the education of a student which emphasizes that he is preparing himself for a particular profession. The studies and practices of one student which reveal that he is to be a teacher and not an engineer are as much 'education' as are the studies and practices of another student which reveal that he is to be an engineer and not a teacher.

The fundamental weakness of the present system is that there are 100 institutions engaged in the training of teachers but they are not related to one another in such a way as to produce a coherent training service.

It is clear to us that the idea of separate and self-contained training institutions must be abandoned. The problem is to retain the services of existing institutions in so far as they are or can be made efficient, to add other institutions which have a contribution to make and, with the cooperation of those whose responsibilities entitle them to an interest in the matter, to weld the whole into an integrated training service.

Our scheme places the training of graduates and non-graduates under the same authority, namely the University School of Education; and it makes institutions which are approved for the training of qualified teachers of all kinds an integral part of the School.

We recommend

(*a*) that each university should establish a School of Education, it being understood that some universities may find it desirable to establish more than one such school;

(*b*) that each University School of Education should consist of an organic federation of approved training institutions working in co-operation with other approved educational institutions; and

(*c*) that University Schools of Education should be responsible for the training and the assessment of the work of all students who are seeking to be recognized by the Board of Education as qualified teachers.

2. *The Joint Board Scheme* (*proposed by Sir Arnold McNair, Dr A. P. M. Fleming, Mrs Lionel Hichens, Miss A. H. Ross and Mrs J. L. Stocks*)

We . . . recommend

that the Joint Board . . . reconstituted should become responsible for the organization of an area training service in which there will be a university training department and training colleges preserving their identity and being in direct relation with the Board of Education and the Central Training Council, and in particular should, in addition to their present duties, make or ensure the making of arrangements for

(i) Practical Training in Schools and Continuous Teaching Practice

(ii) refresher and other courses for serving teachers,

and, so far as distance and other factors may permit,

(iii) enabling the students of one training institution to receive instruction in others,

(iv) enabling members of the staff of one training institution (more particularly specialists) to give instruction in others;

that, with a view to making reciprocally available the resources of the university training department and the training colleges in each area, so far as distance and other factors may permit, the university (in respect of its training department) and the training colleges should through the instrumentality of the Joint Board develop the practice of consulting upon appointments to their staffs and the use of their staffs;

that in each area the university should be invited to nominate representatives upon the governing bodies of the training colleges, and that the university, if its constitution provides for the representation of external bodies upon a Court, should invite the training colleges to appoint representatives;

that the passing of the examinations in the university training departments and in the training colleges, which must necessarily differ in content, should result in obtaining a common professional qualification accepted by the Board of Education, while the term 'Diploma in Education', if retained by a university, should be reserved for rewarding more advanced studies;

that the Joint Board should be responsible for the examination and assessment of students both in the university training department and in the training colleges for the purpose of the grant of the above-mentioned professional qualification . . .

Our approach to the problem is: what is the contribution which the universities, having regard to their experience and their resources and their other present and future obligations to the country, are best qualified to make, and what are the best ways in which they can make it?

. . . Fifteen years ago, the universities . . . at the request of the Board of Education took over from that Department the responsibility for the testing and examination of students in training colleges for the purpose of their recognition as certificated teachers. . . .

It is clear to us that the training colleges value the connection with the universities established by these Joint Boards and the attendant Boards of Studies and that they would welcome closer contact with the universities, provided that it takes the form of a partnership between equals and does not lead to the universities having a predominant influence in the training of the students in the training colleges.

The nation as a whole has woken up to the deficiencies of its public educational system, and at the moment we are witnessing one of the most widespread and insistent of popular demands for its reform. The universities are amongst the bodies to which this demand is addressed, and they have an important contribution to make towards its satisfaction. We appeal to them, in the first place, to ensure that their training departments shall be as efficient as care and money can make them, and shall be regarded as important in every way as a department engaged in preparing students for their degrees; and, in the second place, to accept the view that the universities' contribution towards the improvement of our public educational system should be the concern of the universities as a whole and not be looked upon as the duty of their training departments alone. . . .

We are of the opinion, in the light of the experience of the past fifteen years, that the time has now arrived for going beyond the contact which is concerned with examinations and studies and for developing between the universities and the training colleges and between the training colleges themselves a wider relationship, and we believe that this can best be done by making use of the existing Joint Boards and of any new Joint Boards that may be created. . . .

. . . In each area the university and every training college should become conscious that they are all engaged, each in its different way, in the common task of training teachers, and that the experience, and to some extent the training potentialities, of each should be reciprocally available for the purpose of a more unified service. . . .

. . . The university training departments and the training colleges should preserve their separate identity, and the Joint Boards should exercise, in respect of the final assessment of the students of both (including their practical teaching), the control which they now exercise over the examinations taken by the training college students. . . .

We owe it to our colleagues who differ from us and to those who read this Report to explain why we are unable to accept the University School of Education Scheme. The reasons are as follows: –

(*a*) If the proposed acceptance of responsibility by the universities for the training of all teachers were to become a reality and not remain merely a gesture, the desire to make the most of the university connection would in our opinion inevitably tend to bring about the concentration of the many new training colleges required upon the university cities and towns, which for the most part are crowded industrial areas in which it is already difficult enough to find adequate accommodation for hostels on healthy sites and adequate ground for sports and physical training.

(*b*) The concentration of training colleges upon the university towns would in some cases increase the difficulty of finding adequate facilities for what is described in Chapter 6 as Practical Training in Schools and preclude access to that variety of schools which can be enjoyed by students of training colleges situate in the larger country towns.

[From Chapter 4, pp. 48–60

37 · Education Act. 1944

Many of the legal changes introduced in the Act had been canvassed for many years. The most important was in Clause One, in which the Minister of Education (the President of the Board became a Minister by an amendment in Committee) was made responsible for the education of the people of England and Wales and the local education authorities were required to carry out their part 'under his control and direction'.

The old arrangement of 'elementary' and 'higher' education stemming from different administrative roots was replaced by primary, secondary and further education – 'a continuous process conducted in three successive stages'.

The County and County Borough Councils were made responsible for all stages. L.E.A.s were given the duty to secure 'adequate provision of primary and secondary education' including nursery schools and special schools, and to prepare development plans showing how this was to be done. Tuition fees at maintained schools were forbidden.

The Dual System – i.e. the existence side by side of schools provided by the L.E.A. and schools provided by the voluntary bodies, that is the Churches – was considerably modified. The financial settlement was made more generous to the voluntary bodies. Church schools could choose 'Aided' or 'Controlled' status. 'Aided' schools were to receive grants to cover teachers' salaries and other maintenance charges; a grant of 50 per cent towards the cost of alteration to buildings; the cost of all internal repairs and half the cost of external repairs. Other grants at 50 per cent (increased to 75 per cent in 1959) were payable in respect of new school building when a school was transferred to a new site because the existing premises could not be brought up to standard, or where a new school was to be built in substitution for one or more existing schools.*

In Aided schools, the appointment of staff remained in the control of the Governors or Managers, the majority of whom were to be nominated by the Voluntary body. As for Controlled Schools, their governing bodies were to include a majority of L.E.A. representatives but denominational instruction was permitted to continue. Their schools became the financial responsibility of the L.E.A. The Act laid down that in all primary and secondary schools the day should begin with a corporate act of worship and that religious instruction should be given in county schools according to the syllabus agreed by representatives of the religious denominations.

The leaving age was raised to 15, with special power given to the Minister to delay this for two years. (It was raised to 15 in 1947.) Clause 35 also pro-

* In 1967 this became an across-the-board grant of 80 per cent on all approved Aided school building.

vided for it to be raised to 16 by Order in Council 'as soon as it has become practicable'. The parent's legal duty was changed from that of causing his child to receive 'efficient elementary instruction in reading, writing and arithmetic' to a duty to cause his child to receive 'efficient full-time education suitable to his age, aptitude and ability either by regular attendance at school or otherwise'. A general principle was laid down (see extract) concerning the right of the parent to have his wishes taken into consideration over the choice of school.

Part-time day attendance at County Colleges was to be required at some future date for those who had left school before the age of 18. The Act extended the obligation and powers of the L.E.A.s in connexion with ancillary services, such as medical, school meals, transport, the provision of school clothing and the award of scholarships for higher education. Section 89 gave statutory backing to the Burnham Committee and empowered the Minister to make the scales recommended by the negotiating committee mandatory on the employing authorities.

This Act was the result of prolonged negotiations with interested bodies of all kinds, including the churches, in which Mr R. A. Butler (Conservative) and Mr J. Chuter Ede (Labour) then respectively President of the Board of Education and Parliamentary Secretary in the wartime coalition government succeeded in achieving a large measure of agreement. The Roman Catholic interest never accepted the financial settlement for voluntary school building, but in general the religious clauses aroused less acrimony than past experience had led many to expect.

THE EDUCATION ACT · 1944

Part I

1. It shall be lawful for His Majesty to appoint a Minister (hereinafter referred to as 'the Minister') whose duty it shall be to promote the education of the people of England and Wales and the progressive development of institutions devoted to that purpose, and to secure the effective execution by local authorities, under his control and direction, of the national policy for providing a varied and comprehensive educational service in every area.

THE STATUTORY SYSTEM OF EDUCATION. LOCAL ADMINISTRATION

Part II. 6

Subject to the provisions of Part 1 of the First Schedule to this Act, the local education authority for each county shall be the council of the county, and the local education authority for each county borough shall be the council of the county borough.

THE THREE STAGES OF THE SYSTEM

Part II. 7

The statutory system of public education shall be organized in three progressive stages to be known as primary education, secondary education, and further education; and it shall be the duty of the local education authority for every area, so far as their powers extend, to contribute towards the spiritual, moral, mental, and physical development of the community by securing that efficient education throughout those stages shall be available to meet the needs of the population of their area.

Part II. 25

(1) Subject to the provisions of this section, the school day in every county school and in every voluntary school shall begin with collective worship on the part of all pupils in attendance at the school, and the arrangements made therefore shall provide for a single act of worship attended by all such pupils unless, in the opinion of the local education authority or, in the case of a voluntary school, of the managers or governors thereof, the school premises are such as to make it impracticable to assemble them for that purpose.

(2) Subject to the provisions of this section, religious instruction shall be given in every county school and in every voluntary school.

(3) It shall not be required, as a condition of any pupil attending any county school or any voluntary school, that he shall attend or abstain from attending any Sunday school or any place of religious worship.

(4) If the parent of any pupil in attendance at any county school or any voluntary school requests that he be wholly or partly excused from attendance at religious worship in the school, or from attendance at religious instruction in the school, or from attendance at both religious worship and religious instruction in the school, then, until the request is withdrawn, the pupil shall be excused from such attendance accordingly.

Part II. 35

In this Act the expression 'compulsory school age' means any age between five years and fifteen years, and accordingly a person shall be deemed to be over compulsory school age as soon as he has attained the age of fifteen years*:

Provided that, as soon as the Minister is satisfied that it has become practicable to raise to sixteen the upper limit of the compulsory school age, he shall lay before Parliament the draft of an Order in Council directing that the foregoing provisions of this section shall have effect

* The Education Act, 1962 raised the leaving age somewhat by reducing the leaving periods to two each year, at Easter or at the end of the summer term.

as if for references therein to the age of fifteen years there were substituted references to the age of sixteen years. . . .

Part II. 36

It shall be the duty of the parent of every child of compulsory school age to cause him to receive efficient full-time education suitable to his age, ability, and aptitude, either by regular attendance at school or otherwise.

Part II. 68

If the Minister is satisfied, either on complaint by any person or otherwise, that any local education authority or the managers or governors of any county or voluntary school have acted or are proposing to act unreasonably with respect to the exercise of any power conferred or the performance of any duty imposed by or under this Act, he may, notwithstanding any enactment rendering the exercise of the power or the performance of the duty contingent upon the opinion of the authority or of the managers or governors, give such directions as to the exercise of the power or the performance of the duty as appear to him to be expedient.

Part IV. 76

In the exercise and performance of all powers and duties conferred and imposed on them by this Act the Minister and local education authorities shall have regard to the general principle that, so far as is compatible with the provision of efficient instruction and training and the avoidance of unreasonable public expenditure, pupils are to be educated in accordance with the wishes of their parents.

38 · Report of the Special Committee on Higher Technological Education appointed by the Minister of Education. [*The Percy Report*]

Published: *1945*

Chairman: *Lord Eustace Percy**

Members: *Dr D. S. Anderson; Sir Lawrence Bragg, F.R.S.; Sir Hugh Chance; Sir Charles Darwin, F.R.S.; Dr E. V. Evans; Mr B. Mouat Jones; Mr S. C. Laws; Dr H. Lowery; Mr H. S. Magnay; Sir George Nelson; Sir Frederick Rees; Dr R. V. Southwell, F.R.S.; Mr Fitzherbert Wright*

Assessors: *Mr W. Elliott; Mr H. B. Wallis; Mr F. Bray; Mr H. J. Shelley*

Terms of Reference: ***Having regard to the requirements of industry, to consider the needs of higher technical education in England and Wales and the respective contributions to be made thereto by Universities and Technical Colleges; and to make recommendations, among other things, as to the means for maintaining appropriate collaboration between Universities and Technical Colleges in this field.***

The future of higher technological education in the technical colleges after the second world war – and the added responsibilities of local education authorities in further education generally after the 1944 Act – raised questions about the whole technological basis of industry. The Percy Committee, like the Barlow Committee a year later (see p. 230), found evidence of serious shortcomings in the training of technologists affecting both quality and quantity. Among the recommendations in the report were proposals for the designation of a carefully selected and limited number of technical colleges as Colleges of Technology, which should be allowed to build up full-time courses of degree standard. While remaining under the L.E.A.s, these colleges were to be largely self-governing, but the report envisaged that the L.E.A.s should receive a substantially higher rate of grant from the central government for this work.

There was disagreement about the qualification to be awarded for their high level work: one group wanted a degree (Bachelor of Technology), another, a State Diploma in Technology (Dip. Tech.). The Chairman wanted to make the selected colleges 'Royal' institutions awarding Associateships and Fellowships.

* Lord Eustace Percy (1887–1958) was a former Member of Parliament and President of the Board of Education (1924–9). He left the Commons in 1937 to become Rector of the Newcastle division of the University of Durham (1937–58), being raised to the peerage in 1953 as Baron Percy of Newcastle. While President of the Board of Education he had taken a special interest in technical education.

The Committee was impressed by the difficulties of co-ordination springing from the existence of 146 education authorities with responsibilities in technical education and proposed the establishment of regional advisory councils to avoid wasteful competition between courses and colleges.

This report, with the Barlow Report, effectively made the case for expansion and helped to create a climate of opinion about technical education of which the swing from arts to science subjects in the grammar school sixth forms was only one result. Apart from the proposed regional advisory councils, little came of the other recommendations till, ten years later, the Colleges of Advanced Technology emerged to fulfil the role envisaged for the major colleges, Royal or otherwise.

Action on the main recommendation was delayed by controversy about the nature of the qualification to be awarded by the selected colleges. Proposals for a degree touched the interests of the universities. The professional institutions had their position to safeguard. Lord Cherwell and others were canvassing the idea of a technological university on the lines of M.I.T. In 1950, the National Advisory Council on Education for Industry and Commerce published a report on *The Future of Higher Technological Education* supporting the case for new courses in advanced technology in selected technical colleges. With this was a scheme for a national body to be known as the Royal College of Technologists, which would approve courses in appropriate colleges, and appoint external examiners to assist the colleges in setting and marking examinations. The resulting qualifications were to be the Associateship and Fellowship of the Royal College of Technologists.

Shortly after the Labour Government of the day had accepted this (1951), there was a General Election and a new Government (Conservative) was formed which reopened the whole discussion. The proposals for a technological university were again canvassed and rejected. Meanwhile advanced work was increasing in the colleges and a higher rate of grant was approved for it from 1952.

After various other suggestions had been pressed by bodies such as the Association of Technical Institutions and the Parliamentary and Scientific Committee, the development of colleges of advanced technology, shorn of all junior work, was projected in a White Paper on *Technical Education* in 1956. This provided for the setting up of a Council on Higher Technological Awards to approve courses leading to a Diploma in Technology. The 1956 White Paper also sketched a pattern of regional, area, or local, colleges forming the base of the pvramid of which the Colleges of Advanced Technology were the apex. This followed the announcement of plans for major expansion of technological departments in various universities, notably at the Imperial College of Science in London.

In 1962, the C.A.T.s passed from local authority control to become direct-grant institutions under the Ministry of Education. The following year, the Government received the Robbins Report (see p. 288) and accepted the proposal that C.A.T.s should become autonomous university institutions awarding their own degrees, and a new Council for National Academic Awards should be created to replace the Council on Higher Technological Awards and extend its function to the supervision and moderation of degree examinations in regional and area technical colleges. It is worth noting, in view of Lord Eustace Percy's note of dissent, how little difficulty in the event arose from the method of administering the qualification Dip. Tech., and the ease with which this made its mark as an award of degree-status.

THE PERCY REPORT · 1945

COLLEGES OF TECHNOLOGY

. . . We recommend . . . the selection of a strictly limited number of technical colleges in which there should be developed technological courses of a standard comparable with that of university degree courses. The selection of these colleges must be a matter for the Ministry of Education; but we suggest that for engineering up to six colleges exclusive of any in the Greater London area, might be selected in the first instance. While these technological courses may be a distinctive feature of such colleges they would have many other activities. The conditions in any one college could obviously be adapted to suit local needs; but one would expect to find, in addition, part-time work of an advanced character for Higher National Certificate and other qualifications of similar standard. Further a very important function of these colleges would be the provision of post-graduate courses in special branches of technology . . . full or part-time . . .

[From Section 3, pp. 11–12

DEGREE OR DIPLOMA?

We have not . . . been able to reach agreement regarding the title of the technological qualification which will correspond with the university first degree. Some of us feel that its equivalence of standard should be emphasized by a similarity of title, others that a different title is needed in order to emphasize the difference in content of the courses on which it is awarded . . .

[From Section 6, p. 21

LORD EUSTACE PERCY'S RESERVATION

. . . This disagreement is important only because if our other recommendations are accepted, the issue we have left unsettled will be inherited by the proposed National Council of Technology as a troublesome legacy which will . . . delay energetic action . . .

It is not a disagreement between the University members of the Committee and other members; it is not a conflict of 'interests' . . . The issue, what qualifications are to be conferred on the students of the new colleges of technology, really raises the larger issue, what is to be the ultimate future of these colleges . . .

If higher technological education is to be developed on the scale and with the intensity which we have been convinced are necessary to the well-being of the nation, it is natural to propose that such higher studies, wherever pursued, should lead to a Bachelor's degree. For, obviously, the aim of such a policy must be to ensure that such studies will be pursued only in institutions fully competent to conduct them . . .

In all civilized countries the power to confer degrees is the distinguishing mark of a university . . . Government policy has been based on the principle that a university should be a self-governing community of teachers and students, working together in one place, mature enough to set its own standards of teaching and strong enough to resist outside pressures, public or private, political or economic . . .

A Government can have only one university policy at a time . . .

There is no escape from this in a proposal to grant university powers, not to the colleges individually nor to an external examining body, but collectively to a 'moderating' body, mainly representative of the colleges. If the intention is to develop the colleges into university institutions there need, perhaps, be no great objection to temporary arrangements, however anomalous, designed to alleviate the hardships of their apprenticeship, as the hardships of the University Colleges are alleviated by the anomalies of the external degrees of the University of London. If, on the other hand, it is intended that they should remain municipal colleges, with only such autonomy as is compatible with financial control by the representatives of the ratepayers, the privilege of thus exercising collectively university powers which cannot be entrusted to them individually could not be confined to them alone. It would have to be offered at least to university colleges and to such institutions as the Royal Colleges of Art and Music, and the Architectural Association; and I do not see how it could be logically withheld from institutions of 'Further Education' generally.

[From *Note by the Chairman on Section 6*, pp. 25-6

39 · Report of a Committee appointed by the Lord President of the Council entitled 'Scientific Manpower'. [*The Barlow Report*]

Published: *1946*

Chairman: *Sir Alan Barlow, Bart.*

Members: *Sir Edward Appleton, F.R.S.; Professor P. M. S. Blackett, F.R.S.; Mr Geoffrey Crowther; Sir Alfred Egerton, F.R.S.; Sir George Nelson; Professor S. Zuckerman, F.R.S.*

Assessors: *Dr C. P. Snow; Mr A. Gunn*

Secretary: *Mr M. T. Flett*

Terms of Reference: *To consider the policies which should govern the use and development of our scientific manpower and resources during the next 10 years, and to submit a report on very broad lines at an early date so as to facilitate forward planning in those fields which are dependent on the use of scientific manpower.*

The Committee was appointed by Mr Herbert Morrison, Lord President of the Council, in December 1945 and reported in May 1946. Sir Alan Barlow. the Chairman, was a joint second secretary at the Treasury. He retired in 1948, after a distinguished Civil Service career which had included service at the Board of Education before the first world war.

In effect this report was to determine the immediate post-war policy with regard to university expansion. It is noteworthy that, in the absence of any other instrument for framing Government policy on higher education, it fell to this committee on scientific manpower to shape the first stage in an expansion policy which led, step by step, to the Robbins Report in 1963.

Like the Percy Report, it owed its origin to the awareness that industrial growth demanded more highly-trained scientific and technological manpower. The experience of the war years had shown that this had to be organized rather than left to chance. Of the Committee, Mr Crowther, later Sir Geoffrey Crowther of the Crowther Report, was an economist, and Sir George Nelson (later Lord Nelson) was the chairman of the English Electric Co. The scientists all had extensive experience in the upper reaches of Government science, of the kind described in novels and essays by the scientific assessor to the Committee, Dr (later Lord) Snow. Professor (later Sir Solly) Zuckerman became the chief scientific adviser to the Minister of Defence, and chairman of a Scientific Manpower sub-committee of the Advisory Council on Scientific Policy.

The main recommendation of the Committee was that the universities should be expanded so as to double the output of scientists. With this went the rider, not strictly within the terms of reference, but highly important in the event, that 'a substantial expansion in the number of students studying the humanities should not be sacrificed to the need for an increased output of scientists and technologists'. In a phrase which should be remembered in view of the spate of new university foundation in the 1960s, the Committee observed: 'there is nothing sacrosanct about the present number of universities in the kingdom and we are attracted by the conception of bringing into existence at least one university which would give to the present generation the opportunity of leaving to posterity a monument of its culture'. Lord Lindsay of Birker became Principal of the University College of North Staffordshire in 1949.

The report was accepted by the Government, and the university population which in 1938–9 had numbered 50,000, topped the 100,000 mark in 1958–9.

THE BARLOW REPORT

DOUBLING THE OUTPUT OF SCIENTISTS

. . . An expansion in the output of qualified scientists involves problems that are, to a great extent, common to all faculties faced with a demand for a substantially increased output of graduates. It is hardly open to doubt that many faculties will find themselves in this position and, as we have no desire that science should receive exceptionally favourable treatment, we have in the following paragraphs, spoken where it seemed to us appropriate, in terms of the development of the universities as a whole.

THE TALENT AVAILABLE

We need to form an estimate of the proportion of the population that is inherently fitted to benefit from a university education. We attach very great importance to this question, as whatever happens, the quality of our university graduates must not be sacrificed to quantity. In few other fields are numbers of so little value compared with quality properly developed. Character, temperament and wider qualities of mind are, of course, as important as intellectual acuity and the test of fitness for the universities is not intelligence alone. Moreover, before it enters the university, intelligence must be trained and the associated personal qualities matured to a standard we would not wish to see lowered . . .

We have surveyed the results obtained in recent years on the distribution of intelligence, as measured by 'intelligence tests', among the whole population and among samples of the members of certain universities . . . At present rather less than 2% of the population reach the universities. About 5% of the whole population show, on test, an intelligence as great as the upper half of the students who amount to 1% of the population. We conclude, therefore, that only about one in five of the boys and girls, who have intelligence equal to that of the best half of the university students actually reach the universities. It cannot be assumed that all of them have the other innate capacities necessary to a university career . . . Many . . . would not desire a university career; yet there is clearly an ample reserve of intelligence in the country to allow both a doubling of university numbers and at the same time a raising of standards . . .

[From pp. 8–9

THE HUMANITIES

It is not within our province to consider the future demand for graduates in the humanities, languages and fine arts and we are not qualified to do so. We have been informed, however, that here too there exists a need for a very substantial increase in the available supply of trained ability, and if this should prove to be the case it could be a matter of great satisfaction to us. For we attach the greatest importance to the atmosphere of an association of men and women which takes all knowledge as its province and in which all branches of learning flourish in harmony. Such an atmosphere has a great part to play in completing any student's education and preventing him from becoming a narrow and cloistered specialist. In particular we would deprecate any attempt to meet the increased demand for scientists and technologists at the expense of students of other subjects (even if, as is unlikely, the Universities could be persuaded to make such an attempt) or to give any preference to science students over arts students in such matters as military service.

[From p. 11

40 · Report of the Central Advisory Council for Education (England) entitled 'Early Leaving'.

Published: *1954*

Chairman: *Sir Samuel Gurney-Dixon*

Members: *Mr A. S. Benstead; Lady Bragg; Professor C. F. Brockington; Dr J. Macalister Brew; Miss A. M. Bozman; Mr E. S. Byng; Mr H. E. Clay; Dr F. Consitt; Miss D. E. M. Gardner; Mr T. F. Gilbert; Mr R. Gould; Mr J. C. Jones; Professor A. V. Judges; Mr L. R. Missen; Miss E. H. Molyneux; Mr W. F. Oakeshott; Professor S. G. Raybould; Dr M. E. Reeves; Mr D. R. O. Thomas*

Secretary: *Mr L. R. Fletcher*

Assessor: *Mr D. G. O. Ayerst, H.M.I.*

Terms of Reference: *To consider what factors influence the age at which boys and girls leave secondary schools which provide courses beyond the minimum school-leaving age; to what extent it is desirable to increase the proportion of those who remain at school, in particular the proportion of those who remain at school roughly to the age of 18; and what steps should be taken to secure such an increase.*

The report is notable in retrospect for its presentation of the evidence of the influence of social class on school performance. It made use of a survey to discover information hitherto unknown about the class composition of grammar schools in the years following the abolition of fees.

It recommended better maintenance allowances for needy children staying on at school beyond 15. It called for legislation for the payment of family allowances in respect of all children still at school. It favoured a higher proportion of grammar school places in secondary education.

REPORT ON 'EARLY LEAVING' · 1954

SOCIAL SELECTION

It is clear that part at least of our problem lies in the selection of boys and girls to go to grammar schools. Are there many who would have done well in a sixth form but fail to secure admission to a grammar school? Is the problem of early leaving and poor results the result of admitting many unsuitable pupils to grammar schools? Some relevant evidence is available from our sample. The schools were asked to divide the boys and girls into four groups representing three equal divisions of their original intake arranged in order of merit in the local education authority's selection test and a fourth group consisting of later transfers from secondary modern schools. We can trace the academic record (in terms of the categories defined in paragraph 20 above) of the children in each of these groups (which we call 'selection groups'). . . .

The great majority of boys and girls in the sample can be classified according to the nature of their fathers' occupations; and, armed with this knowledge of circumstances which reflect the social background, we can see what relation it has both to the chances of admission to a grammar school and to a successful career in it.

TABLE J

Occupational Background of Pupils at Maintained and Direct Grant Schools

	Father's occupation					
	Professional and managerial	Clerical	Skilled	Semi-skilled	Un-skilled	
	%	%	%	%	%	
All schools	15	4	51	18	12	100
Grammar schools	25·0	10·3	43·7	15·3	5·6	100
Sixth forms	43·7	12·0	37·0	5·8	1·5	100

The figures in the top line are calculated from the 1951 Census returns; the other figures are derived from our sample. The comparison leaves little doubt that by the time the local education authorities hold their allocation examination at 11 the children of certain social groups have as a whole begun scholastically to outstrip those at the other end of the scale, and that the same process is continued among those selected from grammar schools during their time there. We do not assume that this is solely due to environment. . . .

If the figures shown in the two lower lines of Table J were all the evidence about the performance at the grammar school of children with differing social backgrounds, it might mean no more than that the same boys and girls who had done best in the selection test at 11 continued to excel in their passage through the school and, since there already were more of them from professional and managerial homes than from unskilled workers' (as Table 7 in Appendix II shows), it would not be surprising to find that the proportion staying on for sixth form work was higher.

We have seen, however, in paragraph 34 that many pupils who do well at 11 do less well at 16 and *vice versa*. Table K analyses this by parental occupations.

TABLE K

Comparison of Pupils' Achievements at beginning and end of their Grammar School Life (Maintained Grammar Schools only)

Selection group at 11	Academic category at 16–18	Professional and managerial	Clerical	Skilled	Semi-skilled	Un-skilled
		%	%	%	%	%
1	A B C	79·9	64·6	60·1	46·8	29·6
	D	10·2	16·8	13·6	15·4	16·3
	E F	9·9	18·6	26·4	37·9	54·0
	All	100	100	100	100	100
2	A B C	61·8	53·3	42·6	27·7	25·6
	D	12·8	15·2	16·5	14·6	12·0
	E F	25·4	31·5	40·9	57·7	62·4
	All	100	100	100	100	100
3	A B C	48·3	36·3	32·6	22·8	12·8
	D	18·2	21·5	15·6	15·1	10·7
	E F	33·5	42·2	51·8	62·1	76·4
	All	100	100	100	100	100

It will be seen that the improvement between 11 and 16 which has raised many pupils from the bottom selection group to the highest academic categories is most common (amounting to 48·3 per cent.) among those from professional and managerial occupations, while the corresponding deterioration which has caused many who were placed in the top selection group at 11 to be found by 16 in the lowest academic categories is most common among the children of unskilled workers (54·0 per cent.) and semi-skilled workers (37·9 per cent.). There are, of course, plenty of pupils whose fathers are of professional or managerial standing who were in the lowest selection group at 11 and are still in the lowest academic categories at 16. Similarly, among the children of semi-skilled or unskilled workers 46·8 per cent. and 29·6 per cent. respectively of those who were in the top selection group at 11 were also in the highest academic categories at 16–18.

Table K is concerned solely with actual academic achievements. It might perhaps be suggested that the poor showing of children from the homes of semi-skilled and unskilled workers was caused largely by their family tradition being against a long school life and certainly against a sixth form career; that if they had not had a high proportion of very early leavers their academic performance might have been similar to that of other social groups. Table L, however, shows how closely the schools' estimate of their pupils capacity follows the general pattern of Table K.

TABLE L

Comparison of Pupils' Achievement at beginning and Schools' Estimate of Capacity at end of School Life (Maintained Grammar Schools only)

Selection group	Best suited for course leading to:	Father's occupation				
		Professional and managerial	Clerical	Skilled	Semi-skilled	Un-skilled
		%	%	%	%	%
1	Two Advanced subjects . . .	70·8	55·6	46·6	34·0	21·0
	General sixth . .	12·6	15·7	14·5	11·7	16·8
	Ordinary level only	16·7	28·7	38·9	54·3	62·1
	All	100	100	100	100	100
2	Two Advanced subjects . . .	42·0	33·5	26·4	13·0	15·5
	General sixth . .	20·2	11·9	14·9	12·1	7·3
	Ordinary level only	37·7	54·5	58·6	74·9	77·2
	All	100	100	100	100	100
3	Two Advanced subjects . . .	26·1	20·2	17·1	9·3	4·7
	General sixth . .	21·9	12·5	12·2	9·2	4·7
	Ordinary level only	51·9	67·4	70·7	81·5	90·6
	All	100	100	100	100	100

The figures in Tables K and L show unmistakably how often home background influences the use which a boy or girl will make of a grammar school education. In our analysis we have been concerned only with broad classifications, and we are well aware that many individual children of well-to-do parents find little support at home for hard work at school and academic ambition, while many children from very poor homes have parents who know the worth of the education they themselves missed. Still it is beyond doubt true that a boy whose father is of professional or managerial standing is more likely to find his home circumstances favourable to the demands of grammar school work than one whose father is an unskilled or semi-skilled worker. The latter is handicapped.

[From Chapter 3, pp. 12–20

THE INFLUENCE OF THE HOME

The figures quoted in Table K in Chapter III . . . show clearly the extent to which a child's home background influences his performance at school. One of the significant findings to which we wish particularly to call attention concerns the children of semi-skilled and unskilled workers. Of the 1,621 children in our sample who entered the grammar school from these two classes, 917, or more than half, failed to get as many as three passes at Ordinary level, and of these 520 left before the end of their fifth year. 32 per cent. and 37 per cent. respectively of the failures in these two ways, compared with 21 per cent. of the whole entry, were from these types of homes. Our sample tells us, therefore, that of approximately 16,000 children who in 1946 entered grammar schools throughout England from such homes, about 9,000 failed to get three passes, at Ordinary level, and of these about 5,000 left before the end of their fifth year.

So many of the unskilled workers' children achieved little that it will be worth while considering them separately. The first point to observe is the low rate of entry from the unskilled workers' home. The number of children from unskilled workers' families who might have been found in our grammar school sample if the proportion were the same as in the population as a whole is about 927; the actual number was 436. This suggests that some 5,000 children from unskilled workers' homes who might have been expected, if the yield from unskilled workers' homes were the same from other homes, to enter grammar schools in England in 1946 did not qualify for admission. The second important finding is the high rate of academic failure among those who did. Of the 436 children admitted 284, or two-thirds, left without as many as three passes at Ordinary level. Thus, of about 4,360 children from unskilled workers' homes who entered grammar schools, only about 1,500 obtained the benefit that the grammar school is specifically designed to give. At a higher level the wastage was even more marked: on the same calculation only 230, or one in 20, obtained two Advanced passes or entered for two Advanced subjects. These represent 1·4 per cent. of the

17,000 children who took advanced courses, about one-ninth of the proportion in which unskilled workers' children are found in the population as a whole.

[From Chapter 6, p. 34

We have been impressed above all with the far-reaching influence of a child's home background. We have traced the school records of children in different social groups and we have found that from the children of parents in professional or managerial occupations at one extreme to the children of unskilled workers at the other there is a steady and marked decline in performance at the grammar school, in the length of school life, and in academic promise at the time of leaving. This is not a mere development of the better performance at the age of 11 of children in certain groups; it reflects a widespread changing of places in academic order between 11 and 16 or 18 (paragraphs 40–44, 90–91).

[From Chapter 9, p. 56

41 · White Paper on Technical Education. 1956

The White Paper appeared shortly after a speech by Sir Winston Churchill at Woodford in the autumn of 1955 – one of his few public utterances after he retired from Downing Street – in which he drew attention to Russian advances in technology and technical education. It proposed a five-year, £100m programme of expansion at the technical colleges to go hand in hand with plans announced earlier (1953) for expansion in the technology departments of certain university departments.

The White Paper envisaged an expansion of technical education at all levels. For the higher level technologist, the White Paper sought to increase full-time study by the extension of sandwich courses and in particular by the creation of a new category of college, the Colleges of Advanced Technology, in which the major part of the advanced work would be concentrated (see introduction to extract from the Percy Report, p. 226).

WHITE PAPER ON 'TECHNICAL EDUCATION' · 1956

INTRODUCTION

Between 1938 and 1955 the number of university students in science and technology has doubled and since . . . 1944 . . ., more schools and technical colleges have been built, more teachers have been recruited and more interest has been shown in education by parents and employers than in any corresponding period in our history.

But this is nothing like enough. From the U.S.A., Russia and Western Europe comes the challenge to look to our system of technical education to see whether it bears comparison with what is being done abroad. Such comparisons cannot be made accurately because standards and systems of education vary so much, but it is clear enough that all these countries are making an immense effort to train more scientific and technical manpower and that we are in danger of being left behind. . . .

We do not need the spur of foreign examples. Our own circumstances show clearly the policies which we must pursue. The aims are to strengthen the foundations of our economy, to improve the standards of living of our people, and to discharge effectively our manifold responsibilities overseas. Success in each case will turn largely on our ability to secure a steady increase in industrial output, in productive investment, and in exports of goods and services of the highest quality at competitive prices. One industry after another is being compelled to follow its competitor, supplier or customer in modernizing its techniques, knowing that unless new materials are discovered and new methods applied, British industry may fall behind in the race. The pace of change is quickening, and with it both the need and the demand for technical education.

The demand will be no less urgent from countries overseas. The countries and territories of the Commonwealth look to the United Kingdom for help in the provision of the scientists, engineers and technicians indispensable to the execution of the development projects to which they are already committed and to the further expansion which they will certainly wish to undertake. It is our duty to help them as much as we can. There are many under-developed countries outside the Commonwealth who also look to us for technical manpower. This we must be prepared to supply in increasing quantity by providing more places at universities and technical colleges for overseas students and more British experts to work or teach abroad.

We face, then, an intense and rising demand for scientific manpower and by no means only for men and women with the highest qualifications. Every technologist relies on technicians and craftsmen to translate his plans into products. It would be a great mistake to increase the output of technologists without adequately supporting them at the lower levels from which in any event many of them are drawn. Much therefore depends on strengthening the base of the pyramid of technical education by improving the education in the schools and raising the numbers of school-leavers who are able and willing to take successfully the courses offered at technical colleges.

Here the prospects are good. The romance of science is catching on as can be seen even in the toy shops. Every year parents and children are taking a greater interest in technical education. More boys and girls are staying on at school after the statutory leaving age; more are taking science and more are continuing their education after school; and more are succeeding in the courses on which they have embarked. These are welcome signs that the base of the pyramid is growing stronger. It will also grow larger, since the age-groups from which industry and the technical colleges are now recruiting are the smallest for a hundred years. Soon the figures will climb upwards. Last year the number of 18 year olds in Britain was 640,000; in ten years' time it will be about 850,000.

Technical education must not be too narrowly vocational or too confined to one skill or trade. Swift change is the characteristic of our age, so that a main purpose of the technical education of the future must be to teach boys and girls to be adaptable. Versatility has been the aim of a classical education; technical studies should lead to a similar versatility and should, therefore, be firmly grounded on the fundamentals of mathematics and science. It is much easier to adopt new ideas and new techniques when the principles on which they are based are already familiar.

The range of technical education goes far beyond the study of materials and mechanics. Accountancy, costing, salesmanship, commercial skills of all kinds, including foreign languages, are equally important to a great trading nation. Full employment brings new problems which are more likely to be soluble the wider is the understanding of how our economy works. Such subjects as economics, business management, wage systems and human relations must now be given more prominence. . . .

In a sense, all technical progress rests upon the common foundation of language, and more attention will have to be given to the teaching of good plain English, the use of which saves time and money and avoids trouble. Without it bridges are hard to build over the gulfs that separate experts in different specialized subjects not only from the general public but from one another. Moreover a place must always be found in technical studies for liberal education. The time available often limits what can be done in the way of introducing into the curriculum subjects such as history, literature and the arts, but in any event a wide treatment of scientific and technical subjects is essential if students who are to occupy responsible positions in industry are to emerge from their education with a broad outlook. We cannot afford either to fall behind in technical accomplishments or to neglect spiritual and human values.

[From pp. 4–5

TECHNOLOGISTS

The mixture of earning and learning made possible by technical colleges continues to demonstrate its success. The students have proved their worth in practice and employers want more of them. The present annual output from advanced courses at technical colleges in England and Wales (including roughly 1,000 who gain degrees in science and about 500 who gain degrees in technology) is about 9,500. The proportion of these who ultimately become technologists in the sense in which the term is used in this Paper . . . is not precisely known, but is probably about one half. The Government now propose to raise the capacity of advanced courses at technical colleges as soon as possible from 9,500 to about 15,000.

Advanced full-time and sandwich courses

As technologies grow more complex and the need for versatility increases, the strain of reaching these high qualifications by evening work or by studies on one or two days a week becomes more severe. There will be many, especially those whose ambitions do not extend beyond the Higher National Certificate, who will wish or will be obliged by circumstances to continue to take part-time courses. But the Government believe that for the highest technological qualifications sandwich courses will become more and more appropriate. These are courses lasting four or five years and involving alternate periods, usually of three to six months, of theoretical education in a technical college and specially designed practical training in industry.

These advanced courses will suit the able worker who has already had experience in industry and should also attract an increasing number of boys and girls who, when they leave school at eighteen, feel the urge to start their careers as soon as possible. . . .

Sandwich courses at the highest level will, no doubt, be eligible for the new Award to be given by the National Council for Technological Awards . . . [Diploma in Technology]. . . . This Council has been set up on the recommendation of the National Advisory Council on Education for Industry and Commerce. At the moment, the only national qualification of sufficiently high level for many of the best students attending technical colleges is the London External Degree. This suffers from the disadvantages inherent in external control and is limited to a few technologies. It was therefore considered to be unsuitable as a permanent qualification for colleges of advanced technology. In the National Advisory Council's view the best way of overcoming the difficulty was to create a new qualification of high standing which would allow the colleges freedom to plan their own courses in consultation with industry and the professional bodies and to conduct their own examinations. The National Council for Technological Awards, which is an independent body, was recently established to create and administer this new qualification and to satisfy itself that conditions of teaching, and the syllabuses and examinations, are satisfactory. This is a vital task: the work of the Council will do much to determine the scope and quality of advanced technological studies in the next generation. . . .

Colleges of Advanced Technology

The Government consider that the bulk of full-time or sandwich courses should be carried on in colleges which concentrate on advanced courses of technological level.

Teachers capable of taking charge of such courses are scarce and the equipment they need is often expensive. Moreover, an advanced course in one technology often cannot be efficient unless allied technologies are studied to a similar level in the same college. The college must also be strong in the appropriate fundamental sciences. And opportunities for research are essential in order to promote fully effective cooperation between industry and the staff of the technical college.

The Government now wish to see the proportion of advanced work at these colleges vigorously increased, so that as many of them as possible may develop speedily into colleges of advanced technology. The Minister of Education will discuss forthwith with the local education authorities concerned how this can be done within the framework of the building programme announced in this Paper. . . .

The building up of colleges of advanced technology will not prevent the development elsewhere in suitable cases of advanced courses, particularly those of a part-time nature. Indeed, part-time advanced courses are already provided in some 150 local colleges conveniently placed for the students and part-time staff who work in industry. These courses make a vital contribution to the total output of technologists, especially by the Higher National Certificate route, and they will be expected to continue and develop as long as they are efficient and can attract enough students.

There are those who argue that a college of advanced technology cannot be successfully administered within the framework of local government. The Government do not accept this.* Local authorities take great pride in such colleges and often have been willing to find more money for them than the pressure on national resources has allowed them to spend. To remove these colleges from local control against the wishes of the authorities could be justified neither by past experience nor by the hope of better results from a more central control. This statement is, however, subject to one qualification: the Government rely on the local authorities to work effectively together in planning the provision of courses and – just as important – in making it possible for students to attend the courses which best suit their needs, whether these courses are in their own or another authority's area.

Colleges of advanced technology must also have the independence appropriate to the academic level of their work. Some local authorities have pointed the way by establishing strong governing bodies widely representative of industry and with power to spend within the heads of annual estimates approved by the authority. The Minister is taking steps in consultation with the local education authorities concerned to ensure

* Colleges of Advanced Technology were removed from the control of local authorities in 1962 and became Direct Grant Institutions. Following the Robbins Report of 1963 they became independent university institutions, with access to the University Grants Committee.

the general adoption of this policy for all colleges of advanced technology. He also proposes to review the accommodation and equipment of each such college and to satisfy himself that the staff are adequately qualified and have appropriate freedom to plan their own courses.

[From pp. 15–17

42 · Report of the Central Advisory Council for Education (England) entitled *15 to 18*. Volume One: *Report* Volume Two: *Statistics*. [*The Crowther Report*]

Published: *1959*

Chairman: *Sir Geoffrey Crowther**

Members: *Mr G. S. Bosworth; Mr M. H. Brown; Mr M. H. Cadbury; Alderman S. M. Caffyn; Mr A. B. Clegg; Dr H. Frazer; Mr T. F. Gilbert; Miss B. A. Godwin; Miss M. G. Green; Dr V. M. Grubb; Dr R. Holroyd; Miss E. M. Huxstep; Lord James of Rusholme; Miss A. P. Jephcott; Professor A. V Judges; Mr B. G. Lampard-Vachell; Sir Patrick Linstead, F.R.S.; Professor N. F. Mott, F.R.S.; Mr W. F. Oakeshott; Mr S. H. Porter; Professor S. G. Raybould; Dr M. E. Reeves; Professor T. S. Simey; Mr G. H. Sylvester; Dr P. F. R. Venables; Mr H. A. Warren; Miss E. M. Wedekind; Mr J. V. C. Wray; Mr B. W. M. Young; Mr D. G. O. Ayerst, H.M.I. (Assessor); Mr J. A. Humphreys (Secretary); Miss M. L. Smith (Clerk) (Ministry of Education)*

Miss C. Avent was co-opted by the Council.

Lieutenant-General Sir Kenneth McLean, K.C.B., K.B.E. (who resigned for domestic reasons), Mr O. W. Mitchell (who resigned for reasons of health) and the late Dr J. Macalister Brew (who died in May 1957) were also members during the consideration of the present terms of reference.

Terms of Reference: *The education of boys and girls between the ages of 15 and 18.*

The remit to the Central Advisory Council in March 1956 was made at a time when it appeared that the supply of teachers was improving. The birth rate appeared up to 1956 to be conforming to the general pattern predicted by the Royal Commission on Population in 1949 – that is, it seemed that after the bulge in the immediate post-war years it would settle down somewhere mid-way between the top of the bulge and the pre-war level.

Plans were being laid for the introduction of the three-year course of teacher training on the assumption (which proved far from correct) that during the 1960s the number of teachers entering the service would bring about a rapid reduction in the pupil-teacher ratio.

* Geoffrey Crowther (1907–1972) was educated at Leeds Grammar School, Oundle School, and Clare College, Cambridge, Yale and Columbia. He was President of the Cambridge Union in 1928. Editor of *The Economist* from 1938–56, he subsequently became a director of companies including Economist Newspapers Ltd, Trust Houses Ltd, Commercial Union Assurance Ltd, and Hazel Sun Ltd. He was a member of the Barlow Committee in 1945 (see p. 230). He was knighted in 1957 and made a life peer in 1968.

In these circumstances it was possible to prepare for the further application of the 1944 Education Act and, in particular, to form a view about priorities to be accorded to raising the school-leaving age to 16 on the one hand and introducing compulsory part-time day education to 18 on the other.

By the time the report appeared, the school situation had been transformed by the rise in the birth rate and the steady decline in the marriage age leading to more children and fewer teachers. Far from being enough teachers for a rapid reduction in the size of classes, the schools were faced with a struggle to keep the existing over-sized classes within bounds. By 1964, when the Government announced that the leaving age would be raised in 1970–1,* the prospective dip in school numbers in the late sixties had disappeared. The report unanimously recommended that the school-leaving age should be raised to 16 between 1966 and 1968. For this, the Council was prepared to accept somewhat larger classes than the regulations (not yet enforced) of a maximum of 40 children in a primary and 30 in a secondary class would allow (teacher-pupil ratio of 1 : 19 instead of 1 : 16). They wanted the raising of the leaving age to be followed in the early 1970s by the introduction, area by area, of County Colleges and compulsory continued part-time education. With this, they recommended 'a strong Youth Service'.

They set great store by an early announcement of intention on the part of the Government: the acceptance of the target date for raising the leaving age, and a reaffirmation of belief in county colleges.

The report advocated a 20-year programme of educational development aimed at ensuring that by 1980 half the boys and girls in the country should stay in full-time education to 18. The Council believed that there was a great waste of talent in a situation in which only 12 per cent stayed to 17 and 6 per cent to 20. They were particularly concerned about the 'second quartile' in the ability range, and the extent to which early leaving was a social rather than an academic phenomenon.

They made a lengthy survey of the advanced and extended courses in modern schools, urging that an extra year of compulsory schooling 'should offer new and challenging courses and not be simply a continuation of what has gone before'. They urged that all children able to attempt some subjects in GCE 'O' level should be allowed to do so. They were against national examinations at standards below 'O' level but recognized the value of regional, or better, local examinations at 15 plus for about a third of the modern school population.

A section of the report considered the Sixth Form. It endorsed the principle of 'education in depth' (specialization) but condemned excessive and premature specialization which in large measure it blamed on the shortage of university places. It introduced the concept of 'numeracy', i.e. a general understanding of scientific method and language, which arts students needed to acquire, comparable with the 'literacy' which should be demanded of science students. This led to consideration of the proper use of 'minority time' – sixth form time not earmarked for main examination subjects – and

* The raising of the leaving age was postponed by two years to 1972–3 as part of the budgetary cuts which, in January 1968, followed the devaluation of the pound in November 1967.

the rejection of a general course embracing both arts and science at a more modest level.

The report also examined technical education and in particular part-time technical education, showing the inefficiency of much day-release and evening work and pointing in the direction of block release and sandwich courses. It ended with a strong recommendation for much more educational research.

An important part of the report dealt with the sociological background to education and the extent to which able pupils fail to progress as well as they should for reasons of home background and family attitudes (see extract). The statistical basis for these sections of the report is provided in volume two which includes an analysis of the Survey of National Service Recruits, showing how educational attainment correlates more closely with social background than measured ability.

THE CROWTHER REPORT · 1959

This report is about the education of English boys and girls aged from 15 to 18. Most of them are not being educated. . . . . If we are to build a higher standard of living – and, what is more important, if we are to have higher standards in life – we shall need a firmer educational base than we have today. Materially and morally, we are compelled to go forward. . . .

WHO GETS FULL-TIME EDUCATION?

This all-important group of full-time pupils has four characteristics. . . . The first is . . . that, as far as numbers go, there is no distinction to be drawn between boys and girls – the proportions of each in full-time education between 15 and 18 are very nearly the same. . . .

The second . . . is the extent to which social background enters into the decision about which boys and girls will continue in full-time education beyond the minimum leaving age. This was brought out in the Council's previous report on *Early Leaving* and is further illustrated from the survey of Army and R.A.F. recruits. . . . Table 2 shows clearly that among the families of manual workers it is still the exception for a child to stay at school after he is legally free to go.

The third characteristic is that the available resources of men (and presumably also of women) of high 'ability' are not fully used by the present system. Table 3 makes it clear that, among National Service men entering the Army, while nine-tenths of those in the top 10 per cent in ability stayed at school voluntarily for at least one year more than they had to, over four-tenths of them (42 per cent) left by 16. . . .

The fourth characteristic, at least in maintained schools, is that the great majority of boys and girls whose full-time education extends beyond 15 are the first generation in their families to attend a grammar

TABLE 2

Percentage Distribution of National Service Recruits to the Army and R.A.F. by Age on Leaving School and Father's Occupational Background

Father's occupation	Number = 100 per cent	Recruit's age on leaving school			
		15 or less	16	17	18 or more
		per cent	per cent	per cent	per cent
Professional or managerial	929	*25*	*24*	*17*	*34*
Clerical or other non-manual	882	*59*	*22*	*9*	*10*
Skilled workers	3,666	*78*	*15*	*3*	*4*
Semi-skilled	946	*85*	*11*	*2*	*2*
Unskilled	852	*92*	*6*	*1*	*1*
All above Groups	7,275	*72*	*15*	*5*	*8*

school. The Social Survey brought out the fact that both parents of two-thirds of the boys and girls who attended selective schools (grammar schools and technical schools) themselves left school at 14, which was in their day the legal minimum leaving-age. Only 12 per cent of the boys and girls came from homes where both parents had had a longer education than the legal minimum. This is a measure both of the task that

TABLE 3

Percentage Distribution of 'Ability' among 5,940 National Service Recruits to the Army who Left School at Various Ages

Ability groups	Number = 100 per cent	School-leaving age			
		15 or less	16	17	18 or more
		per cent	per cent	per cent	per cent
1 (highest)	681	*9*	*33*	*17*	*41*
2	1,824	*65*	*22*	*6*	*7*
3	1,014	*94*	*4*	*1*	*1*
4	1,184	*98*	*2*	*Tce*	*Tce*
5	863	*98*	*1*	—	*1*
6 (lowest)	374	*97*	*3*	*Tce*	*Tce*
All Groups	5,940	*77*	*12*	*4*	*7*

Tce = trace, less than 0·5 per cent.

TABLE 4

School-leaving Age for (a) All Men in Ability Groups 1 and 2 and (b) Sons of Manual Workers (except in Agriculture)

	Number = 100 per cent	School-leaving age			
		15 or earlier	16	17	18 or later
		per cent	per cent	per cent	per cent
All men in Ability Group 1	681	9	33	17	41
Manual workers' sons in Ability Group 1	295	19	44	13	24
All men in Ability Group 2	1,824	65	22	6	7
Manual workers' sons in Ability Group 2	1,286	75	20	3	2

confronts English schools at the present, and of the promise that lies ahead of them.

[From Chapter 1, pp. 3-9

RAISING THE LEAVING AGE: INDIVIDUAL CONSIDERATIONS

There are two main arguments for raising the school-leaving age. One starts from the social and personal needs of 15 year-olds, and regards education as one of the basic rights of the citizen; the other is concerned with education as a vital part of the nation's capital investment. As far as the former argument is concerned, nothing has happened in the last twenty years, or could happen, which would weaken our agreement with the view of John Dewey that what the best and wisest parent wants for his own child the community must want for all its children. A boy or girl of 15 is not sufficiently mature to be exposed to the pressures of the world of industry or commerce. . . .

The onset of puberty is earlier than it used to be . . . and there is no doubt that boys also mature earlier . . . But this is not true of the emotional and social consequences of puberty . . .

This is surely the period in which the welfare of the individual ought to come before any marginal contribution he or she could make to the national income . . .

Secondary education is, then, in our view essentially the education of the adolescent. And adolescence coincides much better physically than it does psychologically with the present length of the compulsory secondary course. Until they are 16, boys and girls need an environment designed for their needs. Each extension of the school-leaving age obviously brings the schools increasingly difficult emotional and social problems, especially perhaps with the education of girls. But the difficulty of the problems is no reason for refusing to face them, though it is a reason for considering very carefully what qualities are needed in the teachers who will have to deal with them. We may hide, but we do not solve, teenage problems simply by letting boys and girls leave school. Indeed, we condemn many of them to do without the help they need. It is true that the protective side of education is likely to be quite ineffective if the educational side is unsatisfying, but we are convinced that there are sufficient important, fresh educational interests which can be aroused in boys and girls during their teens which are today often left only half-exploited, or barely touched upon, when they leave school.

[From Chapter 11, pp. 108–16

RAISING THE LEAVING AGE: NATIONAL CONSIDERATIONS

It does not seem likely that we shall achieve our object quickly if we limit ourselves to voluntary persuasion. . . . It would mean a reversal of the present outlook of the manual workers of the country as a whole. . . .

If the abler children of the lower social groups, and if members of large families from all but the highest groups are to receive a full secondary education, it does not look as if it can be achieved without increasing the length of compulsory school life. . . .

All in all, it seems most unwise to rely on the unassisted effects of economic conditions to continue to produce advances in education of the kind that have been seen in the past decade. It is unlikely that, without compulsion, it will become the accepted thing in all classes of society for boys and girls of average intelligence to stay at school until 16. In the majority of neighbourhoods, the question of whether to stay on at school will still have to be individually debated, the presumption being that it is better to leave unless there is a strong reason to the contrary. In such a situation we believe the odds are weighted against the national interest. If there is going to be less pressure from industry for juvenile labour, then the real cost to the country of taking a whole age-group out of the labour market will also be less, especially if this results in their being better equipped when eventually they come into it. It is by no means so clear that, in default of collective action, it will be to the economic advantage of an individual boy or girl to stay longer than he must at school, especially if his ability is marginal to the occupation he desires. Without a rise in the statutory leaving age, the opportunity may be missed.

That the average worker in industry and commerce requires much more education than was needed only a short time ago is the result of two separate tendencies that have combined to produce the same effect.

On the one hand, the people of superior intelligence who used to spend their lives in middling jobs because they were denied educational opportunities in their youth, now pass into the grammar schools and the universities or colleges of advanced technology and finish up in the professions. On the other hand, there has been a great increase in the number of skilled and professional jobs, which have sucked up into higher ranks many whose abilities would never in the past have got them so high. The result has been to create a universal upgrading of the sort of post that is filled by a given level of intelligence.

More time and care must be spent on education and training . . . It is not only at the top but almost to the bottom of the pyramid that the scientific revolution of our times needs to be reflected in a longer educational process.

The case for raising the minimum leaving age is further strengthened by the lack of opportunities for part-time day education for girls. Boys have been more fortunate in securing the help of part-time day release. Roughly a third of all boys in employment under 18 now get it. Few girls have this opportunity – only 8% . . .

The Fifth Year as a Transition

The economic argument for another year of compulsory schooling – the argument from what the public interest demands – therefore seems to us to be a very strong one. There is, however, one condition in it which has been implicit in much that we have written but should now be made explicit. If there is to be a fifth year of secondary education for all, it should not be simply one more year such as the other four have been. When boys and girls left school at 12 to go to work, it would have been nonsense to talk of the last year at school as a transitional year. They were children right up to the time they left school, and beyond. But by 15, and still more by 16, they have already acquired a good deal of independence. There is still an abrupt transition from school to work, but there is no sharp break in the way they spend their spare time – many of them have begun before they leave school to adopt in their leisure hours the patterns of the late teens. This imposes a serious responsibility on the schools, of which they are aware. We single out two aspects from many for comment. The first concerns working hours. It is natural that as boys and girls grow older their waking day and their working day should grow longer. When they pass from the infant school to the junior school, half-an-hour a day is added to the length of lessons. But no further addition is made to official school hours whether a boy is 8 or 18, and he continues to go to school only on about half the days in the year. As soon as he leaves school, however, his hours of work become much longer and his holidays much shorter. Which is right? If the school-leaving age were still 14, nearly everybody would agree, we think, that the school day and year were much closer than industry's to what boys and girls ought to be putting in at the end of their school life. Now that the leaving age is 15, a good many people have doubts whether school conditions should not be brought for everybody (as they already are for a good many) a little nearer to subsequent working conditions. When the school-leaving age is raised to 16 these doubts will, we think rightly, become virtual certainties. They apply, however, only where the actual hours spent in school are the sum total of work done by the pupils. Wherever homework is set, and conscientiously done, the balance is substantially redressed. The experience of comprehensive and modern schools is showing that homework can profitably form part of the education of far more boys and girls than used to be believed, but it cannot be anything like the whole solution for pupils who are markedly below average. Allowance must also be made for other forms of work quite unconnected with school. . . .

The second point concerns the feeling of growing independence and usefulness that 15 year-old boys and girls ought to have, which is often closely connected with the amount of money they have to command. There is no doubt that the world as it has grown to be offers them tempting opportunities for spending considerable sums of money on clothes, sport and entertainment, and that these luxuries have become virtual necessities to many. . . .

Some at least of us feel that the raising of the minimum leaving age to 16 may increase the frustration of prolonged dependence on parents for every penny of spending money. . . .

There is a vital responsibility laid on the local authorities, within the statutory powers they already possess, to see that the conditions under which pupils can earn money are reasonable and do not stand in the way of their education and their healthy physical growth. . . .

There is, then, a strong case on economic grounds for raising the school-leaving age; but, if this were the only reason for doing so, it might not be a sufficient reason. . . .

The economic argument alone, in fact, stops a little way short of being finally conclusive. We come back, therefore, to clinch the matter, to the point from which this chapter started. Our main case is not economic at all. It rests on the conviction that all boys and girls of 15 have much to learn, and that school (in the broadest sense) and not work is the place for this. 'Secondary Education for All' will not be a reality until it is provided for all up to the age of 16. We believe that this is a duty which society owes all its young citizens just as we individually recognise it as an obligation in our own families.

[From Chapter 12, pp. 117–31

PART-TIME TECHNICAL EDUCATION

The first defect – chronologically the first, not the most important – is the lack of integration between the education that students receive in the technical colleges and the education they have received at school. . . .

Here and there examples can be found of close co-operation between the schools of an area and the local college of further education, but we have the impression that in general it is sporadic and not very effectual. We do not believe that the fault lies more on one side than on the other. . . .

The course in which a boy finds himself is all too likely to depend upon accidents of his employment or his unguided choice than upon any deliberate assessment of what he is qualified to profit by. . . .

The second defect of the system as it is today is the very high proportion of effort put into it that is wasted, or at least attains goals far short of what was originally aimed at. Only one student in 11 succeeds in climbing the National Certificate ladder from bottom to top, and only one in 30 does so in the time for which the course was designed. Against the background of the nation's present and future needs for trained manpower, these wastage rates are shocking. . . . There is no escaping from the fact that the ladder of further education is at present too steep for most of those who are attempting to climb it. Something could be done by better methods of selection: many of those who now enter upon courses have not the ability to succeed in them; it should be possible to identify them and steer them towards other courses where their chances will be better. But this is not the only, nor even the main explanation. . . . Very many of those who do succeed, do so only at the cost of giving up to their studies, over many years, the whole of their spare time. Nowhere else in our educational system do we expect such sacrifices for success. Not only does the present system bear very hardly on the young people who are working their way through it, it also deprives the country every year of thousands of potential technicians. . . . . If the ladder cannot be made less steep, the only alternative is to provide more help for the climbers.

For this, the prescription is more time. If we were confined to one comment and one recommendation about English further education, it would be this. At every stage, and on every level, the need is for more time, for less pressure on both staff and students. Even a little more time would, in our opinion, much more than proportionately raise the educational yield. . . . .

There is one aspect of the need for time on which we wish to make a special comment. We are unhappy about the reliance that is still placed on evening classes for this age-group. . . .

The possibility of rising in the world by evening study has historically been one of the great safety-valves of English society. . . . We do not think it is possible (even if it were desirable, which is arguable) to ban all evening classes. But we are glad to observe that much less reliance is placed on them than was the case twenty years ago and we should like to see this progress continued. With this object in view, we make three recommendations. The first is that no boy or girl under the age of 18 should be expected to follow a course of further education that relies entirely upon evening classes; those industries and professions that do now expect this of their young employees should be invited to reconsider their practices. Secondly, we think that any course that requires more than one evening of classes a week of a boy or girl under 18, in addition to part-time day classes, is too heavy and should be rearranged; and even one evening a week may be too heavy if there is a considerable burden of homework or reading. . . .

We do not urge the necessity of providing more time simply as a matter of justice to these young students, but also because it would make possible a great improvement in the quality of the education they receive. This brings us to the third of the major points we want to make. The education provided in the colleges today is far too narrowly concentrated on the immediate vocational target. Some of it is perilously close to the line that separates education from mere instruction. Even where this is not so, the syllabuses are so heavy (inevitably so) and the time so short that the students are unable to lift their eyes from the immediate objectives even to glance at the surrounding intellectual country. More time is an essential condition for any remedy; but more time will not achieve anything by itself. There is need for a great deal of thought about what can be done to make these courses, while still serving their vocational purposes, come closer to the ideal of what a balanced education should be for young people of above average intelligence. We do not think this should be done only, or even perhaps mainly, by the addition of courses in the humanities – though there should be some movement in that direction. We think as much could be done by broadening out the syllabuses in some of the technical subjects themselves.

[From Chapter 32, pp. 366–9

THE APPROACH TO THE SIXTH FORM

It is important to be clear about what happens to boys and girls in the last years of their way to the Sixth Form. Some very important decisions are commonly made in the fourth and fifth years of the main school course, that is at the ages of 14+ and 15+. It is then that routes begin to diverge through the choice of one or other 'option' . . . whether or not to start a second modern language, or whether or not to take additional science. . . .

The pressure to provide the options that look ahead to Sixth Form work . . . inevitably leads to other things being crowded out . . . The practical subjects have become optional. . . . This is true, too, of three quarters of the schools as far as art is concerned; only music remains . . . and that only in right of its secure hold on the girls' schools. . . . It is true that these subjects usually remain as options but in most maintained schools few of the more academic pupils take them, or can find time to do so in school hours. . . . If we regard the development of some pride in workmanship and some aesthetic sensibility as an important part of general education . . . we clearly cannot be content to leave it in day schools to after-school voluntary societies. . . .

The other part of the price paid for planning the curriculum from early days with an eye on university or professional requirements . . . lies in the field where family background and environment count for most. The 'English subjects' tend to go to the wall. After the third year, history and geography commonly become alternatives. . . . Our sample of inspection reports shows that, in 42 per cent of the schools, history ceased to be compulsory and became an option by the fourth year (that is about the age of 14), though in girls' schools the proportion was only 31 per cent. . . . Religious instruction . . . is . . . at this stage limited to one period a week. . . . English itself may be reduced. . . . .

The pressures that lead to this over crowding of the Fifth Form timetable come from outside the Fifth Form. . . . It would not . . . be fair . . . to blame the schools. . . . That does not mean . . . that anybody should be complacent about the effects of this 'pre-specialisation'. In our opinion, they are, on balance, bad not only because 15 is too early for the majority even of able children to say a final farewell to education on a broad front, but mainly because the existence of 'options' in these early years inevitably closes doors and freezes into permanent choices what may be no more than passing inclinations. . . .

If . . . some of the pressure could be taken off the timetable it would be possible to continue throughout the main school to give all pupils the opportunity to carry on those practical and aesthetic subjects. . . . Most 15-year-olds need plenty of time in school and the best teaching in order to become really literate in their own tongue. . . . We are certain that the effect on the schools is to produce a congestion of the main school curriculum in the fourth and fifth years which is detrimental to the real interests of most of their pupils. . . . .

[From Chapter 20, pp. 209–18

THE CURRICULUM OF THE SIXTH FORM

Specialisation . . . is a product of the nineteenth century. . . . Today an all-round education is possible only to a relatively low level. . . .

In this system of specialisation for young people while they are still at school English education is singular. Neither in Western Europe nor in North America is there anything of the sort. Even nearer to home, in Scotland, the schools insist on a much wider spread of subjects in the Sixth Form. . . .

In its essence the argument against the English Sixth Form is that it introduces specialisation too early and on too narrow a front. . . . Not only may specialisation begin before a boy knows his own mind but . . . before anybody can give valid advice on what his best course is. . . .

The other great complaint . . . is that it is on too narrow a front. This can mean two things. It may mean that the actual subjects selected for study themselves are too restricted . . . or the complaint may be about the treatment of the subject. In either case . . . the fear is that specialisation will act as a constricting frame and not a liberating agent. . . . The more he learns, it is said, the more he will be cut off from his fellows. . . .

These are telling criticisms. . . . They apply to good schools as well as bad. A third type of criticism is not the less important because it applies only to below-average schools. In a good school, the argument runs, the really good teacher with the really good pupil may find the present system a grand way of encouraging a boy to think, but in an average school the average teacher with the average pupil will do little more than cram him. If this is true, the educational argument for specialisation, as a tool to sharpen the mind, has to be discarded; and the only defence left is the utilitarian argument that it saves time in the total educational process from the infants' school to the post-graduate course. This . . . is a serious matter. . . . It is not however obvious that to cram in eight subjects would be better than to cram in two or three.

Such are the arguments against specialisation. They are effective; but it is worth noting that the broad curriculum of Europe and America is almost equally under fire. . . .

For ourselves, after considering the matter most carefully we are agreed in accepting and endorsing the English principle of specialisation, or intensive study, as it would be better described . . . There are undoubtedly some abuses. . . . But the best line of advance, in our opinion, is to reaffirm the principle and reform its application. . . .

The first step in the argument for specialisation is that able boys and girls are ready and eager by the time they are 16 – the ablest by 15 – to get down to the serious study of some aspect of human knowledge which, with the one-sided enthusiasm of the young, they allow for a time to obscure all other fields of endeavour. 'Subject Mindedness' . . . is there whether we use it or not. . . .

The second step in the argument is that concentration on a limited field leads naturally to study in depth. The boy embarks on a chain of discovery . . . No longer does he accumulate largely isolated pieces of information . . . In a word, he begins to assume responsibility for his own education . . .

The third step in the case for specialisation is that through this discipline, a boy can be introduced into one or two areas which throw light on the achievement of man and the nature of the world he lives in. . . .

The fourth step in the argument is that, given the right teaching, a boy will by the end of his school days begin to come out on the further side of 'subject-mindedness'. . . . He reaches out for a wider synthesis . . . If a boy turns that corner . . . we can be sure that, narrow as his education may have been during the last few years, he will take steps to widen it as well as deepen it.

The fifth step in the argument is that this process of intellectual growth demands a great deal of concentrated time. It virtually enforces specialisation because the time left for other subjects is bound to be small – rarely can it be more than one-third. . . . The intellectual level of any type of Sixth Form work requires subject teaching by specialists; but, if the specialist teaching is also to be personal teaching, it is necessary that the pupils themselves should also be specialists.

We have two main groups of complaints about things as they are. The first . . . concerns the specialist subjects themselves . . . The attempt is made to pour a quart of professional competence into the pint pot of a very few years . . . What is taught in any subject should be taught because it is right for the pupil at that stage of his development, and not because it will be convenient for his teachers in the next stage. . . .

Our second main criticism . . . concerns the use to which the minority time, amounting usually to between one quarter and one third of the time-table, is put . . . Little is done to make science specialists more 'literate' . . . and nothing to make arts specialists more 'numerate', if we may coin a word. . . . Some of the blame for this relative failure may perhaps rightly be put down to the pressure of the specialist subjects; but more, we feel, belongs to the way in which the minority time is organised . . . We attach great value to the English practice of specialisation. Equally, we attach great importance to those complementary elements in the Sixth Form curriculum which are designed to develop the literacy of science specialists and the numeracy of arts specialists. . . .

In our view, then . . . there should be not two but three elements in a sound Sixth Form curriculum. The first and largest should be the specialist element, on which a boy will spend, say, two thirds of his time in school and much the greater part of his homework. Secondly there should be the common element, when scientists and arts specialists should come together. And thirdly . . . there should be the complementary element, whose purposes – and in our view they must in the main be pursued separately – are to save the scientists from illiteracy and the arts specialists from innumeracy.

[From Chapter 25, pp. 257–75

43 · Report of the Departmental Committee on the Youth Service in England and Wales. [*The Albemarle Report*]

Published: *1960*
Chairman: *Lady Albemarle*
Members: *The Rt Hon. D. F. Vosper, M.P.; Mr M. J. S. Chapman; Mr R. Hoggart; Mr D. H. Howell; Mr R. A. Jackson; Miss A. P. Jephcott; Mr J. Marsh; Mr L. Paul; Rev. E. A. Shipman; Prof. A. G. Watkins; Dr J. W. Welch; Mrs E. M. Wormald*

Terms of Reference: *To review the contribution which the Youth Service of England and Wales can make in assisting young people to play their part in the life of the community, in the light of changing social and industrial conditions and of current trends in other branches of the education service; and to advise according to what priorities best value can be obtained for the money spent.*

The report was the first major departmental inquiry into the Youth Service – the name given to the various forms of voluntary and statutory youth work which were formally brought into a working relationship by the Board of Education's Circular 1486 in 1939.

During the second world war, in response to the stresses of the time, the scope of the youth service was extended, and in the White Paper on Educational Reconstruction a section was devoted to the Youth Service which envisaged its future role on a larger scale as an essential part of the education service.

The McNair Report on teacher training covered youth leaders also, but its recommendations were not put into effect, nor were those of the Jackson Report (1949) nor the Fletcher Report (1951). The first need of the Albemarle Committee, therefore, was to persuade the Government to set up an emergency training college for the training of youth leaders, to set up a Committee for the negotiation of tolerable pay scales, and put in hand long-term plans for the recruitment and training of youth leaders from three main sources: 'teachers, social workers, and mature persons with a natural gift for leadership'.

The report defined the age-range covered by the youth service as 14–20. It called for a 10-year plan, nationally and locally, involving a 'generous and imaginative building programme', and the setting up of a Youth Service Development Council to oversee it. It sought to preserve the essential character of the youth service as a mixture of voluntary and statutory provision, with financial grants from the Minister to national, and the L.E.A.s to local organizations.

The report was important for the sociological background against which it set the youth service. Mr (later Professor) Richard Hoggart's hand is clearly to be seen in Chapter 2 (see below). The Committee rejected the most stringently uplifting concepts of what a youth service should do. They refused to accept its primary aim as educational, or moral in the sense of reclaiming the lost and preventing delinquency. They laid down three legitimate aims, all or any of which justified a youth club or activity: association, training and challenge (see below).

The Government accepted the report on publication. The Emergency Training College was set up at Leicester and brought into action with all dispatch. A committee was set up on which were represented the voluntary organizations and the local education authorities and the youth leaders for the negotiation of salaries, and in due course this led to the publication of agreed scales which were not unrelated to those of teachers. The Youth Services Development Council was set up, and small but regular building programmes for youth centres began to be approved.

THE ALBEMARLE REPORT · 1960

THE WORLD OF YOUNG PEOPLE

. . . Adolescents are the litmus paper of a society . . . Today's adolescents live within a world sharply divided into two immense blocks of power; and a world under a constant threat of nuclear catastrophe. In addition, their own country's power and international status, once so great and indisputable, are now less easily assumed. These issues may only be made articulate by a few. We are persuaded, nevertheless, that they are felt to lie immediately behind the small stage of many an adolescent's activities, like a massive and belittling backcloth.

The society which adolescents now enter is in some respects unusually fluid. Old industries change their nature as new processes are adopted; new industries appear and help to shift the location of industry itself. New towns arise, and new estates on the outskirts of old towns deplete the established housing areas and alter their social composition. A series of Education Acts, notably that of 1944, are causing some movement across class and occupational boundaries and should in time cause more. So British society is beginning to acquire greater mobility and openness. The effects of these changes are not always marked at present; some groups seem to live much as they have lived for many years. Yet as the changes develop, so old habits, old customs, old sanctions, old freedoms and responsibilities will be called in question and new relationships demanded . . . These changes are *of* the new world of adolescents . . .

Yet paradoxically this society is increasingly organised and set into formal patterns . . . As technological needs and social planning increase so does the centralised organisation of individual lives. There is an ironic interaction between this change and that outlined in the preceding paragraph: as older patterns and hierarchies loosen, a new kind of stratification – economic and educational rather than cultural or geographic – begins to emerge from the combined pressure of industrial need and public good intention. To some extent the potentially academic are separated from the rest; so are the technologists, the clerical, the apprentices; and so on with increasing effectiveness. As we have noted earlier, much of this separating into functions is necessary if British society is to maintain and improve its standard of living. But clearly it exacts penalties, unless guided with unremitting care, especially on the emotional life of those who, at the most disturbed period of their lives, are subject to both a new openness and a new stratification.

In such a society – democratic (and so having no official 'philosophy'), commercial, still to some extent expressing traditional forms and values but rapidly becoming more open and demotic – in such a society young people are between conflicting voices. They can often sense a contradiction between what they are assured, at school and in other public organisations, are this society's assumptions and standards and much they are invited to interest themselves in and admire once they leave these sheltered environments. They may recognise a similar contrast between what their parents tell them – if indeed they speak of the subject – are the foundations of a worthwhile personal life and the assumptions made on many a hoarding or at many a work-bench. (In films and advertisements, for instance, how little attention is given to the power of mutual respect and of the affectionate sharing of quite undramatic aspirations in promoting courtship, in comparison with the attention given to immediate physical attraction and its accoutrements.) Meanwhile many young workers have a great deal of spare money, and it has become a sizeable business to cater for their wants and to suggest new levels of need or new ways of spending. . . .

Commercial competition in and by itself ensures that the weight and direction of the appeals now so insistently made to adolescents represent neither the full variety nor the full potentiality of their interests. We do not believe that these interests are so uniform that, left more alone, a vast majority of young people would in exactly the same week be humming the melody of *one* song as sung by *one* momentary 'star'. Yet all these persuasive voices undoubtedly speak winningly to adolescents, and perhaps especially to those adolescents who, not selected for advanced education or training, may feel an obscure but powerful sense of rejection. They have money but little status; not even, as yet, the controlling responsibilities of family life. Why should they listen, they may feel, to the more sober and often drab voices – urging restraint, caution, discipline and (to them) similarly 'old fashioned' attitudes – voices from that very world which has seemed, in its formal classifications, not greatly to care for them?

It is plain that today teenagers receive exceptional attention, of certain kinds. The subject of 'youth' or 'the youth problem' has recently been so much discussed that it has become difficult either to write firmly about those parts of the attacks on young people which have point, or to speak reasonably and responsibly in their defence, to explore what Burns called 'the moving *why* they do it'.

We mention below some of the generalisations commonly made about adolescents today. We believe that most of them are untrue and distorting. But they have hardened into some of the most striking cliches of the last decade. It is frequently said, then, that young people today belong to 'a generation of teenage delinquents'; that they have rejected family life and are 'featherbedded' by the Welfare State; that they are increasingly materialistic; 'couldn't care less'; and have no moral values. Probably the most accurate reply to such assertions is also the most obvious: that today's adolescents are much like those of other generations. Yet we would add this: that when we compare what is so often said about adolescents with the overwhelming unanimity of regard expressed in the evidence of those with long and intimate experience, especially in 'difficult' areas, we are left predominantly with a sense of respect and admiration for most young people's good sense, goodwill, vitality and resilience. Again, a quotation from Burns' poem addressed to the *Unco Guid* is relevant:

> 'What's done we partly may compute
> But know not what's resisted.'

In other words, it is easier to note obvious instances of 'anti-social' behaviour than realise how much worse might well have happened, in present conditions, had young people not made so many positive, often unconscious, decisions to ignore this kind of appeal or resist that unworthy but shiny temptation. It is easier to condemn by a blanket misreading all new forms (in dress, in dancing, in popular singing) than to acquire the close knowledge which will permit an appreciation of the strengths some of these new forms reveal. If those publications, in particular, which now use so much of their space in headlining the aberrations of a small proportion of young people were to exercise as much effort, but a more sensitive imagination, in looking for the signs of positive and worthwhile life, we could assure them that they would have no shortage of exciting material. . . .

It is true that some of the attitudes and actions of young people today do give an impression that they 'couldn't care less'. Yet this attitude is often not so much cynical as sceptical. They feel themselves in a world and society which disagrees about or is unsure about its meaning and purpose (this is not to say that they find their day to day personal life tasteless or without standards). Meanwhile much of the outside world constantly tries to persuade them to believe this or think that, to try this or laugh at that. Yet the realities of their daily work, the small sense of status this gives them, often makes them feel (whatever the friendly public voices say) that at the bottom the outside world regards them as indistinguishable units, a mass. What wonder that they often react into a defensive refusal to give of their inner selves. '*It's all brainwashing*', they say fiercely, equally of those who would 'sell' them soap, records, drink, politics, religion, 'the whole lot are out to brainwash you. Why should I buy it?' Yet the fierceness with which they can say this indicates an acute disappointment. From one aspect it is a sign of health that they throw up so strongly self-respecting a defence against the conflicting mass of public voices. We do not think this attitude much extends to their personal relations with one another, and these are often marked by a vivid and tolerant co-operativeness. And this scepticism towards almost all that does not come within the concrete, particular and known area of local life is not confined to one social or educational group. In different forms it can be seen in undergraduates as in unskilled workers (and in Paris and Chicago as in London – indeed, some of the basic causes are common to countries on both sides of the Iron Curtain). To dismiss the outside world as 'square' is to some extent a natural feature of adolescence, but today's rejections seem often to go beyond this, to have a peculiar edge and penetration. They suggest how strong is the *potential* idealism of young people, that idealism which is now so often baffled and turned back upon itself. At what should be the age for enthusiasm, for attack, for unregarding commitment, in a period offering unparalleled opportunities for young people to see and know and explore, whole areas of human experience have been thus defensively written off. As if in compensation young people often show an intense loyalty to things and people they believe to be of their own kind (ironically, many of the teenagers' own idols have been manipulated into prominence by the machines for promotion and publicity). When something attracts their loyalty and seems not to be a 'sell', they will show and accept leadership and discipline of a high order. Even the elaborate codes of urban gangs illustrate this, and youth workers in tough areas confirm it of many among the 'unattached'. . . .

It would be wrong for us not to say also, what many devoted youth workers, teachers, employers, union officials and clergy know well, that the very existence of these problems can be used by some adolescents, consciously or unconsciously, as a justification for indifference or irresponsibility. . . .

. . . The 'spirit that denies', the mind resolutely closed to the self-discipline necessary for growth, can exist in adolescents as it can in adults; and the more unrestrained behaviour of some young people today cannot be laid wholly at the door of perverse social forces . . .

Change should be a challenge, not a master. Many of the social changes we have discussed were intended to contribute to social justice, and can be made so to contribute if we have the will. We repeat that we believe the great majority of young people have this innate capacity. It is for the Youth Service, in cooperation with parents, other branches of the educational service and many other organisations, to help young people to develop this capacity, the better to meet the challenge of a changing world.

AIMS AND PRINCIPLES

[From Chapter 2, pp. 29–34

We do not, as we shall hope to show, underestimate the value of formal educational effort within the Youth Service. But we believe that the primary basis of such a service is social or pastoral. This is, of course, an educational purpose in a sense wider than that usually understood, and has been comprehensively expressed in Sir John Maud's* well-known statement of Youth Service aims: 'To offer individual young people in their leisure time opportunities of various kinds, complementary to those of home, formal education and work, to discover and develop their personal resources of body, mind and spirit and thus the better equip themselves to live the life of mature, creative and responsible members of a free society.' . . . The aim of the Youth Service is not to remove tensions so as to reach towards some hypothetical condition of 'adjustment' to individual or social life. It is to help towards ensuring that those tensions which are social accidents, often both fruitless and oppressive, shall not submerge the better possibilities of children during their adolescence. The Service should seek first to provide places for association in which young people may maintain and develop, in the face of a disparate society, their sense of fellowship, of mutual respect and tolerance. Such centres may also help to counteract the increasing educational and professional stratification of society. Those who are intellectually or financially well-endowed have as much to gain as others from the opportunity for mixed fellowship, as much to

* Permanent Secretary, Ministry of Education 1945, to 1954. Subsequently British High Commissioner and Ambassador in South Africa, 1954–62, and from 1963, Master of University College, Oxford.

learn from as to give to others. It is very difficult to run a club whose members have mixed educational backgrounds, but it is exceptionally well worth trying.

Yet, as we have said, an adolescent today moves into a society at once formidably restricted and surprisingly permissive, and finds himself canvassed by many agencies which seek to alter his attitudes in ways congenial to them. He needs to develop his capacity for making sound judgments; he needs, to take only one instance, opportunities for realising that some things – slower and more hardly won – are nevertheless more rewarding than the excitements offered in each day's passing show. This is to us the basis of the case for specific education and training within the Youth Service. It does not conflict with the aim suggested earlier, but rather complements it. But clearly this kind of specific education must bè imaginatively conceived and directed. Association in itself may be useless for young people, or it may be immensely educational, according to the imagination of the leadership. And merely formal education may satisfy the letter but kill the spirit of educational development in youth. If educational activity is flexibly planned, we believe it can both connect relevantly with the experience of the students and be tough and demanding. We do not think most young people seek soft options, but that they do want a clear aim in their efforts.

Association of the right kind and training of the right kind – to these two primary aims of a Youth Service we would add a third: challenge. This aspect can inform all others, and we discuss it at greater length in Chapter 5. Here we would stress only two points; that many adolescents have a strong need to find something they can do, individually or in a chosen group, which they feel to be deeply worth while beyond pleasure or personal reward; and that it is immensely important that young people, of different kinds and levels of ability, should have opportunities to display and to respect forms of pre-eminence in fields other than the academic.

To sum up: the question now should not be, ought there to be a Youth Service, but can this country any longer make do with one so plainly ill-equipped to meet the needs of the day. In this time of unprecedented plenty, the lives of many young people are likely to be poorer at 20 than one might have guessed on seeing them eagerly leave school at 15. Young people have never been more in a crowd – and never more alone: without a Youth Service many of them would not be more free but less free. A properly supported Youth Service can help many more individuals to find their own way better, personally and socially. This country must choose to have a Youth Service adequately provided for these most important purposes. . . .

. . . It is a matter of history that strong ethical feelings moved the pioneering voluntary organisations to undertake their hard practical jobs over the years . . .

To this zeal we pay strong tribute. Yet over a period of time there is a tendency for ethical impulses to lose their immediacy and drive, and to seem to young people unrelated to the situations in which they find themselves. . . . At a time when many young people feel tempted to reject adult experience and authority it is plain that the Youth Service should not seem to offer something packaged – a 'way of life', a 'set of values', a 'code', as though these were things which came ready-made, upon the asking, without being tested in living experience . . .

We touch directly now on two related points on which we earnestly hope not to be misunderstood. The first has to do with the spiritual aims of the Youth Service and in particular with the fact that many statements of purpose (not only those of denominational organisations) include reference to the need for 'communicating Christian values'. Obviously we are deeply sympathetic to this aim, and indeed the Education Act of 1944 lays on local education authorities the duty 'to contribute towards the spiritual, moral, mental, and physical development of the community . . .' (section 7). Denominational or specifically committed organisations must remain free to give expression to their spiritual ideals in their youth work. For the Youth Service as a whole, however, we think this way of embodying aims is mistaken. For many young people today the discussion of 'spiritual values' or 'Christian values' chiefly arouses suspicion. In view of the background described in this and the preceding chapter such a response is not altogether surprising. We are not, we need hardly add, implying that young people are immoral or unidealistic: we are saying that the shaky or contradictory expression of 'spiritual values' within society as a whole and the weakening of public speech are so persuasive as to cause many young people to reject habitually a direct approach of this kind. And those with more independent minds are likely to reject the more forcefully. We have been told of those who will say directly that the Youth Service should not be a disguised backdoor to religious beliefs or a form of 'moral exploitation'. We would repeat therefore that it is on the whole better for principles to be seen shining through works than for them to be signalized by some specific spiritual assertion.

We would make similar observations on the frequently stated aim of 'training young people in citizenship'. . . .

Much in the foregoing raises the involved question of communication in a society which has been to a large extent hierarchically divided in its speech and is now becoming, especially through the activities of 'mass communications', almost demotically 'classless'. W. H. Auden has some lines to the effect that:

'All words like peace and love,
All sane affirmative speech
Has been soiled, profaned, debased,
To a horrid mechanical screech.'

We believe this is largely true . . .

[From Chapter 3, pp. 36–9

44 · Report of the Central Advisory Council for Education (Wales) on Technical Education in Wales

Published: *1961*

Chairman: **Mr A. B. Oldfield Davies*

Members: **Principal G. P. Ambrose; Miss Gwennant Davies; Lady Twiston Davies; *Dr G. W. Evans; *Professor C. E. Gittins; Alderman W. Douglas Hughes; Miss A. Wittington-Hughes; Mr E. O. Humphreys; *Professor D. W. T. Jenkins; Professor J. R. Jones; *Mr R. G. Mathias; Lady Hopkin Morris; *Mr A. J. Nicholas; Mr A. D. Rees; *Alderman Mrs D. M. Rees; Professor E. J. Roberts; *Councillor Mrs G. I. Williams; *Dr Gordon Williams*

Co-opted Members of Technical Panel: *Mr R. C. Mathias; Mr Watcyn V. Williams*

Secretaries: *Mr E. O. Davies, H.M.I.; Dr W. J. Thomas, H.M.I.*

*Members of the Technical Panel.

Lady Twiston Davies, Lady Hopkin Morris and Mr E. O. Humphreys died during the preparation of the Report.

Terms of Reference: *In the light of contemporary changes in the industrial pattern of Wales, to consider what educational provisions should be made to serve the best interests of industry and those employed in it.*

This report, based on an investigation by the Technical Panel of the Advisory Council, was significant as one of the only specific proposals from an official source for the reform of apprenticeship training. Criticism of the haphazard way in which craftsmen were trained was widespread throughout the United Kingdom. It was stimulated in the years following the second world war by the Productivity teams which visited the United States under official auspices. Later there was the influence of academic speculation and European comparisons, led by Lady Gertrude Williams and Dr Kate Liepmann.

The Welsh Advisory Council proposed a national craft apprenticeship scheme supervised by the Ministry of Education, working through representative bodies. A feature of the scheme was a network of Apprentice Training Centres, to which, at 16, an apprentice would be admitted for a three-year full-time training.

No action was taken on the proposal which, as the authors noted, was only practical if adopted throughout Britain. But in 1962 the White Paper on *Industrial Training* appeared (see p. 239) which paved the way for the general adoption of first-year full-time courses of training for apprentices, under the supervision of industrial training boards.

TECHNICAL EDUCATION IN WALES · 1961

As already mentioned . . . the Council hopes that block-release courses will increase in number and that employers will release their apprentices to attend them.

Much of what has been said above in relation to the high failure rate on National Certificate courses applies equally to the high rate of failure on craft courses in preparation for the examinations of the City and Guilds of London Institute. The wide range of intelligence among the craft apprentices who pursue these craft courses, and the comparatively high academic standard of some of the examinations, are factors which contribute to the present failure rate. The recent introduction of additional examinations demanding both a lower academic standard and a more practical approach, in some craft subjects, will give the less academically-minded but, nevertheless, capable and satisfactory apprentice an opportunity to succeed, whereas hitherto he would have failed. The Council therefore welcomes this development and hopes that it will spread to craft subjects generally.

Finally, the Council is of the opinion that industry can do much to reduce the failure rate by making every effort to ensure that it makes the best possible choice when selecting craft apprentices. The Council strongly recommends that industry and headteachers of secondary schools, particularly those of secondary grammar schools, make the best possible use of the Youth Employment Service. The Council believes that if industry, schools and parents used the Service to the fullest possible extent and if the Service were extended to provide more fully for all types of schools, then the problem of placing school-leavers in the grade and type of employment best fitted to their abilities and aptitudes would be nearer a solution.

A New Approach to Craft Apprenticeship

It has already been mentioned . . . that recruitment to craft apprenticeships is, in the main, carried out with current needs of industry in mind rather than long-term requirements. If the nation is to maintain its reputation in industrial development and production against keen competition from other countries, its supply of skilled workers must be adequate and must not be influenced by such factors as short-term fluctuations in the country's economy. An example of present practice was the reduction in the number of craft apprenticeships offered to school leavers in the summer of 1958, following the credit restrictions imposed earlier that year. The effect of this reduction will be felt in 1963 when these apprentices complete their apprenticeships and take their places as craftsmen in industry. At that time pupils in the so-called 'post-war bulge' will be leaving the secondary schools and, becoming wage-earners, will increase the demand for consumer goods. This increasing demand will, in turn, call for employment of more workers including craftsmen, and will occur at a time when the supply of craftsmen will be reduced owing to the fall in craft apprenticeships offered in 1958.

Another serious defect in the present craft apprenticeship system is that the standard of practical training given to the apprentice differs greatly from one firm to another. Some apprentices are fortunate in that their employers conduct well-planned schemes of practical training which may include a year or two at a Works Training School. The training received in this way gives them every opportunity to familiarise themselves with various aspects of the craft and prepares them well for careers as craftsmen. Many others however are not so fortunate, and they receive training which is narrow in its concept and is of poor standard. A craftsman so trained often finds himself incompetent to carry out his duties satisfactorily, particularly if he moves to another firm whose methods may be different from those of the firm at which he served his apprenticeship. A system which allows the standard of practical training an apprentice receives to depend completely on the facilities which his employer can offer is unsatisfactory to the trade and unjust to the apprentice.

How can these defects of fluctuating recruitment and varying standards of practical training be remedied? Since the future prosperity of the country depends on, among other things, an adequate supply of competent craftsmen, the Council regards the responsibility of recruiting and training craft apprentices as a national one. The position in Wales differs in many respects from that in many parts of England and in the opinion of the Council the only satisfactory solution would be the establishment of a national craft apprenticeship system which would be administered by the State through the Ministry of Education working in turn through appropriate bodies representative of the interests involved and so free individual industries of the responsibility for providing basic craft training. The Council realises that this system must operate over the United Kingdom as a whole before it can be successful in Wales, but it cannot for that reason refrain from considering it.

In such a scheme as the Council envisages, the apprentice would be admitted to an Apprentice Training Centre, normally at the age of 16, although provision would be made for entry at a later age. The centre may or may not be an integral part of an existing technical college, and would give a full-time course of practical training lasting three years, of which two would be spent on a broad and sound training in the skills and basic requirements of a group of related crafts and the third more directly aligned to the needs of the trade the apprentice intends to follow. Maintenance grants on a sufficiently generous scale to encourage young persons to undertake apprenticeships rather than go into paid full-time employment which would be likely to be blind alley should be provided. Attendance at technical college courses would be on an ampler scale than is the case generally for apprentices at present; two days a week or one month a term, with supervised study in the intervening periods spent at the training centre, would be arranged. It is only on the completion of the three years' course that the apprentice would be given employment and he would continue to be an apprentice for a further two years during which time he would gain experience, and acquire the ability to use the skill and craft knowledge he possesses, in industry.

While the Council is not in a position to elaborate this scheme in detail it hopes that the following ideas, among others, will receive careful consideration. Industry could contribute towards the maintenance of the centres through an Apprenticeship Levy imposed on every firm or organization employing craftsmen and technicians. A National Apprenticeship Council, fully representative, would determine policy concerning the number of training centres required and their geographical distribution, and also what training facilities are to be offered in various areas. From estimates obtained annually from industry of the number of craftsmen and technicians needed, say, in three or four years' time, together with knowledge of the Government's plans for industrial development, the Council would determine the annual intakes into the centres. The selection of candidates for apprenticeships would be made by Area Apprenticeship Committees who would also be responsible to the National Council for the efficient conduct of the centres in their respective areas.

Among the advantages to Wales of a National Craft Apprenticeship system would be:

(i) recruitment to the apprentice training centres could be controlled so as to meet the estimated need for skilled craftsmen and technicians judged by the prospects of establishing new industries and the expansion of existing ones;

(ii) education and industrial training could be more closely related than they are at present;

(iii) the standard of training would be more uniform throughout the country and of a level at least comparable to the best given at the present time. This is of particular importance because of the large proportion of small firms in Wales;

(iv) the training could easily be adjusted, when necessary, to meet the changing needs of industry caused by the introduction of new methods and techniques;

(v) the technical college course, with the additional time allocation, would include subjects other than those concerned directly with the vocational interests of the apprentice;

(vi) it would give the school-leavers in rural areas an equal opportunity of gaining apprenticeships with those from the towns and cities in industrial areas.

The Council is aware of the problems involved in changing from the present system to a national one and it also appreciates the difficulties that would be encountered in administering the scheme. Not the least is finding suitably qualified teachers in sufficient numbers. A necessary preliminary step would be to establish in one of the training colleges of Wales a course designed for such teachers. Furthermore it realizes that the system would succeed only if it were given full and active support by the Government, industry and the trade unions. In spite of the problems and difficulties involved, the Council believes that the change is necessary. In this respect the Council finds that it differs from the conclusions of the Carr Report *Training for Skill** and the recent report of the Central Advisory Council for Education (England) *15 to 18*.

The policy of establishing a national craft apprenticeship system, were it to be realized, must at present be regarded a long-term one, even if only on account of the time that would be taken, among other things, in setting up the training centres. In the meantime, and as an alternative if a national system is unacceptable, the Council recommends that the five-year craft industrial apprenticeship period be reduced to three years provided that all apprentices recruited by industry at 17–18 years of age have had a two years' full-time course in the basic subjects associated with technical education. This two years' course would be given in a place of full-time education staffed and equipped for the purpose. This might be a specially selected school serving an area or a college of further education, depending upon local conditions. The full-time course would begin at between 15 and 16 years of age and extend to between 17 and 18 years when an appropriate examination would be taken. The examination would best be an external examination conducted in Wales by the Welsh Joint Education Committee. Industry would interview applicants for industrial apprenticeship during the last term of the course and make the final selection after its completion.

The basic subjects in the full-time course would be those common to the training of apprentices in practically all branches of industry and

* para. 18. '. . . the responsibility for the industrial training of apprentices should rest firmly with industry. . . .' Her Majesty's Stationery Office 1958.

would include English, mathematics, physics, chemistry, engineering drawing, and an extensive course in workshop practice and technology. The content of each syllabus would be appropriately related to general industrial requirements and would emphasize practical applications. In certain areas a bias towards a particular industry would be acceptable and might be advantageous provided the basic quality of the training is not materially affected. The course would not be confined to the above subjects, but would also include other subjects of cultural importance in the education of future citizens and make for greater adaptability, the importance of which has already been emphasized.

The Council is aware that not all those who pursue this special full-time course would be successful in being accepted by industry for industrial apprenticeship, but it hopes that the number in this category would be small and that industry would cooperate fully in making use of all those who successfully completed the course. In any case the resultant general raising of the level of educational training given to such a large additional section of the community could have nothing but a beneficial influence upon our society. The scheme would bring to technical education an orderliness which is now lacking and would avoid the dilemma, in which many pupils find themselves, of having to decide at 15 or 16 years of age whether to accept an apprenticeship and forgo the opportunity of sitting the General Certificate of Education examination or to remain at school for the latter purpose with the possibility of losing an apprenticeship through age restrictions. Even though the suggested course would be directed towards an apprenticeship examination, pupils wishing to do so would still be able to sit the General Certificate of Education examination at the appropriate time.

45 · White Paper on Industrial Training. 1962

The appearance of this White Paper at the end of 1962 marked the end of a period of transition during which Conservative governments, from 1951 onwards, moved slowly from a determined reluctance to take any steps to control industrial training, to the decision in principle that this could not be left to the unfettered discretion of industry.

Behind the proposals outlined in the White Paper lay a major shift of industrial opinion during the four years which followed the publication, in 1958, of the report entitled *Training for Skill*, which was prepared by a sub-committee of the Minister of Labour's National Joint Advisory Council presided over by the then Parliamentary Secretary, Mr Robert Carr. This had drawn a firm distinction between training and education. It expressly excluded the Government from the former, while urging industry to put their house in order. This report, which was the result of a timid compromise among the employers and the trade unions in the absence of strong leadership from the Ministry of Labour, had the unexpected result of arousing support for some kind of public intervention among those who saw that, left alone, industry would fail to meet the challenge.

The Industrial Training Act of 1964 carried out the proposals of the White Paper, strengthening them somewhat by a Central Advisory Council to advise the Minister of Labour on the operation of the Act. In bringing industrial training (not just apprenticeship) within the public purview, the Bill broke new ground and gave the opportunity for major changes in the lower levels of industrial and technical training. The extent of these changes was bound to depend on the attitudes adopted in different industries and the use made by successive Ministers of Labour of their powers under the Act.

The Bill has a direct family link with the Report of the Central Advisory Council for Education (Wales) with its proposal that first year apprenticeship schools should be set up by L.E.A.s. Linked with proposals for raising the leaving age, it points to the next development in part-time day education.

INDUSTRIAL TRAINING: THE GOVERNMENT'S PROPOSALS · 1962

THE CASE FOR ACTION

Ever since the war industry in this country has been short of skilled labour. This has usually been so even in those parts of the country where the general demand for labour has been relatively small. There is no doubt that shortages of skilled manpower have been an important factor in holding back the rate of economic expansion – not least in those parts of the country where such expansion would have done most to reduce a level of general unemployment higher than the average.

It will be impossible to secure the objective of a steadier and more rapid rate of economic growth unless skilled manpower is available on a growing scale. This means that the rate of industrial training must be increased.

An increase in the supply of skilled labour will need to be matched by an improvement in quality. Whether or not we decide to join the Common Market our exports will be faced with increasing competition. At its best, the standard of training in this country is high; unfortunately this is by no means universal. Much is barely adequate and some definitely unsatisfactory. Many firms do not make adequate use of the facilities for technical education. Our overseas competitors, particularly in Western European countries, have paid great attention to the need to maintain an adequate supply of well trained skilled labour. We must be quite sure that our own arrangements do not fall behind.

At present training for industry in this country is primarily the responsibility of individual firms, though the Government, Local Education Authorities, and other agencies such as the City and Guilds of London Institute are helping. The Industrial Training Council which was set up in 1958 by the British Employers' Confederation, the Trades Union Congress and the nationalized industries, to provide encouragement and help to industries in dealing with the training of workpeople has helped to stimulate interest in the question. In recent years many firms have taken advantage of the rise in the number of school leavers by increasing substantially their recruitment of apprentices. In 1961 there was an increase in the number of apprentices recruited of 12,321 (or 10 per cent) over the previous year and in the first ten months of 1962 there was a further increase of 10,989 (or 9 per cent) over the corresponding period of 1961. These increases have been very welcome. Even so, it remains doubtful whether the number of new entrants into skilled occupations will be sufficient to match future needs. Experience in the United States, for example, suggests that technological progress requires an increasing proportion of trained and technical manpower in the working population, with a correspondingly smaller demand for unskilled and semi-skilled labour. The same is true here. The great majority of unfilled vacancies call for some degree of skill, while a high proportion of the adult unemployed are labourers.

A serious weakness in our present arrangements is that the amount and quality of industrial training are left to the unco-ordinated decisions of a large number of individual firms. These may lack the necessary economic incentive to invest in training people who, once trained, may leave them for other jobs. While the benefits of training are shared by all, the cost is borne only by those firms which decide to undertake training themselves.

That these weaknesses exist, and must be remedied, is increasingly accepted within industry itself. The Government has therefore decided that the time has come to strengthen and improve the existing partnership between industry, the Government and the education authorities in the provision of industrial training. . . .

. . . The objectives . . . can be stated as follows:

(i) to enable decisions on the scale of training to be better related to economic needs and technological developments;
(ii) to improve the overall quality of industrial training and to establish minimum standards; and
(iii) to enable the cost to be more fairly spread.

So that discussions may take place on a realistic basis the Government has drawn up proposals. . . .

A TRAINING BILL

The Minister of Labour would be given statutory power to set up Boards which would be responsible for all aspects of training in individual industries. Before setting up a Board the Minister would be required to consult the organizations principally concerned on both sides of the industry.

The range of functions which the Boards might be empowered to undertake . . . might include:

(1) Establishing policy for training in the industry, including such questions as admission to training (apprenticeship or otherwise) length of training, registration of trainees, and a provision for appropriate attendance at colleges of further education.
(2) Establishing standards of training and syllabuses for different occupations in the industry, taking into account the associated technical education required.
(3) Providing advice and assistance about training to firms in the industry.
(4) Devising tests to be taken by apprentices and other trainees on completion of training and, if necessary, at intermediate stages – for example, at the end of the first year.
(5) Establishing qualifications and tests for instructors.
(6) Establishing and running training courses in its own training centres.

(7) Paying grants to firms to reimburse them all or part of the costs incurred in the provision of approved training.
(8) Paying allowances to trainees not taken on by firms while being trained in public, or the Board's own, centres.
(9) Collecting money from establishments in the industry by means of a levy.
(10) Borrowing.

A levy on firms in the industry is an essential part of the proposals. . . .

The Boards would be empowered to appoint qualified persons to undertake duties in connection with the promotion of industrial training including making reports on the quality of training provided by firms applying for grants. The Minister of Labour would be empowered to appoint officers to satisfy him that the standards of training adopted by the Board were sufficient to justify payment of grant to the Board by the Minister.

The Kind of Scheme which might be operated by the Boards

Legislation on these lines would leave latitude to the Boards in deciding on their activities within the range of functions set out [above] . . . It might well be, however, that particularly in dealing with apprenticeship trades some Boards would find that they could best make progress by concentrating their main attention – at any rate at first – on the improvement of first-year training. This view is based on the experience of firms which have their own training schools and on the success achieved by the Ministry of Labour and many education authorities in the last two or three years in training first-year apprentices on a full-time basis both in Government Training Centres and Technical Colleges.

Experience has shown clearly that if young people on leaving school are given a systematic course of training in the basic principles of their trade, their progress thereafter to full skill will be more rapid and their adaptability within their trade much greater than if they started out on a narrow range of production work. It is difficult for many employers, particularly in small and medium-sized firms, to make available the machinery and instructors to give the apprentice this systematic grounding. The wider provision of opportunities for systematic training in the first year of apprenticeship would do much to improve our whole system by remedying it at its weakest point, that is to say, the haphazard and narrow training given all too often at the beginning.

46 · Report of the Minister of Education's Central Advisory Council entitled *Half Our Future*. [*The Newsom Report*]

Published: *1963*
Chairman: *Mr John Newsom**
Members: *Mr R. H. Adams; Miss C. Avent; Mr D. B. Bartlett; Mr S. W. Buglass; Alderman S. M. Caffyn, Mr A. B. Clegg; Professor B. A. Fletcher; Mr F. D. Flower; Dr H. Frazer; Mr A. J. N. Fuller; Miss M. G. Green, The Rev. H. W. Hinds; Mrs A. J. Hirst; Mr R. M. T. Kneebone; Dr Kathleen Ollerenshaw; Miss B. Paston Brown; Miss E. M. Pepperell; Alderman A. H. Quilley; Mr J. Scupham; Miss E. L. Sewell; Miss A. M. Simcock; Mr W. J. Slater; Mr J. E. Smith; Mr C. A. Thompson; Mr N. G. Treloar; Mr D. Winnard; Miss K. A. Kennedy (Assessor); Mr D. G. O. Ayerst, H.M.I. (Assessor); Mr R. J. W. Stubbings, H.M.I. (Assessor); Mr J. W. Withrington, H.M.I. (Assessor); Miss M. J. Marshall, H.M.I. (Secretary to the Council); Miss M. L. Smith (Clerk).*
The Council began in March, 1961 under the chairmanship of Lord Amory, who resigned in June 1961, following his appointment as High Commissioner for the United Kingdom in Canada. Dame Anne Godwin (resigned November 1961) and Miss N. Newton Smith (resigned December 1961) were also members of the Council during this enquiry.
Terms of Reference: *To consider the education between the ages of 13 and 16 of pupils of average or less than average ability who are or will be following full-time courses either at schools or in establishments of further education. The term education shall be understood to include extra-curricular activities.*

The Central Advisory Council was reconstituted after the completion of the Crowther Report and charged with investigating the education of pupils of less than average ability. There were no special circumstances leading to this remit, except that it was logical to follow a report which dealt mainly with the top half of the ability range with one on the education of less able children.

The report adopted as its first and most forceful recommendation, the Crowther plea for a longer school life. Besides raising the leaving age to 16,

* John Hubert Newsom (1910–71) was educated at Imperial Service College and Queen's College, Oxford. After a variety of jobs in education and social work from 1931–40, he was chief education officer for Hertfordshire from 1940–57. He resigned to become a director, later a managing director, of Messrs Longmans, Green & Co. Ltd, publishers. He was knighted in 1964.

the Council also wanted to take up references in the Crowther Report to the need for a more exacting programme in the last years of school life. They proposed a longer school day, incorporating into the formal curriculum activities now undertaken voluntarily in many schools.

Other recommendations included a joint Working Party on social services in the slum areas; accelerated action to remedy the 'functional deficiencies' of the schools and the improvement of teacher training, with the retention, at all costs, of 'concurrent' academic and professional training.

Much more important than the detailed recommendations was the wealth of factual information which the Report collected. It made extensive use of the Social Survey and the National Service statistics. Other statistics showed that nearly 80 per cent of the school buildings in which the average and below average children were taught were more or less seriously deficient.

They found that these children received less than their share of the resources employed by the education service and that the turnover of teachers – on the whole the least well-qualified teachers – was fastest in the schools they attended. They found evidence of wide differences in attainment (see p. 283) between school and school and area and area.

They also found evidence of a rising average standard as measured by reading tests made regularly between 1948 and 1961, and they firmly associated themselves with those who argued that the educational performance of many of the children in the 'Newsom' group is held back more by social factors than by genetics.

The report is notable for the absence of any assessment of the merits of different forms of organization for secondary education. The Council took the view that secondary modern schools and, even more so, comprehensive schools had not been in existence long enough for any valid judgments to be made about which was better, and preferred to tackle the problem on the assumption that the educational needs of these children would be the same irrespective of the type of school organization adopted. They were encouraged to this *pis aller* by the fact that the questionnaires used to collect the information tabulated in their survey were not constructed so as to give any guidance on the question of organization; and that a unanimous report was facilitated by evading this contentious issue.

THE NEWSOM REPORT 1963

EDUCATION FOR ALL

Despite some splendid achievements in the schools, there is much unrealized talent especially among boys and girls whose potential is masked by inadequate powers of speech and the limitations of home background... If it is to be avoided, several things will be necessary. The pupils will need to have a longer period of full-time education than most of them now receive. The schools will need to present that education in terms more acceptable to the pupils and to their parents, by relating school more directly to adult life, and especially by taking a proper account of vocational interests. . . . Finally, the schools will need strong support in their task, not least from parents, and they will need the tools for the job, in the provision of adequate staff and buildings and equipment . . .

We had difficulty with our terms of reference. 'Average' and 'below average' are full of pitfalls. The words themselves are useful enough, as ways of trying to identify in broad terms two large groups of pupils; but unluckily they often carry emotional overtones: the idea of 'below-average ability' easily suggests 'below-average people', as though the boys and girls so described were being regarded as generally inferior and in some way less worth educating than their 'above-average' brothers and sisters . . .

Another fact, perhaps not often enough emphasized, is that the standard indicated by 'average' is rising all the time, and perhaps never more rapidly than in the last 25 years . . .

In . . . a series of tests designed to show the pupils' capacity to read with understanding, there is a clear record of improvement. A test score which even 14 years ago would have been good enough to put boys or girls well into the above-average category would today put them firmly into the below-average group. Over the intervening years the general level of performance has risen . . .

The point is, could many people, with the right educational help, achieve still more? If they could, then in human justice and in economic self-interest we ought, as a country, to provide that help. Any substantial recommendations affecting provision for half the population are bound to cost money. Are we prepared to foot the bill? We . . . think it essential to state at the outset the economic argument for investment in our pupils.

Briefly, it is that the future pattern of employment in this country will require a much larger pool of talent than is at present available; and that at least a substantial proportion of the 'average' and 'below-average' pupils are sufficiently educable to supply that additional talent. The need is not only for more skilled workers to fill existing jobs, but also for a generally better educated and intelligently adaptable labour force to meet new demands . . .

The results of . . . investigation increasingly indicate that the kind of intelligence which is measured by the tests so far applied is largely an acquired characteristic. This is not to deny the existence of a basic genetic endowment; but whereas that endowment, so far, has proved impossible to isolate, other factors can be identified. Particularly significant among them are the influences of social and physical environment; and, since these are susceptible to modification, they may well prove educationally more important . . .

There is very little doubt that among our children there are reserves of ability which can be tapped, if the country wills the means. One of the means is a longer school life. There is, surely, something of an anomaly in the fact that whereas a five-year secondary course is regarded as an essential minimum both for our ablest children in the grammar schools and for those of very limited capacities indeed, in schools for the educationally sub-normal, less is demanded for the large majority of children who neither progress as quickly as the first group nor are as severely limited in their potential as the second.

Our terms of reference imply, and the whole argument of our report assumes, a school-leaving age of 16 for everyone. We have again considered the position with great care, and we have unhesitatingly come to the same conclusion as the Council reached in 1959: 'This is a duty which society owes all its young citizens'. The evidence presented to us makes it clear that in the last few years there has been a marked strengthening of conviction in this matter, both among those professionally concerned with education and among the interested general public...

The decision to raise the school-leaving age should not therefore continue to be deferred and progress left to follow its voluntary course. There are still too many boys and girls who, otherwise, will leave at the earliest permissible moment, whatever their potential abilities, because outside pressures are too much for them. . . .

If the decision were taken quickly, a leaving age of 16 could be made operative for all pupils who enter the secondary schools in or after 1965: that is, the first year of full-time compulsory education up to the age of 16 would be 1969–70 . . .

There is one other point about our terms of reference which we must make straight away: they appear to leave open the possibility that when the school-leaving age is raised, some pupils below the age of 16 may be following full-time courses in colleges of further education. We are ourselves convinced, and have found almost unanimous agreement among those who have contributed evidence, that the schools should be responsible for boys and girls up to this age. This does not rule out the transitional use of the colleges for the full-time education of 15 to 16 year-olds, in the period before all secondary schools have the buildings, staffing and equipment to provide a fifth year for all their pupils... But when the school leaving age is raised to 16 for all, there will be a fundamental change in the whole educational situation, and the schools must be equipped, staffed and re-orientated in their working to meet it.

[From Chapter 1, pp. 3–8

IN THE SLUMS

There is no need to read the melodramatic novelists to realize that there are areas, often near the decaying centres of big cities, where schools have more to contend with than the schoolboy's traditional reluctance . . .

Nothing that we have seen or heard leads us to believe that the strictly educational problems of the less able pupils are different in slum schools from other schools.

But schools in slums do require special consideration if they are to have a fair chance of making the best of their pupils. They seem to us, for instance, to need a specially favourable staffing ratio.

Even more they need measures which will help them to secure at least as stable a staff as other schools. Perhaps this can be secured simply by making it clear that professionally it is an asset to have served successfully in a difficult area, that work there can be intellectually exciting and spiritually rewarding, that these are schools in which able teachers may want to serve and make their career as so many of their gifted predecessors have done. One headmistress wrote to us; 'the staffing of schools in difficult areas is made more difficult by those administratively responsible who take the line, "It's no good asking folks to come down here – they wouldn't put up with it." In fact this is not true. Four able teachers have *asked* to come to this school, and their request has been ignored.' Perhaps then a change of wind will be sufficient.

But perhaps more tangible inducements may be needed. One suggestion is contained in an appendix to this report.* Another might be the provision of good residential accommodation for teachers near the schools. This is something which ought to be examined, however, not only as a device for recruiting teachers, but also for its bearing on the whole life of the community in which they would then be living as well as working. In helping to solve a purely school problem we might be slightly relieving that uniform residual nature of the population which helps to make a slum.

There is another aspect of the staffing problem which also overlaps strictly education boundaries. There is no doubt at all about the need for a good deal of social work in connection with the pupils. Problems of poverty, health and delinquency are involved. Nearly twice as many fourth-year pupils get free dinners as in modern schools as a whole. Twice as many boys are under five foot high, and twice as many under six and a half stone in weight. Among third-year pupils, half as many again as in modern schools generally missed more than half a term's work – two-thirds of them because of ill-health. There is also a worse problem of truancy: half as many again could not satisfactorily explain their absences. One in six of the third-year girls were in this category.

* A paper by Mr R. F. Goodings and Mr Simon Pratt, outlining a scheme for inducements to be paid to teachers willing to contract to serve anywhere they may be sent.

We have no hesitation in saying that these figures from our survey taken in conjunction with the general picture given by the heads make a good case for the employment of trained social workers. But should they be school-based? This is a different and more difficult problem. Behind each absence there is a story which may well involve several different social agencies...

We are clear, too, that an adequate education cannot be given to boys and girls if it has to be confined to the slums in which they live. They, above all others, need access to the countryside, the experience of living together in civilized and beautiful surroundings, and a chance to respond to the challenge of adventure. They need priority in relation to school journeys, overseas visits, and adventure courses. Clearly this is an educational matter, but it is not solely one. Children below school age, young workers, older people – the whole community – need to have a stake in something more than the streets in which they live . . .

Whatever is decided by the educational authorities in these matters will have repercussions on other social agencies. It is equally true that decisions made in other fields – in housing, for example, or in public health – will have reactions in the schools . . . In the slums the need for reform is not confined to the schools. It is general. Because no social service is 'an island to itself' there may be a case for an inter-departmental working party to plan the strategy of a grand assault, but not at the expense of postponing the opening of the campaign.

[From Chapter 3, pp. 17–26

CONTRASTING ATTAINMENTS

The second general conclusion from the survey evidence is the contrasts which exist between school and school. . . . Nine points, equivalent to five and a quarter years, separated the schools with the highest and the lowest reading test scores. Within each neighbourhood group, the range was considerable. This can be illustrated by comparing the distribution among schools in the problem areas, where the group average is lowest, with that in the mixed neighbourhoods where the group average is highest.

Comparative Tests Scores in Problem Areas and Mixed Neighbourhoods

	Test Scores										No. of
Neighbourhood	*25*	*24*	*23*	*22*	*21*	*20*	*19*	*18*	*17*	*16*	Schools
Problem Areas	—	—	3	7	3	6	4	2	4	1	30
Mixed Neighbourhoods	3	4	7	11	9	5	2	—	1	—	42

[From Chapter 21, pp. 186–7

IN AND OUT OF SCHOOL

A number of considerations lead us to advocate a rather longer school day for boys and girls in their last two years at school . . . A characteristic complaint of this group is that they are 'bored' – with school, with life outside school, and later with their jobs. The peak in the figures for juvenile delinquency persistently occurs in the last year before boys and girls leave school. All our evidence suggests that many pupils are capable of more sustained effort and show themselves able to respond to opportunities of a larger range of activities. The schools on the other hand find themselves short of time in which to undertake all the things they know to be profitable. Finally, young people still have to face a much longer working day when they enter employment, and some bridging of this gap seems desirable.

How should any extra time be used? First, to incorporate into the total educational programme many of those activities which are now called 'extra-curricular' . . .

Secondly, some of the time might be used for what is really a special form of out-of-class activity, 'homework'. The term may be a misnomer for what we have in mind, but again we use it for want of a better. Perhaps some more appropriate name may be found if the concept of what is involved begins to change.

The abler pupils in secondary schools are regularly required to do a substantial amount of homework, which considerably lengthens their effective working day. But large numbers of pupils, and the majority of 'our' pupils commonly do none. We are strongly of the opinion that all boys and girls would profit from undertaking some work for themselves outside what is done in lessons; we also think this work could, and for many of our pupils, especially, should, take more varied forms than what is conventionally recognized now as homework. The task to be undertaken might, for instance, be making a model, or finishing some project in the art or craft room begun in school time. It might be a chance to try some new skill or craft or, for those pupils who wished to learn typing, an opportunity for intensive practice which it may be difficult to provide inside the normal school timetable. It might consist in the group viewing and discussion of a film or television programme. It might be the preparation of material before giving a talk in class, or gathering information for some group project in school: obtaining the information might involve writing letters or direct observation and note making, or visiting a museum, an art gallery, the public library or the town hall. It could be working on the school magazine, or balancing the Young Farmers' Club accounts, or mapping the route of a coming school expedition . . .

We have come somewhat reluctantly to the conclusion that if the school day is extended, some element of compulsion will have to be introduced into what are now voluntary activities . . .

Written evidence we have received, as well as discussions with witnesses, leads us to believe that in some areas local education authorities and schools would be willing to experiment with the idea of a three-session day . . . We think it highly desirable that official encouragement – including financial support – should be given to some experiment . . .

A decisive factor in any scheme would be staffing. Under the present system, many schools have been extraordinarily lucky in the generous voluntary service of the teachers in out-of-school hours. But, as our examples have shown, by no means all schools are as fortunately placed, and extra-curricular activities sometimes founder altogether for lack of people to lead them. We acknowledge the real difficulties which the schools face, but we do not regard the difficulties as insuperable. In our opinion, and we believe in the opinion of the large majority of teachers, these activities represent a proper part of the teachers' professional responsibilities in the education of their pupils, and we do not accept, for instance, that married women cannot be expected to contribute . . .

At the same time, we realize that to extend extra-curricular provision for all pupils on a large scale, particularly if the school day developed on a three-session pattern, would in some schools be to risk placing an intolerable burden on those teachers who are already doing most, unless staffing resources were supplemented in some way.

It is clear that the total number of staff needed for one kind of educational activity or another would be greater. That, in a time of continuing and acute teacher-shortages, must give us pause. But there might be room in the educational scene to draw far more on the special knowledge or skills of persons outside the school.

[From Chapter 6, pp. 41–7

TEACHERS

We have implied . . . that the teachers will be receiving their training in training colleges. We have done so deliberately, because we are convinced that the kind of training the colleges offer, that is a 'concurrent' course in which the personal higher education of the student is combined with pedagogical studies, is likely to provide the most suitable professional preparation for teaching most of the pupils with whom we are concerned. We are also aware that current policies require the colleges to concentrate on the training of primary teachers, and that in the immediate future only a minority of teachers with this type of training, mainly specialists in certain 'shortage' subjects, will be available to the secondary schools. While we recognize the serious teacher shortage which the primary schools face, we are concerned lest an emergency measure which does not rest on any positive assessment of the needs of the secondary schools should be retained as long-term policy.

It was for this reason that at a fairly advanced stage of our deliberations we requested the Minister to make known our views to the Robbins Committee. (The letter is included as an appendix to the report.) Briefly, it argues that a 'concurrent' training, which includes a prolonged study of child development combined with a study of a range of subjects, is more likely to produce effective teachers of less able pupils than the existing 'consecutive' pattern of graduate training which consists of a more specialized course followed by a much shorter period of professional training. We realize that many changes may be contemplated in the future in the relative rôles of the training colleges and the universities, and indeed that altogether new types of training institution may emerge. We are not concerned with types of institution, or with the title of the qualification which trained teachers may eventually claim, but with the preservation of a pattern of training which we are convinced has marked value for the future teachers of large numbers of boys and girls.

It is clear, however, that if current expectations are fulfilled, not only will university graduates, as opposed to concurrently trained teachers, enter the secondary schools in increasing numbers, but also many of them in the near future will be without any kind of professional training. We view with extreme concern the prospect of large numbers of teachers without any training in the craft skills of their profession, whose own educational experience will have given them very little insight into the learning difficulties of many of the pupils they will teach . . .

We therefore urge that a training requirement for graduates be introduced at the earliest practicable moment; that meanwhile the conditions of training, including the financial inducements, be reviewed, in order to make voluntary training more attractive; and that there should be an emergency programme of in-service courses to help the untrained graduates equip themselves better to deal with the teaching problems they will encounter.

We are convinced in any case that the content of many graduate training courses should be re-examined, and the inclusion of some introduction to sociological studies and the possibilities of work in practical subjects be considered. Graduates who are likely to be teaching in secondary modern schools ought to do some part of their teaching practice in those schools; and we believe that the training colleges with their experience of work in this field could have a valuable part to play in the training of these graduates.

[From Chapter 12, pp. 105–6

EVIDENCE OF IMPROVEMENT

Although this report is about the academically less successful, it is a success story that we have to tell. In interpreting our terms of reference perhaps the most important thing to bear in mind is that what an average boy or girl knows is not a fixed quantum for all generations, but something liable to change. There are indications of marked improvement over the last 15 years. There is opportunity for more improvement to come and reason to expect it. The four reading test surveys [1948, 1952, 1956 and 1961] and the National Service Survey [see Crowther, Part II] tell the same story of rising averages. The Army's measure of ability is a battery of intelligence and attainment tests. The tests were standardized in 1947 and recorded in a form in which the top and bottom group each represented ten per cent. of the population and the intervening four groups 20 per cent. each. But ten years later when these tests were used for our National Service Survey, 58 per cent. of the intake instead of 50 per cent. fell into the top three groups, and the bottom two groups comprized only 21 per cent. of the intake instead of the original 30. It is true that men who were 18 in 1947 had spent their later years of elementary education (secondary education for all was yet unborn) in the disorder of the war years so that something would clearly have been wrong if there had not been a sensible improvement in attainment test results between 1947 and 1958. The same argument would apply to the improvement in the reading test results between 1948 and 1952. We were making up obviously lost ground. But the later tests of 1956 and 1961 show that we are now going forward into new territory. The position of pupils aged 14 years 8 months in modern schools at the four dates is shown in the following table . . .

The Reading Tests 1948–1961

Year	Average Score	Gain in Months (7 months = 1 point)
1948	18·0	—
1952	18·4	3
1956	18·9	6
1961	21·3	23

Today's average boys and girls are better at their books than their predecessors half a generation ago. There are reasons to expect that their successors will be better still.

[From Chapter 21, pp. 184–5

47 · Report of the Committee on Higher Education appointed by the Prime Minister. Volume 1: Report. Appendices I–V published separately in six additional volumes. [*The Robbins Report*]

Published: *1963*

Chairman: *Lord Robbins*

Members: *Sir David Anderson; Dame Kitty Anderson; Mr A. Chenevix-Trench; Professor J. Drever; Mr H. L. Elvin; Miss H. L. Gardner; Sir Edward Herbert; Sir Patrick Linstead, F.R.S.; Sir Philip Morris; Mr H. C. Shearman; Mr R. B. Southall; Mr P. S. Ross (of the Treasury) secretary*

Sir Edward Herbert died on April 28 while the Committee was still sitting.

Terms of Reference: *To review the pattern of full-time higher education in Great Britain and in the light of national needs and resources, to advise Her Majesty's Government on what principles its long-term development should be based. In particular, to advise, in the light of these principles whether there should be any changes in that pattern, whether any new types of institution are desirable and whether any modification should be made in the present arrangements for planning and coordinating the development of the various types of institution.*

The Committee was announced by the Prime Minister, Mr Harold Macmillan, at the end of 1960 and was set up early in 1961. The decision to institute the inquiry came after growing evidence of the pressure on the schools which was likely to come from the failure of higher education to expand as fast as the sixth forms. This pressure was discussed in the Crowther Report (1959) under terms of reference which excluded any investigation of higher education. The creation of C.A.T.s and plans for the expansion of the teacher training colleges, following the introduction of the three-year course (1960), were altering the balance between university and non-university institutions in higher education. The case for an inquiry of the kind eventually set up was argued in the House of Lords on a motion put down by Lord Simon of Wythenshawe in 1960 and attracted support from all sides of the House. Sir David Eccles, then Minister of Education, and responsible for non-university higher education was known to be pressing for an inquiry. (Lord Robbins, former professor of economics at the L.S.E., and latter-day chairman of the *Financial News*, in addition to being one of the Prime Minister's most trusted economic advisers, happened also to have taught Eccles at New College, Oxford.)

The Committee's own summary of the report is reprinted here. Having accepted the case for expansion on a large scale, they devoted the body of the report to an examination of how to expand without the loss either of academic freedom or academic excellence.

Elaborate and detailed statistical appendices prepared under the direction of the Committee's statistical adviser, Professor Claus Moser, backed up the Committee's conclusions at every point. The cost of the report – £128,770, of which £45,000 was the estimated cost of sample surveys – was a measure of the research which went into it, research on a scale unprecedented in the study of English education.

The statistics supported the increases in places and showed that any smaller increase must lead to an accentuation of the pressure on the schools. They showed that sufficient able students and staff could be expected to be forthcoming.

The report followed the Early-Leaving Report, Crowther and Newsom, in the recognition of social rather than genetic limitations in the present flow of students. Its proposals raised the percentage of the age group receiving full-time higher education from about 8 per cent to about 17 per cent (12 per cent for girls, 22 per cent for men) by 1980.

Of crucial importance was the recommendation that a new Ministry of Arts and Sciences should be set up, through whom a higher education Grants Commission should approach the Government. This was the subject of a reservation by Mr H. C. Shearman, a former chairman of the L.C.C. Education Committee.

This recommendation added to the significance of the proposals for the teacher training colleges to be removed from the local authorities and integrated, administratively, into the university pattern (an arrangement closely resembling the first scheme put up in 1944 by half the McNair Committee, including Mr P. R. Morris who, as Sir Philip Morris, Vice-Chancellor of the University of Bristol, was a member of the Robbins Committee). The Ministry of Education's interest in teacher training, and that of the L.E.A.s and the churches, was recognized in the report but not sufficiently to prevent this section of the report arousing opposition inside the Ministry of Education as well as in wider educational circles.

Within twenty-four hours of the publication of the report, the Government accepted the Robbins targets up to 1973 and announced that funds would be made available to the University Grants Committee to this end, including £650m for capital expenditure. They accepted the proposals for the C.A.T.s to become university institutions and for the creation of a small group of technological universities.

THE ROBBINS REPORT

SUMMARY

Comparisons with conditions abroad reveal a situation of some complexity. In the United States of America, the Soviet Union and certain Commonwealth countries the provision of higher education greatly exceeds our own, after allowing for differences in population. But elsewhere the comparison is more ambiguous. Judged on grounds of opportunity offered for entry, our system is well down the list of the systems with which we have compared it. Judged on grounds of output of qualified persons, the comparison is not unfavourable: the United States of America and the Soviet Union apart, we stand very high on the list. But when we compare published plans for future development many other countries are far ahead of us. If, as we believe, a highly educated population is essential to meet competitive pressures in the modern world, a much greater effort is necessary if we are to hold our own.

Our calculation of the future requirement for places in this country is based on an estimate of the numbers of young people who, on the present basis of student grants, will both be able to satisfy suitable entrance requirements for higher education and will wish to be admitted. Our investigations have suggested the existence of large reservoirs of untapped ability in the population, especially among girls: they have also shown a most significant increase in the number of young people coming forward year by year from the schools. We recognise that there can be no certainty how strongly this trend will continue up to 1980. With that qualification (and on assumptions which allow for no relaxation in the degree of competition for entry) we have arrived at a requirement of about 560,000 places for full-time students in all higher education in 1980–1, and of about 390,000 places in 1973–4, compared with 216,000 in 1962–3.

We are clear that the main remedy for the serious strains that are placed on the schools must lie in a great expansion of places in higher education. But there are a number of ways in which the processes for selection for higher education might be improved; and the arrangements for co-ordination between institutions of higher education and the schools should be strengthened. The special problems due to competition for places in institutions of outstanding eminence can only be solved by the improvement of other institutions. . . .

Universities

There is much to praise in the universities' central tradition of teaching and research and their provision of honours courses for studies in depth. But there are also two weaknesses: the small proportion of students in the universities of England and Wales taking first degrees of a broader nature, and the inadequate provision for postgraduate study and research.

Broader courses for the first degree are already available to a larger extent than is often realised. But these courses should be taken by a much greater number of students than at present, both on educational grounds and in the interest of their future careers. . . .

A general lengthening of undergraduate courses to four years is undesirable, but a substantially higher proportion of students than at present should proceed to postgraduate work, with appropriate grants. We consequently recommend more provision both for research and, in particular, for advanced courses.

Colleges for the education of teachers

In the rapidly changing colleges for the education and training of teachers there are very different problems. In England and Wales many of the colleges are very small. Some of the students have the capacity to do work of degree standard; and although the colleges will continue to concentrate in the main on courses of the present kind, it is unjust that there should be no facilities for obtaining a degree. But to confer degree-giving powers on all the existing colleges would be inappropriate because of the number involved, the variation in their sizes and the diversity of standards. . . .

We recommend a radical change. The status of the colleges would best be assured and the problem of degrees satisfactorily solved by a closer association with the universities. Our recommendation is that, as a development from the Institutes of Education in which the colleges are at present associated with the universities, there should be set up University Schools of Education under whose auspices degrees would be available to suitable college students. The Schools of Education would receive finance through the grants committee system. Training Colleges, which should be renamed Colleges of Education, would be given independent governing bodies; they would become members of the Schools of Education and would receive finance from them.

We do not recommend a degree for students who complete the present course: to award both a professional qualification and a degree after three years would leave insufficient time for the depth of academic study that characterises a three-year degree course and would give the students concerned an unfair advantage over those university students who, after a three-year course for a degree, take another year's professional training before becoming teachers. We do, however, recommend that such students as – either on entry or after a preliminary period – are found to possess the capacity should be able, if they wish, to take a course of study that, in addition to giving professional training, leads after four years to a degree. For a minority of students transfer to a university may be appropriate.

For the universities these proposals involve an additional administrative burden at a time when preoccupation with their own expansion will be very great. But we are convinced that immense benefit will flow from closer links with the universities and that our proposals offer the best hope of raising the status and standards of the colleges and securing their full integration into the system of higher education of the future. For the local authorities, who have done so much to promote the development of the colleges, and who are so closely involved in the supply of teachers, these proposals involve parting with institutions to which many of their members have devoted long and energetic service. It is essential that, in ways that we specify in some detail, the local authorities should be associated with the Colleges and the Schools of Education. . . .

Technological and further education

There is an outstanding need to attract a higher proportion of first-class talent into courses in technology and to provide for the more effective organization of research and training at postgraduate level both inside and outside the universities.

We recommend the development of five Special Institutions for Scientific and Technological Education and Research, comparable in size and standing and in advanced research to the great technological institutions of the United States of America and the Continent. The bases for three such institutions already exist in the university sphere. We recommend that another, completely new, institution should be planned and that a fifth should be developed from one of the existing Colleges of Advanced Technology.

We recommend that in general the Colleges of Advanced Technology should be given charters as technological universities. They should be placed as soon as possible under the Grants Commission, which is one of our main recommendations for the future machinery of central government, and, as with the new universities, their progress towards complete autonomy should be supervised by academic advisory committees. . . .

The Regional Colleges are to be regarded as at once providing the seedbed for some further growth of institutions to university status and as fostering, in addition to their characteristic work in science and technology, educational experiments in fields such as the teaching of modern languages and many aspects of business studies.

We hope that, for reasons of economy of staff and equipment, the work of university level will be concentrated as far as possible in selected centres. But we attach great value to the continued provision of facilities for work of university level over a wide area. The Area Colleges will develop in a variety of ways, and the opportunities open to students will be enhanced by our proposals that degrees should be available for appropriate courses.

Students taking advanced courses in the Regional and Area Colleges, should have the same opportunity for degrees as those in university institutions. For this purpose, we recommend the creation of a Council for National Academic Awards to perform, for Britain as a whole and with more extended terms of reference, functions similar to those performed so well in England and Wales by the present National Council for Technological Awards. In particular, the new Council would award degrees.

Future pattern

We have carefully considered whether any new categories of institutions should be introduced. We conclude that in general this is not necessary: the present range of institutions, if imaginatively developed, affords the necessary scope for new experiments and opportunities.

In suggesting how the 560,000 students of 1980 should be distributed between different types of institutions, one of our main concerns has been to reduce the pressure on the schools caused by the shortage of places in the universities. Some of this pressure may well be reduced by the extension of facilities for obtaining degrees in other institutions. But we doubt whether it will be reduced sufficiently. We therefore recommend that the universities' share of entrants to higher education should be increased from 55 per cent. in 1962 to 60 per cent. in 1980.

If this is to happen, the necessary first steps must be taken immediately. Of the 350,000 university places needed by 1980, nearly 300,000 might in favourable conditions be provided by the development of existing institutions, which at present contain 130,000 students. In modern conditions it is desirable that universities should be large enough to have an adequate division of labour within departments and to make economical use of buildings and equipment.

It may be that most of the university places that are required in the next ten years can be provided by such developments. But if no further steps are taken, the situation will thereafter be irretrievable, for universities take long to establish. We therefore recommend the immediate foundation of six new universities, of which at least one should be in Scotland. Another would be the new Special Institution of Scientific and Technological Education and Research. Such new foundations might provide 300,000 places by 1980. The remaining places should be provided by the advancement to university status of some ten Regional Colleges and Colleges of Education. If the scale of these recommendations should seem over-ambitious, we would remind the sceptics that demographic projects beyond 1980 suggest no lessening of the rate at which the demand for places will grow.

Except for management studies and languages, we have not made recommendations about the content of courses in particular subjects, holding this to be a matter best worked out in detail within and among the various institutions concerned. But we consider that there is scope for an increase in the proportion of students in higher education engaged in studying science – this will be largely achieved by current plans of development – and that there is scope for considerable increase in the proportion and an improvement in the quality of those taking technological courses of various kinds.

As we have indicated, much of the expansion contemplated will take place by the growth of existing institutions. But, for the remainder that demands new foundations, having regard to the decisions of the last few years, we wish to emphasise the claims of the great centres of population, both because of the advantages that institutions can draw from such an environment and because of the advantages they can confer. As a result of a recent decision, which we endorsed, there will soon be two universities in Glasgow; and there is room for more than one in some other large cities. . . .

We hope that, as in the past, the universities will maintain an active interest in the provision of [Adult education] courses and that the fruitful co-operation of the agencies in this field will continue.

There is no reason to suppose that in the long term the expansion of higher education need be held up by lack of suitable teachers. But in the short term there will be difficulties; and in any event attention will have to be given to the economical use of manpower and the adoption of the most suitable methods of teaching. We repudiate any suggestion that the teaching problem should be solved at the expense of research, but we think that teaching time might well be used more effectively; and we urge that increased attention should be given to the problems of introducing young men and women from families with scanty educational background to the atmosphere of higher education. We also recommend the provision of more extensive residential facilities for students.

Finance

With an increase from eight to 17 per cent. in the proportion of the relevant age group for whom we recommend that full-time higher education should be provided, the cost of higher education will be substantially increased both absolutely and in relation to the gross national product. While we are unable to put a figure on the return on this outlay considered as an investment, we are clear that it will be remunerative, both in its absolute effects on the general productivity and adaptability of the internal working of the economy and in helping to maintain our competitive position in the world at large.

On the assumption of a constant value of money and an average increase in productivity of 3¼ per cent. per annum, our proposals would lead to an increase in public expenditure on full-time higher education from £206 million in 1962–3 to £742 million in 1980–1; the proportion of gross national product devoted to this purpose would rise from 0·8 to 1·6 per cent. A substantial fraction of the rise in expenditure could be carried without increased relative burden by the increase in productivity we have assumed; and although there would remain a proportion not so carried, such expenditure would be well justified. On any broad appraisal of the return both in productivity and increased capacity for enjoyment, many items at present covered by public expenditure have less claim on our resources than this. . . .

Internal government

In discussing the government of individual autonomous institutions, we defend the principle of lay majorities on ultimate governing bodies but emphasise that there should be strong academic representation and that such bodies should not interfere with strictly academic business. We argue that there should be adequate representation of non-professional members of the teaching body on all internal organs of government not concerned with matters of appointment and promotion. We outline a parallel code for other institutions. We draw attention to the importance of the position of vice-chancellors, especially in a period of expansion, and emphasise the need at once to relieve them of superfluous duties and to make adequate provision for appropriate methods of appointment. . . .

The problems of reconciling in modern conditions the claims of autonomous institutions to academic freedom and the need for adequate co-ordination of a system substantially supported from public funds are the subject of a separate chapter. We set out, both in regard to individuals and institutions, the ingredients of academic freedom that, in our view, are essential to a healthy system of higher education. At the same time we indicate the spheres in which consideration of national needs and an economical use of public resources make it necessary to limit completely free action and to provide some machinery of co-ordination. Recognition of this need has made us all the more aware of its dangers. We therefore lay great emphasis on the principle of control through general block grants administered by an independent committee or commission appointed for its expert qualifications, not for its political affiliations. We regard this principle, exemplified in the present system by the University Grants Committee, as one of the significant administrative inventions of modern times: and we attach great importance to its retention and development in the machinery of government of the future.

Grants commission and Ministerial responsibility

We therefore recommend that oversight of the entire body of autonomous institutions, the universities and the Colleges of Advanced Technology, and with the universities the associated Schools of Education, together with the Scottish Colleges of Education, should be placed in the hands of a Grants Commission.

This body, which would be the lineal successor of the University Grants Committee, would have the duty of advising the government on the magnitude of the grants to be made to this sector of higher education and of distributing grants and assessing the correct allocations to the different institutions concerned. The main body of the Commission would be constituted on the same principles as the University Grants Committee, with a suitably augmented staff. Much of its detailed work would, however, be conducted by a structure of the main Commission. In this way we believe that the intimate contacts characteristic of the operations of the University Grants Committee will be retained, although the scope of the Commission will be considerably wider.

The problem of ministerial responsibility for the Grants Commission presents many difficulties. It would be inappropriate for the Chancellor of the Exchequer to be responsible for the Grants Commission, whose scope will be much wider than that of the University Grants Committee. Nor would it be suitable for it to be the responsibility of a minister without portfolio. We have considered therefore with great care whether the whole education service should become the responsibility of a Secretary of State for Education, and we do not wish to minimise the strength of the case that can be made for this. But in the end we have come to the conclusion that for autonomous institutions, involved as they are not only in teaching but also in research and the advancement of knowledge, the more appropriate conjunction for the Grants Commission would be with the Research Councils, the Arts Council and other bodies that have the status of advisory and distributing intermediaries. We recommend therefore the creation of a new ministry with the responsibility for all such intermediaries, with the title of Ministry of Arts and Science. For Scottish institutions, we recommend a special relationship between the new minister and the Secretary of State for Scotland.

With such a structure of ministerial responsibility – the new minister responsible for the Grants Commission and the institutions dependent on it, and the Minister of Education and the Secretary of State for Scotland remaining responsible for the other institutions of higher education and the schools – there will be a need for co-ordination. The prime responsibility for this will rest with the ministers and their departments, advised on specific questions like the supply of teachers by national advisory bodies. But we also recommend the establishment of a small Consultative Council, composed of people representative of various educational and other interests, to which ministers can remit questions concerned with higher education as a whole, as well as its relations with the schools.

The immediate crisis

The report concludes by drawing attention to an educational emergency now confronting higher education because of the arrival at the ages of 17 and 18 of the very large numbers of children born immediately after the second world war. In our judgment, this is an emergency of the same importance as the emergency produced by demobilisation after the last war and demanding the same type of extraordinary measures to meet it. If the needs of this situation are not adequately met by immediate government action, many of our plans for long-term expansion will be seriously endangered.

[From Chapter 19, pp. 265-76

GUIDING PRINCIPLES

Numbers and eligibility

Throughout our Report we have assumed as an axiom that courses of higher education should be available for all those who are qualified by ability and attainment to pursue them and who wish to do so. What type of education they should get and in what kind of institution are questions we consider later on; and the criterion by which capacity is to be judged is clearly a question on which there may be a variety of opinions. But on the general principle as we have stated it we hope there will be little dispute.

If challenged, however, we would vindicate it on two grounds. First, conceiving education as a means, we do not believe that modern societies can achieve their aims of economic growth and higher cultural standards without making the most of the talents of their citizens. This is obviously necessary if we are to compete with other highly developed countries in an era of rapid technological and social advance. But, even if there were not the spur of international standards, it would still be true that to realise the aspirations of a modern community as regards both wealth and culture a fully educated population is necessary.

But beyond that, education ministers intimately to ultimate ends, in developing man's capacity to understand, to contemplate and to create. And it is a characteristic of the aspirations of this age to feel that, where there is capacity to pursue such activities, there that capacity should be fostered. The good society desires equality of opportunity for its citizens to become not merely good producers but also good men and women.

The recognition of individual achievement

Secondly we have assumed throughout the principle of equal academic awards for equal performance. We think that in any properly co-ordinated system of higher education the academic grading of individuals should depend upon their academic accomplishment rather than upon the status of the institution in which they have studied. We are well aware that there are limits to the realisation of this principle, and that the status accorded by the world to a degree from an institution of long standing and established reputation may well be higher than the status of a degree earned in an examination of comparable severity in an institution of more recent foundation. This is in the nature of things. But it is no argument for retaining formal differences in terminology that do not reflect real differences in attainment.

The status of institutions

We wish to see the removal of any designations or limitations that cause differentiation between institutions that are performing similar functions. Distinctions based on adventitious grounds, whether historical or social, are wholly alien to the spirit that should inform higher education. It must, however, be recognised that within the wide field of higher education there is a need for a variety of institutions whose functions differ. There must, therefore, be distinctions between institutions which, though they are all engaged in higher education, have differing functions and a different emphasis. Our concern is that such distinctions should be genuine, based on the nature of the work done and the organisation appropriate to it, and that nobody should think that in recognising the existence of such distinctions by function we are implying that one kind of institution is more important and valuable to the nation than another. All are needed to provide appropriate educational opportunities and to supply national needs. . . .

Opportunities for transfer

If it is true that certain differences of level and function must be expected to persist among institutions, it is also true that such a structure can only be morally acceptable if there are opportunities for the transfer of a student from one institution to another when this is appropriate to his or her intellectual attainments and educational needs. We attach great importance to this.

Organization

The organisation of higher education must allow for free development of institutions. Existing institutions must be free to experiment without predetermined limitations, except those necessary to safeguard their essential functions; and there must be freedom to experiment with new types of institution if experience shows the desirability of such experiments. Our fundamental postulate of the necessity for system and order is not to be in any way construed as conflicting with this. We ask indeed that there should be co-ordination, some principles of policy commonly accepted, some organisation providing for rational allocation of scarce resources. But we should hold it to be the very bankruptcy of constitutional invention if such conditions were thought to be incompatible with that scope for individual and institutional initiative that British tradition has always held to be one of the main essentials of intellectual and spiritual health. . . .

The maintenance of standards

Finally we must demand of a system that it produces as much high excellence as possible. It must, therefore, be so devised that it safeguards standards. We began our discussion by emphasising the claims of numbers. It is only fitting, therefore, that we should close it by emphasising the claims of achievement and quality. The two ends are not incompatible.

[From Chapter 2, pp. 8–10

CASE FOR ONE MINISTER: MR H. C. SHEARMAN'S RESERVATION

What is needed is that the minister who has to sustain with the Treasury and in Cabinet the financial needs of the universities and other related institutions shall be familiar with the complementary requirements of the schools, and *vice versa*. What is to be feared is that each will be fighting for his own hand and both may suffer. The impact of this situation on the schools, whose needs are, and are likely to continue to be insistent, could be serious – particularly if one result should be that the Minister of Education were supplanted as a member of the Cabinet by the minister regarded as responsible for the 'senior' institutions.

Continuity is essential between the schools, further and part-time education, and full-time higher education. The students would gain confidence if such a continuity visibly existed; and there would be, what is no less important, positive encouragement to the movement of staffs in both directions.

This principle of continuity is nowhere more important than in the sphere of teacher training. Here what the Report aims to achieve is the continued raising of the standards of work in the colleges and an improvement of their status, while retaining close contact with the administration of the schools. This aim would be more surely reached, in my judgment, if co-ordination at the higher level were to be through a single Ministry.

It may well be that some local education authorities have not shown a sufficiently liberal attitude to the colleges; if so, it can and should be changed. On the other hand in many material respects (for instance, the provision of residence) the Ministry of Education and local education authorities have no need to apologise for their record; and, on the other hand, if Training College students have rarely been recognised for degrees, that has not been the fault of the education authorities. . . .

I submit therefore that a single Minister for Education – or Secretary of State if that title is preferred (though I find it rather less euphonious) – with one or two Ministers of State to assist him is the more satisfactory answer. He would take over the present sphere of responsibility of the Minister of Education and that of the Chancellor in respect of the University Grants Committee, (and conceivably some of the other functions alluded to) but he would be at the head of a new department from which a forward-looking outlook might be expected. He would, we should hope, adopt in his department the administrative styles appropriate to the different parts of the wide field he would be called upon to survey. Devolution – on the one hand to the Grants Commission with its wide area of independent action, and on the other (through general grant or other appropriate financial arrangements) to the local education authorities and governing bodies – would be the keynote of his Ministry.

As a matter of practical politics it might well be that such an arrangement would be preferable to creating a ministerial post whose relatively light duties might either be unattractive as a full-time occupation for a senior member of the government or alternatively might even prove an irresistible temptation to excessive interference with the affairs of the Grants Commission.

48 · Comprehensive Reorganization. 1965

Some eight months after the Labour victory in the 1964 General Election, Mr Antony Crosland, Secretary of State for Education and Science, issued a circular inviting local education authorities to submit plans for the reorganization of their secondary schools in order to eliminate selection into separate and different types of secondary school at 11.

The draft of the circular was revised several times before it was issued, to take account of objections raised by the local authority associations. Originally the intention had been to call for reorganization plans, with the assumption that to demand them was within the general authority of the Secretary of State. In the final version the Secretary of State only 'requests' authorities to submit plans, giving a suggested 12-month deadline, which in the event proved impracticable or unacceptable for many authorities.

The circular outlined six main forms of comprehensive reorganization which the Secretary of State was prepared to consider: the 11–18 all-through comprehensive school, the three stage – primary, middle and secondary organization with breaks at 8 or 9 and 12 or 13 – and four kinds of two-tier system. During the course of further study and consideration of the plans which were submitted, the initial prejudice in favour of all-through schools was somewhat diminished and experience showed that the middle school arrangement deserved more support than at first was expected.

At the Labour Party Conference at Blackpool in October 1968, Miss Alice Bacon, Minister of State for Education and Science, announced that the Government would introduce a Bill to compel local Authorities to reorganize on comprehensive lines.

A short Education Bill to this end was brought forward in the autumn of 1969, but before Parliament had completed consideration of the Bill, the Government resigned and were defeated at the General Election of June 1970. (See also: Secondary organization 1970, p. 352.)

By December 1969 schemes had been approved for 129 out of 163 education authorities; 108 of these covered the whole or the greater part of the area. The plans of 12 authorities were under consideration and 6 had yet to produce a plan. Eleven authorities had produced plans which were rejected by the DES and three more had declined to submit any scheme.

CIRCULAR 10/65: *THE ORGANISATION OF SECONDARY EDUCATION*. Issued by the Department of Education and Science on 12 July 1965.

Introduction
It is the Government's declared objective to end selection at eleven plus and to eliminate separatism in secondary education. . . .

The Secretary of State accordingly requests local education authorities, if they have not already done so, to prepare and submit to him plans for reorganising secondary education in their areas on comprehensive lines. . . .

I MAIN FORMS OF COMPREHENSIVE ORGANISATION

Six main forms of comprehensive organisation have so far emerged from experience and discussion:

(i) The orthodox comprehensive school with an age range of 11–18.
(ii) A two-tier system whereby *all* pupils transfer at 11 to a junior comprehensive school and *all* go on at 13 or 14 to a senior comprehensive school.
(iii) A two-tier system under which *all* pupils on leaving primary school transfer to a junior comprehensive school, but at the age of 13 or 14 *some* pupils move on to a senior school while *the remainder* stay on in the same school. There are two main variations: in one, the comprehensive school which all pupils enter after leaving primary school provides no course terminating in a public examination, and normally keeps pupils only until 15; in the other, this school provides G.C.E. and C.S.E. courses, keeps pupils at least until 16, and encourages transfer at the appropriate stage to the sixth form of the senior school.
(iv) A two-tier system in which *all* pupils on leaving primary school transfer to a junior comprehensive school. At the age of 13 or 14 *all* pupils have a choice between a senior school catering for those who expect to stay at school well beyond the compulsory age, and a senior school catering for those who do not.
(v) Comprehensive schools with an age range of 11 to 16 combined with sixth form colleges for pupils over 16.
(vi) A system of middle schools which straddle the primary/secondary age ranges. Under this system pupils transfer from a primary school at the age of 8 or 9 to a comprehensive school with an age range of 8 to 12 or 9 to 13. From this middle school they move on to a comprehensive school with an age range of 12 or 13 to 18.

The most appropriate system will depend on local circumstances and an authority may well decide to adopt more than one form of organisation in the area for which it is responsible. . . . An organisation of type (iii) or (iv) is not fully comprehensive in that it involves the separation of children of differing aims and aptitudes into different schools at the age of 13 or 14. ... Such schemes are acceptable as interim solutions, since they secure many of the advantages of comprehensive education and in some areas offer the most satisfactory method of bringing about reorganisation at an early date. But they should be regarded only as an interim stage . . .

(i) Orthodox comprehensive schools 11 to 18

If it were possible to design a new pattern of secondary education without regard to existing buildings, the all-through comprehensive school would in many respects provide the simplest and best solution. There are therefore strong arguments for its adoption wherever circumstances permit.

In practice, however, circumstances will usually not permit . . . There is, of course, some scope for building new schools of this type; and it should be borne in mind that such schools need not be as large as was once thought necessary to produce a sixth form of economic size. It is now clear that a six or seven form entry school can cater properly for the whole ability range and produce a viable sixth form . . . .

It will sometimes be possible to establish a single comprehensive school in buildings designed for use as separate schools. But any scheme of this type will need careful scrutiny. If buildings are at a considerable distance from each other, or separated by busy roads, the disadvantages are obvious. . . .

(ii) Two-tier systems whereby all pupils transfer at 11 to a junior comprehensive school and at 13 or 14 to a senior comprehensive school

Two-tier systems consisting of junior and senior comprehensive schools, each with its own head teacher, and with automatic transfer of all pupils at 13 or 14, have two clear advantages over other two-tier systems. They avoid discrimination between pupils at the point of transfer; and they eliminate the element of guesswork about the proportion of pupils who will transfer to the senior school. They may, it is true, produce problems of organisation, particularly where a senior school is fed by more than one junior school. . . . But this system is attractive in that it will often fit readily into existing buildings; and it can develop into an all-through system of orthodox comprehensive schools in the course of time as new buildings become available.

(iii) A two-tier system under which all pupils transfer at 11 to a junior comprehensive school and at 13 or 14 some pupils move on to a senior school while others remain in the junior school . . .

. . . The Secretary of State will expect certain conditions to be observed:

(a) It is essential, if selection is not to be reintroduced, that transfer to the senior school should be at parents' choice.

(b) Guidance to parents on transfer should be given on an organised basis and should not take the form of advice by one teacher only.

(c) . . . The parents must have the final decision; but parents from less educated homes in particular should have a full explanation of the opportunities open to their children.

(d) The junior school must be staffed and its curriculum devised so as to cater effectively for the whole ability range in the first two or three years. . . . The more able children must not be held back or denied the range of subjects and quality of teaching which they would have enjoyed in a grammar school. Equally their needs must not be met at the expense of other children. . . .

(*iv*) *Two-tier systems whereby all pupils transfer at 11 to a junior comprehensive school with a choice of senior school at 13 or 14 . . .*

These differ from the schemes described [above] . . . in that the junior comprehensive school has the same age range for all its pupils. No children remain in it beyond the age of 13 or 14. All pupils then have a choice of senior school: one senior school will aim at Advanced level and other sixth form work, while the other will not take its pupils beyond Ordinary level, although the dividing line between the schools can be drawn at different points and they may overlap.

(*v*) *Comprehensive schools with an age range of 11 to 16 combined with a sixth form college for pupils of 16 and over . . .*

Two conceptions of the sixth form college have been put forward. One envisages the establishment of colleges catering for the educational needs of all young people staying on at school beyond the age of 16; the other would make entry to a college dependent on the satisfaction of certain conditions (e.g. five passes at Ordinary level or a declared intention of preparing for Advanced level). A variation of the sixth form college pattern is that which attaches the sixth form unit to one school; under such an arrangement pupils from schools without sixth forms can transfer to a single sixth form at another school. . . .

It is essential that no scheme involving the establishment of a sixth form college should lead to any restriction of existing educational opportunities for young people of 16 to 18. Where authorities are considering the establishment of sixth form colleges they should review all the educational needs of the 16–18 group in their area and the provision they have hitherto made for them, both in sixth forms and in colleges of further education. . . .

In this country there is so far little experience on which to base final judgements on the merits of sixth form colleges. Nevertheless the Secretary of State believes that the issues have been sufficiently debated to justify a limited number of experiments. Where authorities contemplate the submission of proposals, he hopes that they will consult with his Department at an early stage.

(*vi*) *An organisation which involves middle schools straddling the primary/ secondary age ranges . . .*

. . . The establishment of middle schools with age ranges of 8 to 12 or 9 to 13 has an immediate attraction in the context of secondary reorganisation on comprehensive lines. In the first place such schools seem to lead naturally to the elimination of selection. In the second they shorten the secondary school span by one or two years and thus make it possible to have smaller all-through comprehensive schools.

Notwithstanding the *prima facie* attractiveness of middle school systems the Secretary of State does not intend to give his statutory approval to more than a very small number of such proposals in the near future. . . .

II SOME GENERAL CONSIDERATIONS

(*i*) *Buildings*

The disposition, character and size of existing schools, particularly of the schools built since the war which must be assumed to remain in use for a considerable time, must influence and in many cases go far to determine the shape of secondary organisation. . . . It would not be realistic for authorities to plan on the basis that their individual programmes will be increased solely to take account of the need to adapt or remodel existing buildings on a scale which would not have been necessary but for reorganisation. . . .

It is for authorities to weigh these considerations and to devise the most satisfactory plans in relation to local circumstances. In doing so, they should appreciate that while the Secretary of State wishes progress to be as rapid as possible, he does not wish it to be achieved by the adoption of plans whose educational disadvantages more than off-set the benefits which will flow from the adoption of comprehensive schooling.

(ii) Staffing

. . . The Secretary of State will not be able to modify the quota arrangements to take account of individual authorities' proposals in response to this Circular. . . .

. . . *(v) The school community*

. . . The Secretary of State . . . urges authorities to ensure, when determining catchment areas, that schools are as socially and intellectually comprehensive as is practicable. In a two-tier system it may be possible to link two differing districts so that all pupils from both areas go to the same junior and then to the same senior comprehensive schools.

(vi) Voluntary schools

In a number of areas which have already introduced or planned a comprehensive organisation the voluntary schools have not been included, but the plans which the Secretary of State is now requesting authorities to prepare should embrace them. . . . The Secretary of State asks that local education authorities and the governors of voluntary schools should enter into discussions to this end at the earliest practicable stage in the preparation of plans.

It is not essential that the same pattern should be adopted for denominational and other voluntary schools in any given area as is adopted for that area's county schools. The disposition and nature of the existing voluntary school buildings may dictate a different solution; . . .

(vii) Direct Grant schools

. . . The Secretary of State asks that authorities should open discussions at an early stage with the governors of direct grant schools in which they take up places; it may be appropriate for such discussions to be in consultation with any other authorities taking up places in the same schools.

(viii) Consultation

The smooth inception and continuing success of any scheme of reorganisation will depend on the co-operation of teachers and the support and confidence of parents. To secure these there must be a process of consultation and explanation before any scheme is approved by an authority for submission to the Secretary of State. An authority should take all those concerned into its confidence at as early a stage as possible. . . .

III PREPARATION AND SUBMISSION OF PLANS

... Plans should be submitted within one year of the date of this Circular, although the Secretary of State may exceptionally agree an extension to this period in the case of any individual authority. Plans should be in two parts as follows:

(a) A general statement of the authority's long-term proposals . . .
(b) A detailed statement of the authority's proposals, whether or not they have already been discussed with the Department, covering a period of three years starting not later than September 1967.

49 · Report of the Central Advisory Council (England) entitled *Children and their Primary Schools*. Volume I: Report. Volume II: Research and Surveys. [*The Plowden Report*]

Published: *1967*

Chairman: *Lady Plowden*

Members: *Sir John Newsom (Deputy Chairman); Mr H. G. Armstrong; Professor A. J. Ayer; Miss M. F. M. Bailey; Mrs M. Bannister; Miss M. Brearley; Dr I. C. R. Byatt; The Hon. Mrs J. Campbell; Professor D. V. Donnison; Miss Z. E. Dix; Professor C. E. Gittins; Miss S. E. Grey; Mr E. W. Hawkins; Miss E. M. Parry; Mr A. Puckey; Mr T. H. F. Raison; Alderman Mrs E. V. Smith; Mr R. T. Smith; Professor J. M. Tanner; Brigadier L. L. Thwaytes; Mr T. H. Tunn; Mr Martin H. Wilson; Mr F. M. White; Dr M. Young; Mr J. E. H. Blackie, H.M.I. (Assessor); Mr. D. H. Leadbetter (Assessor); Miss E. M. McDougall H.M.I. (Assessor); Miss M. E. Nicholls, H.M.I. (Assessor); Mr M. Kogan (Secretary); Mr N. Summers (Assistant Secretary until March 1965); Miss C. K. Burke (Assistant Secretary from January 1964).*

The following members of the Department and H.M. Inspectorate also assisted the Council: *Miss S. M. C. Duncan, H.M.I.; Miss N. L. Goddard; Mr D. T. Jones, H.M.I.*

The Council were appointed in August 1963 and begun work under these terms of reference in October 1963. Mr P. Mursell resigned from membership of the Council in January 1964 and Mr H. B. Rose in February 1965.

Terms of Reference: *To consider primary education in all its aspects, and the transition to secondary education.*

The inquiry into primary education was initiated as a natural successor to the two major inqufries into secondary education. Just as the Newsom Report was the lineal successor of the Hadow Report on the Education of the Adolescent (1926) so the Plowden inquiry was a follow-up of two other Hadow reports, *The Primary School* (1931) and *Infant and Nursery Schools* (1933).

The age of transfer was specifically referred to the Council in the light of suggestions emanating from the West Riding of Yorkshire for a three-tier organization, including middle schools taking children from 9 to 13, spanning the traditional break at 11.

The most important recommendations concerned the impact of social disadvantage on educational opportunity. This was a theme which the Newsom Report had dwelt on (see p. 281) and the Plowden Council carried on where Newsom left off. The report enunciated a new administrative principle – that 'positive discrimination' should be exercised through the educational system to counteract the adverse effects of a bad environment. In so doing it introduced the idea of 'educational priority areas' and suggested how a formula could be devised to define the areas of greatest need to which extra resources – more teachers, more salary allowances, more equipment and minor building works – could be diverted.

The Report advocated a steady expansion of nursery education for the most part on a half-day basis, starting with the priority areas. Other recommendations included an increase in the recruitment of nursery assistants and a programme for the recruitment and training of a new category of staff to be known as teachers' aides, with a training of one to two years, largely of a practical nature.

The Council decided that transfer to secondary education should take place at 12 plus, and that legislation should be introduced to make for a more flexible starting age, with half-day nursery education from three to five, and optional half-day in the 'first' (infants) school up to six. After a three-year course the pupil would transfer at eight to the 'middle' (junior) school. As an interim measure the report proposed that children should begin whole-day school twice a year (September and April) with staggered admission during the first term. Part-time attendance for half a day 'should be available for up to two terms before full-time entry'.

The report also put much stress on the relations between school and home, and on the participation of parents in school activities.

THE PLOWDEN REPORT · 1967

Heredity and Environment

Biologists are now much clearer than they were 30 years ago about the manner in which hereditary and environmental factors interact to produce a characteristic, be that characteristic stature or the score in an intelligence test. What is inherited are the genes. Except in very special instances, such as the blood groups and a few diseases, the chemical substance that any given gene causes to be produced is not directly related to any characteristic of a child or an adult. All characteristics have a history of continuous developmental interactions, first of gene products with other gene products, then of more complex molecules with other molecules, then of cells with cells, of tissues with the environment of the mother's uterus, and finally of a whole complex organism with an equally complex environment during the whole of growth after birth. It is now believed that all characteristics are developed in this way;

none is inherited. And none can develop without the necessary genetic endowment to provide the basis, a basis as essential for characteristics which are learned as for those which are apparently not learned. The effect of this new biological outlook is of particular importance when we come to consider the question of changes in measured intelligence.

From an educational point of view the characteristics which have most importance such as intelligence are those which vary in degree in a population rather than being simply present or absent. Stature is a similar example related to physical characteristics. One cannot meaningfully talk of genes for tallness nor of genes for high intelligence. What we can say about such characteristics is that in a given population, growing up under given environmental circumstances, *x* per cent of the variability in height or intelligence can be attributed to inherited factors (the genotype), *y* per cent to environmental ones, and *z* per cent to genotype-environment interaction. The point is that hereditability is not a quantity that belongs to a characteristic but to a population in its environment. Accordingly it varies with the population and the environment. The more uniform the environment, the greater the proportion of variability due to genotype. In England, for example, the differences in height between adults are largely due to hereditary causes, for most children have had enough to eat. But in many underdeveloped countries, where starvation and disease are rife, more of the adult variation will be environmental in origin and a smaller proportion genetic.

The interaction of genes and environment may not be additive; for example, bettering the nutrition by a given amount may not produce a ten per cent increase in height in each person in a population irrespective of his genetic constitution. There may be genotype-environment interaction. Some people may have a rise of 12 per cent, others of eight per cent, depending on whether they carry genes making them react favourably to this new environmental circumstance. A particular environment, in other words, may be highly suitable for a child with certain genes, but highly unsuitable for a child with others. We do not know if such interactions occur in the genesis, for example, of the variations in measured intelligence in our population. If they do, and in principle this seems likely, it would follow that giving everybody the maximum educational opportunity may mean creating individual educational environments for different children. In the same way deprivation would not necessarily mean the same thing for one child as for another.

Genetic factors operate throughout the whole period of growth. Not all genes are active at birth; some only begin to exert their influence after a period of time. Probably this phased effect accounts for the fact that, physically, and perhaps in other respects, children resemble their parents increasingly as they grow older. Some environmental factors, too, may produce little apparent effect when they are most obviously operative, but a larger effect at some later time. This is known as the 'sleeper' effect.

[From Chapter 2, pp. 13–24

Parents' attitudes

Our argument . . . is that educational policy should explicitly recognize the power of the environment upon the school and of the school upon the environment. Teachers are linked to parents by the children for whom they are both responsible. The triangle should be completed and a more direct relationship established between teachers and parents. They should be partners in more than name; their responsibility become joint instead of several.

The need for this is apparent from the results of the National Survey. This enquiry has taken further the investigations undertaken for the Council in connexion with each of its three last reports. . . .

Everything that can be learned from the survey about parents and their relation to the schools is . . . important as a signpost for action. . . . More than half the parents had left school at 14, yet three-quarters wanted their children to stay at school beyond the minimum age. There was little difference in the number of evenings when parents from different socio-economic groups could spend some time with their children; but it is rather disconcerting to find that only about half the mothers did things with their children for some part of most evenings. Similarly, there was little distinction between the proportion of parents in each occupational group who said they wanted the schools to give their children work to do at home. Yet a far smaller proportion of manual workers than of those in other occupations were in fact given work to do at home by their schools. A quarter of all parents, irrespective of the kind of work done by the fathers, were disinclined to visit schools unless they were specially invited.

There were . . . marked contrasts between manual and non-manual workers, and even more between those in professional and managerial occupations, and semi-skilled and unskilled workers. Perhaps the most noticeable difference was in the part played by fathers in children's education. Over two-fifths of the manual workers had left the choice of school entirely to their wives, as compared with less than a quarter of the non-manual workers. Almost half the manual workers, as compared with less than a quarter of non-manual workers, had not been to their child's present school at all. Less than a quarter had talked to the head.

What is particularly true of manual workers is true in somewhat smaller measure of their wives. The higher the socio-economic group, the more parents attended open days, concerts and parent-teacher association meetings, and the more often they talked with heads and class teachers. . . . Manual workers and their wives were more likely to feel, when they had visited the schools, that they had learnt nothing fresh about their children, or that teachers should have asked them more. Not surprisingly, less help with school work was given at home to children of manual workers. Considerably lower proportions of parents from manual worker homes bought, for use at home, copies of some of the books children were using at school. Two-thirds of unskilled workers had five books or fewer in the home, apart from children's books and magazines, as contrasted with one-twentieth of professional workers.

In view of the fact that 29 per cent of all homes have five books or less, the schools are successful in encouraging children to read. About half of the children borrowed books from school to read at home and four-fifths borrowed books either from the school or from public libraries. Only among the children of unskilled workers was there rather less borrowing of books from school, though a substantially bigger proportion of non-manual than of manual workers' children borrowed from public libraries. It looks as though, despite the good work done, the schools need to provide still more books for home use for the children of manual workers. . . .

Our evidence . . . suggests that parents' occupation, material circumstances and education explain only about a quarter of the variation in attitudes, leaving three-quarters or more not accounted for. This implies that attitudes could be affected in other ways, and altered by persuasion.

Our findings can give hope to the school, to interested parents, and to those responsible for educational policy. Parental attitudes appear as a separate influence because they are not monopolized by any one class. Many manual workers and their wives already encourage and support their children's efforts to learn. If there are many now, there can be even more later. Schools can exercise their influence not only directly upon children but also indirectly through their relationships with parents.

[From Chapter 3, pp. 29–36

Educational Priority Areas

In a neighbourhood where the jobs people do and the status they hold owe little to their education it is natural for children as they grow older to regard school as a brief prelude to work rather than an avenue to future opportunities. Some of these neighbourhoods have for generations been starved of new schools, new houses and new investment of every kind. Everyone knows this; but for year after year priority has been given to the new towns and new suburbs, because if new schools do not keep pace with the new houses some children will be unable to go to school at all. The continually rising proportion of children staying on at school beyond the minimum age has led some authorities to build secondary schools and postpone the rebuilding of older primary schools. Not surprisingly, many teachers are unwilling to work in a neighbourhood where the schools are old, where housing of the sort they want is unobtainable, and where education does not attain the standards they expect for their own children. From some neighbourhoods, urban and rural, there has been a continuing outflow of the more successful young people. The loss of their enterprise and skill makes things worse for those left behind. Thus the vicious circle may turn from generation to generation and the schools play a central part in the process, both causing and suffering cumulative deprivation.

We have ourselves seen schools caught in such vicious circles and read accounts of many more. They are quite untypical of schools in the rest of the country. We noted the grim approaches; incessant traffic noise in narrow streets; parked vehicles hemming in the pavement; rubbish dumps on waste land nearby; the absence of green playing spaces on or near the school sites; tiny play grounds; gaunt looking buildings; often poor decorative conditions inside; narrow passages; dark rooms; unheated and cramped cloakrooms; unroofed outside lavatories; tiny staff rooms; inadequate storage space with consequent restriction on teaching materials and therefore methods; inadequate space for movement and P.E.; meals in classrooms; art on desks; music only to the discomfort of others in an echoing building; non-soundproof partitions between classes; lack of smaller rooms for group work; lack of spare room for tuition of small groups; insufficient display space; attractive books kept unseen in cupboards for lack of space to lay them out; no privacy for parents waiting to see the head; sometimes the head and his secretary sharing the same room; and, sometimes all around, the ingrained grime of generations.

We heard from local education authorities of growing difficulty in replacing heads with successors of similar calibre. It is becoming particularly hard to find good heads of infant or deputy heads of junior schools. We are not surprised to hear of the rapid turnover of staff, of vacancies sometimes unfilled or filled with a succession of temporary and supply teachers of one kind or another. Probationary teachers are trained by heads to meet the needs of their schools but then pass on to others where strains are not so great. Many teachers able to do a decent job in an ordinary school are defeated by these conditions. Some become dispirited by long journeys to decaying buildings to see each morning children among whom some seem to have learned only how not to learn.

Heads rely on the faithful, devoted and hard working regulars. There may be one or two in any school, or they may be as many as half the staff, who have so much to do in keeping the school running that they are sometimes too tired even to enjoy their own holidays.

We saw admission registers whose pages of new names with so many rapid crossings out told their own story of a migratory population. In one school 111 out of 150 pupils were recent newcomers. We heard heads explain, as they looked down the lines, that many of those who had gone were good pupils, while a high proportion of those who had been long in the school came from crowded, down-at-heel homes.

What these deprived areas need most are perfectly normal, good primary schools alive with experience from which children of all kinds can benefit. . . . But, . . . there are special and additional demands on teachers who work in deprived areas with deprived children. They meet special challenges. Teachers must be constantly aware that ideas, values and relationships within the school may conflict with those of the home, and that the world assumed by teachers and school books may be unreal to the children. There will have to be constant communication between parents and the schools if the aims of the schools are to be fully understood. The child from a really impoverished background may well have had a normal, satisfactory emotional life. What he often lacks is the opportunity to develop intellectual interests. This shows in his poor command of language. It is not, however, with vocabulary that teaching can begin. The primary school must first supply experiences and establish relationships which enable children to discriminate, to reason and to express themselves. Placing such children in the right stance for further learning is a very skilled operation. But those who have done remedial work will be aware of the astonishing rapidity of the progress which can be achieved, particularly in extending vocabulary, once children's curiosity is released. The thrust to learn seems to be latent in every child, at least within a very wide range of normality. But however good the opportunities, some children may not be able to take advantage of them. Failure may have taken away from them their urge to learn.

A teacher cannot and should not give the deep personal love that each child needs from his parents. There are ways he can help:–

(a) He can relieve children of responsibility without dominating them in a way which prevents them from developing independence. Deprived children may have been forced into premature responsibility. They are often given the care of younger children and are free to roam, to go to bed or to stay up, to eat when and where they can. This produces what is often a spurious maturity. Confidence can be encouraged by tasks which are fully within their capacity. A measure of irresponsibility has to be allowed for: it will pretty certainly come later, and in a less acceptable form, if not permitted at the proper time.

(b) A teacher can do much by listening and trying to understand the context of the questions the children ask. It will be much easier if he knows the child's family and the neighbourhood surrounding his home.

(c) Children in deprived neighbourhoods are often backward. There is a risk that an inexperienced teacher will think there is not time for anything but the three Rs if the child is not to be handicapped throughout his life. This is quite wrong. These children need time for play and imaginative and expressive work and may suffer later if they do not get it at school.

(d) Teachers need to use books which make sense to the children they teach. They will often have to search hard for material which is suitable for downtown children.

(e) Record keeping is especially necessary for teachers in schools in deprived neighbourhoods. There is so much coming and going by families that a child's progress may depend very much on the amount and quality of information that can be sent with him from school to school . . .

We propose a nation-wide scheme for helping those schools and neighbourhoods in which children are most severely handicapped. This policy will have an influence over the whole educational system, and it colours all the subsequent recommendations in our Report. It must not be put into practice simply by robbing more fortunate areas of all the opportunities for progress to which they have been looking forward; it can only succeed if a larger share of the nation's resources is devoted to education. So far-reaching a set of proposals must be firmly rooted in educational grounds, yet the arguments for them inevitably extend beyond this field into many other branches of the nations' affairs. . . .

Our argument thus far can be briefly summarized. As things are at the moment there is no reason why the educational handicaps of the most deprived children should disappear. Although standards will rise, inequalities will persist and the potential of many children will never be realized. The range of achievement amongst English children is wide, and the standards attained by the most and the least successful begin to diverge very early. Steps should be taken to improve the educational chances and the attainments of the least well placed, and to bring them up to the levels that prevail generally. This will call for a new distribution of educational resources. . . .

The many teachers who do so well in face of adversity cannot manage without cost to themselves. They carry the burdens of parents, probation officers and welfare officers on top of their classroom duties. It is time the nation came to their aid. The principle, already accepted, that special need calls for special help, should be given a new cutting edge. We ask for 'positive discrimination' in favour of such schools and the children in them, going well beyond an attempt to equalize resources. Schools in deprived areas should be given priority in many respects. The first step must be to raise the schools with low standards to the national average; the second, quite deliberately to make them better. The justification is that the homes and neighbourhoods from which many of their children come provide little support and stimulus for learning. The schools must supply a compensating environment. The attempts so far made within the educational system to do this have not been sufficiently generous or sustained, because the handicaps imposed by the environment have not been explicitly and sufficiently allowed for. They should be. . . .

Every authority where deprivation is found should be asked to adopt 'positive discrimination' within its own area, and to report from time to time on the progress made. Some authorities contain schools or even one school of this kind where deprivation is so serious that they need special help. Most of these schools and areas are already well known to teachers, administrators, local Inspectors and H.M. Inspectors. Local knowledge will not be sufficient to justify decisions which are bound on occasion to be controversial. Objective criteria for the selection of 'educational priority schools and areas' will be needed to identify those schools which need special help and to determine how much assistance should be given by the government. . . .

The criteria required must identify those places where educational handicaps are reinforced by social handicaps. Some of the main criteria which could be used in an assessment of deprivation are given below. They are not placed in order of importance, nor is any formula suggested by which they should be combined. They may require further study. The criteria are:

(a) *Occupation.* The National Census can report on occupations within quite small areas, and, for particular schools, the data can be supplemented without too much difficulty. The analyses would show the proportions of unskilled and semi-skilled manual workers.

(b) *Size of Families.* The larger the family, the more likely are the children to be in poverty. Wages are no larger for a married man with young children than they are for a single man with none. Family size is still associated with social class, and men with four or more children tend to be amongst the lowest wage earners. Family size also correlates with the results of intelligence tests – the larger the family, the lower the scores of the children . . .

(c) *Supplements in Cash or Kind from the State* are of various kinds. Where the parents are needy, children are allowed school meals free. The proportions so benefiting vary greatly from school to school, and afford a reasonably good guide to relative need. . . .

(d) *Overcrowding and Sharing of Houses* should certainly be included amongst the criteria. It will identify families in cramped accommodation in central and run-down areas of our cities. . . .

(e) *Poor Attendance and Truancy* are a pointer to home conditions, and to what Burt long ago singled out as a determinant of school progress, the 'efficiency of the mother'. Truancy is also related to delinquency. . . .

(f) *Proportions of Retarded, Disturbed or Handicapped Pupils* in ordinary schools. . . .

(g) *Incomplete Families* where one or other of the parents is dead, or not living at home for whatever reason . . .

(h) *Children Unable to Speak English* need much extra attention if they are to find their feet in England. . . .

Once educational priority areas have been selected, the next step must be to give them the help they need. . . . The most important thing is to bring more experienced and successful teachers into these areas and to support them by a generous number of teachers' aides. Until there are more teachers all round, the possibility for increasing their numbers in these schools will, of course, be limited. . . . To start with, quotas should be raised for authorities with educational priority areas. But the schools in greatest need often cannot recruit their full complement at present, and to increase it, if that were all, would do nothing but cause irritation. Additional incentives are needed. We therefore recommend that there should be extra allowances for teachers and head teachers serving in schools in difficult areas. In many ways their work is already more arduous than their colleagues'. They will in future be expected to assume yet further responsibilities, not only in making contact with parents but also in arranging activities for their children outside the normal limits of the school day, and in collaborating with other local social services. Teachers in such schools deserve extra recognition and reward. . . .

We argue [*elsewhere in the Report*] that part-time attendance at a nursery school is desirable for most children. It is even more so for children in socially deprived neighbourhoods. They need above all the verbal stimulus, the opportunities for constructive play, a more richly differentiated environment and the access to medical care that good nursery schools can provide. The building of new nursery schools and extensions to existing schools should start in priority areas and spread outwards. As a minimum we suggest that all children aged four to five who live in the areas should have the opportunity of part-time attendance and that perhaps 50 per cent should have full-time places. . . .

Positive discrimination accords with experience and thinking in many other countries, and in other spheres of social policy. It calls both for some redistribution of the resources devoted to education and, just as much, for an increase in their total volume. It must not be interpreted simply as a gloss upon the recommendations which follow in later chapters. This would not only be a misunderstanding of the scheme; it would destroy all hope of its success. For it would be unreasonable and self-defeating – economically, professionally and politically – to try to do justice by the most deprived children by using only resources that can be diverted from more fortunate areas. We have argued that the gap between the educational opportunities of the most and least fortunate children should be closed, for economic and social reasons alike. It cannot be done, unless extra effort, extra skill and extra resources are devoted to the task.

[From Chapter 5, pp. 50-65

Survey of quality

We felt the need for an assessment covering all the primary schools. Since H.M. Inspectors were in the best position to undertake a comprehensive survey we asked them to do so.

All the 20,664 primary schools in England were included in the survey, apart from 676 which were either too new to be assessed or for some other reason could not be classified. The whole body of H.M. Inspectors responsible for the inspection of primary schools took part. It is probable that misjudgments which must have occurred in particular cases cancelled each other out. The survey was planned to ensure that the various categories into which the schools were placed were exhaustive and did not overlap, to eliminate as far as possible the idiosyncrasies of personal judgement and to make certain that the identity of individual schools could not be discovered.

In the first category were placed schools described as 'In most respects a school of outstanding quality'. These are schools which are outstanding in their work, personal relationships and awareness of current thinking on children's educational needs. They are the pacemakers and leaders of educational advance. This category contained 109 schools in which there were about 29,000 children, representing one per cent of the total primary school population. The second category, 'A good school with some outstanding features', indicated schools of high quality, far above the average, but lacking the special touch of overall rare distinction needed to qualify for the first category. There were 1,538 of these schools educating nine per cent of the total number of primary school children. That ten per cent of the schools should fall into these two categories of excellence is highly satisfactory. 4,155 schools (23 per cent of the children) were in the third category: 'A good school in most respects without any special distinction'. These are schools marked by friendly relationships between staff and children, few or no problems of discipline, a balanced curriculum, good achievement and an unmistakable recognition of children's growth and needs as they are known. One-third of the children in primary schools go to schools which are quite clearly good.

Category 9 was 'A bad school where children suffer from laziness, indifference, gross incompetence or unkindness on the part of the staff'. Into this category fell 28 schools with 4,333 children, or 0·1 per cent of the whole. We were at pains to discover not so much how such schools had come to be since in any large group of human beings or institutions there must always be a few complete failures, but what was done about them when they were identified. Each of the 28 schools was followed up by the local authorities and by H.M. Inspectors, and action taken. There may always be bad appointments of head teachers; and deterioration in health or character may explain schools such as these. We doubt whether any school in this category would be suffered to stay there long.

[From Chapter 8, p. 101

Streaming

Streaming is, as we have seen, by far the most common way of organizing junior schools, but there is reason to think that practice is changing. Only four per cent of junior schools had rejected streaming according to a 1962 survey. The next year the N.F.E.R. found in their enquiry into junior schools that six per cent did without it. . . .

Teachers' views may be moving faster than practice has done. In the 1962 Survey, 85 per cent of primary teachers favoured streaming, six per cent had mixed views and nine per cent were hostile. Of the replies of teachers to our own enquiry . . . only 34 per cent approved of streaming for all or most junior children, 25 per cent approved of streaming for older pupils and 30 per cent were hostile. . . .

To judge by the parents in the National Survey professional opinion is swinging more rapidly against streaming than is public opinion generally. In 1964, two-thirds of the parents preferred their children to be taught in classes streamed by ability. There was no difference according to social class. A clear majority favoured streaming even among those parents who thought that their children were being taught in classes of mixed ability. . . .

Before the 1939 war, streaming was seen as a device for opening the grammar schools to talented working class pupils. . . . Selection for secondary education has been challenged on three main educational grounds: the accuracy of the selective process, the contrast in the provision made for children of differing ability and the effect of segregating them on their achievement. It has also been criticized as being socially divisive both because it gives middle class children a better chance than manual workers' children to secure grammar school places, and because it gives better career openings to grammar school than to modern school pupils. The same arguments are also used against selection for primary school classes, or streaming. . . .

In coming to our conclusions we have taken into account our impressions of schools which we have visited, the evidence we have received and the results of research. Streaming is almost unknown on the continent of Europe, and repetition of the year's work, which is a form of streaming, is declining. . . .

Streaming involves selecting. In schools which are streamed throughout, children are selected at seven. We know of no satisfactory method of assigning seven year old children, still less those who are even younger, to classes graded by attainment or ability. When head teachers rely on their own judgement and those of the infant school heads, they may underestimate the difference which the home makes to the speed of learning to read. But this is one of the main yardsticks by which teachers compare children. Differences in attainments may be more due to differences in age than heads recognize – after all some seven year olds have had half as much education again as others. Objective tests have the advantages that these tests make allowance for age but few group tests are satisfactory at seven and few primary school teachers can find time to give individual tests. There is, too, a danger that if objective tests are known to be used a seven plus test with its pressures and tensions may be substituted for an 11 plus examination. It is known that of the predictions made at 11, by the best methods available, between 10 per cent and 20 per cent turn out to be mistaken within the next three to five years. The earlier that tests are given, the less relevant they are bound to be to an education which will continue to 15 or later. . . .

If many children are bound to be wrongly placed at seven, the amount of transfer between classes is important. Professor Vernon has estimated that it would be reasonable to expect ten per cent of pupils to be transferred each year. It is clear that the actual proportion of transfer is smaller. One sample of two streamed schools showed an annual rate of transfer of 2·3 per cent between eight and 11. In a small sample of three streamed schools there was a transfer rate of six per cent. The conclusion drawn by the N.F.E.R. from their survey was that there was a relatively small amount of transfer in 1961–62.

The reasons for a small amount of transfer are not clear. Teachers, when asked to estimate a figure, almost always over-estimate it. It may be that assessments as children progress through a school are no more reliable than those first made and give no firm grounds for reversal of judgements. . . .

The system of streaming favours girls who are, age for age, more mature than boys and more disposed to play 'the good pupil role' and therefore to gain the approval of their teachers. Research is certainly not needed to substantiate the evidence of any observant visitor to schools that lower streams and remedial classes contain more than their share of boys. The lower the stream, the younger the average age, and the higher the proportion of children who will have had only six terms in the infant school. Conversely, the higher the stream, the older the average age and the higher the proportion of children who will have spent nine terms in infant classes. Of the children in remedial classes in schools studied by the N.F.E.R. . . . 39 per cent had been at the infant schools for the minimum period of six terms and only 12 per cent for the maximum course of nine terms.

There is also much evidence that streaming serves as a means of social selection. It is not simply that middle class pupils congregate in upper streams and the children of semi-skilled and unskilled workers in lower streams. That might be expected from the association of intelligence with social class and occupation. Evidence is also available that more middle class children are to be found in upper streams and fewer in lower streams than would be expected from their results in objective tests. Similarly a higher proportion of children, known from earlier records to have received poor maternal care in early childhood, were in lower streams than their test scores warranted. How much of this placing was due to characteristics in the children which might have made them unsuccessful in an upper stream, how much to teachers' assumptions that clean and well kept children are abler, it is impossible to say.

Selection will inevitably be inaccurate. If the conditions for upper and lower streams were equally good and if all children stood equally high in the respect and affection of the staff, it would not perhaps matter very much whether children were wrongly placed. One of the principal advantages claimed by teachers for streaming is that it makes possible smaller classes and individual help for the slower children. That significantly smaller classes are in fact organized for these children is demonstrated quite clearly from the N.F.E.R. survey. But it is also true that a bigger class is thought to demand a stronger teacher, and the smaller classes, where almost every child may have difficulty in learning and many also have emotional problems, may therefore fall to the less experienced teachers. Their lack of experience may make it exceptionally difficult for them to set their sights – or rather the children's sights – high enough. The multiplicity of the problems with which some teachers have to deal, their low assessment of the children's capacity and the slow rate of progress at which they aim may explain why, at the end of the year, few children stand out as needing transfer. There are of course many schools where teachers alternate between upper and lower streams and where much thought is given to the selection of teachers for classes of slow learning pupils. Nevertheless experience, borne out by research, suggests that in the main the older and more experienced teachers and particularly the deputy heads and holders of graded posts are assigned to the upper streams. Teachers may be streamed, no less than pupils. The more established the teacher the more probable it is that he will get one of the better classrooms and a generous supply of books and equipment. . . .

Finally what is the effect of streaming on children's achievement and attitudes? In 1959 a summary of research on streaming concluded that it was not possible, on the evidence available, either to establish a case against streaming or to prove that it was a more effective form of organization. Since that date further evidence has been published, but it has not materially altered the conclusion. There has been some indication that the standards of attainment of the weaker children may rise when schools are deliberately unstreamed. But the Manchester Survey, 1964, shows that attainment in objective tests tends to be better in streamed schools and that this association does not disappear when allowance is made for the size of school, which is usually related to the type of neighbourhood and therefore to good attainment. It also gives no support to the view that streaming has an adverse effect on children of low ability. The National Survey in which many more variables are held constant, shows no association, positive or negative, between streamed schools and reading attainment, except for a small positive association in the case of top infant girls. The results of the N.F.E.R. cross-sectional study of attainment in matched streamed and unstreamed schools are particularly interesting. . . . Reasonably enough, the tests chosen are similar to those generally used in junior schools. Both at seven and at ten children in streamed schools did somewhat better than those in unstreamed schools. But in no case save in mechanical arithmetic, which is known to give poor prediction of later success in mathematics, was the average difference more than two or three questions right on a test of 30 or 40 items. The advantage for children in streamed schools was most marked when tests assessed the more formal work such as computation and least marked in reading. By ten the lead of children in streamed schools had been reduced in all tests and there was no significant difference in reading, a result identical with that found in the National Survey. There is other evidence which suggests that children who are taught by informal methods make a slower beginning and catch up towards the end of the primary school.

There is some evidence which suggests that achievement in the limited field of measurable attainment is higher in streamed schools. It is not so marked as to be decisive, and our view – which is supported by the results of the N.F.E.R. enquiry – is that forms of organization are less critical than the underlying differences in teachers' attitudes and practice which are sometimes associated with them.

Nevertheless organization can reflect and reinforce attitudes. Schools which treat children individually will accept unstreaming throughout the whole school. When such an organization is established with conviction and put into effect with skill, it produces a happy school and an atmosphere conducive to learning. Not all teachers are yet ready or able to go so far. Even so, it has now been generally accepted that it is impossible to assess accurately the potential of children of primary school age. The younger the children, the greater the inaccuracy is bound to be. We welcome unstreaming in the infant or first school and hope that it will continue to spread through the age groups of the junior or middle schools.

[From Chapter 20, pp. 287–91

50· Report of the Central Advisory Council for Education (Wales) entitled *Primary Education in Wales*. [*The Gittins Report*]

Published: *1968*

Chairman: *Charles Gittins, Professor of Education, University College, Swansea.*

Members: *Miss M. Anthony; Mr J. Brace; Mr E. D. Davies; Sister Dominica; Mr I. C. Evans; Miss S. E. Grey; Mr E. Humphreys; Alderman D. Jones; Mr J. D. Jones; Dr J. H. Jones; Professor H. D. Lewis; Professor D. C. Marsh; Mr G. I. Thomas; Mrs I. D. Thomas; Councillor W. T. Vaughan; Mr A. Williams; Dr J. A. Williams; Mrs N. H. Williams; Mr A. H. Williams, H.M.I.* (*Assessor*)*; Dr G. A. V. Morgan, H.M.I.* (*Secretary*)*; Dr P. E. Owen, H.M.I.* (*Assistant Secretary from February 1965 to March 1966*)*; Mr G. H. Osborne* (*Administrative Officer*)*; Mr J. B. Davies* (*Full-time assistant to Secretary from July, 1965*)

The Council were appointed in August 1963 and began work under these terms of reference in April 1964.

Terms of Reference: *To consider the whole subject of primary education and the transition to secondary education.*

The Gittins report appeared a year after the Plowden inquiry (see p. 308) and covered the same ground from the Welsh viewpoint. Professor Gittins and Miss Ena Grey also sat on the CAC (England) and the Plowden papers were circulated.

The Gittins Committee gave special attention to the needs of the small primary school in the Welsh, bilingual, context and to the initial and in-service training required for teachers in these schools. In the extract quoted here from Chapter 20, the Council argued in favour of relaxing the legal requirement for religious instruction – the first major public committee to do so. In the annual report of the Department of Education and Science for 1968 – *Education and Science in 1968* – the view of the then Secretary of State, Mr Edward Short was recorded. Mr Short, the report stated, 'made it clear that so long as he was Secretary of State there would be no change in the statutory requirements'.

Welsh language

We accept as a basic principle that every child in Wales should have the opportunity to be taught through the medium of his mother-tongue during the infant stage of education. Similarly, at the junior stage and during the transition to the secondary stage, his mother-tongue should form a substantial part of his education and be the main medium of instruction.

Each child should be given the opportunity of learning effectively his second language, Welsh or English, during the primary stage. To create the conditions for effective bilingualism, the second language should be introduced as early as feasible and be used at the appropriate time and in reasonable measure as a parallel medium of instruction.

Each child should be given sufficient opportunity to become reasonably bilingual by the end of the primary stage, i.e. between 11 and 13 years. For most children whose first language is Welsh, this means full oral fluency in Welsh, with attainment in reading and writing appropriate to their age, together with the ability to speak English reasonably fluently and correctly, to read English with comprehension and interest and to write simple English. None of these skills would necessarily be at the average level expected of first-language English pupils of the same age. For first-language English pupils, the aim should be reasonable oral proficiency in Welsh at the end of the primary stage so that the language may be used with confidence in conversational situations within and outside the school. With such competence, a child could make his way about in a Welsh-speaking area. Whilst such oral skill is the prime consideration, this should not exclude the introduction and use of reading and writing, and the foundations should be laid for these skills, which should be attained at secondary level.

Our ultimate hope is that this concept of bilingualism would extend to the whole of Wales. We appreciate the very real difficulties which confront some authorities in areas in which anglicization has progressed rapidly or is long-established, but we would hope that even these would wish to participate in experiments in bilingualism. We would point out that nearly half of our sample of primary school parents in Monmouthshire held favourable attitudes towards Welsh.

This should not imply any degree of compulsion which, in our opinion, loses the moral issue if it is applied and is likely to be ineffective. There should, indeed, be provision for opting out, but we should hope that policy and practice will be so presented that the great majority of parents will participate fully and be persuaded to support bilingual education. . . .

The situation confronting the Welsh language is critical and the need for action is urgent. We feel the kind of education we recommend, in reinstating a language and integrating a minority culture and a major world culture without forfeiting the indentity of the minority culture, may well become, if it is successful, an experiment of interest to many small countries.

Each education authority should have a language policy which sets out quite explicitly its aims and the measures to be taken. The complexity of the language situation demands a variety of practice and flexibility in order to meet particular needs not only in each area but even within each area, but the principles must be clear and it must be ensured that schools carry them out. If this policy is to be more than a pious statement, authorities must be prepared to spend money on material and equipment, to give adequate priority to Welsh staffing and, above all, to appoint experienced language advisers. Evidence given to us, and our observation of the work of advisers, has emphasized the value of such staff and the central role they can play in in-service training.

[From Chapter 11, p. 239

Religious Instruction

We believe, from the evidence available, that in the primary schools of Wales, the statutory obligation has made hardly any difference. We have seen that religious education and an act of corporate worship were the practice long before 1944, and we believe that the schools would earnestly and sincerely wish to continue this practice. The evidence we have received from individual teachers, Christian societies, the Churches and teachers' professional associations point to this conclusion. In addition, we are reinforced in this belief by the state of public opinion as expressed in surveys, which shows a majority of the public to be in favour of continuing religious education in our schools. We are convinced, in fact, that even without statutory force, an act of corporate worship and the provision of religious education would be universally accepted and practised in the schools of Wales.

If the teacher feels free, he is in the best state of mind to give of his best and, in education, it is only the best that should interest us. We feel that compulsion weakens rather than fortifies attitudes towards religion in school. We emphasize again, therefore, the importance we attach to the retention of religious attitudes and teachings as an integral, if not the central, part of the work of the school, and we reiterate our view that this is more likely to happen when schools and teachers are not under compulsion. This is the view we take as a Council now, more than twenty years after the legislation of 1944. In looking back at the achievements and the failures of our schools, we realize that there is an obvious need to take a critical look at our approach in the past, and that much rethinking is necessary, particularly on the question of clarifying our objectives realistically in response to the challenge of modern technological change, improving our methods, and, if necessary, revolutionizing our entire outlook.

[From Chapter 20, p. 369

51· Report of the Committee of Enquiry into the Flow of Candidates in Science and Technology into Higher Education. [*The Dainton Report*]

Published: *1968*

Chairman: *Dr F. S. Dainton, F.R.S.**

Members: *Professor G. A. Barnard; Mr G. M. Goatman; Mr G. M. A. Harrison; Lord Jackson; Professor L. Rosenhead; Mr G. A. T. Hanks (Assessor); Mr J. F. McClellan (Assessor); Mr R. D. Potter (Assessor); Mr W. K. Reid (Assessor); Miss J. M. Scrimshaw (Assessor); Miss J. R. Weatherburn (Assessor); Mr D. W. Tanner (Secretary); Miss I. E. Morris (Secretary)*

Mr G. M. Goatman was a member until December 31, 1967.

Mr G. M. A. Harrison succeeded Professor C. A. Moser on April 13, 1967.

Mr W. K. Reid succeeded Mr G. J. Spence on October 16, 1967.

Miss J. M. Scrimshaw succeeded Mr C. Priestley on October 4, 1967.

The Committee was set up by the Council for Scientific Policy, through whom it reported to the then Secretary of State for Education and Science, Mr Patrick Gordon Walker.

Much of the Committee's work was directed at the secondary school curriculum as a whole in the light of evidence that choices between science and other subjects were effectively taken between the ages of 13 and 15. This led to recommendations for a broad span of studies which would postpone irreversible decisions for or against science 'as late as possible'. In particular, the Committee urged that mathematics should be continued throughout the school life.

Other recommendations aimed at improving the quality of sciencc teaching at the earlier stages of the secondary school period, including financial inducements for science teachers. Universities were urged to revise their courses to make them more attractive to uncommitted students.

The Committee was set up in 1965 to look into the evidence about the alleged swing away from science in the sixth forms of secondary schools which was going counter to the expansion of the science and technology departments in the universities.

The evidence collected by Dr Dainton and his colleagues confirmed that

* Dr Dainton was born in 1914, and became Vice-Chancellor of Nottingham University in 1965. A chemist by academic training, he became a Fellow of thc Royal Society in 1957.

the number of pupils in the sixth forms who were taking the full science options – i.e., those who were being prepared in the ordinary way for entry to university science and technology faculties – was not increasing *pari passu* with the growth of sixth forms and that the actual numbers in the first-year science sixth forms might begin to fall from 1968 onwards.

The report called for changes in the sixth form, less specialization and some mathematics for all. The recommendations were not well received in the schools. They came up against the manifest shortage of specialist teachers needed to carry out the changes proposed and the strong determination on the part of the grammar and public schools to defend the Crowther concept of sixth-form study in depth (see pp. 255–8).

Nevertheless, the report was influential at the university level and helped to guide a joint working party set up by the Schools Council and Standing Conference on University Entrance in 1968 to study plans for sixth-form reform.

Later Choice, and Greater Attractiveness of Science, Engineering and Technology

The investigations we have undertaken show clearly that while the output from the sixth-forms of the secondary schools is continuing to grow rapidly, the output of specialists in science is not. The annual age groups from which sixth-formers are at present drawn are smaller than those of the 'bulge' of the immediately preceding years. Even as a proportion of those smaller age groups, science specialists have increased only slightly, and the remarkable growth which has been achieved over the past decade in sixth-form education has been largely devoted to the development of studies which, under present conditions, in effect disqualify for higher education in science and technology.

Against this situation must be set the increasingly important role of science and technology in everyday affairs and in the economy. Discovery and invention in these fields, and their exploitation, depend upon an adequate force of scientists and technologists and their effective use in employment. This country, to a greater extent than many others, depends on its qualified manpower as a national resource for the creation of wealth. High level scientific and technical jobs form the fastest growing occupational group in Great Britain. . . . The 1965 Triennial Manpower Survey showed an increased forecast demand for scientists and technologists unlikely to be met by the supply. In particular fields, notably in industry and in the schools, the shortage of recruits of good quality is likely to prove critical.

In such a situation are we justified in recommending that there should be a national effort to influence the choice and selection of the individual in relation to his studies and hence his career? The tradition of respect for the choice of the individual is rightly embedded in our educational as well as our political institutions. We esteem that tradition and would not wish to see it altered. But we think it right to insist that the individual, in choosing the subjects that he studies at school, should have as mature an appreciation of those subjects and of the implications for his career as it is possible to give. National requirements do, after all, determine the opportunities for individuals. We feel strongly that considerations of curriculum organisation which have remained substantially unchanged in the last forty to fifty years should not force a premature and largely irrevocable decision for or against science and technology.

In considering possible remedies we were moved at first by a desire to correct the swing away from science. In the later stages of our study this aim has become subsumed within the wider objective of meeting the needs of the individual pupil. The remedy we propose has two main elements. The *first* is that all pupils in the sixth form should follow broad courses of study that keep open the options (both for subjects of study in higher education and for eventual occupation) as late as possible in the individual's educational career. We see this as desirable for the student of the arts or social studies as well as for the potential scientist and technologist. In consequence, decisions for or against science and technology would be deferred to an age of greater maturity than is at present the case. Such a change would have implications for the present patterns of 'O' level study and, in the sixth form, the continued study of mathemetics, a key subject in maintaining flexibility, would become the norm for the great majority.

We are here concerned both with the desirability of higher standards of scientific and mathematical attainment for all well-educated people and with the prospects for subsequent specialisation in science and technology arising from a wider general basis in sixth-form education. We have seen that France has succeeded, against the general trend, in increasing its university intake in science and technology on the foundations of a massive educational effort in these fields at the secondary level. The general continuation in England and Wales of mathematical studies alone would immensely increase the base from which qualified manpower could spring.

There is a clear risk that such a change towards a more mature and rational choice of career could work to the disadvantage of science and technology. Radical changes have taken place over the last decade. Ten years ago there was a severe shortage of university places, a policy of providing two-thirds of all new places in universities in science or technology, and a clear national objective (since achieved) of doubling the output of scientists and technologists. In the sixth forms there was very little alternative to the traditional science–arts dichotomy. Now we have a situation of expanding opportunity in the social sciences, clear and popular alternatives in the sixth forms, renewed debate on the exact nature of the relationship between the supply of and demand for scientific and technological manpower, together with a sense of doubt on the attractiveness of careers in science and technology. In a much more open and indeterminate situation than has existed hitherto the individual's choice and the factors which bear upon it have become critically important. The deferment of choice and of specialisation will provide us with a larger reservoir: but we shall not be able to draw upon it unless science and technology courses in sixth form and university, and the careers to which they lead, are able positively to attract the uncommitted student. There will, we hope, always be a strong stream of able students who by their attainments at school are naturally directed to scientific or technological careers. Schools must continue to ensure that these pupils are fully satisfied in their studies and in their work; and that any remedial measures that may be adopted should not jeopardise the high motivation of this group. What is additionally necessary is to attract those who have less clearly defined motivations or whose abilities are ambivalent.

This then is the *second* and vital part of our remedy, that engineering, technology and science must be made more attractive throughout the whole of education and in employment. We recognise that unless the several issues of curriculum, teaching resources, university entrance requirements, and career opportunities are dealt with, continuing sixth-form studies in science and mathematics would simply hold open options which would not be taken up. Indeed to increase the exposure of young people to inadequate science teaching resources, problematic university selection, unnecessarily rigorous undergraduate programmes, and uncertain or unattractive career prospects would certainly work to the detriment of science and technology. . . .

Mathematics

In our view normally all pupils should study mathematics until they leave school and only in exceptional circumstances should it be held to be possible or desirable for a pupil to opt out. At present a high proportion of pupils with 'O' level passes in the subject abandon it in the sixth form, and some pupils drop it even earlier. We believe that the overwhelming majority are capable of benefiting from the continued study of this subject. We do not mean that everyone should specialise in mathematics, but all pupils need to develop an enhanced capacity to use mathematical techniques for a wide range of purposes in science and technology and outside, and greater appreciation of its relevance to human affairs. Progress is being made in discovering how to make good the shortcomings caused by insufficient or interrupted study of mathematics; but in our view the only sensible solution (and this is reinforced by our international comparisons) is not to create the problem by abandoning the subject. The content of the curriculum is beyond the scope of the Enquiry; but we distinguish some characteristics of mathematical achievement in relation to future demands of employment:

(i) Mathematics as a means of communicating quantifiable ideas and information.
(ii) Mathematics as a training for discipline of thought and for logical reasoning.
(iii) Mathematics as a tool in activities arising from the developing needs of engineering, technology, science, organisation, economics, sociology, etc.; the growth of numerical analysis and electronic computation is a powerful example.
(iv) Mathematics as a study itself, where development of new techniques and concepts can have economic consequences akin to those flowing from scientific research and development.

[From Chapter 8, pp. 84–6, 88

52· First Report of the Public Schools Commission. Volume I: Report. Volume II. [*The Newsom Report*]

Published: *1968*

Chairman: *Sir John Newsom*

Members: *Dame Kitty Anderson; Lord Annan; Dr K. Bliss; Mr J. C. Dancy; Mr J. Davies; Professor D. V. Donnison; Dr T. E. Faulkner; Dame Anne Godwin; Mr W. S. Hill; Mr T. E. B. Howarth; Dr H. G. Judge; Mr G. H. Metcalfe; Mr J. Vaizey; Mr B. Williams; Mr G. F. Cockerill* (*Secretary*); *Mr G. Etheridge* (*Assistant Secretary*).

The Commission was appointed in December, 1965. Mr N. Cook resigned from membership of the Commission in January, 1967.

Terms of reference: *To advise on the best way of integrating the public schools with the state system of education. For the immediate purpose of the Commission public schools are defined as those independent schools now in membership of the Headmasters' Conference, Governing Bodies' Association or Governing Bodies of Girls' Schools Association.*

The Commission will be expected to carry out the following tasks:

(*a*) *To collect and assess information about the public schools and about the need and existing provision for boarding education; forms of collaboration between the schools* (*in the first instance the boarding schools*) *and the maintained system.*

(*b*) *To work out the role which individual schools might play in national and local schemes of integration.*

(*c*) *If it so wishes, and subject to the approval of the Secretary of State, to initiate experimental schemes matching existing provision with different types of need.*

(*d*) *To recommend a national plan for integrating the schools with the maintained sector of education.*

(*e*) *To recommend whether any action is needed in respect of other independent schools, whether secondary or primary.*

In carrying out its task the Commission will be expected (*while respecting the denominational character of the schools*), *to pay special attention to the following objectives:*

(*a*) *To ensure that the public schools should make their maximum contribution to meeting national educational needs, and in the first instance any unsatisfied* *need for boarding education in the light of the Martin* and Newsom reports.†*

(*b*) *To create a socially mixed entry into the schools in order to achieve* (*a*) *above and to reduce the divisive influence which they now exert.*

(*c*) *To move towards a progressively wider range of academic attainment amongst public school pupils, so that the public school sector may increasingly conform with the national policy for the maintained sector.*

(*d*) *To co-operate closely with local education authorities in seeking to match provision with need for boarding education.*

(*e*) *To ensure the progressive application of the principle that the public schools, like other parts of the educational system, should be open to boys and girls irrespective of the income of their parents.*

Additional terms of reference (*October, 1967*)

To advise on the most effective method or methods by which direct grant grammar schools in England and Wales and the grant-aided schools in Scotland can participate in the movement towards comprehensive reorganization, and to review the principle of central government grant to these schools.

The Public Schools Commission was set up in December 1965 to carry out a promise by the Labour Party (victors of the General Elections of 1964 and 1966) to investigate the future of these schools in the light of the comprehensive school policy and the aim of equal educational opportunity. The Party had been divided between those who wished to integrate the public schools into the maintained system, those who wished somehow to abolish them, and those who were inclined to leave them alone while taking care to withdraw any fiscal reliefs they might enjoy. Appointed as a result of this pledge, the Commission received terms of reference which pointed towards integration. The first report covers the boarding public schools. The report should be read in conjunction with the Fleming Report (see p. 210).

Though starting from very different premises, Newsom (like Fleming) sought ways of introducing state-supported pupils into the public schools. The Newsom proposals, however, went a long way beyond Fleming. They assumed that there would be a limited number of public schools which would become 'integrated'. These would be supervised by a boarding schools corporation which would assist in the administration of a scheme for the allocation of pupils. All integrated schools would have to admit publicly-assisted pupils from maintained schools to at least half their places. They would also have to broaden their academic range to take a more nearly comprehensive intake.

As with Fleming the basis of the selection of pupils was a key consideration. The Public Schools Commission held that 'the only justification for public expenditure on boarding education should be need for boarding for either social or academic reasons'.

* Report of the Working Party on Assistance with the Cost of Boarding Education, H.M.S.O., 1960.

† Half Our Future – A report of the Central Advisory Council for Education (England), H.M.S.O., 1963.

The Commission calculated that 47,000 assisted boarding places would be required – 9,000 in preparatory schools and 38,000 in secondary schools – after 15 years.

The full cost of the proposals was estimated at £18·4 million, of which £6·4 million was already being spent by local or central government authorities on aid to pupils.

The report contained two notes of dissent. Mr John Davies, director general of the Confederation of British Industry, Dame Kitty Anderson, former headmistress of the North London Collegiate School, and Mr T. E. B. Howarth rejected outright integration, while supporting the idea of publicly-assisted pupils. Professor John Vaizey, Professor of Economics at Brunel University, while signing the main report, opposed most of the specific recommendations including the attempt to link the assistance of pupils with 'boarding need'.

The report was not well received, being criticized for a variety of often conflicting reasons. The Commission was reconstituted during the summer of 1968 under the chairmanship of Professor David Donnison (vice-chairman during the period of the first report) and went on to consider the future of the independent day schools and, in addition, the Direct Grant Schools.

Integration

At a comparatively early stage in our discussions we came to certain conclusions which differ radically from those of the Fleming Committee

. . . Our first conclusion was that integration was meaningless if only 25 per cent of places in a school were available for children assisted from public funds. They should be there in large numbers if they came at all. Whereas the Fleming Report conveyed the impression that it was a privilege for assisted children to be able to enter a public school, we believe that the fee-paying children will benefit as much as the assisted children by the fact that they will be meeting, perhaps for the first time, their contemporaries from other strata in society. Whereas Fleming did not contend that the public schools should alter or adapt themselves to meet the needs of assisted pupils, we believe that the schools will have to change considerably and that the mere fact of very large numbers of assisted pupils being in the schools will help them to change.

Our second conclusion . . . was that, by degrees, assisted pupils entering public schools in the future should be admitted only to schools accepted for integration. As the number of assisted pupils increased, so should more schools be integrated. Unless this was done, the assisted pupils would be scattered over the face of the public schools like confetti, and there would be no true marriage between the independent and the maintained sectors . . . . Indeed there are some independent schools which are not fitted for integration and which would have to be radically changed before any children were sent to them by the State.

Our third conclusion was that all independent schools recognised as efficient by the Department of Education and Science should be regarded as eligible for integration and not just those who happen to belong – or whose heads happen to belong – to the Headmasters' Conference or the other organisations named in our terms of reference. . . .

Our fourth conclusion was that integration of the public schools is impossible unless there is a general administrative settlement – a settlement which can be publicly debated and costed before legislation is passed. If there is not a central settlement, and the piecemeal arrangements between local education authorities and independent schools which have followed the Fleming Report continue, very little will change. If change is to be effective, it must be nationally accepted and nationally implemented. How else can the schools plan ahead for the new role which they should play?

[From Chapter 1, pp. 20–1

Social divisiveness

The most striking division between the children of this country occurs at eight or nine years old. For that is the age at which so many public school children start to board at preparatory schools. From then on they rarely get the chance of meeting their contemporaries in other social classes, as they would do if they went to a maintained school. They do not mix with them in term time and not often in the holidays. And this lasts for ten years. . . .

Public schools play games chiefly against other public schools: they rarely exchange pupils or fraternise with maintained schools in their area. They belong, in a remarkable degree, to a world of their own. The schools may not seek this status; but it is thrust upon them partly by their history and partly by the class consciousness which surrounds them.

The masters in these schools are no less isolated from their colleagues in the nation's schools. . . . They stick in the public schools, as pupil and master, just as the masters in the maintained system stick in those schools; and neither system learns from the other.

A single sex boarding school must enforce another kind of divisiveness, and a common criticism of the public school system has been that, from 8 to 18, boys are cut off from girls except during the holidays. . . . The segregation of boys from girls in boarding schools for ten of their most formative years must have a socially divisive effect.

The public schools are accused of hogging all the most important positions in the country. Is this true? . . .

The simplest case to take, since it is well documented, up to date, and should be free from any suspicion of deliberately biased selection, is recruitment to the public services, and in particular to the Administrative Classes of the Home Civil Service and the senior branch of the Diplomatic Service. The proportion of successful candidates for the Administrative Class who had been at public schools (as defined) was 35 per cent in 1936, 39 per cent in 1956 and 43 per cent in the years 1963–67 taken together. The entry from maintained schools in the years 1963–67 was 30 per cent; the remaining 27 per cent of successful candidates were almost all from direct grant schools or independent schools other than public schools. The Diplomatic Service entry in the same five year period comprised 88 successful candidates from public schools, 27 from maintained schools and 26 from other schools. For the Administrative Class, competitors from independent and maintained schools were roughly equal; in the case of the Diplomatic Service, there were about 70 per cent more candidates from independent than from maintained schools.

[From Chapter 3, pp. 55 – 8

Civil Service/Diplomatic Service Recruitment

	Ratio of successes to competitors Administrative Class (1963–1967)	Ratio of successes (1963–1967) to school leavers entering university in 1962
Public schools	1:4·6 }	1:99
Other independent schools	1:7·8 }	
Direct grant grammar schools	1:4·4	1:171
Maintained schools	1:7·5	1:483
	Diplomatic Service	
Public schools	1:9·3 }	1:287
Other independent schools	1:23·3 }	
Direct grant grammar schools	1:10·8	1:1106
Maintained schools	1:20·6	1:2970

Source: Civil Service Commission evidence.
Department of Education and Science Statistics 1962, Part III.

The public schools are only one link in a chain of selective processes. . . . Among those at maintained schools who go on to university (on the basis of recent years) less than 10 per cent go on to Oxford or Cambridge. Of those at Headmasters' Conference independent boarding schools who go to universities nearly half go to Oxford or Cambridge.

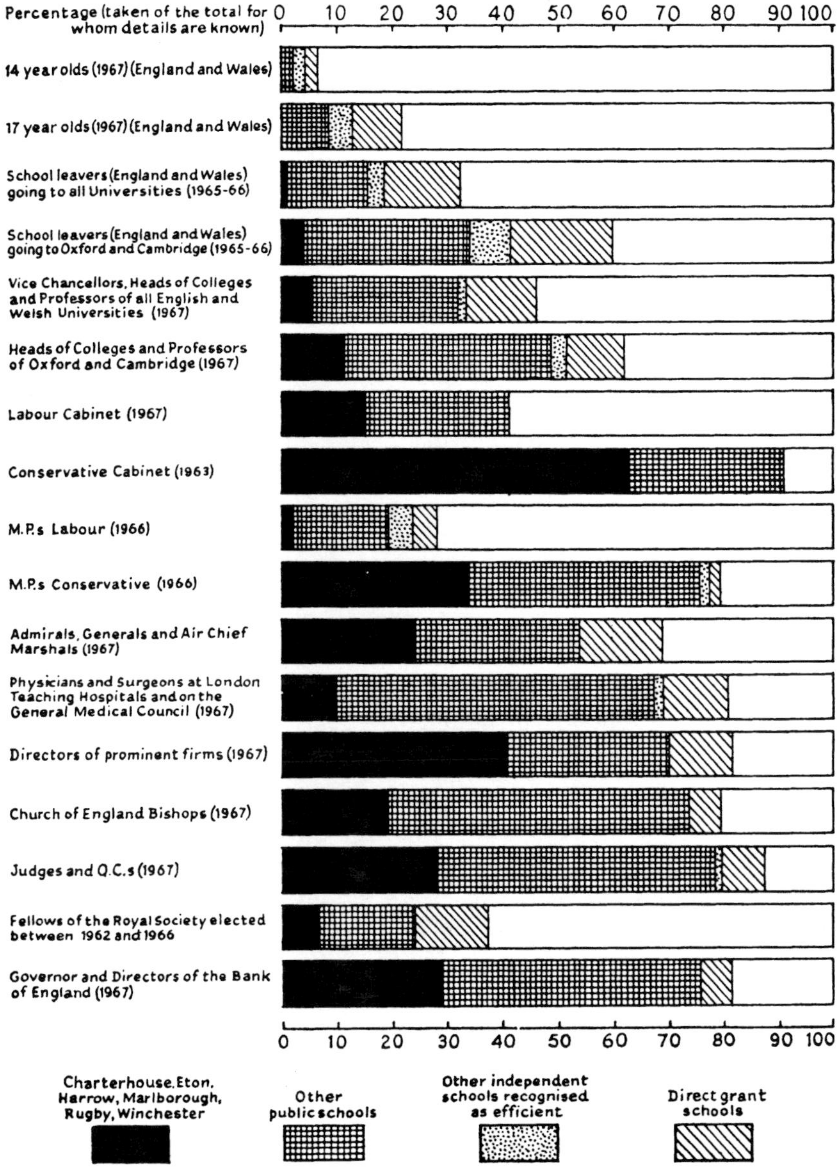
Percentage (taken of the total for whom details are known)
0 10 20 30 40 50 60 70 80 90 100
14 year olds (1967) (England and Wales)
17 year olds (1967) (England and Wales)
School leavers (England and Wales) going to all Universities (1965-66)
School leavers (England and Wales) going to Oxford and Cambridge (1965-66)
Vice Chancellors, Heads of Colleges and Professors of all English and Welsh Universities (1967)
Heads of Colleges and Professors of Oxford and Cambridge (1967)
Labour Cabinet (1967)
Conservative Cabinet (1963)
M.P.s Labour (1966)
M.P.s Conservative (1966)
Admirals, Generals and Air Chief Marshals (1967)
Physicians and Surgeons at London Teaching Hospitals and on the General Medical Council (1967)
Directors of prominent firms (1967)
Church of England Bishops (1967)
Judges and Q.C.s (1967)
Fellows of the Royal Society elected between 1962 and 1966
Governor and Directors of the Bank of England (1967)
0 10 20 30 40 50 60 70 80 90 100
Charterhouse, Eton, Harrow, Marlborough, Rugby, Winchester
Other public schools
Other independent schools recognised as efficient
Direct grant schools

From the most famous public schools, the chances of entry to these universities are even higher. A high proportion of those entering these famous public schools come from a small number of well-known preparatory schools. Thus the hold of public school men on senior posts in many fields is the outcome of a process which begins in the home and leads through preparatory school and public school to the universities and beyond. The public schools play a central part in this process. Their success in securing entry to Oxford and Cambridge is one of the biggest advantages they offer to those who pay their fees, and one of the main reasons for the subsequent success of their pupils. While they recruit from so limited a section of the population, these advantages will remain a divisive influence. . . .

The public schools are not divisive simply because they are exclusive. An exclusive institution becomes divisive when it arbitrarily confers upon its members advantages and powers over the rest of society. The public schools confer such advantages on an arbitrarily selected membership, which already starts with an advantageous position in life. There is no sign that these divisions will disappear if the schools are left alone. They themselves deplore this. It is time we helped them to change a situation which was not of their making.

[From Chapter 3, pp. 60 – 2

Boarding need

In recent years [Local Education Authorities] have been guided by the Report of the Working Party on Assistance with the Cost of Boarding Education, 1960,* in which the categories of need which should 'most readily be entertained' by authorities were defined as follows:

(i) Cases in which both parents are abroad.
(ii) Where the parents are in England and Wales but are liable to frequent moves from one area to another.
(iii) Where home circumstances are seriously prejudicial to the normal development of the child.
(iv) Where a special aptitude in the child requires special training which can be given to the child only by means of a boarding education.

Categories of need

We accept the Working Party's definitions as general lines of guidance; but we think they might with benefit be elaborated, and this we shall attempt. . . . Within the broad band of those eligible *to be considered* for boarding education as assisted pupils, we would include the following categories, which elaborate but do not go beyond the Working

* The Martin Report (see terms of reference on p. 333).

Party's criteria. They are drawn partly from suggestions made by Dr. Royston Lambert . . .

The categories are as follows:

(i) If both parents are dead or have abandoned their children. Children in such circumstances might be better settled with relations, with foster parents or in a residential home. However, for some children, boarding school would be the right answer, provided holidays could be spent with relations or alternative arrangements made either by the local authority or the school.

(ii) If the child is living with a lone parent having full responsibility for the family; for example, a parent widowed, divorced, separated or deserted. At the time of the 1961 census (Table 31 of the Household Composition Tables) there were 661,700 children in this category, either below the age of 15 or in full time education over that age. A considerable proportion of these children would be of an age (i.e. 8 upwards) to be considered for education while living away from home. For many of them attendance at a boarding school might be irrelevant to their needs and could be positively damaging if it meant breaking up the family group still further. Nevertheless, this group quite certainly includes some children who are neglected because a single-handed parent cannot give them sufficient attention, or for other reasons, and whose needs should entitle them to be considered for boarding school places.

(iii) If the child's parents are too ill, mentally or physically, to provide a tolerable home background.

(iv) If both parents live abroad in the course of work (subject to paragraph 168 below).

(v) If there is a reasonable certainty that the nature of the parents' employment will involve the child in frequent and educationally disruptive changes of school. The justification for boarding might depend upon the child's course of study and the stage he had reached; but as a broad guide we think the case would be made out if a child would otherwise have to change schools once every two years, or more frequently, during the remainder of his or her school life.

(vi) If travelling between home and school imposes undue strain or fatigue on the child. This must depend upon the child's age and physical condition, and the length of the school day, rather than upon an absolute time factor. The Department of Education and Science, in a Manual of Guidance (revised 1960) suggested that a journey which took more than three-quarters of an hour for primary age pupils, or more than one and a quarter hours for secondary pupils (including time spent waiting for transport) would be unreasonable; but we do not think this should be interpreted rigidly.

(vii) Where conditions of housing are so exceptionally grave as to impair a child's proper educational development. Boarding education is no substitute for good housing; but society cannot ignore its *educational* responsibility to those children living in the worst conditions.

(viii) If the child's aptitude or intended course of study requires some special educational provision not available in an accessible day school or college of further education.

(ix) If there is extreme tension in personal relationships within the child's home, and the child would benefit by being away during term time.

It is not difficult to think of family circumstances which would not be covered by these criteria, but which might be equally serious in their impact on a child. We therefore attach great importance to a final criterion, which we deliberately do not try to elaborate, because to do so would inevitably limit the range of its application. It is:

(x) Where there are any other exceptional circumstances which severely impede a child's educational progress. . . .

[From Chapter 6, pp. 87–9

Need and desire

We are asked to consider what contribution independent schools might make towards meeting any unsatisfied *need* for boarding education. By need is clearly meant need of a kind sufficient to justify public expenditure – the spending of much more on certain children than on the great majority of their contemporaries. A desire for boarding education for a child who is or who would be at no substantial disadvantage in a day school would not be sufficient.

Yet, to be successful, boarding education requires that need be accompanied either by desire on the part of the parents and child for a boarding education, or at least a clear willingness and readiness to co-operate. It would be not only an infringement of liberty to remove children to boarding school against their wishes or those of their parents, but would be foredoomed to failure, and would be greatly to the detriment of the schools they attended.

The demand for boarding education is not clear cut or easily predictable . . . Once the decision is taken to open the public schools to a wider range of children in need of the education they can provide, the greatest care must be taken to explain the opportunities to parents and to show them what the schools have to offer. If the initiative is left entirely to parents, without sympathetic guidance, the opportunities available will not reach some of those in greatest need of them. We cannot overstress the importance of the part to be played by primary and secondary school heads and teaching staff, on whose guidance so many parents rely.

[From Chapter 6, p. 92

Comprehensive

Our terms of reference require us to propose ways by which the public schools should conform 'increasingly' with [comprehensive] principles. We also have to ensure that the schools 'make their maximum contribution to meeting national educational needs'.

We found this problem the hardest of all which have confronted us. On the one hand we are faced by the plea of the public schools that while they are willing to broaden their entry they cannot easily become fully comprehensive because the vast majority of the schools are too small. They also plead that, if they became fully comprehensive and admitted children from the lowest to the highest range of ability, they would not be exploiting what is in a number of schools their strongest suit, namely a well-staffed and large sixth form. On the other hand it would clearly be unacceptable to schools in the maintained sector if, at the very time when they are moving towards a comprehensive system, the public schools were to be excluded and placed in a special position. In this situation we believe that a compromise must be struck. Those independent boarding schools in the process of integration which are not large enough to be fully comprehensive should nevertheless significantly widen both their curriculum and their examination objectives in order to include a substantial amount of work directed at the Certificate of Secondary Education. . . . Since it could, within the environment of a boarding school favoured by a good staffing ratio, provide the framework for the education of some three-quarters of the ability range, it follows that the schools we are here describing should expect to admit something like this proportion of the ability range. But they would not be expected to admit assisted pupils for whom meaningful work within the C.S.E. context would be impossible. . . .

[From Chapter 10, p. 125

53. Second Report of the Public Schools Commission. Volume I: Report on Independent Day Schools and Direct Grant Grammar Schools. [*The Donnison Report*]

Published: *1970*

Chairman: *Professor David Donnison*

Vice-Chairman: *Lord Annan*

Members: *Mr C. R. Allison; Dr K. Bliss; Dr T. E. Faulkner; Mr M. Arnold-Forster; Dame Anne Godwin; Mr W. S. Hill; Alderman F. H. Hutty; Dr H. G. Judge; Mr R. M. Marsh; Mr B. H. McGowan; Reverend Mother Angela Mary Reidy; Councillor T. Taylor; Mr L. E. Waddilove; Miss J. Wilks; Professor B. Williams; The Very Reverend Robin Woods; Mr R. W. Young; Mr D. E. Morgan (Assessor); Mr G. S. V. Petter, H.M.I. (Assessor); Mr G. Etheridge (Secretary); Mr R. D. Horne (Assistant Secretary).*

Mr D. Neylan was Secretary to the Commission until his death in February, 1969.

The Commission was appointed in 1965 and reconstituted in the summer of 1968, under the chairmanship of Professor David Donnison, then professor of social administration at the London School of Economics from 1961–9, and from 1969 director of the Centre for Environmental Studies. The terms of reference, including the additional terms given in 1967 when the Commission's remit was extended to the Direct Grant Schools, are printed on pages 332–3.

The original intention of the Secretary of State in setting up the Public Schools Commission had been to restrict its field to those schools traditionally known as public schools – schools belonging to the Headmasters' Conference, the Governing Bodies' Association and the Governing Bodies of Girls' Schools Association. The direct grant schools, a minority of which belonged to the H.M.C., were expected to negotiate about their future directly with local education authorities, in accordance with Circular 10/65 (page 306). As very little progress was made in these local negotiations, the Commission received additional terms of reference in October 1967 and the second report – on direct grant schools and independent day schools – appeared shortly before the General Election of 1970.

The Commission was expressly charged with finding the means for these schools to participate in the movement towards comprehensive reorganization. A few of the schools had extensive boarding departments and for them the same considerations applied as for the boarding schools considered by the

Newsom Commission. But the main body of the Donnison report is taken up with the issues of comprehensive education and their implications for a group of selective schools now enjoying quasi-independent status, with substantial numbers of fee-paying pupils.

The Commission was divided about what to recommend.

Two main schemes were put forward on the basis that the schools were to become non-selective up to the school-leaving age, with a variety of roles and covering a variety of age groups corresponding broadly to the choice set out in section one of Circular 10/65. Seven members, including those most directly connected with direct grant schools, urged Scheme A under which the schools would be allowed to retain a special 'full grant' status, receive their money directly from a central 'School Grants Commission' in order to preserve their semi-independence but without giving them any more affluence than maintained schools.

Under Scheme B, urged by seven members, the direct grant schools would lose their special status and become controlled or aided maintained schools (this was backed by the maintained school and local government interests on the Commission). Four members, including the chairman and vice-chairman, were happy with either scheme.

Five members also favoured allowing a few direct grant, independent and maintained schools to survive as schools for specially gifted children – a solution which might have ensured a continuing role for outstanding institutions such as Manchester Grammar School.

Two members – Mr Allison, a former head of a direct grant school (Brentwood), and Mr Woods, Dean of Windsor (later Bishop of Worcester) opposed the principles adopted by the Commission on the subject of comprehensive education and wished to preserve the possibility of some schools continuing as selective grammar schools. They also opposed the abolition of all fees and instead favoured a common means-tested scale for all pupils at these schools.

Before the Government had time to discuss the recommendations with teachers and local authorities the General Election campaign began and a Conservative victory ended any serious consideration of the proposals. The most interesting section of the report, however, had not been the administrative recommendations but the discussion of policy aims in secondary education as a whole and the implications of a commitment to comprehensive education in particular. Till the Donnison report appeared no comparable public document had set out reasoned arguments for comprehensive education or attempted to lay down principles on which policy should be based.

Following the General Election of 1974, the Labour Government went ahead with the ending of the Direct Grant arrangements. Some 117 former direct grant schools chose to become independent; a number of others entered the maintained system as voluntary schools.

Staying on

The most striking feature of the British system, when compared with those of other countries, is the heavy loss of pupils at the minimum leaving age. Comparisons between the proportions of pupils staying on at school in different countries, with different educational systems and presenting statistics in different ways, must be hazardous. Figure 1 offers only a rough guide. Nevertheless one conclusion can reasonably be drawn from the figures – that smaller proportions of our children are still at school between the ages of 16 and 18 than would be found in almost any comparable economy. Comparison of such figures is complicated by the fact that many young people in these age groups are in this country and in Scotland educated in colleges of further education for which comparable figures are not available from other countries. But the effect of any errors arising from this gap in the statistics is small. Even if full-time students in colleges of further education are added to this country's figures, and their counterparts in other countries ignored, our place in the rank order shown in Figure 1 is scarcely altered. The proportion of children remaining at school in Britain has risen considerably since 1965–6, the year adopted for Figure 1. Data for later years are not available for all the other countries appearing in this comparison, but it is clear that staying-on rates are rising fast in most places. Thus, if data for more recent years are used for all countries, our place in the rank order shown in the Figure is unlikely to change greatly.

Since they start a year earlier, pupils in this country who stay on at school will generally have had one more year of education by the time they reach the age of 16 or 17 than their counterparts elsewhere. It is tempting to assume that they will therefore be a year ahead of children in other countries in their general intellectual development. We have found no evidence to support this view. A study of mathematical attainments at the ages of 13 and 17–18 in twelve countries* suggests, for this subject, that children who start at age five have no advantage over those who start at age six. This study also suggests that our average attainment in mathematics among pupils still in school is close to the averages for other countries. But our results showed a greater spread from top to bottom than most; i.e. our good performers are very good but we have far too many bad performers. . . .

In general, the proportion of a country's age group attaining the highest standards by the age of 17 or 18 appears to depend heavily on the proportion who continue their education to this age. Early selection and early specialization, if they are achieved at the cost of high wastage from

* 'International Study of Achievement in Mathematics' edited by Torsten Husén: John Wiley and Sons, 1967.

BOYS AND GIRLS AT SCHOOL AS A PERCENTAGE OF AGE GROUP IN TOTAL POPULATION IN DEVELOPED COUNTRIES

Age 16

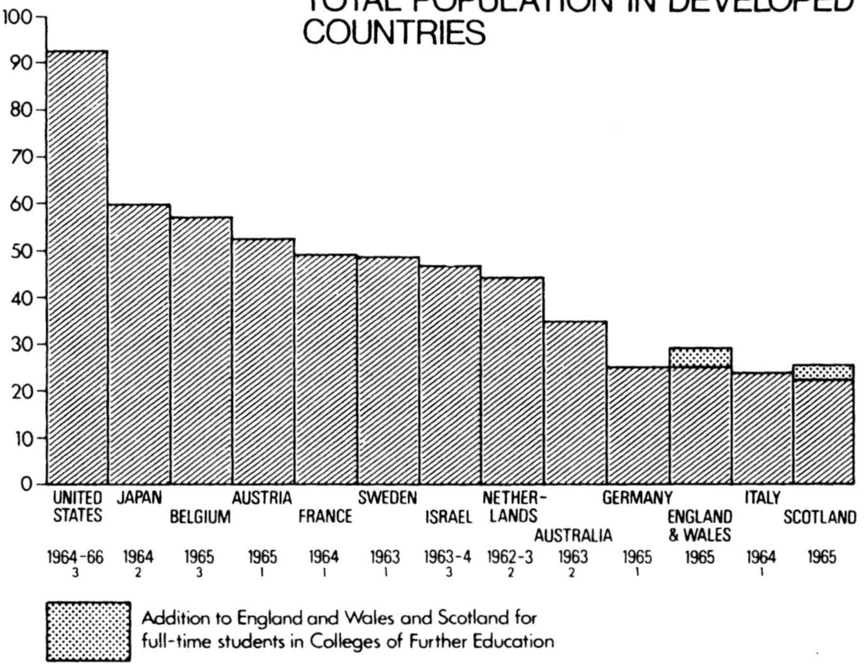

Age 17

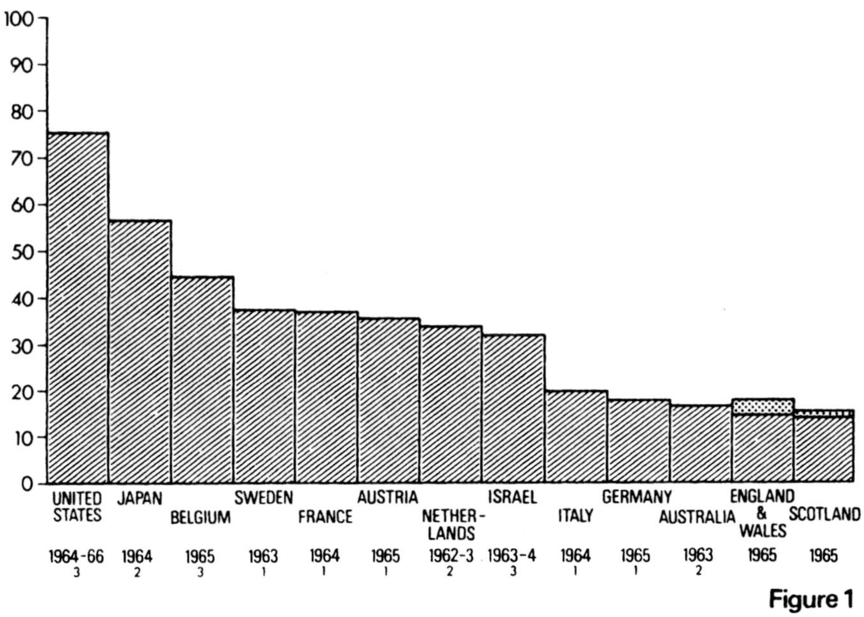

Figure 1

school at ages 15–16, tend to *reduce* the numbers attaining these high standards.

When European education first took shape the majority of children were not expected to pursue their schooling far. Each country has therefore had to incorporate schools which originally met the needs of different social classes into a national system for all children. First, the aim has been secondary education, with fairer opportunities of higher education, for all children. It is after this has been achieved that something akin to our own movement towards comprehensive education takes place. It is no longer enough to give children opportunities to compete for entry to the more academic forms of secondary education: they must be enabled and persuaded to take their education as far as they can. The United States of America, Australia, Japan, Sweden, Norway, France and the East European countries all have or will shortly have largely comprehensive educational systems, up to age 15 or 16 at least. Other countries (Denmark and Italy, for example) have introduced, or are introducing, common schooling up to the age of 14. Other countries (Germany and Israel, for example) are experimenting with forms of comprehensive schooling or (as in Austria) with ways of making parallel systems more flexible and facilitating transfer between schools after the age of selection. All are engaged in the movement towards comprehensive education.

[From Chapter 2, pp. 22–4

Comprehensive principles

Comprehensive organization takes different forms in different places and new forms are constantly evolving. Before we can say whether, let alone how, the schools in our terms of reference should 'participate' in this process, we must explain what we mean by 'the movement towards comprehensive reorganization'.

For the next decade or two, the chief and fundamental aim not only of secondary reorganization, but of our whole educational endeavour, must be to get more and more children to take their education to a point that enables them to go on learning and adapting throughout their lives. Ultimately all, except some of the severely subnormal, should continue systematic education (in which paid work, if they do any, plays an educational or clearly subordinate part) until the age of eighteen, with good opportunities for further education thereafter. This must be our aim because more and more children and their parents will want a full secondary education; because gross inequalities of education in an urban, industrial society produce pervasive social inequalities and destructive conflicts; because our economy will need more and more people capable of adapting, training and retraining throughout their lives, and will offer poorer opportunities to those incapable of doing this; and because Britain allows larger proportions of her young people to drop out of school at the ages of 15 and 16 than her neighbours and major competitors, and is already severely handicapped by this waste of talent. An educational system which enables a minority of the most fortunate children to take their education a long way while turning the rest out into the labour market as soon as it is socially tolerable for them to start work is as obsolete as the early industrial era from which it originated. There is no time to be lost in creating the new system we need: the pupils going to school for the first time this year will go on working, under present retirement arrangements, until about the year 2030. Long before that date our economy will have scant opportunities to offer the untrained and unskilled worker.

This is what the movement towards reorganization is all about. The forms and patterns of education now evolving must be judged by their capacity to attain these aims. The essential features of the movement can be briefly outlined.

First we must postpone irrevocable, and nearly irrevocable, decisions about children's educational opportunities to as late an age as possible. The earlier we select, the more mistakes we make; and those errors cannot be much reduced by better techniques of selection. Early selection by academic criteria tends to be a wasteful, self-fulfilling prophecy. (Self-fulfilling because however well-intentioned our endeavours to give different schools equal treatment and status, experience shows that better teaching resources tend to be concentrated upon the children selected, and their morale and performance tend to improve. Wasteful because the excluded majority are penalized and their opportunities tend to be restricted despite the excellence of many secondary modern schools.) Procedures for late transfer, designed to remedy errors in selection, seldom work well in practice and in any case fail to correct the fundamental handicaps which selection imposes on the excluded.

Precisely how far can selection be delayed? This is trickier ground. We believe that selection at 11 is too early, and international comparisons indicate that most countries share this view. But by the age of 18 a good deal of selection is taking place, and will already have taken place. For one thing, because of the scarcity of resources we cannot yet offer higher or further education to all; and even when (or if) we can, some institutions of higher education (those in particular which combine teaching and research) will make academic demands on their entrants not necessarily made by other institutions. Even if it is true that at present the downward pressure of university entrance on school work is too severe, it is appropriate that boys and girls who aspire to higher education should begin serious preparation for it by the age of 16, and acquire suitable intellectual dispositions before that age. More generally, the interests, abilities and vocational aims of many students are differentiated well before the age of 18, and the diverse aspirations that they foster suggest that there should be some differentiation at an earlier age (between 14 and 16), and many other countries have found this to be so. Differences of curriculum, educational style and pace will be found in comprehensive schools before the age of 16 – though they should not be of a kind that unnecessarily creates barriers or limits choices.

If more and more children are to continue their education to the age of 18, our second aim must be to offer them a greater variety of subjects, learned in a greater variety of ways, than the traditional sixth form provides. Some of the new children staying on at school will not want to pursue a course of studies designed mainly for those entering universities, and should not be expected to do so. But encouragement to excel, in varied ways, must be as keen as ever.

Third, if selection is to be postponed and the way to an education continuing beyond school is to be opened to all, then children from a wide range of social classes must be educated together wherever this is possible. Children tend to advance together, adopting the aspirations of their peers, and we must therefore try to place all in an environment where high attainment and intellectual interests are sufficiently common and respected to be 'catching'. Social segregation of young people in their formative years is also likely to impoverish their education in more fundamental ways: it makes it harder for them to understand their fellow countrymen.

Parents, teachers and administrators are moving towards an increasingly general agreement about these fundamental aims of educational planning. Difficulties arise when it comes to applying them. In practice there are many obstacles to be surmounted. Some of the main ones must be briefly listed.

Our system of education is geared to public examinations, giving entry to higher education and professional training, which assume early specialization, early entry to sets and classes studying particular syllabuses, and advanced work which attains standards – in relatively few subjects – that would in some countries be found only in universities. This system is changing; in future, children will not specialize so soon or so severely. But continuing competition for entrance to the universities (which are unlikely to expand fast enough to meet the demand for their places) will make these changes a slow and difficult process.

Our grammar schools have long been organized specially for this system. They are small. Most of them have less than 600 pupils and fewer than 4 forms of entry. If they cease to be academically selective from the age of 11 or thereabouts and become comprehensive schools, most of them must either be greatly enlarged or must cover a shorter age range. In that event their adaptation to new tasks is not simply a question of numbers and logistics. The strengths they have developed over the years may initially restrict what they can do for the four-fifths of young people who have hitherto been excluded from them – young people whose aspirations and interests cannot all be met within the more academic culture of a traditional grammar school. We shall argue that schools can only remain academically selective if they recruit at the age of 16+ within a system which makes really good provision for carrying forward the education of all young people. Even as sixth form colleges, they should be larger than most of the present direct grant schools if they are to make the most effective use of their teachers and equipment. Schools taking only sixth formers have to provide a wide range of specialist staff at a high academic level. In sixth forms attached to a lower school, these teachers also teach children in lower forms. If they are to be fully employed in a self-contained sixth form college, there will have to be more than one group in their subject and this calls for a college which is much larger than the usual sixth form.

Some of the non-grammar schools are large, well-equipped comprehensive schools recruiting plenty of able children and teachers. Others are only beginning what may be a long haul from secondary modern to full comprehensive status. They may also be handicapped by social deprivations afflicting the neighbourhoods in which they stand. Unless other schools or colleges of further education come to their help, their pupils may be as severely handicapped as those in some of the old secondary modern schools.

The schools facing these different problems are scattered unevenly across the country. Some of the strongest grammar schools stand in the middle of big cities, often alongside small secondary modern schools. But the proximity of these contrasting problems seldom offers ready scope for mutually helpful solutions. If the schools serve different religious denominations, collaboration and combination may be difficult or impossible. If the population of a central neighbourhood has been falling for many years there may be a surplus of school places, dictating contraction rather than expansion of the schools there. If expansion is possible there may be no room on their restricted sites for the buildings required.

These and many other difficulties mean that the process of bringing hitherto selective schools into a comprehensive system is likely to be a slow one. How fast we can proceed depends on the determination of the central and local authorities concerned, and particularly on the resources they can bring and are willing to bring to the task. Existing buildings may be unsuited, without adaptation, to the new demands to be made on them. More staff may be needed. Teaching methods may have to be revised. All these things take time and money. Reorganization which fails to give all children better opportunities of taking their education further is reorganization in name only. Only when local education authorities receive finance on as generous a scale as they receive exhortation will thoroughly satisfactory advances be made.

From this analysis of the task before us and its difficulties we derive the following general principles for evaluating schemes for reorganization and proposals for the future of individual schools. Such schemes and proposals should:

(a) ensure so far as possible that children of all abilities are educated in such a way as to develop their talents to the highest possible degree;
(b) avoid the segregation of pupils before statutory school leaving age into schools (or clearly distinguishable sections or 'sides' within schools) which are designed, staffed, equipped or organized to provide separately for particular levels of ability;
(c) ensure, wherever possible, that all pupils are educated in schools which offer adequate opportunities of progressing to further and higher education, opportunities which are actually taken by an appreciable number of pupils;
(d) avoid unnecessarily depressing the expectations and drive of children and their teachers;
(e) avoid deliberately placing schools in a hierarchy of esteem;
(f) prevent, wherever possible, any school becoming a 'one class' establishment;
(g) whenever the normal secondary age range (11–18) has to be divided into different, tiered schools, ensure that transfers occur at a point and in a way that encourages children to continue their education, and avoid frequent movement of pupils which permits only a short stay at any one school;
(h) in such cases also ensure that there is the closest possible collaboration between teachers in the different schools over curriculum, teaching methods, guidance of pupils, etc., including opportunities for teachers to teach in both schools whenever this is appropriate;
(i) ensure that suitable buildings and staff are available before new schemes come into operation;
(j) whenever the foregoing objectives cannot soon be attained, create situations which encourage development in these directions, and avoid situations which frustrate development in these directions.

It follows from our principles for reorganization that there can, ultimately, be no place for fee-paying in schools coming wholly into a comprehensive system. . . . Here we need only point out that to permit the payment of fees to play any part in selection would clearly threaten the aims of reorganization . . .

We must make our position clear on the question of 'creaming'. It has often been said to us that even the most selective direct grant schools recruit so small a proportion of the most able pupils in their large catchment areas that they have a negligible influence on the numbers of talented children entering comprehensive schools. . . . But to defend the retention of selective direct grant schools on these grounds is to neglect the national character of the reorganization in which we are engaged. If maintained grammar schools are being reorganized all over the country under policies strongly pressed by the central government – and they are – it is indefensible for that government to preserve and support other grammar schools, having similar aims and functions. The maintained grammar schools are as selective, as well-staffed and as successful as most direct grant schools. The two groups of schools cannot justifiably be treated differently in this respect. The creaming effects of the direct grant schools cannot be considered in isolation from the broader questions of selection and segregation throughout secondary education.

But the creation of a wholly comprehensive system of secondary schools cannot eliminate the tendency of schools which have a better reputation to attract more able pupils than other schools in their neighbourhood. There will always be some schools that are better than others. Where these differences arise from remediable handicaps in the recruitment of staff or pupils, in scarcities of resources or poor leadership, then remedies must be sought. Where they arise only from the fact that some schools advance more strongly than others, in a system in which admission procedures are as fair as possible, no school is severely handicapped and all are encouraged to develop as far and as fast as possible, there is no cause for concern. We have never suggested that all schools should, or could, be the same.

[From Chapter 7, pp. 108–14

54 · Secondary Organization. 1970

The Conservative success in the General Election of June 1970 brought a new Secretary of State to the Department of Education and Science, Mrs Margaret Thatcher, whose first action was to cancel Circular 10/65 (see p. 301) and issue her own circular on the organization of secondary education.

This withdrew the formal instruction to education authorities to submit reorganization schemes (and the guidelines for secondary building schemes issued the following year as Circular 10/66) and returned to them the discretion to decide whether to bring forward schemes or not.

It was presented as means of restoring powers to the local education authority and a deliberate retreat from excessive central government interference. ('Authorities will now be freer to determine the shape of secondary provision in their areas.') But the Secretary of State's powers under Section 13 of the Education Act remained unabated and, though the circular did not spell out how concepts like 'educational considerations in general, local needs and wishes in particular and the wise use of resources' were to be interpreted, it was left to the Department of Education to judge each scheme on its merits. As time passed the new Secretary of State showed herself reluctant to sanction schemes which involved a break at 14, schemes which involved schools using more than one site if this meant much movement between sites, and schemes which aroused strenuous, if partial, local opposition to the change of role by grammar schools.

Circular 10/70: *THE ORGANISATION OF SECONDARY EDUCATION*. Issued by the Department of Education and Science on 30 June 1970.

The Government's aim is to ensure that all pupils shall have full opportunities for secondary education suitable to their needs and abilities. The Government, however, believe it is wrong to impose a uniform pattern of secondary organization on local education authorities by legislation or other means. Circular 10/65 is accordingly withdrawn. Consequential restrictions on the character of secondary building projects will no longer apply.

Authorities will now be freer to determine the shape of secondary provision in their areas. The Secretary of State will expect educational considerations in general, local needs and wishes in particular and the wise use of resources to be the main principles determining the local pattern. Recent rapid changes in secondary school organization have in many areas imposed considerable strains within the education system. Where a particular pattern of organization is working well and commands general support the Secretary of State does not wish to cause further change without good reason.

Authorities which have had reorganization plans approved by the Department may either proceed to operate them unchanged or notify the Department of their wish to modify them. Those with plans currently lodged with the Department are invited to say whether they wish to have them further considered or to withdraw them. The Secretary of State will be pleased to consider any new plans which may be submitted. Officers of the Department will be available for consultation at any stage at which this would be helpful.

Whatever course local education authorities adopt the Secretary of State trusts that they will maintain close consultation with those representing the denominational and other voluntary schools in their area. Any proposed changes should also be discussed with the teachers. Full opportunities should be given to parents to make their views known before decisions are reached.

55 · Report of a Committee of Enquiry into Teacher Education and Training. [*The James Report*]

Published: *1972*

Chairman: *Lord James of Rusholme**

Members: *Miss E. Aggett; Mr C. R. English; Dr H. G. Judge; Mr C. P. Milroy; Mr J. F. Porter; Prof. J. R. Webster; Mr A. G. J. Luffman, H.M.I. (Assessor); Mr R. Dellar (Secretary); Miss M. E. Gummer (Assistant Secretary).*

The Committee was appointed at the end of 1970 with the following terms of reference:

> 'In the light of the review currently being undertaken by the Area Training Organizations, and of the evidence published by the Select Committee on Education and Science, to enquire into the present arrangements for the education, training and probation of teachers in England and Wales and in particular to examine:
>
> (i) what should be the content and organization of courses to be provided;
>
> (ii) whether a larger proportion of intending teachers should be educated with students who have not chosen their careers or chosen other careers;
>
> (iii) what, in the context of (i) and (ii) above, should be the role of the maintained and voluntary colleges of education, the polytechnics and other further education institutions maintained by local education authorities and the universities
>
> and to make recommendations.'

The Committee owed its origin to disquiet about standards of reading in schools, and evidence that many teachers could be shown to enter primary schools with inadequate training in methods of teaching reading. To some extent this reflected research work carried out in the sixties by Miss Joyce Morris, Mrs Vera Southgate Booth and others who had sought to measure the incidence of reading failure. To this were added the more general complaints about progressive primary methods put forward by contributors to a series of Black Papers published by the *Critical Quarterly* in 1969 and 1970

* Lord James of Rusholme, Vice-Chancellor of the University of York from its foundation in 1962, was born in 1909; a former high master of Manchester Grammar School and a member of the Crowther Committee (see page 245), he was knighted in 1956 and made a life peer in 1959.

(leading on to the formation of the National Council for Educational Standards).

Mr Edward Short (Secretary of State for Education from 1968 to 1970) responded in February, 1970, by inviting the Area Training Organizations to carry out their own inquiry.

At the same time the Parliamentary Select Committee on Education and Science chose teacher training as its main topic of inquiry and received and published a large amount of evidence. The dissolution in May 1970 prevented it from reporting.

It was against this background that the Conservatives promised, if they won the 1970 election, to set up a committee to look into the whole field of teacher education and training. Unlike most educational commissions in the past, the James Committee was small and intensive. Five members were seconded full-time to work on the inquiry. Lord James and Mr (later Sir Cyril) English were half-time members. They were asked at the outset to present their report within 12 months. This time-table was adhered to and the finished document was presented to the Secretary of State on December 14, 1971.

The James Report proposed a radical reorganization of teacher education within three successive cycles: the first cycle, general higher education; the second cycle, professional training; and the third cycle, in-service training.

First priority went to in-service training – the third cycle – with the recommendation that every teacher should be released with pay for in-service training for the equivalent of one term every seven years (to be raised to one term every five years as soon as possible).

For the first cycle the Committee envisaged two alternatives. For some future teachers the first cycle would be taken in a university or polytechnic, taking a first degree (which might, but would more likely not, include education studies). For others (those going to the colleges of education) the first cycle would lead to a new qualification, the Diploma in Higher Education, taken at the end of two years. It was envisaged that the normal entry requirements would be two A levels, but that generous exceptions should be allowed. It was also envisaged that courses leading to the Dip.H.E. might be offered in polytechnics, Colleges of F.E. and other institutions of higher education, as well as in colleges of education.

The assumption was that the first cycle (though it might include some education and child development studies) would be general in character in the colleges, and therefore, that professional training should follow consecutively, rather than be provided concurrently as had been the case.

Recruitment to professional training would take place at the beginning of the second cycle, from among all those candidates who had obtained a first cycle qualification (generally speaking, a Dip.H.E. or university or C.N.A.A. degree). The second cycle (of two years) consisted of one year of professional studies, not necessarily in the same college as that in which the first cycle had been pursued. On completion of this, the student would be designated a 'licensed teacher', and would then seek a school appointment. In the first year of employment the licensed teacher would be given a restricted timetable; his work would be supervised by a school-based professional tutor and he would be released one day a week to attend at a professional centre accessible to his school.

On successful completion of the two-year second cycle the student would qualify for a 'professional degree', the B.A. (Education), the same qualification going at the end of the second year to all students without regards to whether they were holders of the Dip.H.E. or degrees.

The report discussed the administrative structure required to operate such a system and the validation of the qualifications offered at each stage. It recommended that a National Council for Teacher Education should be set up, empowered to award the degrees of B.A. (Ed.) and M.A. (Ed.), to determine the conditions of entry to teacher training, and to advise on which second and third cycle qualifications were professionally satisfactory. The National Council would also advise the Secretary of State generally on teacher training matters and the recognition of licensed teachers for registration.

Below the National Council, the Report envisaged some 15 Regional Councils for Colleges and Departments of Education, on which the main bodies concerned with teacher education would be represented – universities, polytechnics, local education authorities, teachers. The Regional Councils would carry out functions similar to those hitherto undertaken by Area Training Organizations and plan the future development of the colleges.

In a Note of Extension, two members of the Committee, Professor J. R. Webster and Mr James Porter, argued in favour of closer ties between the colleges and the universities including the opportunity for some colleges to merge with universities if acceptable schemes were put forward. They hoped that the universities would validate the Dip. H.E. in many colleges and that some colleges would be encouraged to do three-year degree work, together with four-year honours degrees which included education as a course of study.

In the widespread controversy which followed the publication of the report, the discussion centred on the principle of concurrence, the currency of the proposed Dip.H.E., the validating bodies, the character of the fourth year (replacing the probationary year) and the credibility of the B.A. (Ed.). The report aroused strong hostility in the National Union of Teachers, where the licensed teacher proposals were roundly condemned and the B.A. (Ed.) rejected. It was apparent early on that the possibility of a national council combining the tasks that James envisaged (including the validation of the Dip.H.E. and the B.A. (Ed.)) attracted little support. The in-service training proposals were generally welcomed and action was promised on cycle three before the rest of the report was formally considered.

The third cycle

Much of the argument of this report depends upon the proposals made for the third cycle. To none of our recommendations do we attach greater importance than to these . . .

The third cycle comprehends the whole range of activities by which teachers can extend their personal education, develop their professional competence and improve their understanding of educational principles and techniques . . .

All teachers ought to have opportunities to extend and deepen their knowledge of teaching methods and of educational theory. When special studies of teaching methods have identified improved techniques it is important that the results should be widely communicated to teachers in the schools. All teachers should have the opportunity to acquire a better understanding of the principles and methods of educational technology, especially if this was not imparted to them in initial training. All teachers need to keep abreast of the results of educational research and experiment, and to be informed about the use of new books, materials and equipment. Teachers in the primary schools – and those in secondary schools who are faced with illiteracy or semi-illiteracy in their pupils – will need to continue to improve their understanding and competence in the language arts, i.e. language development and the teaching of reading and writing. Although this deeper understanding, however much emphasized in initial training, cannot be fully acquired without prolonged experience, suitable in-service training, rooted in the experience teachers have already had, can be a powerful aid.

All subject specialists will need to refresh and extend their knowledge of their special interests, and general teachers to widen their command of the content of what they teach. The single-subject graduate will find gaps in his background knowledge of some parts of his subject, and he may be called upon to teach one or more subsidiary subjects in which he may understandably be less confident. There are many other ways in which teachers may wish – or need – to acquire new subject specialisms. Changes in curriculum may make new demands which teachers have to be equipped to meet. Particular examples of this are the introduction of modern mathematics, the development of science and French in primary schools . . .

Any scheme for the third cycle should be flexible, as well as being as systematic and comprehensive as possible. The application of such a scheme would depend on the development, very largely from existing resources, of a network of new agencies, on the use of facilities for further and adult education and on access to adequate advisory services. It would also have implications for existing institutions and organizations, not least for the schools . . .

In-service training should begin in the schools. It is here that learning and teaching take place, curricula and techniques are developed and needs and deficiencies revealed. Every school should regard the continued training of its teachers as an essential part of its task, for which all members of staff share responsibility. An active school is constantly reviewing and reassessing its effectiveness, and is ready to consider new methods, new forms of organization and new ways of dealing with the problems that arise. It will set aside time to explore these questions, as far as it can within its own resources, by arranging for discussion, study, seminars with visiting tutors and visits to other institutions. It will also give time and attention to the introduction of new members of staff, not only those in their first year of teaching but all those who are new to the school. Heads of schools, heads of departments and other senior teachers should be especially concerned to assess the needs both of their schools and of teachers on their staff and to encourage teachers to take the opportunities offered outside the school for in-service education and training, whether these involve part-time day release, attendance at full-time courses or participation in vacation, weekend or evening activities.

It would be unrealistic to expect hard-pressed schools to take on additional responsibilities without an increase in teaching staff. Nevertheless, this degree of involvement in the purposes and practices of the third cycle is a responsibility which the schools will not wish to evade. It is fortunate, therefore, that there is now a prospect of a steady increase in the supply of teachers. A high priority should be given to improving staffing ratios so that schools are able to play their full part in the third cycle and thus help to raise the status and standards of the teaching profession as a whole. As soon as better staffing and the expansion of full-time courses allow, all teachers should be entitled to release with pay for a minimum of one school term or the equivalent (a period of, say, 12 weeks) in a specified number of years. The immediate aim should be to secure teachers' entitlement to a minimum of one term or the equivalent in every seven years, but this should be regarded as only an interim target. As soon as possible, the level of entitlement should be raised to one term in five years . . .

Every school should have on its staff a 'professional tutor' to co-ordinate second and third cycle work affecting the school and to be the link between the school and other agencies engaged in that work. Whether the professional tutor were the head or deputy head, as might be the case in a small school, or a designated member of the staff in a larger school, it would be important for all teachers designated as professional tutors to be among the first to be admitted to third cycle courses, so that they could be trained for their new tasks. Among the responsibilities of the professional tutor would be that of compiling and maintaining a training programme for the staff of the school, which would take account both of the curricular needs of the schools and of the professional needs of the teachers . . .

[From Chapter 2, pp. 5–12

The second cycle

The recommendations which . . . we make for the pre-service training and induction of teachers (distinguished from the higher education of the potential teachers which precedes it and the in-service education which it inaugurates) are based upon three propositions. The first is that the needs of our society and the implicit standards of a key profession require that no young man or woman should be accepted for training as a teacher until a full course of higher education, . . . has been completed. The second is that, whatever methods of educating and training teachers may be developed in future, the time has come to abandon the formal distinctions between the two main existing types: that is, three years of concurrent training for non-graduates and one year of consecutive training for graduates. These present distinctions, although increasingly blurred during the last decade by the development of degree work within the colleges and of concurrent courses in some universities, run sharply through the whole profession (in its career and salary patterns, for example) and are obsolete. The third proposition . . . is that no teacher can in a relatively short, or even in an unrealistically long, period at the beginning of his career, be equipped for all the responsibilities he is going to face. This familiar truth has been given a disturbingly sharper edge in a world of rapidly developing social and cultural change.

These three propositions underlie all our recommendations and can best be illustrated by reference to the evidence produced for this Inquiry. In much of this evidence, the present concurrent pattern of training in the colleges has been the subject of strongly expressed and divergent views: it has been both vigorously attacked and stoutly defended. Objective study of the facts leads inescapably to the conclusion that while there are great virtues in the present pattern, there are also a number of serious weaknesses. Study of the evidence and observation of the situation in the colleges make it clear that most of these weaknesses are symptoms of structural inadequacies in the present system rather than of incompetence in its administration or operation. That system in its present form, as has already been affirmed, is linked to a dual pattern of teacher training. The concurrent form of training within the colleges of education suffers from a conflict and confusion of objectives. The colleges are required at one and the same time to extend for three years the personal education of the student and to train him as a teacher. Exegesis may soften this distinction – for example, by emphasizing the role of 'Education' itself in the enrichment of the intellectual life of the student, or by relating the main subject to the problems of teaching it to pupils in the secondary schools. Discussion with college of education lecturers, and even more with students, suggests that such exegesis sometimes glides into special pleading . . .

The conflicts between education and training, the unrealistic width of subject and other offerings in many colleges and the poverty of in-service training conspire to impose severe limitations on the present effectiveness of initial training. At the same time, there is a proliferation of suggestions for the inclusion of new, or the restoration of old, elements in the programme of training . . . In such a hubbub of competing priorities it may not be surprising, although it is certainly alarming, that such matters as the teaching of reading should sometimes appear to be neglected. The assertion that such essentially relevant and practical elements are not presented with sufficient clarity and emphasis is widespread. It may be concluded that, with things as they are, the colleges are asked to do too much, are left with no rational basis for discrimination and are often unable to give enough time to aspects of training which they and the profession recognize as central. . . .

Nothing has impressed, or depressed, us more than the gross inadequacy of the present arrangements for the probationary year. This inadequacy has hampered even the most enlightened of current procedures and has sometimes left unchecked practices which are so much less enlightened as to imply incompetence and irresponsibility. To assume that any of the large scale changes that are needed can be produced merely by exhortation is to misunderstand completely the nature of the problems with which we have been concerned. What is true of the probationary year is true, as has been argued throughout this chapter, of pre-service training as a whole. The faults are faults of structure, and only changes in that structure could permit us to hope for genuine reform. The division between graduate and non-graduate training, the confusion between education and training, the diffusion of educational effort within the colleges, the inevitable incompleteness of initial training by itself, the multiplication of desirable objectives and the relative neglect of necessary ones, the frustrations of teaching practice and of the probationary year: these collectively produce a problem to be solved by changes based on the principles outlined in this report. . . .

The second cycle should concentrate on preparation for work appropriate to a teacher at the beginning of his career rather than on formal courses in 'educational theory'. To make such a statement is to invite the charge of philistinism, of undervaluing the intellectual content of educational studies, of depriving the young teacher of the conceptual framework within which he may integrate his learning and his experience. This is, it may well be objected, to court disaster by exposing the intellectually under-prepared teacher to a barrage of conflicting advice and practices. These objections have force, and must be met here since the assertion that second cycle training should be both specialized and functional is central to the position adopted in this report. The argument should be about balance and timing rather than about rigidly exclusive alternatives. It is not suggested that educational studies – that is, the history, philosophy, psychology and sociology of education – should be banished from the second cycle curriculum but only that their role should be seen as contributory to effective teaching. The study of these disciplines is of great value. Indeed, we urge in Chapter 4 that they should become more commonly integrated in undergraduate and other first cycle studies, and have already argued in Chapter 2 that they should be encouraged in the third cycle. It must be doubted, however, whether such studies, especially if presented through the medium of lectures to large groups of perplexed students are, in terms of priorities, a useful major element in initial training. A rudimentary introduction is all that can realistically be attempted at this stage, even if some part of that introduction has already been given in the first cycle. For most students, reflection is more likely to be illuminating after, not before, the experience of teaching and this is why it would be better in any case for the bulk of such studies to be deferred from the second to the third cycle. It is not their importance but their placing which needs to be challenged. The present system, unless and until it is fundamentally reformed, with the confusions inherent in concurrence and the inadequacy of in-service provision, inhibits any such deferment. The argument is, however, that the system needs to be changed. . . .

At the end of that first year the student would take up an assignment in a school and begin to receive a salary. . . .

The second year of the second cycle would be an essential part of the initial training course and as such must demonstrably be very much more than merely an improved version of the probationary year. Moreover, it would not be enough simply to identify the second year of initial training as being school-based, and to insist that each school must take measures to give effect to such an identification. Chapter 2 has already described the strong supporting network of professional centres, including the existing professional institutions, which must be developed, to meet both the general needs of the third cycle and the specific needs of licensed teachers in the second. The new teachers with whom we are here concerned would be assigned to specific professional centres, released to them for at least one fifth of their working time, which does not necessarily mean one day a week, and look to them for the reinforcement of the on-the-job training already available in their schools. Although it would be an over simplification to describe a year in the conditions here outlined as being an extension and deepening of what is now called 'teaching practice', it is because of this new approach to meeting the needs of licensed teachers that the formal commitment to such practice in the first year of the second cycle could, and should, be limited . . . .

Students who, at the time of growing competition for places in higher education and for the available places in teacher training, had successfully completed at least two years in the first cycle and two in the second should enjoy graduate status. They would have entered the second cycle as holders of an acceptable qualification in higher education and would thereafter have demonstrated, in their first appointments as well as in their college-based or department-based work, their mastery not only of a range of disciplines but also of the fundamental skills and insights of teaching. We therefore recommend that all such successful students and teachers should be awarded a general degree of B.A. (Education). Such an award would presuppose that the regional body had considered with favour not only the reports submitted by his school and his employers on a teacher's performance in his first year of practical work but also a certificate from his professional centre that he had completed an approved programme of further studies during that same year. . . .

[From Chapter 3, pp. 18–32

The first cycle

For the man or woman who will be mainly concerned with the teaching of one or two subjects to a relatively high level, a degree course, whether in a university or elsewhere, may well provide the most appropriate educational base and we would expect that for many teachers success in obtaining a university or C.N.A.A. degree would be the most suitable way of satisfying the requirements of the first cycle. . . .

For very many teachers a different kind of preparation is needed, and it is suggested that this could be provided in a two year course leading to the award of a Diploma in Higher Education. Such a course would be a more appropriate foundation, not only for many teachers in first and middle schools, but also for many of the non-specialist teachers of adolescents who are needed in secondary schools and F.E. colleges. It is a course which the colleges of education will be especially well fitted to provide, since it develops naturally from the present pattern of their work and makes use of the expertise which they have already built up. A common course of professional training, extending over two years for all, would thus be preceded by a diploma course for some teachers and a degree course for others. There should be no implication that one route is more difficult or more prestigious than the other. The distinction means simply that different kinds of teaching, not necessarily related to types of schools or to the ages of the children to be taught, may require different kinds of preparation.

The main concern of this Committee has been to study and reflect on the education, training and probation of teachers and our terms of reference have encouraged us to consider whether it is possible to break down what is often described as the 'isolation' in which many teachers are at present educated. Many voices have urged that prospective teachers should not be obliged to commit themselves at the age of 18 to a course which can lead only to a teaching qualification. It is argued that students following courses which may lead to teaching should have the opportunities enjoyed by students in other sectors of higher education of moving in other directions without disadvantage and that the presence in institutions attended by potential teachers of students proceeding to other careers would end the 'isolation' of which complaint is made. Such criticisms and proposals point towards a consecutive pattern of preparation for teaching, in which a student's formal commitment to professional training need not come until after a period of 'uncommitted' education.

We have at the same time been urged to protect the interests of those students who, from the outset, have a teaching career clearly in view. Many students do embark on their higher education with the clear intention of becoming teachers. It would be curiously unjust and unwise to place arbitrary obstacles in the way of those very students whose strong and early motivation gives promise of their becoming some of the most effective and dedicated teachers. Proposals for the first cycle must make it possible for such students to choose from among the available options a course which is similar in many important respects to the concurrent courses now offered in the colleges of education. The arrangements for the diploma course outlined below would allow such a choice to be made. Some colleges should have the opportunity to concentrate on courses of this type. . . .

Three examples may be given of the ways in which the 'committed teacher' may be helped to see the relevance of either his general or his special studies to the career he proposes to follow. First, there cannot be any barrier between 'a subject' and the methods by which a lecturer can communicate to others the satisfaction he gets from it. The study of philosophy for intending teachers, to give another example, is rightly defended as of great value in introducing students to a variety of fundamental problems and to the technique of asking and answering questions in the pursuit of truth. It so happens that some of the questions of most absorbing interest to the intelligent student arise from a study of education. One of the greatest of philosophical works is also perhaps the most stimulating of all books on education. The Republic. In the first cycle, those who are intending teachers and those who are not can profit from a common course in which some examples of philosophical questions are drawn from the one experience they all have in common, that is the experience of being educated. To give a third example, some of the novels that should be introduced to all students, either in a literature course or elsewhere, concern the experiences of childhood and youth, and will be of professional interest to the intending teacher even if the main purpose of reading them is to enrich the personal lives of a whole group, whether teachers or not. Indeed, the teaching of almost any subject, to intending teachers and other students alike, should be illuminated by some awareness of its relationship to other areas of knowledge and its reference to the social, political, economic, cultural and technological conditions of contemporary society. Given the right kind of teaching, the problem of reconciling the virtues of concurrent and consecutive courses becomes much less formidable, even if the main solution of it must be the inclusion among the special subject choices of the study of subjects closely related to education. . . .

Currency of the diploma

It has been emphasized that, in accordance with our terms of reference, our first concern in devising the diploma that is discussed here was to ensure that it would be a suitable educational base on which the subsequent professional training of many teachers could rest. It must also be stressed that such a diploma could fulfil several other important functions. That it would do so is central to our recommendations.

The course described here would provide a higher education of value in itself: for a number, perhaps an increasing number, of students the diploma could well be a terminal qualification. It is one of the curiosities of higher education in this country that for the 18-year-old school leaver who does not want to enter employment immediately there is virtually no alternative, apart from certain kinds of training that are specifically vocational, to a 3-year course leading either to a degree or to a teaching qualification. The diploma suggested here would offer a 2-year course consisting of both a general education and some specialized elements, which themselves might look to future occupational choices, for example languages or economics for students thinking of a career in business. It has been suggested that such a qualification would be welcomed not only by business, industry and the public service but also by the schools. The schools may see it, for many of their sixth formers who require higher education, as a welcome alternative to the present university courses which are not necessarily well-suited to the aptitudes and aspirations of all those who are formally qualified to take them. It would be naive to disregard completely the weight of responsible university opinion questioning whether there is sufficient motivation for university courses, as at present conceived, on the part of many of the formally qualified students who choose to follow them. If these misgivings are justified one solution might be to modify entirely the idea of a university. Another would be to offer a different course, equally suitable for able students but so broadened in scope that it would provide a more satisfying educational experience for many of them. The latter solution is the one recommended here.

The Diploma in Higher Education, given its content and character, would not only be a terminal qualification for many students and the basis for the professional training of many teachers, but could also increasingly provide an appropriate educational basis for training in other professions. If so, this professional training would often be given in institutions other than those in which the students had taken their diplomas.

Some students following the diploma course might wish to continue rigorous academic study to a higher level. Of these, some might be acceptable candidates for university or C.N.A.A. degree courses and it is to be hoped that, although the number of transfers would probably be small, institutions offering these courses would feel able to accept such students and give them credit for their two years' higher education. For some others, there should be opportunities within the college system to pursue degree courses based on, and developed from, the new courses designed for the Dip.H.E., which would often meet their needs better than existing degree studies.

[From Chapter 4, pp. 40–7

The need for change

One strong reason for changing the system is that the colleges have outgrown the pattern designed for them. Since the Robbins Report, and even more plainly since the McNair Report, the colleges have grown in status and confidence. . . .

As the colleges have grown and developed, the whole system of higher education has become very different from that in which the area training organizations were established. The development of the binary system, the designation of polytechnics and the growing interest of the polytechnics in teacher education are changes that raise new questions. What does it mean, and why is it desirable, for the teacher training department to have a relationship with a university, here represented by the A.T.O., which is apparently not felt necessary by other departments within the same polytechnic? Similarly, the growth of the university sector, including the foundation of the Open University, raises important questions . . . There are now well over 30 universities in England and Wales: why is it good for some to be bases for A.T.O.s and not others? . . .

Nor are the shortcomings of the present system at regional level alone: there is no national agency, apart from the D.E.S., to co-ordinate all teacher training activities and it is doubtful whether the functions of central planning and control should be exercised indefinitely, in however efficient and enlightened a manner, by the D.E.S. There is a clear need for a national body in which central government decisions, once formulated, can be elaborated in terms of the action to be taken throughout the system. The lines of planning and control running between colleges, universities, L.E.A.s, schools, A.T.O.s and the D.E.S. are not as clear as they need to be, more especially as the number and complexity of decisions grow. . . .

Several factors . . . point towards a more fundamental review of regional and national organization than that already known to be necessary. First, the development of third cycle work changes very substantially the general pattern for the continuing education and training of the teacher. What is envisaged is not a minor adjustment to be painlessly accommodated within the present system. Although many A.T.O.s are as active in providing and co-ordinating in-service training as the limitation of their resources allows, the comprehensive and very much expanded scheme of opportunities in the third cycle which is now proposed could not be planned and managed within their present pattern. Nor, given the scope and variety of the work known to be involved, is it self-evident that universities would themselves welcome such a role or wish to accord to it a high priority in the allocation of their own resources.

Secondly, one of the implications of that expansion, as of the proposals for the second year of the second cycle, is the establishment and growth of a network of professional centres which will include not only all the professional institutions but also centres set up in schools, F.E. colleges, teachers' centres and elsewhere. The work of the professional centres must cohere in an effective regional and national pattern and the establishment of that pattern will be a major responsibility of the new agencies proposed in this report.

Thirdly, an implication of equal importance is the creation of an effective partnership in teacher training to include the active participation of teachers working in the schools and F.E. colleges. The agencies must include those teachers in the process of policy-making as well as in its detailed application. . . .

Fourthly, if the proposals of this report are adopted, a completely new approach to qualifications for students and for teachers will be introduced, and new patterns of study established in colleges. There must be reciprocity between regional agencies in the acceptance of the Dip.H.E. and the B.A. (Ed.) as qualifications for entry to second and third cycle courses in their constituent professional institutions, and the establishment of that reciprocity will require the creation of new and authoritative organs of consultation. With the introduction of the Dip.H.E., the colleges will include students who are not intending teachers and, in the course of time, other institutions may incorporate the diploma in their programmes of work.

Fifthly, the new patterns of study will often depend upon a grouping of colleges and, in some cases, the transfer of students between them. Some students, for example, will wish to transfer from one college to another in order to follow the appropriate specialist course for the first year of the second cycle. The economies and higher standards flowing from specialization presuppose rationalization which in turn requires machinery to ensure that wise decisions are not only taken in theory but also applied in practice. The agencies must therefore have a clearly recognized responsibility for making to their constituent members recommendations on the distribution of the resources made available by central policy decisions. . . .

In the course of our studies, our visits to institutions and our discussions we have given careful attention to the arguments in favour of a universal retention of the present system.

Those arguments include that of prestige by association. It is said that lecturers in the colleges feel that their position as scholars is enhanced by a formal university connection . . .

The argument from academic freedom asserts that the universities exert not a dictatorial power but a beneficent influence in protecting the colleges' academic integrity from improper interference by L.E.A.s or by the D.E.S. A development of this argument is that the removal of the present university dominance of the area training organizations would create a 'power vacuum': to end the dominance of one partner would invite the dominance of another . . .

The colleges rightly see themselves as places of learning. The universities are, or should be, the highest manifestation of the life of learning and it seems to follow, therefore, that it is right for the colleges to work under the auspices and ultimately the guidance of the universities.

Our rejection, after prolonged reflection and discussion, of some of the conclusions alleged to follow from the arguments summarized here is based upon two convictions. First, we are persuaded that the reality of the present situation is very different from the theory which those arguments propound. Secondly, we recognize that the situation has already changed, is still changing and, if our other proposals are adopted, will change so radically as to call for major reforms. The case for maintaining the present arrangements must be examined in greater detail. The argument from prestige by association, for example, raises difficulties. Whatever theoretical advantage college lecturers may derive from their link with a parent university, it is often more apparent than real, except in the extremely important matter of the opportunities given for personal and professional relationships between college and university staff. It is precisely these opportunities which the proposed system, so far from restricting, should do much to enhance and extend. . . .

Placing undue emphasis on the present link with universities has its own attendant dangers. The most obvious of these is that some colleges have been encouraged to strive for the wrong kind of excellence. Their courses have in many cases become too academic, in the bad sense which that word should never have acquired . . .

The relationship enjoyed by a college through its A.T.O. is not, in practice, with the university itself but with the Institute or School of Education which in some cases is an appendage whose function is only dimly understood by many university teachers. The creation of the B.Ed. degree has made a greater number of those in universities aware that they have a share in the training of teachers, by bringing the regulations for that degree directly before senates and by involving, as examiners, numbers of university teachers who are not concerned with the certificate in education. But whether all, or indeed many, of the universities responsible for A.T.O.s feel a widespread and deep involvement with the education and training of teachers, our evidence leads us to doubt . . .

The argument from academic freedom would have had greater force a few years ago, before the changes brought about as a result of the Weaver Report. In our visits to colleges very little evidence was found that principals or members of their staffs felt their freedom to innovate or to develop within present resources threatened either by local education authorities or by the D.E.S. There has been no indication that the colleges need the kind of bulwark against outside pressures that the present structure is said to provide . . .*

[From Chapter 5, pp. 49–54

A note of extension by J. F. Porter and J. R. Webster

First . . . we hope that many universities, whether or not the base of present A.T.O.s, would wish to form an association for this purpose

* Note of Reservation: Two of us do not share the view expressed in paragraphs 5.16—5.19 of the influence of the universities on the colleges. Our experience of teacher education suggests that any examples of false academicism or enervation that may exist have far more complex causes than merely the nature of a college's link with a university. J.F.P. and J.R.W.

with a college or group of colleges in their area. We are more sanguine than our colleagues that a number of universities, given adequate financial support, will wish to undertake the new tasks described here. Universities have shown their concern for teacher education both by their response to the McNair Report in the 1940s and to the Robbins Report in the 1960s. We cannot believe that, at a time when all institutions of higher education are becoming increasingly sensitive to social needs, they would wish to reverse this history. This is not to suggest that the colleges could not flourish if they were to offer awards under the auspices of the Council for National Academic Awards. We have been impressed, as our colleagues have been, by the liberal attitude of the C.N.A.A. towards the award of degrees. We think it necessary, however, to emphasize the very real institutional and educational advantages that could result from an association between the universities and the colleges, an association perhaps ranging from the validation of the Dip.H.E. for some colleges to full amalgamation with others. The colleges of education are certainly in no doubt of the value of their connection with universities. We have also formed the view that this association is most likely to meet the wishes of the majority of the teaching profession.

Secondly, we wish to emphasize the implications of the proposal contained in the report that some colleges of education should develop both general and honours degree courses, built on the unit structure of the Dip.H.E. . . . The college of education system should be fully involved in the expansion of higher education and enabled to admit not only Dip.H.E. students, intending teachers and others, but also undergraduates reading for first degrees of many kinds.

Thirdly, we would think it important that within this range of new-style degree courses in the colleges there should be courses leading to honours degrees which included the study of education.

Fourthly, although we endorse the report's proposals for ending the divisiveness of teacher training, we are disturbed that divisiveness will persist in that area where it causes most concern: differences in the length of initial higher education received by teachers of different kinds which are in turn reflected in differences of salary and career expectations. During the next few years of expansion in higher education, possibly accompanied by some contraction in the demand for teachers, it is both inevitable and desirable that the profession should recruit an increasing proportion of teachers who have received three years' higher education before their professional training. Indeed, there is some danger that it might recruit more holders of specialized degrees than were needed, in preference to teachers whose higher education was better suited to the work they were going to do. . . . We think it entirely feasible that within a decade all intending teachers should have the opportunity to pursue higher education courses of the same length, sufficient to attain that breadth of knowledge, creative skill and awareness which is needed for the teaching of children at all stages. We go beyond our colleagues in stressing the likelihood and desirability of such a development. . . .

[From pp. 78–9

56 · Report of a Committee of Enquiry appointed by the Secretary of State entitled *Adult Education: A Plan for Development*. [*The Russell Report*]

Published: *1973*
Chairman: *Sir Lionel Russell**
Members: *Mr Clifford H. Barclay; Mr Jim Conway; Mr R. D. Salter Davies; Mr Tom Ellis, MP; Mr Brian Groombridge; Mr David Heap; Mr J. W. Henry; Mr H. D. Hughes; Professor H. A. Jones; Mr H. J. Marsh; Alderman Mrs Ellen W. Mitchell; Dr Elizabeth M. Monkhouse; Sir Alfred Owen; Mr E. E. H. Jenkins (Secretary)*
Assessors: *Mr F. A. Harper (until 1 January 1970); Mr S. P. Whitley (from 1 January 1970); Mr J. A. Lefroy, H.M.I.; Mr J. A. Simpson, H.M.I.; Mr C. W. Rowland, H.M.I.; Mr R. W. Evans, H.M.I.*

Mr H. J. Marsh resigned on 1 February 1972; Mr J. A. Lefroy, H.M.I., served as an Assessor to the Committee until his retirement from H.M. Inspectorate on 30 September 1970; Mr J. A. Simpson retired from H.M. Inspectorate on 30 September 1971 but continued to serve with the Committee until its Report was completed; Mr C. W. Rowland, H.M.I., was Secretary to the Committee until 7 September 1970 after which he served as an Assessor.

The Committee was apointed in February 1969 with the following terms of reference: *To assess the need for and to review the provision of non-vocational adult education in England and Wales; to consider the appropriateness of existing educational, administrative and financial policies; and to make recommendations with a view to obtaining the most effective and economical deployment of available resources to enable adult education to make its proper contribution to the national system of education conceived of as a process continuing through life.*

The Russell Committee was set up in 1969 in the last year of Mr (later Sir) Harold Wilson's second administration. It betokened more a desire to hold out hope to the adult educators (who had suffered badly as a result of public expenditure cuts and the raising of fees) than any firm intention on the part of the Government to follow forward policies in adult education.

* Sir Lionel Russell, educated at Clifton College and Christ's College, Cambridge was Chief Education Officer for Birmingham from 1946 to 1968.

The terms of reference confined the enquiry to non-vocational adult education – a major limitation within which to work. The Committee was entrusted first with the King Charles's head of adult education: reviewing the 'appropriateness of existing educational, administrative and financial policies' meant reconsidering the division of responsibility between the local education authorities, the university extra-mural departments and such voluntary bodies with a long record of service in the field as the Workers' Educational Association. Given the due representation of the principal interests on the Committee, there was no surprise when little change was recommended beyond the suggestion for a national Development Council and a network of local bodies to coordinate the existing institutions. Though it included a section on the possible development of new techniques relying on the audio-visual media, for the most part it assumed more of the same.

The proposals envisaged the doubling of student numbers over a period of five to seven years at a cost of £22 million a year (from £16 million to £38 million) at 1968/9 prices. Being committed to the continuation of a variety of providing bodies, with the central government financing some by direct grant and funding the local authorities through the Rate Support Grant, the Committee had to put a clear and consistent lead by the Secretary of State as a prime requirement. This, in itself, assumed a commitment, never hitherto forthcoming, to steady financial support and firm guidance to local education authorities on their responsibilities.

By the time the report appeared a change of government had brought Mrs Margaret Thatcher to the Department of Education and Science. She took no action on the recommendations. It was not till 1977 that Mrs Shirley Williams appointed Dr Richard Hoggart to be the first chairman of the Advisory Council for Adult and Continuing Education, a body with a central stimulant role, similar to that of the proposed Development Council, but lacking support from the Government of the unmistakable kind demanded by the Committee.

By terms of reference and timing, this major review of adult education was doomed to miss the tide. The growing interest in recurrent education on the Continent had failed to strike a political chord in Britain and the Committee had to work within the traditional framework of adult education. Had the task been taken up a few years later, against a background of international recession and high unemployment, the approach might have been different and the priority attached to continuing education by such powerful bodies as the Trades Union Congress would certainly have been much greater. As it turned out, the most important developments in adult education in the years immediately after the appearance of the report, such as the adult literacy programme initiated in 1975 and the large expansion of the activities of the Manpower Services Commission, owed little to the deliberations of the Russell Committee.

THE RUSSELL REPORT · 1973

GENERAL STATEMENT

Underlying our Report and the recommendations that spring from it are the following key propositions:

...The explicit and latent demands for all kinds of adult education have increased and will continue to increase. Adults...have claims for the provision of a comprehensive service which can satisfy these demands in appropriately adult ways: all areas of education will be enriched if demands for the education of adults are met.

Within our community there exists an enormous reservoir of human and material resources: a relatively modest investment in adult education ...could release these resources to adult education for the benefit of individuals and the good of society.

The successful development of adult education depends in very large measure on a consistent lead and direction being given by the Secretary of State.

The most important recommendations we make are:

A Development Council for Adult Education for England and Wales should be established and a Local Development Council for Adult Education should be set up in the area of each local education authority. Regional Advisory Councils in England and the Welsh Joint Education Committee in Wales should establish sub-committees for adult education where these are not already in being.

Adult education should continue to be provided by a partnership of statutory and voluntary bodies: the latter should receive increasing financial support from the Department of Education and Science towards general expenditure and from local education authorities towards local expenditure.

The Secretary of State should use the many ways open to her to stimulate the development of adult education and in particular should give guidance to local education authorities regarding their responsibility to secure the provision of a varied and comprehensive service of creative, intellectual and physical activities....

There should be a planned increase in the number of full-time staff... particularly in the local education authority sector where as quickly as possible numbers should increase substantially, suitable career and salary structures should be introduced and opportunities for training and staff development should be extended. The service should, quite properly, continue to rely heavily on part-time teachers and more opportunities should be created for them to undergo training, while their salaries should reflect the extent of their training and their accumulated service and experience.

Adult education programmes should provide opportunities for adults to complete secondary, further and higher education and offer access to qualifications at all levels.

More positive effort should be directed towards the disadvantaged.

Additional accommodation should be provided for adult education partly in purpose built or specially adapted buildings but mainly in association with educational plant used for other purposes....

The universities have an important and expanding contribution to make which should continue to be financed partly from University Grants Committee funds and partly by direct grant from the Department of Education and Science.

The Workers Educational Association should continue as a providing body and should be allocated resources to expand its work especially in certain priority fields.

Opportunities for both short and long periods of residential adult education should continue to expand and there should be an improvement in the residential facilities provided especially for this purpose.

[From Recommendations, pp. ix–x

THE GENERAL STRUCTURE

We have had to ask whether the present pattern, with its variety of providing bodies and sources of finance, should be scrapped or radically altered....

Alternatives to the present pattern have been suggested to us. These include first, a single national providing body for adult education funded directly by the central government; second, a similar provision administered regionally; and third, sole provision by the local education authority, somewhat after the practice in Scotland. We have considered these in detail and have decided not to recommend them.

We make no apology of our rejection. We see substantial advantages in the present system over any other, and we indicate these...below. We have however examined seriously and dispassionately the three possible variants suggested to us. The proposals for a single national providing body or for regional providing bodies are both open to the same fundamental objection. Either of them would be divisive in its effect, separating the administration of adult education from the rest of the educational service. Either would presuppose finance wholly from exchequer grant or partly from national funds and partly by a precept upon local authorities which would be quite without precedent for an educational service and could well be a disastrous beginning to a new era in adult education....

...The argument for making them [the local authorities] the sole providers is a strong one; nevertheless we are not convinced....

...None of the bodies representative of local authorities has put this case to us; on the contrary they have expressly commended the contributions of the universities and the voluntary providers. They recognize that the educational needs of an area are so diffused and the activities of the providing bodies so diverse that something important would be lost under unilateral direction, above all the enterprise and accumulated experience of the bodies involved. Certain of these are national bodies serving specific types of need over a wider area than that of the local education authority and this wider vision may often import a freshness and flexibility into the purely local initiatives from which so much of adult education derives. Moreover each of the providing bodies has access to resources of its own – be they premises, teaching staff or voluntary workers – which can be released into the mainstream of adult education by a conscious policy of cooperation. We consider the traditional partnership between statutory and voluntary agencies to be a valuable feature of social organization in this country and particularly appropriate to adult education. Partnership in this sense could not exist if the voluntary organizations operated only as agents of the local education authority. This view is also in accord with our principle that adult education should draw on the total cultural resources of each community. We believe that the administrative and financial structure should recognize this principle and that the local education authorities should therefore be seen, as we know that they would wish to see themselves, as major partners rather than as monopolists. Finally we draw the lesson from community development projects as well as from the traditions of adult education itself that there are situations in which voluntary organizations can work, at any rate in the first instance, more freely than statutory bodies, especially in controversial fields.... Adult education is emasculated if it cannot venture into areas of social, political, industrial, religious or moral controversy: the right to do so is implicit in the word 'adult'. Boldness in these matters is often easier for voluntary organizations. For these reasons we have come to the conviction that the variety and flexibility demanded by the range of needs for adult education in England and Wales are not compatible with a single type of providing body.

Adult education, by its voluntary nature and the extent of its potential relevance to all areas of adult life, is different from the rest of education. A structure of variety and complexity is inescapable. This general structure we see as a series of interlocking contributions from a number of providing bodies of different kinds. The lead in general policy and in the establishment of national standards of adequacy must come from the central government, and there must be means of consultation at a national level. Since adult education must be seen as part of the total education service, which in England and Wales is a locally administered service, it follows that the local education authority will be the major provider and should take the initiative in cooperative planning with the other providing bodies. These will exist at three levels: a certain number of national agencies in receipt of direct grant from central government; a larger number of voluntary bodies aided by local education authorities; and a further range of local societies and clubs whose work will be supported by the adult education service of the local education authority through some form of affiliation.

[From Part III, pp. 49–51

SOCIAL ASPECTS OF ADULT EDUCATION

ADULT EDUCATION IN RELATION TO INDUSTRY

The education of trade unionists has traditionally been a function of adult education, and in cooperation with the T.U.C. and major trade unions, is one of the fastest growing points in 'role education'....

In a period when industrial relations are becoming increasingly complex, it is of vital importance that the large numbers involved on both sides of industry should be given the opportunity to study the problems and acquire the necessary techniques. It is a multi-disciplinary study, embracing elements from economics, psychology, sociology and political science....

The T.U.C. regard trade union education as 'a distinct sector within the total provision of adult education', separate from vocational training on the one hand and liberal adult education for trade unionists on the other. The evidence of the educational agencies concerned is that this work could be rapidly expanded if increasing resources were made available.... We regard this partnership between the trade unions and the adult education movement as a fruitful one, ensuring that genuine educational values and an objective approach are fostered....

The bulk of non-vocational adult education has always taken place outside working hours, in evening classes, at weekends, or in summer schools. For many years, however, the principle of day-release for young workers up to eighteen has been embodied in education legislation in this country.... The growth of such schemes however is disappointingly slow, and affects only certain industries and sections of workers.... The International Labour Organization...has under active consideration a proposed international instrument concerning paid educational leave.... Minimum rights of paid educational leave would have to be established by law or by collective agreements, and the arrangements would be the joint concern of the public authorities, educational institutions, and organizations of workers and of employers. For trade union education the unions would be fully involved in the selection of candidates and the approval of programmes.

Some countries in Western Europe have anticipated these recommendations by introducing legislation which provides for specified periods of paid leave for approved courses of social, trade union or vocational training, and which is usually supplemented by collective bargaining agreements between national employers' associations and trade union centres....

ADULT EDUCATION AND THE DISADVANTAGE

We have...indicated...our particular concern for the disadvantaged, whose participation in adult education is at present minimal. We give a wide interpretation to the term 'disadvantaged' and include in it the physically and mentally handicapped as well as those who, on account of their limited educational background, present cultural or social environment, age, location, occupation or status, cannot easily take part in adult education as normally provided. Here again the lines of approach are clearer if they are related to the total range of needs rather than to the offerings of particular bodies....

First-line provision for identified groups of disadvantaged adults. The initial impetus may come from social service agencies, voluntary action groups, community and social organizations, employers or the explorations of the adult educators. It will then be for the adult education service to determine whether, by suitable adaptation of its arrangements, the disadvantaged can be brought to join in its normal activities or whether special provision has to be made for groups with common needs. Often such special provision will be an inescapable starting-point but the objective should be, wherever possible, to integrate the members of such groups into the full life of the community and not to segregate them longer than is necessary....

In what we have called first-line provision, for example, the W.E.A., with its traditions of the critical study of society, will have a special and important role.... This will lie especially in providing the educational background for those interested in community action in deprived urban areas, and in work associated with places of employment.... In planning this work the focus must always be upon the disadvantaged individual in the context of his own community, and we therefore see the area organizations of adult education as occupying the central role in exploring the diverse educational needs of the area and in drawing together and facilitating the provision of the various educational agencies....

The same approach seems to us to be practicable for determining the place of adult education in community development areas, especially as social deprivation is often associated with other disadvantage, physical, mental, economic or educational. The approach must be based on the ascertained needs of individuals and must lead to a flexible and varied provision related to that range of needs. It will aim always at the creation of learning situations, maintaining an essentially educational rather than social or political role. . . . The work will include the kind of experiments that have been made in some areas in bringing informal adult eduction into community development projects, but it will be wider than those, having as its objective not only social action upon the local environment but also the attainment by the individual of a sufficient level of self-realization to join confidently in the active life of the groups he chooses to belong to.

. . . If occupational mobility is to be achieved without social and political friction and without personal distress it must mean more than direction to a new job and re-training for it. The individual will need an understanding of the processes of change, of the need for change and most importantly of the range of opportunities open at each moment of change. Second chance education must include this general educational objective. Vocational education will usually be concerned with preparing people, especially young people, for entry to a specific career after a choice has been made by them or for them, and with the 'in-service' development of those already embarked on an occupation. Adult education has the function of helping to clarify choices before transfer is made and of assisting in the process of transfer by preparing for entry to the training needed.

In this kind of education three different objectives can be stated. First there is the improvement of general education from the point where initial schooling ceased. For some this may go back to basic education of an elementary kind, including functional literacy and numeracy. Secondly, there must be an opportunity for those contemplating further formal study to try themselves out and assess not only their ability but the strength of their motivation before embarking on it. And thirdly there will be specific forms of preparation for formal courses. In this connection it has been suggested to us that the G.C.E. syllabuses which are commonly regarded as the basic qualifications for advanced study are not always wholly suitable for adults, being designed primarily for full-time study in schools. We therefore welcome the experiments being made by certain of the examining boards in devising courses of a more flexible character and forms of assessment more appropriate to adults. . . .

At the level of basic and remedial education there will be an evident role for the area organizations, many of which are already active in it. But also the total programme of an area organization of adult education must contain the elements of continuing general education that may be required by adults with an eye on later formal qualification. This may be achieved in a number of ways according to the local circumstances: direct provision by the area organization; the incorporation of appropriate W.E.A. or university courses in the programme; or active collaboration with other educational institutions in the area. Some authorities, whose secondary schools are organized as neighbourhood schools or community colleges, have begun to admit adult students alongside sixth-formers in advanced level courses in the schools; the practice could well be extended to activities in art and music, craft work and certain forms of science. The colleges of further education however are of the greatest importance here, for they already provide many of the courses leading to formal qualifications that the adult student may aspire to. . . . The development of a full service of adult education and the links it should forge with other parts of the education system will produce a great demand for access to qualifications by part-time study. But regrettably the opportunities for acquiring professional qualifications in this way seem to be diminishing. We would urge all those bodies who are concerned in the award of professional qualifications to reflect upon the situation we are here considering – the period of social and occupational change that lies ahead, the possible advantages in a new profession of the adults' broader experience of life and work, and the effect of the more direct motivation that commonly characterizes the mature student – and to review the opportunities they afford for adults to qualify by part-time study or by combinations of part-time study and practical experience.

The universities, because of their activity in adult education already, are considerably involved here. We have seen evidence of the way in which participation in adult education of university quality will generate a desire for graduation in the subject, which may not necessarily be directed to a change of occupation. Access to such awards is a logical consequence of the universities' provision of adult education. The basis of this must necessarily be part-time study, though we would urge the consideration as a long-term aim of combined periods of part-time and full-time study. Moreover if the forecasts of generally shorter working hours and our recommendations for day-release and educational leave take effect, more adults will be able to undertake day-time study in universities, either in courses especially for them or alongside the internal students.

The Open University has of course clearly demonstrated the existence of demand here but we have reason to think that the demand goes much wider. Adult students do not necessarily want to engage in the wide spread of subject matter that Open University degree courses at present include. Their motivation will often be narrower and more specific, more akin to the single-subject or combined honours degrees of traditional universities, and, in our view, legitimately so. . . .

In two respects the experience of the Open University offers useful guidance. The credit system that it operates is appropriate to the circumstances in which adults study, especially as it also allows for certain prior study elsewhere to count for credit. Since part-time students must necessarily take a long time over a degree course, perhaps five years, there will be many who, through change of employment or promotion, will be unable to complete their course in the institution in which they began. A credit structure that allows for transfer of credit has the flexibility that adult students require. Secondly, the Open University's unique combination of centrally prepared study materials and local personal tuition is particularly suited to the needs and ways of working of the adult part-time student.

We would urge all universities to create opportunities for adult students to read for degrees, diplomas or other awards by part-time study and to expand such opportunities where they exist already. To meet some of the problems of such students we believe a transferable credit structure is appropriate. . . .

The multi-media approach of the Open University has shown the possibilities of this form of learning in higher education. We believe they exist at other levels too. We have elsewhere recommended that the Development Council for Adult Education should take the initiative in bringing together those concerned in educational broadcasting . . . in adult education and in relevant commercial interests such as publishing, to explore these possibilities and to make available to adult education appropriate learning materials. Since such provision would be made on a national scale it has a particular application in this field of adult qualifications.

We see this as an important area of adult education in which the partnership and inter-relation of the various participating bodies are more important than the contribution of any one of them. Only through such a partnership can the progressive needs of the individual student be met.

[From Part II, pp. 89–99

57 · Industrial Training Act. 1973

By the time the Conservative Government, led by Mr Edward Heath, took office in 1970, pressure had built up for a revision of the Industrial Training Act of 1964. In particular the operation of the levy-grant system was held to be onerous to small firms and to lead to unnecessary bureaucracy among the Industrial Training Boards. Initial Government plans, outlined in a Green Paper in February 1972, reflected a desire among vocal Conservative industrialists to see a reduction in intervention on the part of the Industrial Training Boards and of Government supervision of training. These were among those (according to the Green Paper, 'probably the majority') who believed that financial sticks and carrots were no longer necessary to encourage employers to attend to training because 'a permanent shift in attitude in British industry has been achieved'.

In the event, as the result of extensive public discussion, the eventual legislation compensated for the weakening of the training boards by the creation of a strong Manpower Services Commission. It became the main executive agency of the Secretary of State for Employment with functions which came to impinge more and more on education. In the years which followed, its budget rose rapidly from an initial £125m to reach £1,769m by 1983–84.

The extract below is from *Employment and Training: Government Proposals*, 1973, the White Paper, setting out the rationale behind the 1973 Act.

MANPOWER SERVICES COMMISSION

The Manpower Services Commission will be directly responsible to the Secretary of State for Employment for the employment and training services at present run by the Department of Employment. The main purpose is to give responsibility to representatives of employers and workers and of local government and education interests for the management and development of these services. . . .

There will be 10 members of the Commission – a chairman, three members appointed after consultation with the Trades Union Congress, three after consultation with the Confederation of British Industry, one each appointed after consultation with local authority associations in England and Wales and in Scotland respectively, and one after consultation with professional education interests. It is envisaged that at least one of the people appointed after consultation with local authority associations will have experience of education matters. The members of the Commission will be expected to retain the confidence of the organisations consulted before their appointment. They will not, however, be delegates of those organisations, and will have to take decisions without continual reference back....

The Secretary of State for Education and Science will be responsible for consultation on the representation of professional education interests.... All the members will be appointed by the Secretary of State for Employment.

FUNCTIONS OF THE COMMISSION

The Commission will have powers to provide services in the employment and training field broadly comparable with those which the Secretary of State for Employment has at present under the Employment and Training Act 1948.... The main duty of the Commission will be to make such arrangements as it considers appropriate for assisting people to select, train for, obtain and retain employment, and for assisting employers to obtain suitable employees....

The Commission will have a general responsibility for promoting training for employment. The Commission will be responsible for the Training Opportunities Scheme which enables individual men and women to prepare for new employment by undertaking full-time courses of training and education related to their intended employment. The Commission will also co-ordinate the work of industrial training boards established under the Industrial Training Act 1964. ... It will meet the administrative expenses of the training boards, and provide funds for selective grants to stimulate key training activities....

RELATIONS BETWEEN THE COMMISSION AND THE GOVERNMENT

The Commission will be directly responsible for carrying out its functions within a general policy framework agreed with the Secretary of State for Employment. The Secretary of State will be responsible for the Government's dealings with the Commission; on matters of concern to other Ministers he will act in consultation with them. He will not be involved in the detailed operation and day-to-day management of the Commission and Agencies.

The Commission will be responsible for expenditure in excess of £100 million a year. It will submit each year to the Secretary of State for Employment for his approval a programme of work together with a budget for the coming year, and it will be its duty to act in accordance with the approved programme, and with any directions given by the Secretary of State. There will also be five-year forward projections, as in the case of other publicly financed services, covering both the

Commission's expenditure and, so far as is possible, the wider implications of its work, e.g. in the education field....

The Secretary of State will answer to Parliament on his functions in relation to the Commission and Agencies, including matters of general policy and expenditure....

[From pp. 1–3

58 · Education Act. 1976

On returning to office in 1974 the Labour Government once again took up the task of legislating on secondary reorganization, and prepared a new version of the abortive education Bill of 1969 (see p. 301). The result was the 1976 Education Act. This laid down the principle and set out a procedure by which the Secretary of State could require local education authorities to submit schemes in accordance with it. For enforcement, the Secretary of State had to continue to rely on powers of direction and order provided by the Education Act of 1944 in Sections 68 and 99.

Tacked on to the Bill were six further, miscellaneous sections – one of these limited the independent powers of L.E.A.s to pay for places in independent schools; another, Section 10, inserted at a late stage in the House of Lords, was aimed at encouraging the education of handicapped children in ordinary schools.

The Warnock Committee (p. 401) was still sitting when the Act was passed.

EDUCATION ACT · 1976

COMPREHENSIVE SCHOOLS

1. (1) Subject to subsection (2) below, local education authorities shall, in the exercise and performance of their powers and duties relating to secondary education, have regard to the general principle that such education is to be provided only in schools where the arrangements for the admission of pupils are not based (wholly or partly) on selection by reference to ability or aptitude.

(2) Subsection (1) above shall not be construed as affecting—

(*a*) the provision, whether in special schools or otherwise, of special educational treatment as mentioned in section 8(2)(*c*) of the Education Act 1944 (provision for pupils suffering from disability of mind or body); or

(*b*) the provision of education in any school where arrangements for the admission of pupils to the school are based on selection wholly or mainly by reference to ability or aptitude for music or dancing.

2. (1) If at any time it appears to the Secretary of State that progress or further progress in giving effect to the principle stated in section 1 above is required in the area or any part of the area of any local education authority, he may require the authority to prepare and submit to him, within such time as he may specify, proposals for the purpose of giving effect to that principle in the area of the authority or in any part of that area specified by him.

(2) Before submitting any proposals under this section a local education authority shall consult the managers or governors, or persons representing the managers or governors, of every voluntary school (whether or not in their area) which is in the authority's opinion affected by the proposals; and, if the managers or governors of any voluntary school in their area so request, the authority shall transmit to the Secretary of State with their own proposals any proposals made by the managers or governors for the purpose mentioned in subsection (1) above.

(3) If it appears to the Secretary of State—

(*a*) that, having regard to any proposals submitted to him under this section by a local education authority, a significant change in the character, or a significant enlargement of the premises, of a voluntary school in their area is required; and

(*b*) that no satisfactory proposals for that purpose have been transmitted to him under subsection (2) above,

the Secretary of State may require the managers or governors of the school to prepare and submit to him, within such time as he may specify, proposals for that purpose. . . .

(6) Where at the passing of this Act the arrangements for the admission of pupils to schools in, or in any part of, the area of a local education authority are based partly on selection by reference to ability or aptitude, the Secretary of State shall not, for such period as he thinks fit, require the authority to prepare and submit proposals under this section in relation to those schools if it appears to him that the purpose of the arrangements is to secure the even distribution between the schools of pupils of different degrees of ability or aptitude. . . .

Miscellaneous

4. (1) Section 13 of the Education Act 1944 shall have effect with the following amendments (being amendments requiring the implementation of approved proposals as to the maintenance of a school or as to changes in its character).

(2) For subsection (8) there shall be substituted—

'(8) When proposals for the maintenance of a school or proposals that a local education authority should cease to maintain a school have been approved by the Secretary of State under this section, it shall be the duty of the local education authority to maintain or, as the case may be, to cease to maintain the school in accordance with the proposals.'...

(3) After subsection (9) there shall be inserted—

'(9A) When proposals for the making of any change in the character of a school have been approved by the Secretary of State under this section, it shall be the duty of the local education authority or, in the case of a voluntary school, the managers or governors to give effect to the proposals.'...

10. (1) For section 33(2) of the Education Act 1944 there shall be substituted—

'(2) The arrangements made by a local education authority for the special educational treatment of pupils of any such category shall, subject to subsection (2A) of this section, provide for the education of the pupils in county or voluntary schools.

(2A) Where the education of the pupils in such schools as aforesaid—

(*a*) is impracticable or incompatible with the provision of efficient instruction in the schools; or
(*b*) would involve unreasonable public expenditure,

the arrangements may provide for the education of the pupils in special schools appropriate to the category to which the pupils belong or in schools not maintained by a local education authority and for the time being notified by the Secretary of State to the authority as in his opinion suitable for the purpose.'...

(3) This section shall not come into force until such day as may be appointed by the Secretary of State by order made by statutory instrument.

59 · Report of the Committee of Enquiry entitled *A New Partnership for Our Schools. [The Taylor Report]*

Published: *1977*

Chairman: *Councillor Tom Taylor*

Members: *Professor G. Baron; Miss J. Barrow; Mrs M. B. Broadley; Mr D. P. J. Browning; Councillor E. Currie-Jones; Mrs A. E. Edwards; Mr F. D. Flower; Councillor P. O. Fulton; Mr J. E. Hale; Mr G. M. A. Harrison; Mr R. N. Heaton; Councillor E. G. Hett; Councillor J. R. Horrell; Mr J. A. R. Kay; Miss B. Lynn; Mr J. Macgougan; Miss A. C. Millet; Mr M. J. Moore; The Rev. P. J. Reilly; Mrs J. Sallis; Mrs J. Stone; Mr K. J. Turner; Canon R. Waddington; Mr J. K. Sawtell (Secretary)*

Assessors: *Mr M. W. Hodges; Mr C. A. Norman H.M.I. (from November 1976); Mr S. K. Bateman (until September 1975); Mr J. B. Davies (from January 1976)*

Mr J. A. R. Kay resigned on 24 September 1975.

Terms of Reference: *To review the arrangements for the management and government of maintained primary and secondary schools in England and Wales, including the composition and functions of bodies of managers and governors, and their relationships with local education authorities, with head teachers and staffs of schools, with parents of pupils and with the local community at large; and to make recommendations.*

The Committee was set up in 1975. It was a response to an apparent growing interest in lay participation in education as a part of a wider consumer movement. A National Association of Governors and Managers had been formed as a pressure group in 1970, some of whose leading members were influential in Labour Party circles. By the time the report appeared in 1977, the educational consumer movement had taken a somewhat different tack, with more emphasis on stronger control at the level of the central Government and the local authorities rather than the school level where active governors might intervene.

The recommendations included a marked strengthening of the powers of governing bodies, with membership divided equally between representatives of the local education authority, the staff, the parents and the local community. The wide powers which the Committee recommended Governors should exercise in respect of the curriculum (see extract) aroused strong opposition among the teachers' unions, notably the National Union of Teachers. (The N.U.T. general secretary hung the label a 'busybodies' charter' on to the report when it first appeared.)

A Labour attempt to put some of the recommendations into effect failed when an Education Bill was lost at the dissolution of Parliament in March 1979. The following year the Conservatives' 1980 Education Act revised the legal provision for governors, requiring the election of parent and teacher governors. The same Act also laid down the standard information which local authorities should provide in respect of each school, and a new procedure for dealing with parental preferences in the allocation of pupils to primary and secondary schools.

THE TAYLOR REPORT · 1977

What the reader will seek, in following our statements of our findings and our thoughts, is evidence of a recognizable guiding philosophy.... The principles which seemed to us important after studying all the evidence, ...were these:

(i) within the framework of national and local policies, however these may change with time, the special character of the individual school is precious to most people and should be protected;

(ii) that character is essentially a product of *local* considerations and of the skill, support and concern of all those on the spot who care about its success;

(iii) one body should have delegated responsibility for running the school, and in forming that body no one interest should be dominant – it should be an equal partnership of all those with a legitimate concern, local education authority, staff, parents, where appropriate pupils, and the community;

(iv) the governing body thus formed should be responsible for the life and work of the school as a whole: we did not consider that a school's activity could be divided, and neither could accountability for its success;

(v) the decision-making role of the governing body is only part of its functions: equally important is its responsibility for promoting and protecting good relationships both within the school and between the school and its parents and the wider community: where we recommend particular measures to achieve effective communication and harmonious relationships, we therefore charge the governors with the task of ensuring their satisfactory operation;

(vi) while the detail of the new arrangements which we recommend should be left to a considerable extent to local discretion, the essential features should be universal.

[From the Preface, pp. xi and xii

CURRICULUM RESPONSIBILITY IN ACTION

...Our preferred concept of the school curriculum effectively comprehends the sum of experiences to which a child is exposed at school. Strictly speaking therefore in exercising, as we propose, responsibility for the education provided in the school the governors will always have the whole curriculum before them since no single aspect of the life and work of the school can be properly understood if considered in isolation. In practice, however, the planning and development of a school curriculum can be broken down into four basic, and to a large extent overlapping, stages;

(i) establishing the school's aims;

(ii) translating those aims into more specific goals and organizing the school and developing teaching methods and other practical steps to achieve them;

(iii) keeping the education provided under continuous review and making periodic appraisals of the school's progress towards its goals and aims;

(iv) deciding upon and taking action to facilitate such progress.

We take it as given that policies decided nationally and at the local education authority level will provide the framework within which individual schools and their governing bodies will operate.... Within this general framework we *RECOMMEND that the governing body should be given by the local education authority the responsibility for setting the aims of the school, for considering the means by which they are pursued, for keeping under review the school's progress towards them, and for deciding upon action to facilitate such progress....*

SETTING THE AIMS OF THE SCHOOL

We propose that when looking to the governing bodies to set the aims of the schools for which they are responsible, the local education authority should alert them to the difficulties experienced, first, by schools whose aims are too frequently questioned and changed and, second, by schools whose aims become unalterably fixed. We believe that both extremes could be avoided if the governing bodies were to reconsider the particular aims of the school periodically....

TRANSLATING THE SCHOOL'S AIMS INTO PRACTICE

When the governing body has reached conclusions on any of the aims which it wishes its school to follow, it should consider whether the organization, teaching methods, disciplinary practices and other measures used in the school are appropriate for the pursuit of their aims.

Obviously there can be no question of a simple, staged progression from an agreement on the aims of the school, in their totality, to the preparation and adoption of a 'master plan' for pursuing them. We have in mind a fluid procedure in which action on any aim could be initiated as and when it was agreed by the governors.

We RECOMMEND that the governing body invite the headteacher in consultation with his staff to prepare papers setting out the means by which they propose to pursue the aims adopted. In the case of well-established aims, the school's existing practice might need no revision but where some new aim was being considered it would be necessary to examine whether its pursuit required the introduction of new activities into the school. After discussion and consideration of any alternative suggestions it would be for the governing body to decide whether to adopt (or confirm) these proposals.

In considering the arrangements for pursuing the school's aims, the governing body's attention would focus upon the setting of specific goals or objectives and upon the school's organization and teaching methods, examining both the educational experience and pastoral care available for the children and the educational and social effects of particular ways of arranging the provision of teaching.

These operations would, in our view, be of considerable educational value. Teachers would have an opportunity to discuss, explain and justify their decisions in terms which could be understood by people not belonging to the teaching profession; their skill as professionals can only grow from such an experience. Lack of confidence may often have lain behind the reluctance of many teachers in the past to discuss their work with people from outside the school. The latter also would come to recognize the importance and difficulty of reconciling the different objectives of the school and of producing unified plans for achieving them....

As regards teaching methods we must draw a distinction between the methods adopted by the individual classroom teacher and broader questions of method which affect the education provided by the school as a whole (or at least large departments within it). Obviously the individual teacher should continue...to be responsible for deciding how to teach the members of his class, in the light of his own capacities and any general teaching policies adopted generally in the school. Nonetheless we believe there are at least two other considerations which should influence and could limit the making of decisions by individual teachers or even by the school's teachers in general. First, all decisions involving questions of consistency of approach and continuity of method are likely to be of sufficient importance to concern the governing body. Second, we believe that people not engaged in education have an important contribution to make in expressing public opinion and concern generally on how children are taught and we hope that the governing body will become the forum for considering the suitability of new educational ideas and methods for the school. Proposed innovations might originate within or without the school. The governing body should encourage a two-way flow of ideas, examining developments initiated by its own teachers and discussing with them the implications of developments elsewhere. We believe that the governing body should concern itself with the professional development of the teachers in its school and should be active in promoting this, for example by encouraging them to take full advantage of opportunities for in-service training.

The construction of a timetable for a secondary school is a complicated task which is properly carried out by senior teachers; the purpose is clearly to provide the organization within which teachers can teach and children can learn. It might be thought that this is a technical process which concerns only the teachers and pupils. But in fact there are often much wider issues involved, including the ordering of curricular balance and priorities to secure the fair distribution of opportunities for children of all abilities. The effectiveness of the timetabling from both the educational and the social points of view is, we believe, a matter of concern for the governing body.

We stress throughout this report the indivisibility of a school's activities. To be effective the learning experience must be supported first by an organization which directs resources in accordance with the needs of each child, second by sensitive pastoral care, and third by the encouragement, through precept and example, of the consideration for others which alone in the long run can ensure pleasant and orderly behaviour. Put conversely, the best guarantee that high standards of conduct will be observed by the majority is a curriculum devised to give every child experience of success, and a structure of care which not only seeks to deal with any personal problems which jeopardize that success, but also makes him feel valued as an individual. We therefore regret that so often 'discipline' should be equated with the treatment of indiscipline, and urge that part of the governors' responsibility is to ensure that theirs is the kind of school in which the more positive concept outlined above is consciously promoted. We also emphasize – and have set out elsewhere – the need to involve parents and the community in supporting schools in their task. In such conditions we believe that pupils will increasingly be encouraged to become identified with the work of the school, to participate fully, and to feel responsible for their own conduct. The growth of such involvement we consider to be vital to their development as individuals and to the success of their school.

Accordingly *we RECOMMEND that within the framework of any*

general policy made by the local education authority the governing body should have the responsibility for formulating guidelines which promote high standards of behaviour and for making such minimum rules and sanctions as are necessary to maintain such standards in the school. It must also be their responsibility to ensure that staff, parents and pupils are made fully aware of these policies and rules and the reasons for them and have an opportunity to express their views. In this way we should hope to bring about not a weakening of the head's authority, but rather an increase in the support he received in a task which is not becoming any easier.

KEEPING UNDER REVIEW THE LIFE AND ACTIVITIES OF THE SCHOOL

As a first step in keeping under review the degree to which the school is achieving its goals and making progress towards its aims, the governing body will want to decide what information and advice it will need in respect of those activities of the school which it considers of particular importance as indicators of the school's progress.

The primary source for this information and advice will be the headteacher and especially his staff, and the success of the operation will depend upon their contribution. Like all other organizations, schools produce in the course of their everyday business a great deal of information about many aspects of their work. Often this serves a single, specific purpose and is then discarded. Even when preserved it is not always in a form which facilitates its further use. We think that this represents a lost opportunity. The information flowing into and within the school, on those matters which can indicate progress in important respects, should be assembled and processed in such a way that it can be readily used by the governing body. Whilst the information required by the governors will vary from school to school it might be helpful to mention a few obvious items which we would expect to be collected. In all schools information about applications for places at the school, records of attendance and suspensions would be helpful, together with records of out of school activities including details of school societies and educational visits. In the case of primary schools information about relevant secondary provision and, in the case of secondary schools, information about examination results and employment opportunities in the area, might be added. In addition to basic information of this kind, the governors would no doubt also wish to have periodic reports of a more qualitative nature on the major departments of the school and its pastoral system as well as the headteacher's assessment of the school's general progress.

The governing body would also be concerned to obtain information on how the school is seen by the community which it serves. It would be for the governing body to decide upon the type of information required and the means of obtaining it but again, for purely illustrative purposes, we note some possibilities: the views of the school's parents, pupils and supporting staff: the pre-school provision available locally; the views of the governing bodies of other schools, to which pupils, in the case of primary or middle schools, normally transfer; the views of local people (based on observation and experience) and, in the case of secondary schools, the views of employers and institutions of higher and further education.

We believe that it will help individual governors to gain insight into the nature of the educational opportunities being provided and into the complexities of the teacher's task if they visit classes in progress. We therefore *RECOMMEND that where the governing body considers it appropriate and desirable and has worked out with the teachers procedures for the purpose, individual governors should have the opportunity of seeing classes at work.* It should be emphasized that governors should not see themselves in the role of inspectors. Where the attention of a governor is drawn to difficulties affecting a particular class or teacher, he should inform the chairman in order that the matter can if necessary be taken up in the first place with the headteacher and perhaps with the local education authority adviser concerned.

[From Chapter 6, pp. 52–6

60 · Education in Schools – A Consultative Document. 1977

This document, known as the 'Green Paper', emanated from the Department of Education and Science as the culmination of the so-called 'Great Debate', initiated by the Prime Minister Mr James Callaghan in a speech at Ruskin College, Oxford in October 1976.

The burden of the speech was the need to re-open public discussion of educational issues which had become 'professionalized'. Mr Callaghan voiced public anxiety on standards and priorities, echoing (while expressly rejecting) criticisms put forward by radical conservative critics in the series of publications known as the Black Papers (1969–77). He implied that the professionals had tried to keep the control of the curriculum to themselves, resisting attempts to get them to explain themselves and their actions to their paymasters and clients.

This major speech was, in its turn, based on a confidential memorandum from the Department of Education and Science, entitled *School Education in England – Problems and Initiatives*. Leaked to the Press on the eve of the Ruskin speech, this concluded by arguing that the D.E.S. should be allowed to give 'a firmer lead' and that the Inspectorate should 'have a leading role to play' in bringing forward ideas on curricular matters.

After the Prime Minister had spoken, the Secretary of State for Education and Science and her colleague, the Secretary of State for Wales, embarked on an elaborate programme of public and private discussions including a series of one-day regional public meetings at which educational issues were canvassed. These meetings used as the basis of the discussion a series of papers put forward by the Department. The regional meetings highlighted anxieties about basic standards and examinations and in particular, the criticisms of employers about the educational standards of school-leavers.

Having orchestrated the debate and largely shaped the discussion, it fell to the D.E.S. also to sum it up and outline future intentions. This was the purpose of the Green Paper. It covered *inter alia* Curriculum (see extract) Standards and Assessment, Teachers (foreshadowing stronger managerial control) and School and Working Life.

Subsequent D.E.S. papers on *A Framework for the Curriculum* (1980) and *The School Curriculum* (1981) were aimed at persuading local education authorities to develop curriculum policies within broad guidelines, and (Circular 6/81) ensuring that every school should prepare a statement of curriculum objectives.

EDUCATION IN SCHOOLS · 1977

CURRICULUM

PRIMARY SCHOOLS

Primary schools have been transformed in recent years by two things: a much wider curriculum than used to be considered sufficient for elementary education, and the rapid growth of the so-called 'child-centred' approach. The primary curriculum has been enriched by a feeling for colour, design and music, and by the introduction of simple scientific ideas. Children engage in work designed to increase their control over themselves physically and mentally, to capture their imagination and to widen their knowledge and understanding of the world about them. The child-centred approach takes advantage of the child's individual stage of development and of his or her interests: it complements the wider curriculum by harnessing the natural enthusiasm of young children for learning things by their own efforts instead of merely being fed with information. In the right hands, this approach has produced confident, happy and relaxed children, without any sacrifice of the 3Rs or other accomplishments – indeed, with steady improvement in standards. Visitors have come from all over the world to see, and to admire, the English and Welsh 'primary school revolution'.

Unfortunately, however, the work has not always been in the hands of experienced and able teachers. While only a tiny minority of schools adopted the child-centred approach to the exclusion of other teaching methods, its influence has been widespread. It has proved to be a trap for some less able or less experienced teachers who applied the freer methods uncritically or failed to recognize that they require careful planning of the opportunities offered to children and systematic monitoring of the progress of individuals. While the majority of primary teachers, whatever approach they use, recognize the importance of performance in basic skills such as reading, spelling and arithmetic, some have failed to achieve satisfactory results in them. In some classes, or even some schools, the use of the child-centred approach has deteriorated into lack of order and application.

The challenge now is to restore the rigour without damaging the real benefits of the child-centred developments. This does not imply any great change in the range of what is taught, but the following features, already recognized by the most effective schools, need to be accepted throughout the system.

(i) In all schools teachers need to be quite clear about the ways in which children make and show progress in the various aspects of their learning. They can then more easily choose the best approach for their pupils.

(ii) Teachers should be able to identify with some precision the levels of achievement represented by a pupil's work. In parts of the curriculum such as arithmetic, it is relatively easy to organize a series of targets for the pupils according to a logical sequence of difficulty. In other parts of the curriculum where teachers are planning to develop their pupils' imagination and social awareness, it may not be possible to be so precise. Teachers can nonetheless plan a progression in these parts of the curriculum and so ensure that they make their proper contribution to the child's education.

(iii) Teachers in successive classes or schools need to agree about what is to be learned. They should as a matter of professional habit pass on clear information about work done and levels of achievement.

(iv) Even allowing for local and individual needs, children throughout England and Wales have many educational requirements in common. It is therefore reasonable to expect that children moving from a primary school in one part of the country to another elsewhere will find much that is familiar in kind if not in detail.

(v) There are some skills for which the primary schools have a central, and indeed over-riding, responsibility. Literacy and numeracy are the most important of these: no other curricular aims should deflect teachers from them. By definition they must form part of the core of learning, the protected area of the curriculum. . . .

SECONDARY SCHOOLS

Four fifths of our boys and girls now attend comprehensive schools. The comprehensive school is at the centre of the Government's policy on secondary education. The objective of the comprehensive system is to offer to every boy or girl educational opportunities appropriate to his or her ability, aptitudes and personal motivation. It recognizes the importance of educating together young people from different backgrounds, as an essential preparation for a more united and understanding society.

The rapid development of comprehensive schools has required great efforts by local education authorities, teachers, and the churches, and could not have been achieved without their co-operation. Ideas about the reorganization of schools naturally continue to evolve. The end of selection for secondary education, to which the Government remain wholly committed, is in sight. . . .

The curriculum is not the school's sole means of realizing the purposes of comprehensive education. The creation of a lively and caring community, where the pupils have opportunities to exercise initiative and responsibility; the sensitive organization of groups for learning and other activities; the establishment of an unobtrusive system of effective guidance and support for the adolescent are crucial to success. But all these serve the cause of the pupils' learning, which is the school's main business and which is embodied in the curriculum. The comprehensive school's curriculum must reflect the diversity of its pupils' individual needs. In educational terms, the comprehensive school aspires to educate all our children to the highest standards of which they are capable. Whatever the difficulties and problems on the way, and this paper does not seek to minimize them, that remains the Government's goal.

Secondary schools, like primary schools, have been transformed. The curriculum now generally offers a greater spectrum of learning and a broader range of choices than did the traditional selective system. A much higher proportion of pupils now take public examinations, the C.S.E., or the G.C.E. Ordinary or Advanced levels. New content and new styles of learning in the sciences and mathematics have helped to make these subjects more interesting and more accessible to many pupils. The opportunity to learn a modern language has been given to a much wider range of pupils of different abilities than in the past. There has, in general, been a good deal of curriculum experiment and diversification and the early years of C.S.E. stimulated fundamental and valuable study of the needs of those leaving school – and often formal education – at 16.

These advances have not been without attendant weaknesses. Further progress must build on the achievements of recent years and take account of current criticism. . . .

The pace of change has outstripped the supply of appropriately qualified and experienced teachers. Some did not understand sufficiently clearly the nature of the changes on which they were embarking, nor did they all have the benefit of adequate support from in-service courses. This is particularly true of teachers changing from a grammar or secondary modern school to a comprehensive one, usually faced with teaching pupils of a wider or different range of ability.

In addition, the secondary curriculum has been under great pressure from the constantly growing demands upon it. These reflect the complexities of adult life which await the pupils when they leave school. But there has been considerable criticism on the grounds that the curriculum has become overloaded and that essential educational objectives may have been put at risk.

The balance and breadth of each child's course is crucial at all school levels, and this is especially so during the later years of compulsory education. In most secondary schools the curriculum of the main school course is broadly traditional for the first two or three years. Options begin to shape the curriculum significantly in the fourth and fifth years. English and religious education are in most schools a standard part of the curriculum for all pupils up to the age of 16, and it is not true that many pupils drop mathematics at an early stage. But the offer of options and the freedom to choose do lead some boys and girls to abandon certain areas of study at an early age. This is questionable in a society like ours where the rapidity of change puts a premium on the sound acquisition of certain basic skills developed in up-to-date terms to the limit of the pupil's ability and understanding. Few, inside or outside the schools, would contest that alongside English and mathematics, science should find a secure place for all pupils at least to the age of 16, and that a modern language should do so for as high a proportion as practicable.

These thoughts were reflected in much of the discussion on the curriculum at the regional conferences. Unease about the curriculum is expressed in many forms but the principal points of concern appear to be:

(i) the curriculum has become overcrowded; the timetable is overloaded and the essentials are at risk;

(ii) variations in the approach to the curriculum in different schools can penalize a child simply because he has moved from one area to another;

(iii) even if the child does not move, variations from school to school may give rise to inequality of opportunities;

(iv) the curriculum in many schools is not sufficiently matched to life in a modern industrial society.

Not all these comments may be equally valid but it is clear that the time has come to try to establish generally accepted principles for the composition of the secondary curriculum for all pupils. This does not presuppose uniform answers: schools, pupils, and their teachers are different, and the curriculum should be flexible enough to reflect these differences. But there is a need to investigate the part which might be played by a 'protected' or 'core' element of the curriculum common to all schools. There are various ways this may be defined. Properly worked out, it can offer reassurances to employers, parents and the teachers themselves, as well as a very real equality of opportunity for pupils.

The creation of a suitable core curriculum will not be easy. Pupils in their later years of secondary schooling have a wide range of interests and expectations. Many of them will need help to see the relevance of what school offers and to understand how their skills can be used for their adult and working life. This can contribute to overcoming the lack of motivation and unco-operative attitudes displayed by some pupils. It is not the task of schools to prepare pupils for specific jobs but experience has long shown that studies and activities that are practical and obviously relevant to working life can be valuable as a means of learning, including the learning of basic skills.

Apart from the central question of curriculum planning up to the age of 16 there are other aspects of the problem that need more study.

(i) Some narrowing of the range of subjects studied after 16 is legitimate and perhaps inevitable, but traditional practice in England and Wales may have gone too far in this direction. Some of those who follow academic sixth form courses devote almost all their time to only two or three closely related subjects, without even the substantial broadening element of general studies provided in many schools. There has however been much discussion elsewhere of this feature of secondary education, and it will come under scrutiny again in relation to possible changes in the examination system.

(ii) Both before and after 16, care must be taken to see that girls do not by their choices limit the range of educational and career opportunities open to them. Positive steps may be necessary to encourage girls to broaden and modernize their aspirations and to feel confident of success in unfamiliar fields of science and technology. This is particularly important now that there are many fewer places available in colleges of education to which a large number of girls have traditionally gone for their higher education.

(iii) The curriculum for the less academic sixth former is not well defined. The same general principles apply as at earlier stages in the secondary school but particular care has to be taken to ensure that the education given to this very wide range of pupils furthers their career prospects as well as their personal development. It is important that they understand the range of opportunities open to them and what they stand to gain or lose by following one or other course.

ACTION ON THE CURRICULUM

Action to improve the planning and development of the curriculum will be successful only if it takes into account fully the division of responsibilities for education in schools. The control of secular instruction in maintained schools – aided secondary schools apart – rests with the local education authority, subject to the provisions of each school's rules of management or articles of government. In practice, much of the responsibility for deciding the curriculum of each school is devolved by the local education authorities and the governors or managers upon the teachers or head teachers in the schools.

It would not be compatible with the duty of the Secretaries of State to 'promote the education of the people of England and Wales', or with their accountability to Parliament, to abdicate from leadership on educational issues which have become a matter of lively public concern. The Secretaries of State will therefore seek to establish a broad agreement with their partners in the education service on a framework for the curriculum, and, particularly, on whether, because there are aims common to all schools and to all pupils at certain stages, there should be a 'core' or 'protected part'.

In their turn, the local education authorities must co-ordinate the curriculum and its development in their own areas, taking account of local circumstances, consulting local interests and drawing on the work of the Schools Council and other curricular research and development agencies. In this way the proper professional freedom of individual schools and their teachers can be exercised to the best advantage.

As the next step the Secretaries of State propose to invite the local authority and teachers' associations to take part in early consultations about the conduct of a review of curricular arrangements in each local authority area. The Schools Council will be invited to play a part in these consultations. Appropriate provision will also be made for other interested organizations to express their views.

The intention of the Secretaries of State is that, following these consultations, they should issue a circular* asking all local education authorities to carry out the review in their own areas in consultation with their teachers and to report the results within about twelve months. The Departments would then analyze the replies as a preliminary to consultations on the outcome of the review and on the nature of any advice which the Secretaries of State might then issue on curricular matters.

[From Chapter 2, pp. 8–13

* Circular 14/77

61 · Report of the Committee of Enquiry into the Education of Handicapped Children and Young People. [*The Warnock Report*]

Published: *1978*

Chairman: *Mrs H. M. Warnock*

Members: *Mr G. V. Cooke (Vice-Chairman); Mrs J. D. Bisby; Sir Edward Britton; Miss M. F. Cairley; Dr I. Chesham; Mr D. Coe; Mr G. H. Dalziel; Mr R. A. Davis (until December 1976); Dr R. M. Forrester; Professor P. J. Graham; Mr D. Guthrie (resigned May 1975); Mr J. E. Harding; Mr L. Macho; Dr J. B. Meredith Davies (appointed June 1975); Mr J. A. D. Michie; Mr G. P. Newton (resigned April 1975); Mr P. H. Priestley; Mr E. J. Richards; Lady Roth J.P. (until July 1977); Mrs M. E. Thruston; Mrs W. Tumim; Dr M. C. Tyson; Professor P. Williams; Mr D. Winnard (until September 1974); Mr D. P. T. Woodgate; Mr P. W. Young*

Secretary: *Mr J. C. Hedger (until May 1976); Miss I. Luxton (from May 1976)*

Assessors: *Mr M. A. Walker (until September 1976); Mr V. H. Stephens (from October 1976); Mr J. R. Fish, H.M.I.; Mrs N. Munro (until May 1976); Mr R. P. C. Macnab (from May 1976); Mr A. Milne, H.M.I.; Mr M. W. Stone, H.M.I.; Mr P. Tansley (until June 1977); Mr S. Loveman (from June 1977); Dr E. E. Simpson; Mr G. M. Bebb; Mr R. B. Brown; Dr J. Ward (until May 1975); Dr J. H. Grant (June 1975 to August 1977); Dr M. Hennigan (from September* 1977)

Terms of Reference: *To review educational provision in England, Scotland and Wales for children and young people handicapped by disabilities of body or mind, taking account of the medical aspects of their needs, together with arrangements to prepare them for entry into employment; to consider the most effective use of resources for these purposes; and to make recommendations.*

The Warnock Committee was set up in November 1973. Mrs Mary Warnock, senior research fellow at St Hugh's College, Oxford and a philosopher by training, had, for a time, been the head of Oxford High School, a girls' direct grant grammar school, before returning to academic life.

Prior to publication, much attention had been directed to the issue of the integration of handicapped pupils within the ordinary schools, an issue which had, to some extent, been pre-empted by Section 10 of the Education Act, 1976 (p. 384). Mrs Warnock and her colleagues accepted the integration ideal, while playing down the rhetoric. They concluded that the majority of handicapped children could and should be taught in ordinary schools. Their definition of handicap suggested that up to 20 per cent of all children would at some time require 'some form of special educational provision'. The logic of such a conclusion demanded efficient special provision within ordinary schools. To back it up, the Committee paid much attention to the initial and in-service training required, and to the support services which would be needed. It recognized that these could not be instituted quickly. Both the integrationists and the special education lobby, therefore, could find comfort in the report, but it leaned towards caution rather than boldness.

The Education Act, 1981, gave effect to recommendations of the Warnock Committee on the identification and assessment of children with special educational needs.

THE WARNOCK REPORT · 1978

GENERAL APPROACH

The criterion by which to judge the quality of educational provision is the extent to which it leads a pupil...towards understanding, awareness of moral values and enjoyment and towards the possibility of independence. It is progress towards these goals which alone can justify a particular course of education for anyone, whatever his abilities or disabilities. For some children, enjoyment and understanding may be confined to the hard-won, taught capacity to recognize things and people, and perhaps to name them. For some, independence may in the end amount to no more than the freedom of performing a task for oneself rather than having someone else do it, even if the task is only getting dressed or feeding oneself. For others the concepts of imaginative understanding, enjoyment and freedom have an infinitely richer content. But the direction of progress is the same.

Though the general concept of education may remain constant, its interpretation will thus be widely different in the case of different children. There is in our society a vast range of differently disabled children, many of whom would not have survived infancy in other periods of history. In the case of the most profoundly disabled one is bound to face the questions: Why educate such children at all? Are they not ineducable? How can one justify such effort and such expense for so small a result? Such questions have to be faced, and must be answered. Our answer is that education, as we conceive it, is a good, and a specifically human good, to which all human beings are entitled. There exists, therefore, a clear obligation to educate the most severely disabled for no other reason than that they are human. No civilized society can be content just to look after these children; it must all the time seek ways of helping them, however slowly, towards the educational goals we have identified. To understand the ways in which help can be given is to begin to meet their educational needs. If we fail to do this, we are actually increasing and compounding their disadvantages.

Moreover there are some children with disabilities who, through education along the common lines we advocate, may be able to lead a life very little poorer in quality than that of the non-handicapped child, whereas without this kind of education they might face a life of dependence or even institutionalization. Education in such cases makes the difference between a proper and enjoyable life and something less than we believe life should be. From the point of view of the other members of the family, too, the process of drawing a severely handicapped child into the educational system may, through its very normality, help to maintain the effectiveness, stability and cohesion of the family unit.

We have been concerned, however, not only with the severely handicapped but with all those children who require special education in any form. The help needed may range from continuous support from specialist services, including an intensive educational programme in a special school for a child with severe and multiple disabilities, to part-time assistance from a specially trained teacher for a child with mild learning difficulties. It is perhaps useful to regard this range of special educational need as a continuum, although that is a crude notion which conceals the complexities of individual needs.

Our concept of special education is thus broader than the traditional one of education by special methods appropriate for particular categories of children. It extends beyond the idea of education provided in special schools, special classes or units for children with particular types of disability, and embraces the notion of any form of additional help, wherever it is provided and whenever it is provided, from birth to maturity, to overcome educational difficulty. It also embodies the idea that, although the difficulties which some children encounter may dictate WHAT they have to be taught and the disabilities of some HOW they have to be taught, the point of their education is the same.

Whatever else may come out of our report, we hope that one thing will be clear. Special education is a challenging and intellectually demanding field for those engaged in it. . . . Those who work with children with special educational needs should regard themselves as having a crucial and developing role in a society which is now committed, not merely to tending and caring for its handicapped members, as a matter of charity, but to educating them, as a matter of right and to developing their potential to the full.

[From Chapter 1, pp. 5–7

A BROADER CONCEPT OF SPECIAL EDUCATION

The view which we have stated of the nature and range of special educational needs and our estimate of the proportion of children who are likely to have such needs during their school career amount to a much wider concept of special education than any currently in use. We must therefore consider the precise way in which special education may be delineated.

We start from the concept of 'special educational treatment' defined in Section 8(2)(c) of the Education Act 1944 as 'education by special methods appropriate for pupils suffering from disability of mind and body'. We note in passing that the definition is in the context of education in schools, and that there is no equivalent formulation applicable to further education. It has an institutional connotation, being linked to the provision of schools (principally special schools) and fixes the framework for later provisions in the Act for the ascertainment, categorization and placement of the pupils covered by it.

Our concept is not tied to particular educational methods or particular categories of children. Nor is it associated with any particular institutional setting; the majority of children who are likely to require special educational provision in the wider sense that we are advocating will be in ordinary primary and secondary schools, which are not approved as providing a particular kind or kinds of education. The traditional view of special education as exclusively separate full-time provision in special schools or classes has in any case been substantially modified by recent practice, and has been explicitly called into question by Section 10 of the Education Act 1976. . . .

Our view of special education . . . encompasses the whole range and variety of additional help, wherever it is provided and whether on a full or part-time basis, by which children may be helped to overcome educational difficulties, however they are caused. It thus embraces educational help for children with emotional or behavioural disorders who have previously been regarded as disruptive, as well as for children who have hitherto been seen as requiring remedial, rather than special, education. Both these groups in our view require special education.

At present 'remedial' groups include children with a variety of difficulties which, though different in origin, are frequently treated alike. There are children who have been absent from school and need to make up work which they have missed; children with physical or sensory disabilities, sometimes temporary, sometimes permanent; children with varying degrees of learning difficulties and children who need to be temporarily withdrawn from the normal class for specific purposes. The term 'remedial', like the term 'treatment', suggests that these children have something wrong with them that can be put right. It is true that some of them are suffering only a temporary learning difficulty and, given appropriate help, are able to return rapidly to their previous classes having completely overcome their disability. Others, however, require special help and support throughout their school lives and to say that these children require 'remedial' education is misleading. Children in these so-called 'remedial' groups have a wide variety of individual needs, sometimes linked to psychological or physical factors, which call for skilled and discriminating attention by staff – in assessment, the devising of suitable programmes and the organization of group or individual teaching, whether in ordinary or special classes. For these children the provision of special support is just as important as for those who have been ascertained as requiring special education. We conclude that a meaningful distinction between remedial and special education can no longer be maintained.

In attempting to delineate special education, we have sought to identify those features which make up its distinctive character wherever it is provided. Our approach is based upon the principle that if it is to be special, special education should afford access to teachers with additional training and, where appropriate, to other professionals; or access to an educational or physical environment appropriate to a particular child's special needs – for example, an environment where adequate physical support is available, or one in which a particular educational regime is followed. We propose that special educational provision for the children with whom we are concerned should, therefore, be understood in terms of one or more of three criteria:

(i) effective access on a full or part-time basis to teachers with appropriate qualifications or substantial experience or both;

(ii) effective access on a full or part-time basis to other professionals with appropriate training; and

(iii) an educational and physical environment with the necessary aids, equipment and resources appropriate to the child's special needs....

[From Chapter 3, pp. 46–7

SPECIAL EDUCATION IN ORDINARY SCHOOLS

In this chapter we move to the central contemporary issue in special education which has been earnestly debated far beyond the frontiers of the education service. The principle of educating handicapped and non-handicapped children together, which is described as 'integration' in this country and 'mainstreaming' in the United States of America, and is recognized as part of a much wider movement of 'normalization' in Scandinavia and Canada, is the particular expression of a widely held and still growing conviction that, so far as is humanly possible, handicapped people should share the opportunities for self-fulfilment enjoyed by other people....

The wider concept of special education proposed in this report, embracing as it does all those children in ordinary schools who, though not at present accounted handicapped, need additional support in a variety of forms, is directly in line with the principle that handicapped and non-handicapped children should be educated in a common setting so far as possible....

THE DIFFERENT FORMS OF INTEGRATION

We have distinguished three main forms of integration. They are not discrete, but overlapping, and although each has a validity of its own they represent progressive stages of association....

The first form...relates to the physical LOCATION of special educational provision. Locational integration exists where special units or classes are set up in ordinary schools. It also exists where a special school and an ordinary school share the same site. It may be the most tenuous form of association, especially if contact with other children is not carefully organized. Even so it can bring worth-while gains. In the case of children attending special units or classes, their parents may be encouraged by the mere fact that their children attend an ordinary school; it is good that a child with a disability or significant difficulty should be able to attend the same school as his brothers or sisters of like age; moreover there is opportunity for children in the ordinary classes to be aware of children with special needs, and for children with disabilities to observe the behaviour of their contemporaries. These outcomes can be promoted by careful planning of the disposition of ordinary and special accommodation. In Sweden, where it is often claimed that the integration of even severely handicapped children has been widely achieved, the form which it takes is, in many cases, mainly locational, as those of us who visited that country observed. Some of the special classes are effectively separated from the rest of the school in all respects; those which are imaginatively planned and organized, however, offer handicapped and non-handicapped children the opportunity of familiarizing themselves with the other, and they represent a first stage towards full integration....

The second form of integration...relates to its SOCIAL aspect, where children attending a special class or unit eat, play and consort with other children, and possibly share organized out-of-classroom activities with them....

The third and fullest form of integration is FUNCTIONAL integration. This is achieved where the locational and social association of children with special needs with their fellows leads to joint participation in educational programmes. . . .

TYPES OF SPECIAL EDUCATIONAL PROVISION IN ORDINARY SCHOOLS

The three forms of integration . . . can be illustrated by examples of different types of special educational provision. . . .

(i) *Full-time education in an ordinary class with any necessary help and support*

Full-time education in an ordinary class should be the aim for many children with special educational needs. It should be possible to achieve this aim in the case of the majority of children with mild learning difficulties, many of whom are at present the concern of remedial services, provided that adequate support is available from teachers with additional training or expertise in special education and from members of the special education advisory and support service. . . . Some children with mild learning difficulties, however, will need more specialized provision of the type described in (ii) and (iii) below, as will most of those with moderate learning difficulties.

For many children with other handicapping conditions full participation in the curriculum of an ordinary class can be made possible by various measures like the provision of ramps and other aids to movement, space for a wheel-chair, special equipment such as a hearing aid, the presence of non-teaching aides, and individual teaching within the ordinary class, supported where necessary by special materials, such as books with large print. Already many children with handicapping conditions, particularly those with physical disabilities, have been successfully placed in ordinary classes in this way.

A small number of children with more severe disabilities, in very favourable conditions, have also been successfully placed in ordinary classes. . . .

We regard it as an important condition of the success of all schemes for integrating children with disabilities or significant difficulties into ordinary schools that there should not be so many of these children in any one school as will change the nature of the school, or even encourage the formation of á separate sub-group. We make a recommendation to this effect in relation to special classes and units. . . . Any special arrangements for the integration of a child with a disability into an ordinary class must be compatible with the interests of other children in the class, and specialist teachers must be available to review the arrangements, to support the ordinary teacher in his work and to tutor the child, where necessary.

(ii) *Education in an ordinary class with periods of withdrawal to a special class or unit or other supporting base*
Some children, though enabled by measures of the kind described in (i) to profit from substantial attendance at an ordinary class, need at least some additional provision which the ordinary class cannot offer. They are likely to include those who require a form of modified or supplemented curriculum, specialist teaching techniques in particular areas of learning, access to some types of special apparatus, materials or accommodation, or perhaps simply the occasional enjoyment of the intimate influence of a smaller teaching group.

(iii) *Education in a special class or unit with periods of attendance at an ordinary class and full involvement in the general community life and extra-curricular activities of the ordinary school*
This arrangement implies that a pupil's special needs are such that the major part of his education must take place outside the ordinary classes of the school. In most cases he will therefore be on the roll of the special class or unit, in contrast to the arrangement in (ii) where the ordinary class will be the home base. Nevertheless we take the view that the slightest participation in ordinary class activities can be strikingly beneficial to children with special needs, and that their total exclusion should therefore not be accepted before every possibility has been thoroughly considered. Of necessity the range of educational opportunities available in a special class or unit may be limited. It is therefore important that children who are able to do so should take part in a wider range of activities, particularly at the secondary school stage. We recognize that the provision of these wider opportunities may present practical difficulties, which will vary according to the nature and extent of the children's disabilities and their age; the problems will be different in secondary schools, where frequent class changes are necessary, from those in primary schools. We believe that these difficulties can, and should, be overcome and we see scope for making arrangements of this kind for children with a wide range of difficulties and disorders, including emotional and behavioural disorders. . . . Full involvement in the communal life and extra-curricular activities of a school is clearly an important feature of the education of all the pupils, particularly those with special needs: but it acquires additional significance

where such involvement is the major or only means whereby a severely handicapped pupil is able to establish his place as an active member of the school....

(iv) *Full-time education in a special class or unit with social contact with the main school*

Where a child's special needs are such that he is quite unable to join an ordinary class for any part of his education he may, for the same reasons, be prevented from full involvement in out-of-class activities. If such children are to live in the community, and if their fellows are to understand their problems, some special interaction is essential. Particularly if the attendance of children with very severe disabilities at the ordinary school is to have any justification they must be allowed opportunity for regular contact with other children and teachers in the school. This contact might be achieved through other children and teachers coming into the special class or unit or through the teachers and children in the special class or unit visiting the main school, if only for social interchange. Careful arrangements to this end will need to be made which take into account individual conditions and capabilities. The arrangements will require to be consciously planned no less than the pupil's formal education, and for this reason should be the responsibility of a particular member of the school staff. Every effort must be made to ensure that the special class or unit is an integral part of the school.... We cannot envisage any substantial move towards the integration of children with disabilities or significant difficulties unless these conditions, which we discuss in greater detail below, are satisfied.

The children

Special educational provision, in whatever shape, will be effective only if informed by an accurate assessment of all the factors – physical, mental and emotional – which condition a child's performance. Teachers must have full information about any special educational needs of the children for whose education they become responsible. The assessment procedures...should enable this condition to be met. For most of those children, up to one in five of the school population, who are likely at one time or another to experience special educational difficulties, assessment at one of our school-based stages should be sufficient; a child with more severe difficulties who requires regular specialist support over and above what the school itself can offer will have been assessed by a multi-professional team. The team will have completed a profile of his needs which, if he is subsequently recorded by the local education authority as requiring special education, will form the basis of the authority's duty to provide it. . . .

It is important that, where children with severe or complex disabilities are accepted, the other pupils should be helped to understand that, while they have certain special needs, these children are in other respects no different from them.

The parents

Throughout this report we have consistently stressed the need for the closest possible involvement of parents in the assessment of the child's educational needs and in the provision made. It follows that we regard such involvement as an important feature of any form of special educational provision in ordinary schools, no less than in special schools. Moreover, the parents of children who are on the roll of a special class or unit should be treated in exactly the same way as parents of other children in the school with regard, for example, to invitations to school functions and membership of governing bodies. . . .

Since problems in integrating individual children with disabilities or significant difficulties in ordinary schools may sometimes stem from their incomplete acceptance by the family, parents must be assisted to understand their child's difficulties. They must also be helped to adopt attitudes to him most conducive to his feeling that he is accepted and has the same status in the family as any brothers or sisters. This sense of acceptance by the family is likely to be a prerequisite of the successful integration of an individual child in an ordinary school. . . .

The integration of children in ordinary schools, particularly those with severe or complex disabilities or disorders, may be prejudiced if the parents of other pupils are not conversant with the arrangements. It is important that they should be clearly informed of the nature of the special provision being made and should have the opportunity to discuss this with the staff.

The staff

Without whole-hearted commitment by teachers to the reception of children with disabilities, particularly severe or complex ones, the most careful planning is unlikely to be successful. An understanding by teachers of what will be involved is essential, and in Chapter 12 we suggest how this might be developed in the course of training. Understanding does not however go the whole way: it must be combined with helpful and constructive attitudes which encourage but do not patronize. A recent survey of special classes and units for physically handicapped children found that although many of the handicapped children were benefiting academically and socially from attendance at ordinary classes, much greater interaction with non-handicapped children would have resulted had integration been a major objective of all the staff, and had more thought been given, from the planning stage onwards, to the means of its achievement. Since the aim of integration is to enrich the education of both handicapped and non-handicapped children this loss of opportunity represents a double deprivation. *We recommend that before a child with a disability or severe difficulty enters an ordinary school the teaching staff should discuss among themselves and agree a plan for securing the maximum educational and social interaction between him and others in the school, and should strive collectively thereafter to implement the plan.* . . .

We strongly endorse the need for adequate staff and resources to be made available to ordinary schools to meet the needs of children assessed as requiring special educational help. These staff must have additional training or substantial experience in special education. . . .

If there is to be a FUNCTIONAL UNITY within an ordinary school, there must be close relations between teachers responsible for children with special educational needs and other members of staff. Where a special class or unit is attached to a school, teachers in the class or unit should have the opportunity to do some teaching in other parts of the school; conversely teachers in the ordinary classes should have the opportunity to share in some of the teaching in the special class or unit. Such interchange will promote the unity of the school, help teachers to understand each other's interests and concerns, and encourage children in the special class or unit to regard themselves as equal nembers of the school. . . .

[From Chapter 7, pp. 99–108

62 · White Paper on a New Training Initiative. 1981

The rise in unemployment and, especially, the rise in youth unemployment during the second half of the 1970s led to a succession of programmes mounted by the Manpower Services Commission aimed at improving industrial training and taking young unemployed people off the unemployment register.

The main focus of attention was the Youth Opportunities Programme which brought together a series of schemes aimed at providing alternatives to unemployment for young people, and within YOP, on the offer to unemployed school-leavers of periods of work experience and a subsistence allowance. Ideally, but not universally, this was accompanied by some form of training and/or education.

The MSC recognized the need to go beyond the improvised YOP to create a more comprehensive Youth Training Scheme which would guarantee a longer period of paid vocational preparation and training.

The White Paper gave Government backing to the idea; the actual form of the scheme was to be worked out by an MSC Task Force. While the White Paper's commitment was for a YTS with prime obligations to unemployed school leavers, the Task Force attempted to extend the character of the scheme to serve as the first stage of training and vocational experience for all young people entering employment at 16. The success of this more comprehensive approach would depend on whether a YTS could be combined (as the White Paper hoped) with a complete overhaul of apprenticeship and other forms of long-term initial training.

Note the foreshadowing in the paragraphs headed 'Staying in full-time education' of the Certificate of Pre-Vocational Education, which came into operation in September 1985.

A NEW TRAINING INITIATIVE: A PROGRAMME FOR ACTION

A NEW TRAINING INITIATIVE

Last May [1981] the Government endorsed the Manpower Services Commission's consultative document 'A New Training Initiative'. This set out three major national objectives for the future of industrial training:

(i) to develop skill training including apprenticeship in such a way as to enable young people entering at different ages and with different educational attainments to acquire agreed standards of skill appropriate to the jobs available and to provide them with a basis for progress through further learning;

(ii) to move towards a position where all young people under the age of 18 have the opportunity either of continuing in full-time education or of entering a period of planned work experience combined with work-related training and education;

(iii) to open widespread opportunities for adults, whether employed or returning to work, to acquire, increase or update their skills and knowledge during the course of their working lives.

... There has been overwhelming support for these three objectives from employers, unions, educational and training bodies ...

PROGRAMME FOR ACTION

The Government's 10-point programme for action comprises:

(i) *a new £1 billion a year Youth Training Scheme, guaranteeing from September* 1983 *a full year's foundation training for all those leaving school at the minimum age without jobs;*

(ii) *increased incentives for employers to provide better training for young people in jobs;*

(iii) *development of an 'Open Tech' programme to make technical training more accessible to those who have the necessary ability;*

(iv) *a working group to report by April* 1982 *on ways of developing the Youth Training Scheme to cover employed as well as unemployed young people, within available resources;*

(v) *setting a target date of* 1985 *for recognised standards for all the main craft, technician and professional skills to replace time-serving and age-restricted apprenticeships;*

(vi) *better preparation for working life in initial full-time education;*

(vii) *more opportunities for vocationally relevant courses for those staying on in full-time education;*

(viii) *closer co-ordination of training and vocational education provision nationally and at local level;*

(ix) *a £16 million fund for development schemes in particular localities or sectors;*

(x) *examination of longer-term possibilities for more effective, rational and equitable sharing of the costs of training between trainees themselves, employers of trained people and the general taxpayer.*

THE NEED FOR ACTION

. . . Our major competitors lay much greater emphasis on training young people than we do. In France and Germany 80 per cent or more of young people reaching minimum school leaving age receive further education or training of some kind. In Britain in 1979 on the most favourable interpretation the figure was less than two-thirds.

In Britain the training provided is mainly apprenticeship in traditional craft and technician skills, for many of which there is declining demand. Opportunities for day release to Colleges of Further Education are limited and sometimes lack co-ordination between the college and where young people work. Full-time college courses often seem financially unattractive to many young people compared with the immediate rewards of an unskilled job.

Training for adults is also inadequate. We have until now assumed that the training given in a person's first job is all he will need for the rest of his working life. Entry to some craft and other occupations is so restricted that there is little point in providing training for adults or for adults to seek it.

Who has the responsibility to train? At the moment the position is muddled. Individual employers, local education authorities, joint negotiating bodies, industrial training bodies, the Manpower Services Commission and Government Departments are all involved. The cost of training is basically a matter for the individual employer, but a wide variety of grants, subsidies and courses is provided at the taxpayers' expense or from Industrial Training Board levies on particular industries.

We must have clearer goals, better means of delivery, a fairer allocation of financial responsibilities and, above all, a will to work together and to get on with it.

THE TRANSITION FROM FULL-TIME EDUCATION TO WORK

The years of compulsory education

The last two years of compulsory education are particularly important in forming an approach to the world of work . . . The Government is seeking to ensure that the school curriculum develops the personal skills and qualities as well as the knowledge needed for working life, and that links between schools and employers help pupils and teachers to gain a closer understanding of the industrial, commercial and economic base of our society.

Staying in full-time education

Nearly one-third of young people between 16 and 19 are still at school or in other full-time education. The Government has made available for 1982–83 additional public expenditure resources totalling £60 million to enable more to do so. Larger sums have been included in our plans for later years, and their adequacy will be kept under review in relation to the number of young people choosing this option.

Good academic results are prized by many who recruit direct from school. They can earn entry to technical and professional courses with appropriate exemptions. They also constitute the principal route to degrees and full professional qualifications.

But increasing numbers of students are taking full-time vocational courses, combining the theory and practice of particular occupational skills with general education in subjects which have hitherto been studied mainly part-time.

There is also a need for vocationally-orientated courses of a more general kind. The Government intend to secure development of a new pre-vocational examination for young people aged 17-plus in schools and colleges in England and Wales. This will be designed particularly for those with modest examination achievements at 16-plus who are not looking towards higher education and are not yet ready for specific vocational education or training, perhaps because they have not yet formed a clear idea of the sort of work they might do. . . .

The first year in employment

. . . Young people need to be equipped not merely to do the immediate task required by the job, but with a basic competence and flexibility which they can build on as they change jobs.

The best way of providing this training is through arrangements made by employers for their own young employees. *Yet in 1979 nearly 40 per cent of the 700,000 school-leavers who found jobs received no training at all. About another 20 per cent were receiving training for only eight weeks or less.* Our efforts must therefore be directed not only to creating jobs for young people but also to ensuring that they are properly trained for them. . . .

A NEW YOUTH TRAINING SCHEME

The young unemployed will remain a priority group in terms of new training arrangements. The Youth Opportunities Programme was introduced in 1978 especially to help the minority of young people who were unemployed and quite unprepared or ill equipped for working life by means of a relatively short period of work experience or work preparation. Since then it has become clear that we need a full-scale training programme that provides for an increasing number and range of unemployed young people . . . a new and better Youth Training Scheme should be introduced by the Commission to cover all unemployed minimum age school-leavers by September 1983.

Training content

The new scheme will build on the experience gained from the Youth Opportunities Programme and the Unified Vocational Preparation programme. It will aim to equip unemployed young people to adapt successfully to the demands of employment; to have a fuller appreciation of the world of industry, business and technology in which they will be working; and to develop basic and recognised skills which employers will require in the future.

These aims require an effective integration of skills, knowledge and experience through planned and supervised work experience and properly designed opportunities for off-the-job training or further education. Young people have different abilities and learning aptitudes and local labour market needs also differ. Both will have to be taken into account in designing and operating the scheme, but for young people with no experience of work a training programme of up to a year will generally be needed.

There will be five main elements:

Induction and assessment. Individuals will receive a proper induction to the programme and to each element of it. Their skills and attainments will be assessed. This may include opportunities to sample different skills or jobs in order to establish aptitudes.

Basic skills. The programme will aim to ensure that basic skills like numeracy and literacy have been acquired; to develop some practical competence in the use of tools and machinery and in some basic office operations; and to foster skills in communication (in interviews for example).

Occupationally relevant education and training, both on and off the job. This will provide opportunity for personal development and use of the basic skills in a variety of working contexts, adapted to the needs of the local labour market. It will be integrated with planned work experience, with young people being given a minimum of three months off-the-job training or relevant further education. Arrangements will be flexible, so that the training can be given in the form of day or block release and can take place in a company training school or at a college.

Guidance and counselling. Young people will receive advice and support throughout the programme under arrangements agreed with their sponsors.

Record and review of progress. Each young person's progress will be recorded, reviewed and assessed as he or she goes through the programme. A document of progress will be given to the young person on leaving the programme and will record standards achieved in a way which is recognisable both to the young person and to potential employers.

Training allowances and benefit arrangements

The new scheme is first and last a training scheme. This is reflected in its structure, its delivery and the terms and conditions for the young trainees. The young people catered for by the scheme will benefit from having a wider range of skills and experience. As trainees, it seems right that they should receive allowances that reflect their learning role. That is how they will make their contribution to the cost of a foundation training which improves their prospects of employment....

FUTURE DEVELOPMENT

Our ultimate objective must of course be to provide proper training on a comprehensive basis, not only for the unemployed but for all young people in employment too; and to do so in a way which gets many more of the young unemployed into jobs with proper training.

[From pp.3–10

63 · Report of the Review Group on the Youth Service in England entitled *Experience and Participation*. [*The Thompson Report*]

Published: *1982*
Chairman: *Mr Alan Thompson*
Members: *Rev. E.F. Cattermole; Mr J. Collins; Mr A.B. Hampton; Mr E. Hopwood; Mr W.R. Knight; Ms J.D.J. McKenley (appointed February 1982); Mrs J. Walpole*

A Private Member's Bill in the House of Commons put forward by Mr Trevor Skeet M.P. in the 1979–80 session caused embarrassment to the newly elected Conservative Government by seeking a clearer definition of local and national responsibilities in regard to the Youth Service – 'clearer' in this context almost certainly meaning a definition which placed greater administrative and financial obligations on local authorities.

The Thompson Committee was set up as part of the Government's attempt to assuage the Conservative Youth lobby and head off the Skeet Bill. Its main recommendations – for legislation to clarify national objectives for the youth service, and for a national advisory council to advise Ministers on youth affairs – were not regarded with favour by those to whom they were addressed and were rejected in the Government's formal response in 1984.

YOUTH AND SOCIETY – THE SITUATION TODAY

Most of the bodies and individuals who have given evidence to us have commented on the main features as they see them of the society in which young people have to make their way. In doing so they have tended to stress the negative features, pointing out the various ways in which our society is becoming a more difficult and dangerous place for the young to grow up . . .

But it is necessary to remember the positive side of the balance sheet. Young people today are in general healthier than they were in the past, they are better educated, they have wider horizons and more opportunities. They are better protected against the worst things that can befall families – starvation, disease, cruelty, harsh working conditions, untimely death. These improvements, inestimable though they are, do not however necessarily go with steadier and more complete personal development. It is the latter factor which is the concern of the Youth Service; and, in order to see what is happening in that respect, we have to try to take a balanced view of what society does to and for young people, and of what the young people make of it.

Against the positive features of modern society noted above must be set a number of factors which are, to say the least, perplexing and confusing to adults, and which must seem all the more menacing to those who are still reaching out for a secure identity....

It is generally accepted, for example, that society is more *mobile* than it was, both physically and in matters of life-style. Sons and daughters less frequently follow their parents' occupations or live within the same community as their parents. Coupled with this is the frequent complaint that the *family* is declining as an institution. No doubt this is true in the sense that in general families are smaller and meet together (*i.e.* as an extended family) less often. Divorce and remarriage are more common; as a result, more children live with single parents or have a number of step-parents. But it is by no means clear to what extent these changes in the family, or in social mobility, really do limit or injure the experience of the adolescent. There has also been a decline in the sense of belonging to a *community*. There are specific reasons for this: the break-up of established communities in the interests of improving the physical environment, changes in the pattern and location of employment, and so on....

But again there are gains as well as losses here. There are areas where there has been positive rejuvenation. It is indeed true that for some the *physical environment* has not only changed but worsened; and no account of the situation of modern youth would be complete which did not recognise that for many of them their immediate environment is devoid of physical attraction, allows little or no scope for pleasurable activity or adventure, and is sometimes loaded with danger and incitements to violence. Unfortunately this was often true for many young people in the past. What is indisputable about this situation is that some young people are deeply affected by factors such as these and find them a serious obstacle to their own personal development.

There are other features of our society which also tend to affect adversely the development of a secure sense of identity in young people. It is a very *materialistic* society, given to measuring success by the number of things which people acquire. A whole industry is devoted to persuading people that they must have this or that product, and to creating *anxiety* in the minds of those who do not have it. Another industry, the media, often feeds on the anxiety with which it manages to surround the events of our daily lives.

THE CONCERNS OF YOUNG PEOPLE

... There are, however, a number of specific issues which impinge on the lives of young people; and in order to learn what these are we have only to listen to what young people say about the things that worry them....

Unemployment

... Half of those leaving school at the minimum age have, at the present time, little prospect of getting a job, though they have a guaranteed place on a scheme funded by the Manpower Services Commission.... The largest growing group of long-term unemployed is in the 18–25 age-group, and relatively little is being done for them. The possibility of being unemployed, or the actual experience of unemployment, is without doubt the chief worry of the great majority of young people today. Throughout his or her conscious life, work will have been held up as the essential badge of adulthood. It stands for the end of dependence and the beginnings of real responsibility and freedom. It brings with it financial means, status and the chance to choose within a range of opportunities. It also combines in itself many of the kinds of experience which are requisite for personal development. Its absence is the more keenly felt; and it is meaningless to say to the youngster who has no employment that the 'work ethic' is over-valued in our society. Faced with the challenge of continuing high rates of unemployment, it may be that society will evolve new patterns of work and leisure and new approaches to employment. But in the meantime many young people are being denied the opportunity of financial independence and with it many of the most important attributes of adulthood.

Racism

By racism we mean the manifestation of a negative attitude towards an ethnic group in the community, accompanied by discriminatory action on the part of individuals or institutions. Racism has become more significant in this country since parts of it have become much more racially mixed than was the case up to, say, the late 1950s.... The large-scale immigration of family groups especially of Asian and Afro-Caribbean origin since the early 1960s has meant that these groups form a significant and sometimes a dominant proportion of the population in some areas, especially in large industrial conurbations. These peoples along with groups already indigenous looked for, and were officially assured they had, equal rights and an equal place in society with those of traditional British origin. Though there were obviously distinctive cultural traits which they wished to preserve, they looked forward to being part of the community. They looked on Britain as a homeland, and their young people are already predominantly of British birth. Unfortunately it does not appear that British society was as prepared to assimilate these peoples as they were to be assimilated. Deep-seated attitudes are no doubt in some cases compounded by feelings of insecurity and resentment springing from lack of good housing, educational disadvantage and a shortage of jobs. The undeniable fact is that there is a significant amount of racial prejudice and racial discrimination, and it is the effect of this on young people which we have to keep in mind. For the young people within an ethnic community the experience of racism may result in frustration, anger and despair leading possibly to a deep-seated alienation. They have indeed to face many serious problems associated, for example, with job opportunities, relations with the police, and the active antagonism of extremist right-wing groups. It is important to recognise that this effect spreads far wider than the immediate consequences for young members of ethnic communities. Racism damages those who practise it as well as those who suffer from it....

Homelessness

Though our survey shows that young people in general value their homes and spend a lot of their time there, quite a number leave home for long or short periods for a variety of reasons – not only because of family conflicts, personal crises, tensions arising from overcrowding and other emergencies, but also for reasons which are part of the process of growing up, such as a desire to be independent. We have been faced with evidence of this in rural areas just as much as in the inner cities.... Young people are not in general seen as a priority group for housing. Young people give homelessness a high place amongst the factors which affect their personal development.

These three problems – unemployment, racism and homelessness – figure predominantly in all the representations we have received from young people, but other factors, no less significant than these in their impact on particular individuals, may be mentioned. Many young people worry about their *education*, about their level of achievement and their relationships at school and college; for many, schooling will not have been the enlarging experience that we often like to think it is. Many feel that there is little logic at present in the pattern of *age-thresholds* governing many aspects of work, education, leisure and domestic rights. Some young people feel that the *police* discriminate against them.

Leisure provision for young people is often inaccessible and expensive. In rural areas especially, but also on large isolated housing estates, the lack of public *transport* and its high cost is a prime cause of isolation, depriving young people of activity and companionship. For many young people, boys as well as girls, attitudes in society towards the appropriate roles of *men and women* are seen as changing and confused. Some girls in particular feel that their personal development is considered relatively unimportant. For both sexes, sexual relations are a source of anxiety as well as bewilderment. Finally, mention must be made again of the growth of *extremist political organisations*, some of which set out deliberately to capture the allegiance of young people. The impact of these organisations is as damaging to those young people whom they succeed in winning over as to those who are the victims of their attentions. . . .

The key to much that we are about to say lies in the gulf, vividly apparent to many young people, between the ideals and the realities of society. Schooling, for example, is presented as a preparation for life and subsequent employment. For many it brings real opportunities, but for some, disappointment and the stigma of failure. Moreover, some of the variations in school experience appear to mirror divisions in society itself, so that schooling comes to seem for some not the ladder of opportunity it was held up to be, but a foretaste of the frustrations which will be experienced later on. The experience of unemployment may be a test and a challenge, but it may equally produce a strong awareness of the futility of growing up into society's 'ideal person' – well-educated and hardworking, when neither good education nor employment are real possibilities.

Outside school and work, young people have to bear the image of being beyond the control and immune to the influence of parents and other responsible adults. This picture is wildly exaggerated by the media. Our opinion survey has shown how strong an influence parents and relatives continue to have; and a certain tension between parents and children is normal and reasonable. There is a good deal of hypocrisy about, and young people often feel that they are the victims of 'double standards' and are not valued as individuals.

Our survey has also shown that young people are well aware that progression to maturity is marked by a growth in both freedom and responsibility. Only a caring personal relationship can guarantee both. Problems arise in many areas of behaviour – in sexual relations, in the resort to alcohol and drugs, in relations with the law – when this progression is monitored not through personal relationships with caring adults, but through the more impersonal manifestations of social observance and 'law and order'. The gap between expectation and reality then widens, irrationalities and inequalities become harder to bear, the young person may begin to feel an 'outsider' in society, and a process of alienation is set on foot. This may lead in extreme cases to a rage against society, which may find expression in delinquency or violence, or more often in apathy and disillusion...

LESSONS FOR THE YOUTH SERVICE

... We have paid particular attention to what young people themselves have said to us. We certainly do not accept that the outlook is bad for all of them. Many young people continue to enter into adult society without undue difficulty or strain, as they have always done.

Nevertheless the negative factors are significant and cannot be brushed aside. For those young people who are affected by them it is important that the Youth Service should address the question of how to help them to react positively and constructively. This may be done partly by relieving the incidence of the factors involved and partly by developing in the young people concerned the capacity to play an active part in altering their condition. For those young people this is going to be a crucial part of their personal development. But the fact that a significant proportion of their peers suffer multiple disadvantages is also an important fact for *all* young people, and one which should inform the *general* experience of transition from dependency to adulthood. In considering its contribution to the personal development of young people in general, the Youth Service must bear particularly in mind the negative experiences of some of them, because young people must be helped to achieve a comprehensive and realistic sense of identity with society and an understanding of all its aspects.

[From Chapter 2, pp. 8–12

Political Education

Politics is the term we apply to the forces which give society the shape and direction it has – *i.e.* which tend to change it or keep it as it is. These forces are based on attitudes – of individuals and of groups – and spring from the activity resulting from those attitudes – *i.e.* from people acting on their convictions. That activity can take certain institutionalised forms, such as voting in an election, joining a political party, engaging in canvassing etc. This is what most people think political action is. But political action can take place in a number of institutions in the community – for example, in industry or the churches – and can take forms such as making representations, getting up petitions, and in general trying to change the aspect of an institution, community or society which impinges on the participant in an unacceptable way. Just as there are social skills which enable one to feel at home in society, so there are political skills which enable one to change it or keep it as it is if someone else is trying to change it.

... Our political tradition depends on consensus being reached on various issues.... This implies a certain level of political literacy. Yet amongst the adult population there is widespread political illiteracy and indeed a failure to understand what 'politics' is. Political education then is necessary. Our opinion survey seems to suggest that most young people see themselves as uninterested in politics but paradoxically hold strong views about a variety of issues which might be called political. We believe that, if they had a better knowledge of the processes by which change can be effected and greater skill and confidence in using them to put their views into effect, they would be less likely to resort to more violent methods of expressing their views about society.

The amount of political education actually carried on within the Youth Service seems to be relatively small. One national youth organisation estimated that only some 5% of its local units included any element of it in their programmes. The majority of LEA responses painted a similar picture with comments like 'we have to be wary of that'. We believe that this is dangerous.

Political education is not the same thing as political studies or civics though it may include some elements of civics. Much of the political education in schools or even within the Youth Service has this passive character. It is not enough. What is required is experience of such a kind that the young people learn to claim their right to influence the society in which they live and to have a say in how it is run. It is active participation in some form of political activity, formal or informal which really counts....

Through the internal machinery of their youth clubs or centres, through the wider scope offered by various forms of youth council in the locality, through participation in local and national issues, the Service can offer young people a real opportunity to express their views in the relatively 'safe' context appropriate to the inexperience of those taking part.

... For political education to be effective, risks have to be taken with the decision-making machinery of the youth club or local youth council. But to the extent that it is effective, young people and their leaders will naturally be led to look beyond the confines of the Youth Service itself and take part in wider issues. This inescapably incurs the risk of controversy and conflict. Where there are contending groups in the adult world, involved in economic, environmental or community questions, the dangers for young people are obvious. There is a real problem here which those who advocate political education within the Youth Service must surely face.

There is obviously no ready-made solution to this dilemma ... We can offer some reflections and suggestions which may be helpful to youth workers, their managers and their employers, recognising that if political education is not a 'safe' thing, neither is democracy, and one will not flourish without the other.

(1) There should be more national recognition of the essential place of political education and of its implications....

(2) There should be more local discussion.... Discussion and intercommunication between workers and management – with the full involvement of young people – are essential.

(3) Management committees and other structures devised to help the individual worker should play a more active part and not leave the problem to the conscience of the individual.

(4) More attention should be paid in training courses, both initial and inservice, to the complexities and difficulties of the problem and the responsibilities of all interests concerned.

... Training, experience and the supporting apparatus of supervision and management can reinforce personal integrity, but not supplant it.

[From Chapter 5, pp. 44–7

A YOUTH SERVICE FOR THE 1980s

OBJECTIVES

... What is lacking is a public acknowledgement of and a general consensus about what the Service is trying to do.

We believe that a basis for this consensus undoubtedly exists. There is virtual unanimity that the fundamental purpose of the Youth Service is to provide programmes of personal development comprising, in shorthand terms, social and political education.... We reiterate here that in our view there need not and should not be any antithesis between personal development and social education.... Social education does not mean social control any more than personal development means anarchy. The twin aims of this process are thus *affirmation* and *involvement* – affirming an individual in his or her proper identity and involving an individual in relationships with other individuals and institutions.

We see social education as essentially an experiential process, as opposed to the passive reception of ideas, impressions and norms. It involves experimentation – the trying out of modes of behaviour and styles of action in a way calculated to help young individuals to know themselves and be able to cope with (though not necessarily to accept all the implicit values of) the society of which they find themselves a part. From this premise it follows that the process of social education must above all be *participatory*. It is not enough to provide places to go to and things to do. The Youth Service must make it its business to create opportunities for young people to have a say in their affairs ...

It follows also that what we have described as *political education* has an essential place within the Youth Service's curriculum.... Basically it must mean the process whereby a young individual learns how to claim the right of a member of a democratic society to influence that society and to have a say in how it affects him or her. This requires practice as well as study. Like all social education, political education is an active, participative process.

A further aspect which we should not overlook is what we may loosely call *spiritual development*.... In some groups or organisations it may take a very specific or doctrinal form: in others such forms are eschewed, but the underlying values are strongly emphasised. What is in point here is the need, explicitly or implicitly recognised, to acknowledge aspects of the human condition which are not purely practical and prudential. There are two propositions which are basic.

(1) It is necessary for the process of human development that the individual should preserve a sense of wonder and gratitude for life and what it brings: this sense lies at the root of enjoyment, interest and appreciation, and without it an individual may well be thought to be maimed in some essential way.
(2) It is equally essential that human relationships should be based on an absolute respect for other human beings, and indeed for other living things.

In our increasingly multi-cultural, multi-religious, multi-ethnic society it must be part of the Youth Service's function to uphold both propositions in all it says and does, and to enable young people to formulate and develop their own beliefs.

OFFERINGS

It may be useful here to summarise the main elements as the five 'A's:
association,
activities,
advice,
action,
access.

Association

By this we mean, as Albemarle meant, a place to go, a place to meet, a place to be with friends, a place of refuge other than the home, a place for socialising and enjoyment. There is no doubt that this is one of the features of the Youth Service by which young people themselves set store....

Activities

These again in all their increasingly rich variety are a vital as well as a traditional feature of youth provision. They may not be ends in themselves, but they are a basic element. The Youth Service must offer young people interesting things to do, new things to test their prowess and adaptability, opportunities of fresh experience, things to exercise the body and mind. For all the increasing range of youth activities, the variety is probably not sufficient in most areas. The range should include popular sports and pastimes, but not be confined to them. The arts should have an important role. The provision of an appropriately wide range of activities is a challenge to the ingenuity and administrative expertise of providing bodies.

Advice

We use this term in a wide sense to denote the whole process of providing information, advice and personal counselling. Young people need all these, and receive much, through home, school, the churches, official services such as the careers service, and various specialised agencies. This is not a reason for the Youth Service to opt out. It may equally be a first resort or a last resort – somewhere to go when you don't know where to get advice, or somewhere to go when other sources fail.... There is therefore much to be done to put the pattern of provision in this field on a satisfactory footing. It must henceforth take its place as one of the mainstream forms of youth provision.

Action in the Community

... The concept of service presupposes a sense of obligation to the established order of society which may be a product of personal development but cannot be taken for granted. The concept of action has many roots – in some, simple compassion for other individuals, in others a desire to acquire an identity as part of a larger community, in others again a wish to remove the causes of distress by changing aspects of the environment or the society. Whatever activities are built upon this basis, it is essential that they should be freely chosen by the young themselves, should be undertaken in a context which encourages reflection on the experience gained, and should encourage a wider and deeper involvement in community affairs....

We envisage community action taking place within the Youth Service in many shapes and forms. Much occasional activity falls within the scope of clubs and units of the uniformed organisations. At local level many young people are involved in youth councils which are active in the local communities. Regular part-time experience can be provided through locally based and financed organisations, a number of which have come into existence over the past 10 to 15 years. Substantial periods of full-time service are most often associated with large-scale national organisations. To make this diversified array meaningful and known to the general public and especially to young people is an administrative challenge which we think the Youth Service must face. It seems likely that the key to future development will lie with local agencies, sometimes statutory, sometimes voluntary, acting in collaboration with other organisations including schools.

Access to Life and Vocational Skills

By virtue of its personal style of approach, the Youth Service seems to us to have a vital role to play in all initiatives designed to mediate the transition from full-time education to adult life.... This is an area where the Manpower Services Commission and other sponsoring agencies need help from the Youth Service: conversely, it seems essential that the Youth Service should look on access to vocational and life skills as part of its mainstream provision, as it already does in certain areas. The extension and development of this work will be a difficult process; but we think that the Youth Service should take the long view and play its part in an overdue step towards a comprehensive system of vocational training and experience for the employed and unemployed alike....

[From Chapter 7, pp. 68–71

64 · White Paper on Teaching Quality. 1983

Following on from the attempts to improve the quality of teacher training which followed the publication of the James Report (see pp. 354–70), the Department of Education and Science began to turn increasing attention to the controls which the D.E.S. and the Welsh Office could exercise over initial teacher training, and the conventions under which the teaching force was managed by the local education authorities.

One of the levers available to the Secretaries of State concerned the recognition of courses offered by universities and colleges, as conferring on a successful participant, 'qualified teacher status'. It was decided, therefore, to use this legal power to establish criteria (see extract) which courses would have to satisfy to be accredited for this purpose. The following year (1984) a Council for the Accreditation of Teacher Education (C.A.T.E.) was established under the chairmanship of Professor William Taylor to preside over the accreditation process.

CRITERIA FOR THE APPROVAL OF INITIAL TRAINING COURSES

The Secretaries of State propose to promulgate criteria, drawn up in consultation with the appropriate professional and academic bodies through A.C.S.E.T. [Advisory Council on the Supply and Education of Teachers] against which they will in future assess initial training courses before deciding whether to approve them. These criteria will relate to both professional and academic content of courses, and to good working relationships with schools. They will provide a framework within which training institutions and professional committees will be able to plan and scrutinize courses before submitting them to the Secretaries of State for approval. The Secretaries of State propose to re-establish the professional committees with fresh guidelines and with constitutions to be approved by them. In approving courses they will not seek to duplicate the work of the institutions and committees, but rather to satisfy themselves that individual course proposals are consistent with the published criteria. Once the criteria are published, the Secretaries of State will initiate a review of all existing approved courses of initial training. They may withdraw approval from those courses which do not conform to the criteria.

The Secretaries of State intend that the criteria should impose three broad requirements:

(i) that the higher education and initial teacher training of all qualified teachers should include at least two full years' course time devoted to subject studies at a level appropriate to higher education. For the primary years a wide area of the curriculum might constitute the student's specialism, whereas for secondary teaching the two years should be spent in the study of either one or two subjects of the secondary curriculum. This requirement would recognise teachers' need for subject expertise if they are to have the confidence and ability to enthuse pupils and respond to their curiosity in their chosen subject fields. For P.G.C.E. [Post-Graduate Certificate of Education] courses, the requirement would be expressed in terms of the preceding first degree course and its relationship to particular P.G.C.E. courses and the curricular needs of schools. For B.Ed. and other concurrent courses, the requirement would be expressed in terms of course structure and content; and in the case of courses for teaching pupils of primary school age the content should include the application of the subjects involved to the learning of young children;

(ii) that the initial training of all qualified teachers should include adequate attention to teaching method in the chosen main subjects, differentiated by age of intended pupils. All primary training courses should include a sufficient, and substantial, element concerned with language and mathematics development;

(iii) that the initial teacher training of all qualified teachers should include studies closely linked with practical experience in school, and involving the active participation of experienced practising school teachers. Satisfactory local arrangements to this end would have to be established. The Department of Education and Science has recently commissioned a research project to monitor and evaluate four examples of such arrangements, so as to assist the development of good practice.

The Government believe that these requirements can only be met if the teaching staff in the training institutions are themselves equipped to educate and train the entrants to an all-graduate profession. In addition, in order to satisfy the third requirement, a sufficient proportion of each training institution's staff should have enjoyed success as teachers in schools, and their school experience should be recent, substantial and relevant. Many of the staff do not now have such experience. Those of the staff who are concerned with pedagogy should also have continuing regular contact with classroom teaching. This will not be easy to achieve at a time when total staff numbers in training institutions are either constant or decreasing. The training institutions should therefore now take steps, in consultation with local education authorities and schools, to ensure that there is sufficient recent teaching experience among relevant staff through, e.g., secondments, the use of joint teacher/tutor appointments and schemes of teacher/tutor exchange. The establishment of close links between training institutions and suitable schools in their vicinity will facilitate arrangements along these lines. When considering courses for approval the Secretaries of State will expect an indication of how the training institution provides the recent teaching experience needed.

The Government are also concerned that the training institutions should improve the selection of students for training; and should recommend for qualified teacher status only those students who have displayed the requisite practical and personal qualities as well as academic competence. At present some 20 per cent of those who enter training courses fail to complete them satisfactorily. The Government recognise the difficulties of selection, but they believe that all institutions should now review their procedures for assessing the intellectual and personal qualities of candidates, and their professional potential. Participation of suitable practising teachers in the selection process is desirable. Where mature students are recruited to undergraduate training courses they may bring with them the advantages of a wider experience; but training institutions should satisfy themselves that those who lack the formal academic qualifications normally required are intellectually capable of completing a degree course successfully. The appraisal of a P.G.C.E. applicant should include an examination of the suitability of the first degree for the training sought.

Entrants to higher education often benefit from a year or so outside the education system between obtaining A levels and entering higher education. It is particularly helpful for intending teachers to break the cycle of school-college-school with some experience of industry or commerce. Young people thinking about a career in teaching should also seek to gain experience of the classroom. At an early stage, working with the teaching staff of a school may assist their choice of career. Candidates accepted for a course of initial training should whenever possible acquire teaching experience before their course begins.

Some persons who are judged to complete the training course satisfactorily then prove unsuccessful when appointed to teaching posts: in some cases this may be because the training institutions are reluctant to fail students who have performed satisfactorily from an academic point of view throughout a three or four year B.Ed. course, when their classroom performance is suspect. More rigorous selection at the point of entry to training should reduce such cases. Where they do occur, the training institution should consider the transfer of the student to a course or, in consultation with its validating body, the award of some form of qualification, which does not lead to qualified teacher status. The Secretaries of State will expect institutions not to award to a student whose practical classroom work is not satisfactory a B.Ed. degree or P.G.C.E. which entitles him to recognition as a qualified teacher.

THE QUALIFICATION OF TEACHERS

A course approved under the new criteria will prepare teachers to work with pupils within a specific age range, and in the case of secondary courses to teach specific subjects. As now, the Secretary of State for Education and Science will issue formal letters notifying those who successfully complete courses of initial training that they have been recognised by the Secretary of State as qualified school teachers. These letters will specifically draw attention to the phase and subjects for which the course of initial training was intended, and in the case of primary courses indicate any relevant curricular specialism. This action will not formally limit the teacher to teaching programmes within the indicated phase or subject areas, but it will be important to the teacher's employer in relation to his obligations under the Education (Teachers) Regulations 1982.

These Regulations require the employment of a staff of teachers in any school suitable and sufficient in numbers for the purpose of securing the provision of education appropriate to the ages, abilities, aptitudes and needs of the pupils. The Government propose to amend the Regulations so as to require employers to have regard to the formal qualifications of teachers in determining whether or not the staff of teachers in any school is suitable. HM Inspectors, following their formal inspections of schools, will be asked to report on the extent to which the qualifications of the teaching staff conform to the requirements of the amended Regulations. After a five-year period the Secretary of State will institute a general review of progress in the light of the reports received.

[From pp. 19–21

65 · White Paper on Training for Jobs. 1984

This followed up points raised in the 1981 White Paper ('clearer goals, better means of delivery, a fairer allocation of financial responsibilities') and marked another important milestone in the rise of the Manpower Services Commission, now dubbed a 'national training authority'. The most controversial paragraph (46) announced changes in the funding of some work-related non-advanced further education, removing funds equivalent to a quarter of the money allocated to the L.E.A.s for this purpose in the Rate Support Grant and giving control of this money to the Manpower Services Commission to allocate.

This proposed change was justified on the basis of the need to make training and vocational preparation more sensitive and responsive to national and local employment needs. It was strongly contested by the local authority associations, with whom there had been no consultations. They persisted in refusing to accept that their colleges were unresponsive, or that MSC control would make them more attentive to local needs.

RÔLES AND RESPONSIBILITIES

If we are to improve vocational education and training, *everyone concerned must have a clear understanding of what his or her own responsibilities are and what part others are expected to play*. . . .

In 1980 employers were estimated to be spending around £2½ billion a year on training. Central and local government provide about £4 billion a year for further, higher and adult education, all of which directly or indirectly prepares people for employment. The Government has also been drawn more and more into financing training, from about £10 million in 1960 (at constant 1983 prices) to some £580 million in 1980 and (with the advent of the Youth Training Scheme) nearly £1 billion this year. Yet we may still face shortages of particular skills and deficiencies in quality.

Training is an investment. It must be seen to pay for itself by making people better able to produce the goods and provide the services that other people are prepared to pay for. Thus, the decisions as to who is trained, when and in what skills are best taken by the employers (and indeed the individuals concerned) who have to satisfy the needs of the market, rather than by central direction. If training costs are excessive or if there are unnecessary institutional obstacles, the quantity and quality of the training provided will be inadequate. Then skill shortages will again hold us back.

So investment in training needs to be attractive financially. That means keeping training costs down, including the acceptance by trainees of levels of income which reflect the value to them of the training given. It means continuing to remove artificial restrictions on the time taken to complete a training programme and on the subsequent use of the skills acquired, so as to give the employer a better assurance of recouping his investment in training people who are always free to leave and market their skills elsewhere. And it requires further development of cost-effective methods of giving and assessing competence.

These improvements are all attainable provided industry and commerce play their part. Most depend on the decisions of *employers*. It is for them to make the investment in training people to do the work that they require; to see that the training they buy is provided economically and to standard; and to act collectively through employers' organisations and, in association with others concerned, through voluntary training bodies and Industrial Training Boards where this may be necessary, for example, in setting standards required throughout an industry or in reforming outdated institutional arrangements.

It is for *central and local government*, at the expense of taxpayers and ratepayers, to ensure that general and vocational education are provided in such a way as to improve the transition to work and respond to the changing needs of employment. The Government is also arranging foundation training for young people under the Youth Training Scheme, with the taxpayer bearing most of the costs. And it will remain the Government's rôle, exercised largely through the Manpower Services Commission, to assist the flow of information about skill needs, training provision and jobs, especially at local level; to encourage the application and development of nationally recognised standards of competence, complementing those set by professional bodies; to fund experimental courses in new technologies and new techniques; and, where necessary, to provide special help for training the unemployed and disabled people.

Trainees themselves need to accept that the total costs of training must be taken into account in determining the level of their pay or allowances. They can also show individual enterprise in the use they make of opportunities such as those offered by the Open Tech programme, including training for self-employment. Adult trainees may also wish in appropriate cases to consider financing their own training by means of a loan . . .

[From pp. 5–6

NEW ARRANGEMENTS WITHIN VOCATIONAL EDUCATION

If the important developments described in this White Paper are to be carried through successfully, *public sector provision for training and vocational education must become more responsive to employment needs at national and local level.* The public sector needs a greater incentive to relate the courses it provides more closely to the needs of the customer and in the most cost effective way.

The Manpower Services Commission, which consists of representatives of employers, unions and local authority and education interests, is now the main agency through which the Government institutes action and monitors progress in training. Since its establishment, and particularly in the last three years, the Commission has developed increasingly close relationships with the Education Departments, local education authorities and local colleges in implementing the new Technical and Vocational Education Initiative, the Youth Training Scheme and the Open Tech, as well as the longer established Training Opportunities Programme. The Government is now asking the Commission to extend its range of operation so as to be able to discharge the function of a national training authority.

For this purpose we have decided to give the Commission important new responsibilities by enabling it to purchase a more significant proportion of work-related non-advanced further education provided by local education authorities. Non-advanced further education (NAFE) comprises the provision offered by local education authorities through colleges of further education at qualification levels below degree, higher diploma, higher certificate and professional courses of equivalent level. The 'work-related' NAFE referred to in this White Paper includes the technical and vocational courses (full and part time, including short courses and evening classes) offered by the great majority of colleges....

At present total expenditure on NAFE in England and Wales is about £1·2 billion per annum, of which some £800 million is devoted to provision that is work-related. The Manpower Services Commission itself currently spends about £90 million as a customer, direct or indirect, on NAFE courses or services. *We have decided that the amount to be devoted by the Commission to such provision in England and Wales should increase to £155 million in the financial year 1985–86, and to £200 million in 1986–87. The intention is therefore that the Commission should by 1986–87 account for about one quarter of the total provision in this area.* The resultant reduction in the need for local authority expenditure will be taken into account in settling the relevant rate support grants; the arrangements for this will be subject to consultation with the local authority associations through the normal consultative machinery....

Under the new arrangements in England and Wales the Commission will be responsible for ensuring that these resources are used to support vocational education and training at NAFE level closely geared to labour market needs. Decisions on what specifically should be supported in this way will be taken in consultation with the education service, employers and other interested parties. These decisions must reflect particular needs, especially at local level, and will change as the needs change.

We expect the Commission to give priority to provision for newly emerging skills, *e.g.* in electronics and robotics; to provision for occupations where traditional programmes no longer match modern industrial and commercial needs, *e.g.* some parts of business studies; and to arrangements for keeping courses and staff training up-to-date and relevant to work needs. It is envisaged that the great bulk of the resources, though not necessarily all, will continue to be spent within local authority colleges. The Commission will also want to take account of local authorities' own plans for expenditure on NAFE, and to maintain reasonable continuity of provision as regards both location and types of course....

The Commission will continue to report on the whole of its activities to the Secretary of State for Employment. The Secretary of State for Education and Science will be fully involved in the consideration and approval of the Commission's Corporate Plans and in proposals substantially affecting NAFE provision in England. Education Ministers will continue to exercise their statutory responsibilities for policy and standards in further education....

[From pp. 13–15

General Index

Index of Members of Committees, Assessors, etc.